MADAGASCAR

NATIONS OF CONTEMPORARY AFRICA
Larry W. Bowman, Series Editor

Madagascar: Conflicts of Authority in the Great Island, Philip M. Allen

Kenya: The Quest for Prosperity, Second Edition,
Norman Miller and Rodger Yeager

*Zaire: Continuity and Political Change
in an Oppressive State*, Winsome J. Leslie

Gabon: Beyond the Colonial Legacy, James F. Barnes

*Guinea-Bissau: Power, Conflict, and Renewal
in a West African Nation*, Joshua B. Forrest

Namibia: The Nation After Independence,
Donald L. Sparks and December Green

Zimbabwe: The Terrain of Contradictory Development,
Christine Sylvester

*Mauritius: Democracy and Development in
the Indian Ocean*, Larry W. Bowman

Niger: Personal Rule and Survival in the Sahel, Robert B. Charlick

*Equatorial Guinea: Colonialism, State Terror, and the Search
for Stability*, Ibrahim K. Sundiata

Mali: A Search for Direction, Pascal James Imperato

Tanzania: An African Experiment,
Second Edition, Rodger Yeager

*São Tomé and Príncipe: From Plantation Colony
to Microstate*, Tony Hodges and Malyn Newitt

Zambia: Between Two Worlds, Marcia M. Burdette

Mozambique: From Colonialism to Revolution, 1900–1982,
Allen Isaacman and Barbara Isaacman

MADAGASCAR

Conflicts of Authority in the Great Island

Philip M. Allen

Westview Press
BOULDER • SAN FRANCISCO • OXFORD

Nations of Contemporary Africa

All rights reserved. No part of this publication may be reproduced or transmitted in any form or by any means, electronic or mechanical, including photocopy, recording, or any information storage and retrieval system, without permission in writing from the publisher.

Copyright © 1995 by Westview Press, Inc.

Published in 1995 in the United States of America by Westview Press, Inc., 5500 Central Avenue, Boulder, Colorado 80301-2877, and in the United Kingdom by Westview Press, 36 Lonsdale Road, Summertown, Oxford OX2 7EW

A CIP catalog record of this book is available from the Library of Congress.
ISBN 0-8133-0258-7

Printed and bound in the United States of America

The paper used in this publication meets the requirements of the American National Standard for Permanence of Paper for Printed Library Materials Z39.48-1984.

10   9   8   7   6   5   4   3   2   1

To Rakotojameson and to Susan
*One of them drank of the Manangareza;
the other understands.*

Contents

List of Tables and Illustrations		xi
Preface and Acknowledgments		xiii

1   *The Virtue of Insularity*   1

The Lie of the Island, *1*
Enigmas of Malagasy Settlement, *7*
An Archipelago of Localities, *13*
Emergence and Supremacy of the Merina, 1787–1896, *15*
Notes, *26*

2   *Politics: From Paternalism to Revolution*   31

Imposition of the French, 1885–1905, *32*
Colonial Architectonics, *35*
Nationalism in the Anxious Empire, *42*
The PSD Republic, 1958–1972, *50*
Revolution: A Congeries of Nationalism, *57*
Urban Revolt and the Ramanantsoa Interregnum, *64*
Notes, *74*

3   *Ratsiraka's Republic: Revolution as Myth*   79

The Structures of Socialism, *79*
Collapse of the Revolutionary Myth, *86*
Military and Political Players in the 1980s, *91*
Metamorphosis of the Republic, *100*
Anticipating the Third Republic, *109*
Notes, *117*

4   *Society in Modern Madagascar*   121

An Itinerary of Ethnic Groups, *122*
Authority of Ancestral Tradition, *130*
Landscape of Classes and Minorities, *140*

Impacts and Transformations in Malagasy Society, *144*
Notes, *162*

5   *Madagascar's Economy: Flight from Reality*   168

Economic Endowments and Inhibitions, *170*
Preparing for Development, *175*
Economics of the Ratsiraka Charter, *180*
Recovering Stability: Structural Adjustment and
    Global Dependence, *193*
From Stabilization to Development, *206*
Notes, *213*

6   *Conclusion: Continuity as Revolution*   220

Apogee of the French, *223*
Revolution and Continuity in International Relations, *229*
The Third Republic: Regions and Localities, *231*
Notes, *236*

Glossary	239
Selected Bibliography	242
About the Book and Author	247
Index	248

Tables and Illustrations

Tables

5.1	Madagascar's GDP at current market prices, 1985–1993	169
5.2	Madagascar's population, estimated and projected, 1900–2025	173
5.3	World Bank and IMF structural adjustment lending for Malagasy stabilization	196
5.4	Production in Madagascar, 1985–1992	199
5.5	Madagascar's external trade, 1980–1992	201
5.6	Madagascar's direction of trade, 1989–1991	202
5.7	Madagascar's external debt and debt service, 1975–1991	204
5.8	Foreign assistance disbursements from OECD, OPEC, and multilateral sources, 1986–1991	210

Maps

	Madagascar and surrounding region	xv
1.1	Provinces and cities of Madagascar	3
4.1	Ethnic groups of Madagascar	123

Photos

Sailing boat harbor of the island of Nosy Be	6
Betsileo musicians	11
Palace of the Prime Ministers	23
Traditional houses	66
Modern quarter near Lake Anosy	66
Zoma market	88
Fruits and vegetables at Zoma market	89
Plateau landscape, with bags of charcoal at roadside	124
Traditional tombs and grave markers	132
Traditional houses	139
Young women and boys parading with drums	154
Valiha player of the Bara people	161
Ringtail lemurs	176
Sisal drying	186
School children visiting Antananarivo Zoo	223

Preface and Acknowledgments

On April 1 many years ago at a very large American embassy in a very important European capital, a very senior Foreign Service officer handed to a very junior subordinate an incoming dispatch from American Embassy Tananarive (now Antananarivo). The dispatch complained about our Foreign Service's habitual misuse of the names "Malagasy" and "Madagascar"; painstakingly, it gave all the rules for appropriate usage. Handwritten on this copy was the following annotation addressed to the junior officer:

> The Ambassador suspects you to be among those who habitually abuse the term "Malagasy" as a noun for the country, rather than, as appropriate, for its inhabitants and language only. He has been advised, further, that you may have even resorted to the improper neologism "Madagascan." I needn't remind you of the consequences entailed by such insensitivity.

The incoming dispatch from Tananarive had been trusting, even plaintive. Naively, it presupposed some sympathy in the great halls of U.S. diplomacy for the sensibilities of obscure Third World societies. The junior officer was of course entirely innocent of the nomenclatural abuse. His superiors enjoyed this April Fool's jest less at his expense than at the expense of the remote Indian Ocean islanders—the point of the jollity being: So the complicated title of a fussy funny country has been misused. Who cares?

The junior officer took the point and learned to use "Malagasy" with considerable respect. Interviewed on CBS Radio shortly thereafter, the junior officer tried to explain why he and his family had responded to a State Department appeal for volunteers to work at new embassies burgeoning throughout formerly colonial Africa. Vaguely, he told the radio audience something about his family's interest in expanding its concept of civilization. Eventually, he was indeed assigned to the island place where the inhabitants, their republic, and their language had the same name, not to be used as a noun for the country itself. That was 1962 and the beginning of a love affair with a great island that has resulted at long last in this book.

Many people have contributed to the shaping of this book over more than three decades. They include some who were dead before we got there but who inhabited the island as ancestors do—artists like the great suicide poet Jean-Joseph Rabearivelo; the much-vilified nineteenth century "nationalist" queen Ranavalona I; and her contemptuous French amanuensis, Jean Laborde. Others closer to our time never realized how much they helped shape my understanding—Richard Andriamanjato, who leads still; his old nemesis, the late André Resampa, so different from Andriamanjato and yet so like him; André Ravatomanga, the prescient Jesuit journalist; and Monja Jaona, who contested everything and does so still.

I owe much to companions of the early years: Benjamin Razafintseheno and Lucien Roux of the Foreign Office; Henri and Bèbe Razanatseheno, the perfect Tananariviens; Sirine and Asgar Barday among the gracious Ismaelite community; Zèle Rasoanoro ("toujours dans la lutte"); the exquisite poet Flavien Ranaivo; Césaire Rabenoro, who rose above it all; Max Croce of Radio Université; Bob Eisenberg and Heather Bond, who made sense of the American Embassy; Jeannot Rabeson, the nonpareil jazz pianist; Shelby, who saw things I would have missed; Alison and Richard Jolly, who have done more to save the world than anybody else I know.

Later on, there were many who helped ideas to form—Colin Legum, Aidan Southall, John Ostheimer, Robert LeBlond, and Aaron Segal, who still sends me books, clippings, and inspiration. Thanks to Bill Watson of Raymond and Whitcomb, who sent me back repeatedly to the beloved island; and to the African-American Institute, which appointed me to the 1993 election observer team. Thanks especially to Lily Razafimbelo, who taught me so much during and after that visit.

Among my most valuable interlocutors were the Indian Oceanists of the CERSOI at the Université d'Aix en Provence— especially Louis Favoreu, Jean Benoit, Marc and Isabelle Besson, and CERSOI's generous librarian, Monique Girardin. I'm indebted for critiques of ideas to the World Bank's structural adjustors Abderraouf Ben Brahim, Philippe LeHouérou, and Pierre Demangel. Other precious resources turned up at the CHEAM library in Paris and the CeDRASEMI collection at Sophia Antipolis. Pam Williams at my own university's library was especially helpful, as was René Atkinson of WFWM-FM. The librarians at the IMF/World Bank in Washington offered refuge among their excellent collection when conventional repositories failed.

Patience and encouragement came when sorely needed from the admirable team at Westview Press—especially from Barbara Ellington, who never gave up even when I was tempted to do so; and series editor Larry Bowman, who approved the first outline then waited and worked hard whenever something else emerged. Michelle Asakawa and Diane Hess labored over the manuscript well after I was wishing it were done. All these significant contributions notwithstanding, I take full responsibility for what is reported here and how it is presented. That includes the arduously compiled statistical tables and all translations not otherwise attributed.

Philip M. Allen

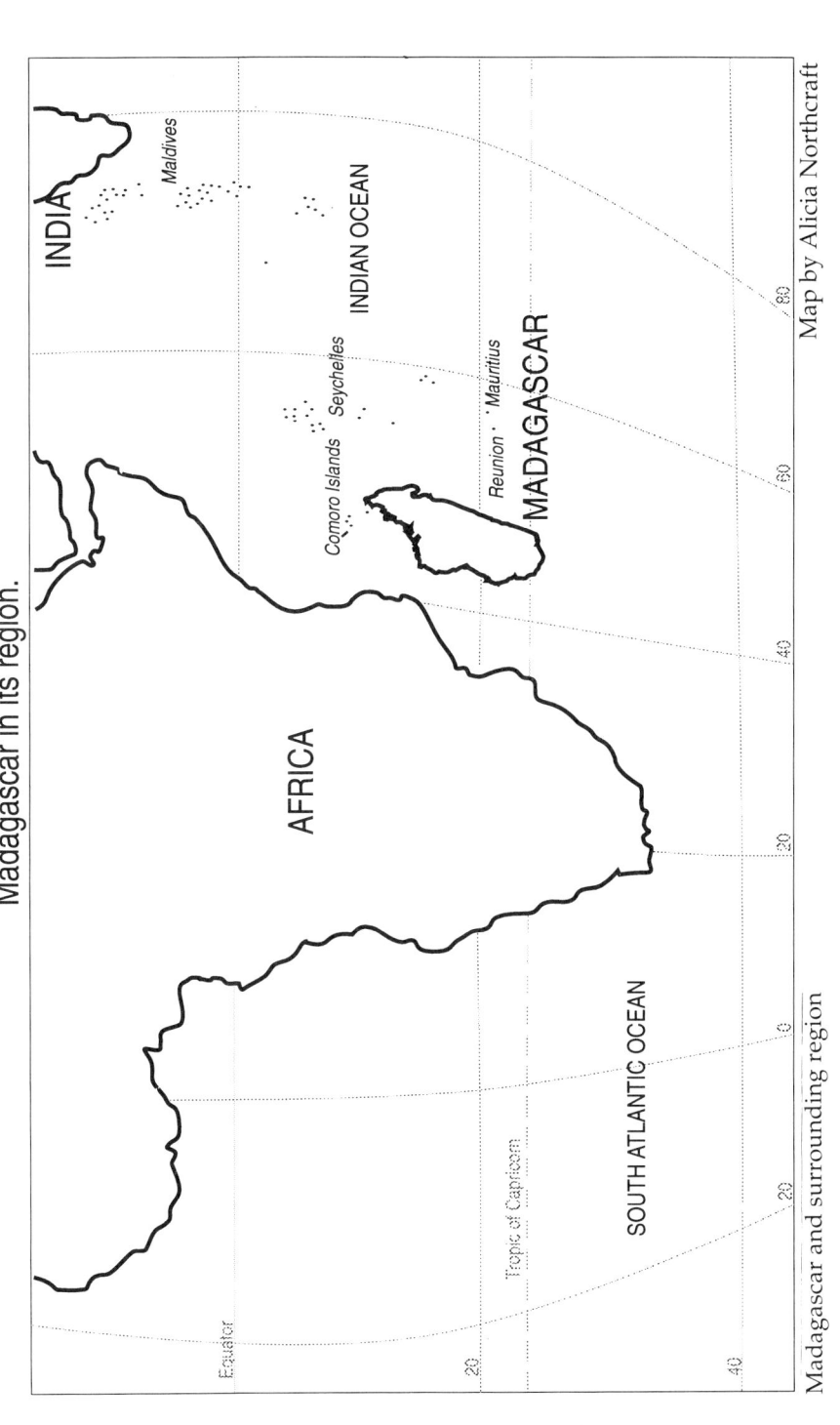

Madagascar and surrounding region

1
The Virtue of Insularity

THE LIE OF THE ISLAND

Africa's largest island—fourth in the world after Greenland, New Guinea, and Borneo—Madagascar marks the southwest corner of the vast Indian Ocean triangle, flanking the long coast of Mozambique. The hourglass channel between them narrows to 400 kilometers between Cap St. André and Moçambique Island, billowing wide to 1,000 kilometers at its northern and southern apertures. Tantamount to a small continent both in extent and complexity, Madagascar spans from north to south as far (1,606 kilometers) as the distance between Boston and Atlanta. Its people, the Malagasy, consider their island as a continental expanse rather than as a maritime spot surrounded by ocean. In French, it is familiarly known as "the great island" (*la grande île*).

A typical insular people, the Malagasy have been able to live their own unique history while communicating fruitfully with nearby shores and distant lands. In the north and west coast towns, Muslim merchants commerced over medieval centuries with the Comoro Islands and the greater Indian Ocean world. Viewed from the exterior, this northern façade of Madagascar appears as a remote frontier of the international system that connected Arabs, Indians, Indonesians, and Chinese, together with Swahili- and Bantu-speaking Africans for more than a millennium.[1] In fact, the island's permanent population settled there only quite recently from points in Africa, South Asia, and the Indonesian archipelago. Madagascar's interchange with the Indian Ocean littoral is being belatedly documented, for the island lay far from the core of the great monsoon system.[2] It took a more central role in the world only after Europeans had rounded the Cape of Good Hope to defeat that system and link the Indian Ocean with the Eurafrican west. And even that distinction evolved slowly.

Madagascar's insularity is more than a geographical platitude. A hundred million years of biophysical isolation permitted the evolution of a unique natural environment, just as several centuries of political separation allowed the development of a civilization unlike any other. Lying so snugly alongside southeastern Africa, Madagascar nevertheless kept its distance and became something quite different. Apart from curious moments of interchange, the two land masses developed—or rather deviated—in parallel. As the zoologist Alison Jolly describes it, "The world of Madagascar tells us which rules would still hold true if time had once broken its banks and flowed to the present down a different channel."[3]

During the Upper Cretaceous period, some 50 to 80 million years after the disruption of the ancient unified landmass of Gondwanaland, Madagascar actually broke free from the present area of Tanzania-Kenya. This major fragment of earth carried off a cargo of plants and animals from the contemporaneous stock of East Africa. Some of those species survive to the present time on the island, long after their extinction on the parent continent with its far older population of humans. In most cases, they evolved their own new forms adapted to the hospitable, temperate insular continent. Madagascar thus became a kind of sea-secured museum.

Despite this separate evolution, new species also crossed to the island on winds and tides, at least until the end of the Eocene (40 million years ago). Humans arriving there over the past fifteen centuries have brought their own biological entourage and in their millennium added a new wing to the museum of Madagascar. Records still do not tell us clearly who the original inhabitants were or precisely when they arrived. The second-century *Periplus of the Erythrean Sea*, the earliest documentary source for the commercial world beyond the Roman Empire, remains silent on the subject. Its maps show Africa rounding off to the west after Cape Guardafui to balance an Asia rounded off at India to the east, leaving no room for Madagascar.[4] The island may have been first identified by Arabs, who called it the Isle of the Moon. No doubt people lived on that moon by then, but they weren't consulted on its name. Portuguese captain Diogo Diaz, encountering the big island on August 10, 1500, called it after Saint Lawrence, whose day it was in the Roman Catholic calendar. How or why the good saint's name gave way to "Madagascar" remains uncertain. Marco Polo may have mistaken the island from afar and confused it with "Mogadiscio," actually on the Somali coast to the north.

Shaped like a great footprint in the sea, the island slopes toward a toe-point at the north; the vast bay here is Antsiranana harbor (once called Diego Suarez). The contour bulges westward toward Africa below Mahajanga; it tucks in again at the river delta of the Tsiribihina in the midwest and pushes out once more at the mouth of the Mangoky River and the town of Morombe (see Map 1.1). Upstream along these western rivers, the midregions contain grassy savannas with rare remaining deciduous patches begging for moisture. In the southwest, which receives less than 400 millimeters (16 inches) of rain a year, a unique desert of spiny thorn trees is ravaged by periodic drought, and life quivers on the brink of extinction. By contrast, along the even-edged east coast, a steep escarpment deflects the Indian Ocean trade winds into a rain forest that receives from 1,500 to more than 3,500 millimeters of precipitation a year.

West of that escarpment, the land flattens into high plateaus, including the area around Antananarivo (Tananarive in French) at roughly 1,250 to 1,500 meters. Two clusters of volcanic mountains point upward from the plateaus to a peak of 2,880 meters in the northern Tsaratanana range and slightly lower along the island's central vertebrae from the Ankaratra range south of Antananarivo to the Andingitra around Fianarantsoa. Some of the granite up-

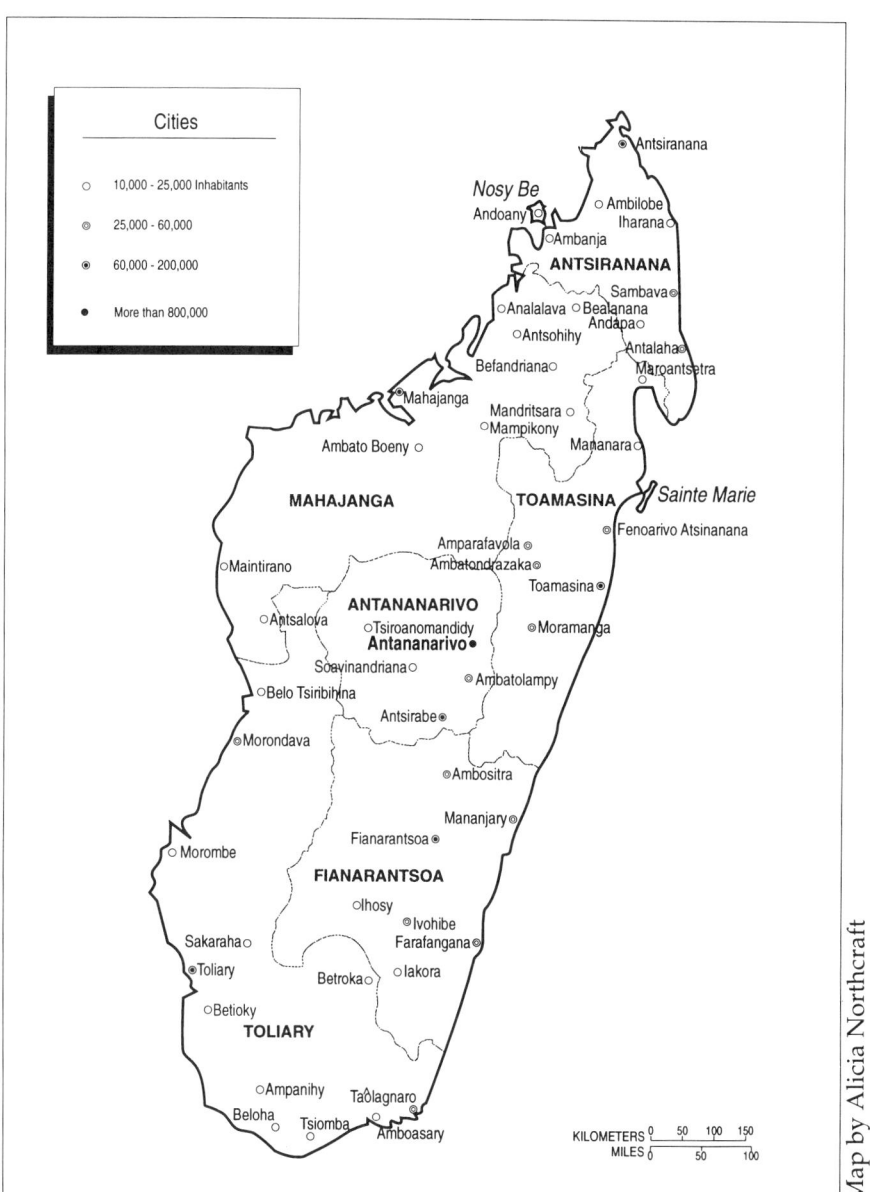

Map 1.1 Provinces and cities of Madagascar

bucklings of central and eastern Madagascar date back more than 3,000 million years, representing "perhaps the oldest rocks on the face of the earth."[5] Ravaged by fire, overgrazing, and erosion, the mountains are often entirely devoid of vegetation.

What forest remains after a millennium of such abuse amounts perhaps to 125,000 of the 587,000 square kilometers of total area. There are about 29,000 square kilometers of arable land to support more than 12 million people (barely one acre for each member of a farming family) and an equal amount of prairie for 10 million head of cattle. Rural per capita income has stayed under $100 a year—including the nominal value of subsistence crops—for as long as statistics have reflected Malagasy poverty.

This virtual continent wears a loose wreath of smaller-island satellites about its coastline. Some of the neighboring islets are truly tributary to Madagascar. Others are relatively autonomous. Independent Mauritius, 800 kilometers to the east, once had historical importance as the Île de France, headquarters of the short-lived eighteenth-century French empire in the Indian Ocean. Halfway between the two lies hat-shaped Réunion, equally lovely step-sibling of Mauritius in the Mascarenes archipelago.[6] Dependent for long periods on sugarcane for their mark in the world economy, both Mauritius and Réunion have grown steadily apart since 1811, the year of Britain's decision to retain the one (Mauritius) and toss the other back to the defeated French.

After generations of economic and demographic vicissitudes, both of these diminutive neighbors have done well for themselves—Mauritius as an indomitable example of pluralist microstate democracy, Réunion as an overseas department of France.[7] They have recently grown somewhat closer to their bigger, less-privileged Malagasy neighbor in a western Indian Ocean network favored by European and UN development assistance.

Strewn across the northern mouth of the Mozambique Channel, the four Comoro Islands have bridged that space for warfare, civilized trade, and piracy during a millennium. From Zanzibar or the Tanzanian mainland (Tanganyika), settlers, traders, missionaries, and predators hopped to the Grand Comoro, Moheli, or Anjouan, and finally to southeasternmost Mayotte, where they became intimate with Madagascar. Called Mahore or Maore in the old sea-going literatures, Mayotte has been a French possession since 1841, and its majority has voted three times to remain so in perpetuity. Hence, the island was retained by France after the other three Comoros declared their independence in 1975.[8]

Several archipelagoes stretching from 300 to 1,500 kilometers north of Antsiranana compose the modern Republic of Seychelles, tiny outpost of nonalignment in a seascape beckoning urgently to Western tourist affluence.[9] Together with Mauritius, Réunion (France), and the Comoros, these Seychelles cooperate with Madagascar in regional development undertakings through the Indian Ocean Commission (IOC). Unlike Madagascar and the Comoros, the Seychelles and Mascarenes have blended Asian, African, European, and Malagasy elements into variegated examples of "Creole culture," with a lingua franca based on French, a position of potency for the Roman Catholic

Church, and a thoroughly maritime idiom in their institutions.[10] By contrast, the Comoros extend Islamic and Swahili culture into the penumbra of southeastern Africa up to the portals of the Malagasy microcontinent.

Two of Madagascar's own offshore islands have the size and carrying capacity for historical noteworthiness. Both Nosy Be—westward from the northern tip—and Sainte Marie (also known as Nosy Boraha) off the northeast coast were fortified early in the nineteenth century by France well before French seizure of the great island itself in 1895-1896. In the centuries before this, however, both offshore islands had served other international maritime purposes. Nosy Be (the name means "big island") was an important component of the Sakalava kingdom of western Madagascar and was used for slave raids and pillage of the nearby Comoros—and probably the African mainland as well. In 1840, as the central Malagasy monarchy of the Merina surged outward to the coasts, French admiral de Hell, governor of Réunion, occupied Nosy Be and offered a refuge there to his ally, the besieged Sakalava queen Tsiomeko.

In a somewhat different, more maritime mode, Sainte Marie and the corresponding northeast coast were capitals of Eurasian piracy in the Indian Ocean during the eighteenth century. Here was enacted the stirring story of the pirate republic of Libertalia.[11] Later, Sainte Marie was a favorite colony and emporium for French nationals, many of them descendants of the buccaneers and their Malagasy clansfolk. Hence, through the first thirteen years of Malagasy independence, Sainte Mariens were by treaty endowed with dual nationality. But even though the ex-pirate stronghold maintained that privilege, it suffered from severe economic neglect, whereas charming Nosy Be was being cultivated into Madagascar's prime tourist attraction.[12]

Still another fringe of islets adorns the outskirts of Madagascar, although scarcely with the historical or cultural significance of Nosy Be and Sainte Marie. These are virtually uninhabited, forlorn flecks—the *îles éparses*—that France persisted in retaining for its own scientific, strategic, and meteorological purposes until 1990. The islets were in fact detached from Madagascar in 1960, just before Malagasy independence, and added to the jurisdiction of France's prefect in Réunion. After three decades of futile protests, the Malagasy have recovered them for whatever purposes they may serve. Several of these islets—Juan de Nova, Bassas da India, and Europa—perch advantageously inside the Mozambique Channel; from them one can view petroleum tankers plowing the seas around Good Hope. The Glorieuses sit just outside the channel to the north. At most, the islets have housed weather research and radio stations, nature sanctuaries, and small detachments of lonely marines or gendarmes who kept the watches of empire along the frontiers of a still strategic sea. But these insular territories give their proprietors important oceanic exploitation rights under the prevailing law of the sea.

Spaciousness and complexity allow Madagascar some independence from its maritime nexus with the outside world. So people came, some of them to stay, and then lost touch with their own origins. An original civilization developed in that space over a period of relative isolation after the first human intrusions. Somehow, it also became a single civilization, cohesive if

Sailing boat harbor of the island of Nosy Be, beyond Hellville (Andoany). Photo courtesy of the Embassy of Madagascar, Washington, D.C.

not uniform in its character. Described in Chapter 4, Malagasy culture is neither Asian nor African despite abundant affinities with both continents. Notwithstanding historically celebrated disparities between coastal and interior peoples, it is one culture. As judged by one of its most assiduous scholars, "Even if undeniable centrifugal forces persist in Madagascar, the society as a whole must be perceived above all in terms of geographic, linguistic, and cultural homogeneity, a phenomenon which places the great island very much on the margin of Black Africa."[13]

ENIGMAS OF MALAGASY SETTLEMENT

Lacking direct evidence of the actual lines of immigration into the great island, scholars continue to dispute the unresolved mysteries of Malagasy origins. European, American, and (a few) Malagasy archaeologists, historians, anthropologists, and linguists have debated lustily over the importance of Asian sources (Alfred Grandidier and more recently Jean Poirier and Paul Ottino) versus African (Gabriel Ferrand and Raymond Kent). The answer seems to favor a judicious synthesis of the two.[14] What we know is this: For a millennium and a half, Madagascar has been the Indian Ocean's authentic demographic melting pot. Its indigenous population is a blend of migrant people from Southeast and South Asia with East Africans; subsequently, Arabs, Europeans, and others joined the mix. The actual place of contact of these constituent peoples—and the degree of interpenetration among them after arrival on the island—remains open to speculation. Malagasy oral tradition is strangely silent on the fact of the ocean itself, let alone on how and when the ancestors managed to cross it.[15] We must indeed still conjecture over the points of arrival and the precise timing of the several waves of settlers on Malagasy shores.

The most plausible of the speculators, Pierre Vérin, accepts the probability of an original Afro-Indonesian population in Madagascar as early as A.D. 400 and no later than A.D. 900.[16] Given the antiquity of the trade system linking the Red Sea and the Indian east, these Indonesian peoples probably came with the monsoons in outrigger canoes along the coasts of southern India, Northeast Africa, and the Comoro Islands. There is no direct evidence to confirm the route, however, and no trace of human habitation in the eastward Mascarenes before the seventeenth century to suggest a more direct transoceanic crossing. Physical and linguistic evidence verifies both the Indonesian and African origins of this Malagasy population. Yet no important traces of Indonesian cultural influence can be found in East Africa to confirm the theories of George Murdock, Ralph Linton, and Hubert Deschamps (supported by Raymond Kent and Pascal Chaigneau) attributing the fusions to a sojourn on the continent.[17] The blending of continents occurred either on the island or in the Comoros, or in both places.[18]

Vérin and others thus posit two waves of arrivals between the fifth and twelfth centuries: first, a paleo-Indonesian people who intermarried with Africans in Africa, in the Comoros, or on the island to form a proto-Malagasy people, sometimes identified as the Vazimba; then a neo-Indonesian group, ancestors of the contemporary Merina, who came perhaps more directly (viz., from India to the east coast of the island) between the eighth and twelfth centuries or even later. Bringing the characteristic social organization of the *fukun* (clan, or deme), the second contingent (sometimes dubbed Deutero-Malayan) retained relative physical integrity, with fairer skins—hence the term *fotsy*, or "white people," sometimes attributed to them. Still, they too are blends of African and Asian ethnicity.[19]

The neo-Indonesian Merina appear to have overwhelmed the technologically less advanced Vazimba. Migrating to the high plateau far from their shores of arrival, they acquired the Borneo-based Maanjan language over a long period of contact with those Afro-paleo-Indonesians. The name Vazimba has been applied at times to the entire first wave, at other times to anybody found on the land by the migrating proto-Merina.[20] But no aboriginal population of Pygmies, Bushmen, or other "little people" has ever been confirmed. Indonesian maritime excursions into the western Indian Ocean appear to have stopped in the twelfth century—blocked, perhaps, by Arab sea power.

In addition to hunting and gathering, the original Afro-Indonesians cleared land for cultivation of rice, yam, taro, and arrowroot, planted in recently burnt fields (the practice of *tavy*). Paddy rice and banana cultivation came later, as did American roots such as cassava. The seventeenth-century plateau seems to have experienced a surge of population and a corresponding expansion of rice fields. Tavy technology spread throughout Madagascar. It has aggravated the deforestation that so sternly marks the central plateau and threatens to devastate the east and west despite efforts by all governments over two centuries to save the forests. Although it pressed hard upon the land, the island population remained sparse, widely disseminated, and recalcitrant to authority. All governments have been obliged to obtain labor for public works through domestic slavery, village conscription, and even coolie immigration.

Slave trading by Arabs extended to Madagascar even into the late nineteenth century despite British efforts to sweep the seas in alliance with the Merina monarchy. But the Arab role in this part of the world extended beyond slaving. Islamic peoples probably joined the Afro-Indonesian population before the close of the first millennium.[21] These included Arabs, Islamic Africans (Swahili and sea-going Bantu), and Persians from Shiraz. Omani and other denizens of the Arabian peninsula brought erudition and a flair for enterprise to combine with the contemplative, poetic, syncretistic spirit of the island. Like the earlier Indonesians and Africans, however, these Muslim immigrants adopted the original Indonesian language—an assimilation that testifies to the strength of the Afro-Indonesian cultural matrix. They also intermarried with and converted indigenous Malagasy to Islam, although without shattering the traditional culture of the islanders.[22]

Within 500 years, Muslim Malagasy—the Antalaotse, or sea people (the Antalaotra in Merina)—dominated all trading towns on the island.[23] Their civilization was particularly brilliant in the northwest, facing traditional East African and Comorean counterparts in the Indian Ocean system. The

Antalaotse also settled in the south and in the highlands, but current archaeological evidence there remains scanty and belated (none earlier than the sixteenth century on the plateaus). Scholarly descendants of Arab immigrants in the east traveled the island as priests, wizards, and royal counselors (called *ombiassy* or *ombiassa*).

Latter-day Muslims also arrived under colonial aegis. They originated in the Comoros, which had come under French domination during the mid- and late nineteenth century, and from Gujarat and Bombay. Starting as imported coolie labor, the Indo-Pakistani Muslims stayed on and established themselves into a colony of some 10,000 by independence time, passing 18,000 by 1972. Some of them acquired French or Malagasy citizenship; others remained stateless. Most entered retail trade in small towns of the west, south, and the central plateau; some (especially the Ismailis) became important industrialists and captains of import-export trade in the major cities. Together with the Europeans, these so-called Karana (people of the Koran) represent the least assimilated ingredient in the great Malagasy melting pot.

The Comoreans came through Mahajanga (Majunga) as small tradespeople, domestic servants and guardians, messengers, and laborers in the cities of the north and center; they grew to over 43,000 by 1972, but their numbers were reduced by pogroms at Mahajanga in the late 1970s. Cantonese and other mainland Chinese began arriving as coolies in the 1860s, even before the French period of control, but they, too, took advantage of colonial policy, skillfully converting their wages into business investments on the east coast and in the highlands. Numbering over 10,000 by 1972, they have tended to integrate with the Malagasy population to a greater degree than have the Karana.[24]

Early penetration of Madagascar by Bantu peoples is likely, since Bantu words appear in all dialects of Malagasy. Migrations from Africa also undoubtedly persisted until the sixteenth century, stopping because of Portuguese and later European mastery of the seas.[25] By then, however, Madagascar had already brewed a global hemisphere of cultural sources into a civilization, innovating as well as recycling, challenging anthropologists and art historians to the utmost. The rectangular shape of virtually all Malagasy dwellings and the practice of divination and number magic may have Middle Eastern astrological origins, for instance; the marvelous anthropomorphic grave statues of the west could be either African or Indonesian in inspiration.[26] Musical instruments and games can be traced to all continents.[27] Social and political systems are evident mixtures of imported influences and existential innovation. Real kingdoms of diverse derivation developed in the seventeenth and eighteenth centuries in all parts of the island.[28] Territorial clustering has produced impressive variations in the Malagasy language.[29] The documents of history, poetry, and religion of southeast Madagascar known as the *sorabe* (great scripture) use Arabic script for Antaimoro and Antambahoaka dialects, not for the official Merina.[30]

Yet, while studying the Bara people of the southwest, the most ostensibly African of all the Malagasy groups, Huntington found commonality greater than diversity. His summary statement is acceptable to most scholars of Malagasy culture:

> All of the peoples of Madagascar (excluding the recently immigrated Chinese, Indian, European, and Comorian populations) have more in common with one another than does any one of them with any overseas population. Although important linguistic, cultural, and physical variations occur in Madagascar, they are more a product of local historical and ecological factors than results of different racial or geographical origins. African, Arabic, and Indonesian institutions have been thoroughly blended into a unique and variable culture on the island of Madagascar.[31]

Far from being predominantly African or Asian, says Paul Ottino, Madagascar represents an autonomous amalgam of its entire cultural neighborhood, as "virtually all the countries bordering on the Indian Ocean have left their perceptible mark in material technologies, in vocabulary, in familial and political structures, in religious concepts, etc."[32] Probably, John Mack's advice is soundest: Rather than seeking to break Malagasy culture down into historical or ethnic components, it's more helpful to assemble it and see it whole.[33]

For centuries, Europeans trickled into the great island whenever they were permitted to do so by local rulers. They brought mysterious powers of the world, powers over things (*mahay zavatra*), and a disrespect for ancestral custom. These powers extended to the bodies of people taken by stealth or in combat. Even in the seventeenth century, Dutch and Portuguese records speak of vigorous economic and cultural activity at the Sakalava port of Nosy Antsoheribory in Boina Bay, where 6,000–7,000 Muslims were ruled by trader kings who spoke the languages of the European slave trade.[34] Arabs alone are believed to have taken 40,000 to 150,000 slaves from that area. Slaves also went from western Madagascar to the Cape colonies of the Dutch and to the Americas. British freebooters, shunted out of the West Africa trade, set up briefly at St. Augustine in the southwest corner of the island, disputing for slaves with the southern Sakalava. Monarchical Sakalava power increased as the Europeans paid for the captives in firearms.

Plying the Indies routes to the north and east of the island, Portuguese, Dutch, Americans, Hanseatic Germans, and British had their turns at refreshment stations and trade staples along the Mozambique Channel and later on the east coast facing the Mascarenes. At first, Portuguese power in the channel forced the Dutch into the Bay of Antongil on the island's east coast. They were nonetheless able to obtain footholds in the northwest within two decades after their establishment of the South African Cape Colony in 1652. The vast majority of the thousand or so "Magelagie" taken out of Boina were pressed to service by the Cape Company. Apparently, however, few Malagasy were carried on the long, pirate-plagued routes to Batavia, and very few of them arrived alive.

Well before European domination of the island, eighteenth-century Madagascar had served as a major source of slaves and of food for its more Europeanized neighbors. Malagasy beef, rice, corn, and even salt were essen-

African, Asian, and European influences are seen among Betsileo musicians, at fair near Fianarantsoa. Photo by Philip M. Allen.

tial for the survival of Bourbon and Île de France, especially during the long, exhausting, late-century wars with England.[35] An eighteenth-century French outpost on Sainte Marie and precarious trading posts along the Betsimisaraka coast brought firearms and cloth to chiefs who traded Malagasy captives for the new technology. Even after the British conquest of the area in 1810–1811 and the humiliation of France in 1815, British and French parties vied for influence at the nineteenth-century court of Antananarivo. The foreign parties were identified with Protestant and Catholic mission activity and with the various industrial plantation ambitions of their venturesome citizens. England's interests were relatively limited—enforcement of the antislave trade treaty signed originally with Merina King Radama I in 1817, protection of missionaries and their schools (which date back to 1818), and sustenance for the island of Mauritius, which had been retained by the British in 1811 after their conquest of the year before.

For the French, protection of national interests became increasingly problematic at court during the latter part of the century, stimulating frequent appeals via Réunion and directly to Paris for intervention against the "odious" monarchy. Following the conquest, French administrators and military personnel joined settlers, traders, teachers, and missionaries in virtually all districts of the island, bringing it close to the status of a settler colony (*colonie de peuplement*).[36] Overcrowded and resourceless Réunion needed Madagascar's empty spaces and a French establishment for decanting surplus Creole populations. Réunionnais champions pressed Paris relentlessly for privileges in Madagascar, stimulating cycles of antagonism with the Malagasy.[37] As Bloch put it, the 1890 treaty by which Britain authorized French imperial action in Madagascar (in exchange for a free hand in Zanzibar) abandoned the island to "the sordid intimidation of France, egged on by Réunionnais commercial interests."[38]

Like the earlier Arab arrivals, the French grafted privileged cosmopolitan layers onto a fundamental Malagasy culture. France's impact here was not the Francophonia indispensable to Réunion, Mauritius, Seychelles, and the tightly knit Creole islands of the Caribbean, but a prestigious "second culture" acquired by elites in a civilization neither European nor Islamic at its core. Madagascar remained, and remains, Malagasy. This ability to resist cultural conversion gives Madagascar a second powerful affinity to the Indo-Malaysian world; the great island remains Afro-Oceanic, not a grand specimen of Francophonia in the southwestern Latin Quarter.[39] Political unity and linguistic codification of the fundamental culture were in fact enhanced more by early nineteenth-century British policy than by the more ambivalent, less-privileged French of the time.[40]

Without imposing a Creole matrix on the island, France has an extended history of implants on Malagasy soil. As early as 1638, King Louis's entrepreneurs had landed the first of 4,000 metropolitans on the Tanosy coast of the southeast, establishing the settlement called Fort Dauphin in honor of the future Louis XIV. By 1674, disease and the hostile Antanosy had driven the last of these settlers to nearby Bourbon (now Réunion), from where their descendants never ceased to contemplate recovering access to the larger, richer place to the west. The original Dauphin colony did leave an important work of scholarship, Etienne de Flacourt's *Histoire de la grande île de Madagascar* (1661), containing the first dictionary of the language among many other revelations. French trade staples and concessions followed at Sainte Marie and at Fenerive and Foulpointe on the Betsimisaraka coast in the mid-eighteenth century to link Madagascar with the more intensively settled Mascarenes and Seychelles.

British conquests of the early nineteenth century drove a political barrier among those archipelagoes and kindled eight decades of rivalry between the European powers in the court of Antananarivo itself. Malagasy slaves were illegally incorporated into the Creole islands until full mid-century. In return, superfluous Réunionnais and others were periodically dumped on the great island. Miserable nests of white colonists dotted the entire east coast of Madagascar, and Creoles dominated the business of the great port of Tamatave (now Toamasina) into the present century. The ruling aristocracy at Antananarivo concentrated on internal island relations, pressing against competitor kingdoms in all directions. By and large, the indigenous monarchies left maritime linkages to the Europeans and Creoles—and to what remained of the Antalaotse in the west and north. Eventually, great transportation companies, from Messageries Maritimes to Air France, inherited those networks. Step by step, beginning in the 1880s, the French came to determine how Madagascar was to inhabit the modern world.[41]

AN ARCHIPELAGO OF LOCALITIES

Most of the economic and cultural vitality of the Malagasy people is distributed along the dorsal spine of their island—the high plateaus—and its coastal estuaries. More than a millennium of slash-burn agriculture has produced 100,000 square miles of virtually useless space where once people encountered forest. Having done what Jolly compares to "mining the environment,"[42] the descendants of those people now must fit their livelihood into the remaining pockets of ecological support. These favored localities occupy five major population zones—a tropical rain forest along the east coast facing the prevailing maritime winds, a central highlands of prairies and jagged mountain eruptions, the arid desertlike south, the vast savanna of the west broken by fertile river valleys, and the mountainous yet tropical northwest.[43]

In time, the early Afro-Asian settlers fanned out over these areas, joining and separating, absorbing occasional accretions of people along the coast, and concentrating into some eighteen population groups. These geographically localized societies are defined by their relation to an explicit environment, a relation that evolved over centuries. They cohere in a kind of terrestrial archipelago, a virtual continent of pasture and desert punctuated by cultural and economic fertility. In discussing the ways in which two plateau societies, the Betsileo and the Merina, colonized new territory, Jean-Pierre Raison refers to Madagascar as "a sequence of populated islets lacking systematic interrelationships."[44]

The resulting collectives have what Raison terms a strictly geographic reality, organizing and defining their ethnic particularity by lineage or by communal territory. Each of these ethnic groups has developed a cultural personality of its own, but they are not really "tribes" as defined on other continents. None of them is "pure" in distinction from any of the others. They all speak a variation of one language. All retain combinations of African and Asian ethnic and cultural quality, all founding their society on patrilinear and patrilocal clan loyalties; they are all Malagasy. The fact that one group, the Merina, obtained predominance in pre-colonial Madagascar, retaining privileged access to political and cultural opportunity under the French, has little to do with racial or tribal distinctions, let alone "superiority." Lighter pigmentation and pronounced Asiatic features of many (not all) Merina have suggested to some a simple racial explanation for Malagasy achievements; denying Africa its role as a source of island institutions, this "myth of the white king" (as Kent calls it) has proved inadequate to explain Malagasy history.[45]

By the mid-sixteenth century in at least three areas, the Malagasy had developed monarchical institutions of rule. In a process not unlike that of high feudal Europe, village chiefdoms on the east and west coasts and on the plateaus collected into broader state organizations with dynastic lineages. These states are identified with the Antaimoro, Sakalava, and Merina people, respectively, but the pattern was later followed by the Bara and Betsileo of the southern interior and by the Betsimisaraka of the east coast. These original political cultures all emerged from a synthesis of Indonesian and African factors. Much research is needed to define them precisely; their evolution may have started with the arrival of new Africans or Africanized Asians on the coasts.

Those belated immigrants (forebears of the Antalaotse or Antalaotra) probably introduced Islam and other Arab influences into the insular communities of Afro-Asians—the *tompon'tany* (masters of the land). The results were first felt along both coastlines through the impositions of Koranic literacy and the commercial concomitants of the slave trade. In any case, as Kent argues with vigor against conventional race-oriented European theories, lighter-skinned Asians cannot alone be credited with cultural advances in Madagascar.[46]

The early development of Malagasy states proved exceptional along the northeast coast and the offshore island of Sainte Marie. There, Betsimisaraka leaders joined forces, and nuptials, with English, French, and American pirate crews who used the island for refuge beginning in the late seventeenth century. After establishing one of the first republics in history, known as Libertalia, the enterprising buccaneers were virtually expelled from these waters by a British expedition in 1721.[47] Their cohabitation with indigenous populations bequeathed a caste of Euro-Malagasy called Zana-Malata (mulatto children), one of whom, Ratsimilaho, forged the Betsimisaraka into a state in the mid-eighteenth century.

In southeastern Madagascar, the Antaimoro recorded the development of theocratic institutions from the early seventeenth century in their sorabe. Arriving a century earlier, probably from Islamic Africa, they diffused highly advanced technology into the island. Readily dominating the tompon'tany of the Matitana locality, they traded with the Europeans and Muslim Africans ("Moors") of the larger region and lived in precarious proximity with their Antanosy, Tanala, Antaifasy, and Antaisaka neighbors. Hemmed in by hostility, the Antaimoro exported their robust culture through itinerant sorceror-priests (ombiassa) as far as the lofty levels of Imerina, where they probably penetrated in small numbers by the mid-seventeenth century. In about 1800, they were again invited there by the mighty Merina king Andrianampoinimerina. The Antalaotse doubtless influenced the rougher-hewn, decentralized, cattle-based kingdoms of the Bara, a people subdued only in part and never fully controlled by Sakalava, Merina, French, or modern republican suzerains.[48]

Both the southern Menabe and the northern Boina kingdoms of the Sakalava originated in the Maroserana dynasty, known also as the kingdom of the gold (Volamena). The royal line traces its sacred power to ancestor kings of the sixteenth century and earlier. These monarchs are credited with conquering and absorbing indigenous Vazimba, Vezo, and Antanandro chiefdoms in the sparsely inhabited country to the north and south. Sakalava tradition tells of the wisdom of the ombiassa, consulted by founding rulers to establish the boundaries, rituals, and institutions of the realm.[49] Even after the collapse of the empires, ancestor sovereigns visited the loyal living in seances of possession called *tromba,* expressing their pleasure or dissatisfaction with the way of the world.[50] These were times when the west coast maintained frequent commercial contact with "Moorish" Africa, supplying rice, cattle, and slaves across the channel. Ombiassa invoked the Arab zodiac and other sources of continental lore in their divinations on behalf of ambitious monarchs. They still serve Sakalava society in its contemporary senescence as diviners and healers.

After the mid-seventeenth century, when Malagasy rulers and their Antalaotse communities began controlling the southwest corner of the Indian Ocean trade, the Sakalava states enjoyed a century of maturity. Helped by French and Swahili African partners, the Maroserana kings expanded their dominion into vast reaches of hinterland, covering perhaps a third of the great island. European witnesses testified to the splendor of the Volamena court at Boina (near present-day Marovoay) and the activity of Mahajanga, the port established by the Volamena kings.[51] Sakalava serenity was interrupted by occasional vassal revolts and by Tsimihety antagonism in the northeast. It was broken finally by invasion from Imerina in the early nineteenth century.

Slave-seeking Boina raided the Comoro Islands to the north, earning firearms by the sale of captured people for the conquest of still more people, in repetition of the most sordid of historical patterns. Slaves were also brought back into Boina, working the earth to feed an otherwise pastoral, warrior empire. A cosmopolitan western Indian Ocean culture flourished in that prepared soil, although oral tradition yielded to written history only after the decline of Sakalava power. The African-influenced Sakalava language, Sakalava forms of celebration and art, their ways of building state institutions, keeping cattle, and honoring the dead all penetrated Bara and lands farther south. Sakalava culture entered remote Tsimihety refuges and influenced even the hitherto unimpressive upland societies of central Imerina.[52]

EMERGENCE AND SUPREMACY OF THE MERINA, 1787–1896

The Merina are the largest, historically most prominent, and most exhaustively studied of the Malagasy people. They dwelt on Madagascar's central plateau and were virtually unknown to the outside world until the late eighteenth century. Oral tradition characterizes an older Imerina (their territory) as a loose aggregate of chiefdoms supported by a combination of pastoral and rice-growing economies.

Merina culture seems to have scored an important breakthrough some three centuries ago through the extension of inundated (paddy) rice cultivation. This complicated technology gradually supplemented the ruinous practice of slash-burn agriculture (tavy), which had by then virtually deforested the entire central plateau. Cattle are still pastured on the periodically burnt prairies of lean grass, but the staple food of Imerina grows green in the paddy fields. The use of iron for tools and weaponry may have been acquired from the Antaimoro or Antalaotse of the Muslim southeast. Technological innovation allowed small principalities to develop around fortified centers of food production, including Antananarivo. Security was provided by clan militias called *fokon'olona*, which were to evolve into political and economic institutions with broad communal participation.

In ethnic and cultural traits the contemporary Merina represent a convergence of ancient Afro-Indonesians (Vazimba) with at least one major immigration of lighter-skinned Asians. The later immigrants are probably the original *hova*, although that name was subsequently applied to all freeborn Merina commoners. This convergence probably took place in intermittent combat from the late sixteenth through the late seventeenth century.[53] The synthesis eventually produced a new dynasty of monarchs who emerged from mortal competition among contenders in the *andriana*, or nobility. A reigning monarch's legitimacy was renewed annually in the purgative rite of the *fandroana*, or royal bath.[54] Andriana elders formed a class of royal advisers, called *ray aman'dreny* (literally, fathers and mothers). Vazimba tradition supplied much mythical content for later Merina culture—including a devotion to founding ancestor-kings who remained present in the world as an invisible foundation for community. Through this synthesis of tradition and technology, the Merina developed a dynamic of superiority that survives to this day. When the great king Andrianampoinimerina looked out from his provincial throne at Ambohimanga in about 1780, the Merina were ready for military, economic, and administrative expansion. Unified under his dynasty, they moved beyond their treeless, windswept hills and intricate green rice fields to the very shores of the land. Within a half-century, the Merina had overwhelmed all but the island's most southern peoples, eventually including the proud Sakalava.[55]

An enigmatic man of vast ambition and corresponding personal resources, Andrianampoinimerina (Nampoina for short) easily imposed authority on his major rivals for control of Imerina. The beneficiary of a palace coup against the hova clans, he combined personal command with organizational genius in military, economic, and administrative matters of state. He sent for Antaimoro scribes from the renowned country of the sorabe, installed markets and corresponding systems of taxation, law courts, labor mobilization, and irrigation technology to expand the capacity of Imerina to feed armies, colonists, and specialized townsfolk. A head tax had already been levied on some Merina subjects by his distant predecessor Ralambo (ca. 1610–1650) to support a standing army and keep it supplied with firearms. Subdividing Imerina into directly administered monarchical lands (*menabe*) and allocated land (*menakely,*) Nampoina administered through loyal agents, called *vadin'tany*. Colonies of peasants, soldiers, and merchants sprang up around the great Merina citadels of the central plateau—Antananarivo, Ambohimanga, Ambohidratrimo, Ambohidrabiby.[56]

In a strategy that has influenced Malagasy administrative thinking to this day, Andrianampoinimerina adapted the ancient fokon'olona system of peasant militias for public works purposes.[57] Communal institutions among the conquered Tsimihety, Sakalava, Bara, and Betsimisaraka were re-formed along Merina fokon'olona lines to integrate newcomers and outcasts into village structures. This integration gave them an identity with the physical space they inhabited (the *fokontany*), in addition to their customary lineage ties.[58] The Merina king also skillfully used traditional institutions of legitimacy for his own purposes—especially the ancient rite of the *kabary* (royal speech making). Codifications of kinship practices, marriage laws, and rules of landholding were given new (royal) patronage, always in favor of the central authority of the monarch.[59]

Once Imerina was under control, Nampoina's legions forged eastward in order to preempt the lucrative slave traffic, supplying both the labor needs of warlike Imerina and those of the French colonies of Bourbon (Réunion) and Île de France (Mauritius). Revenues from slave exports helped buy firearms to pursue the familiar cycle. Merina victories caught the eye of France's principal Indian Ocean rivals, and there soon was agitation, especially at the British court. Andrianampoinimerina's kingdom had little interest in the momentous wars that preoccupied Indian Ocean Europeans during the Napoleonic period, but Madagascar profited from the needs of both sides. Although the Île de France became Britain's Mauritius in 1810, it still needed Malagasy rice and beef and, despite growing antislavery pressures in England, conscript labor. French Réunion proved even more dependent on provisions from Madagascar.

By obliging Europeans to deal for these commodities at his court, Andrianampoinimerina's son and heir, Radama I (1810–1828), brought Madagascar into world history on favorable terms. He continued the conquests of his father, bequeathing to his heirs a realm that covered more than two-thirds of the island. Boina was invaded in 1822 and Mahajanga captured two years later, thus erasing the Sakalava empires of the west. The march of centralization was inexorable. A vast landscape holding perhaps 4 million people at this time also underwent a cultural transformation based on the Merina dialect of Malagasy as lingua franca. Asserting direct control over administrative and economic resources, Radama weakened the influence of the feudal nobility and used the vadin'tany as magistrates in local justice proceedings. The Merina never succeeded in fully dominating the south, where warfare remained endemic. Foreign slave raiding afflicted the west coast throughout the nineteenth century, even after the Merina state had undertaken to bring it to an end.

Radama used foreign lesson and example to organize his dominions. He imposed labor duties and taxable commerce on subject populations, sent Merina agents into the hinterlands under extraterritorial protection, and maintained diplomatic contact with France and Britain. His cabinet and armed forces adopted the structures of modern European monarchies, and he employed foreign missionaries to codify laws and to reduce the Malagasy language to a standard written form—in Latin script, not the Arabic used by the ombiassa or *ampandrano* (diviners) of his father's time. His army was trained by British advisers sent by the astute governor of the new Mauritius colony, Sir Robert Farquhar. Appreciating the Merina empire's need for military buttressing, Farquhar committed capital, armaments, textiles, and technical assistance to help Radama compensate for the loss of revenue from the slave trade. He kept the king's commercial rivals away from the slave-hungry French along the east coast. Thanks to Farquhar, Radama had a Mauritian named Robin as his secretary and British sergeant James Hastie to drill his squadrons.

Acting like a twentieth-century Cold War superpower on the margins of the Third World, England declined to extend herself to dominion in Madagascar. Britain settled, rather, for comity with the Merina sovereign so long as provisions flowed from the great island into Mauritius and the Merina seemed to keep their promises to eliminate their once lucrative slave trade. Unusually deferential to such a "native" prince (compared, for instance, with its treatment of Sri Lanka at the time),[60] London even recognized Radama as king of Madagascar in 1817. Although Britain protected Radama's monarchy from direct attack, it did not challenge French machinations on the edges of his island. In 1816, five years after the British navy had ousted French merchants from Tamatave (Toamasina), England permitted them back; it allowed France to retain Sainte Marie and even to foment trouble for the Merina in Sakalava and Comorean country to the west and north. Under Radama's less cosmopolitan successor, Ranavalona I, Christians and refugees from Betsimisaraka and Sakalava country sought refuge under the Tricolor at Nosy Be and Sainte Marie. Great Britain stood aside while France shelled several sites on the east coast in 1829, supporting claims of Creole slave traders against the Merina.

Beginning in 1817, Welsh Congregationalist clergymen arrived as "artisans" in response to Radama's request for technical assistance from the London Missionary Society (LMS). The brightest of Merina aristocratic youth began going to Mauritius, and even to Europe, for schooling. They returned to the island bearing overlays of sophisticated technology and veneers of values, but the best of them—Secretary of State and historian Raombana, for example—could synthesize British culture and ancestral Malagasy tradition into reverent, intellectual, gentlemanly equilibrium.[61] By 1820, pastors and priests were allowed to open schools on the European model. Outright conversions to the religious beliefs of the Europeans were soon to follow as missionary groups from Anglican, Methodist, Quaker, and Roman Catholic persuasions arrived on the heels of the LMS. Not everybody was able to achieve the cultural syncretism of a Raombana, so the progress of Christianity among the andriana and hova aristocracy threatened traditional ways of conceiving the world. This antagonism engendered a long-lasting political conflict in Antananarivo between pro-European parties and Malagasy traditionalists.[62]

But Radama died in serenity, as the political factions waited for subsequent succession crises to make their respective moves. His wife and cousin, Ramavo, became queen in 1828 under the name Ranavalona. Courageous, strong-willed, Ranavalona I lacked her predecessor's understanding of the European direction that the Southern Hemisphere was taking. Her thirty-three-year reign suffered under continuous dispute among the court nobles (andriana) and several caucuses of commoners (hova). The latter could and did manipulate policy, hold office, even marry a queen, but could not rule in their own name. Ranavalona deployed her own admirable powers of statecraft to play these factions against one another, but she was never strong enough to dominate Antananarivo politics. The chief item of contention was the presence of Europeans both at the capital and in the exploitable countryside. Catholic and Protestant missionaries trekked to Antananarivo to offer services and seek souls. Adventurers sold bills of goods. Timber, cattle, rice, and spice concessions proliferated under the authority of the court. The Lambert Company (French, although based in Mauritius) monopolized production and trade along a substantial portion of the east coast. There was a printing press in Radama's capital, and the Bible was being translated into Malagasy.

But to acquire favor, the foreigners had to negotiate through one political party or another, and each had its rivals. The French persisted in "catching up" with the conquering British, using and defending the interests of their Réunion colony. St. Denis's Catholic diocese was deployed politically against the Protestant missionary phalanxes serving the honor of England. Although never consenting to European-inspired social or cultural change, Ranavalona inclined toward French in preference to British claims for much of her reign. In 1828 she denounced, then renegotiated, the treaties of 1817 and 1820 (which among other provisions, enjoined her from the export of slaves) and in the following year bestowed a gigantic east coast concession on the French colonist Napoléon de Lastelle, representing the firm de Rontaunay of Réunion. She insisted, however, on shorter-term contracts renewable at her own pleasure and on limiting the number of foreigners privileged to dwell in or visit the capital.

Although Ranavalona governed ably with the help of highly skillful counselors, some of them schooled in Europe, she remained a savage in the eyes of uncompromising Christians and an obstacle to the growth of colonial interests based in Réunion and Mauritius. The French navy began troubling Ranavalona's east coast on behalf of slave raiders and land concessionaires from Réunion. France also defended interests in the Comoros and on the islands of Sainte Marie and Nosy Be. The French even tried to weaken Merina control over the west coast. They befriended the deposed Sakalava king, Andriantsoli, who subsequently bequeathed to them sovereignty over his sultanate of Mayotte (southernmost of the Comoros)—thus beginning a Comorean irredentist conflict that remains unresolved to this day.

Eventually, the whole process degenerated into competing British and French bids for a "protectorate" over a monarchy that, ironically, had no enemies except those same predatory British and French. To be pro-European came to imply disloyalty, not merely because Europeans ridiculed the royal rituals and symbols (*sampy* and *sikidy*) but because, unlike the patriotic Raombana, second-generation Christians were identified with the ambitions of foreign powers. As P. M. Mutibwa concludes, "Ranavalona I had tried to protect her country's traditions from foreign ideology, and, forced to make a choice, she had preferred her nation's independence, as she and her government understood it, to the white man's technical knowledge offered to them only through Christianity."[63]

As Ranavalona pursued her predecessors' campaigns for complete control of the island, Christian subversion became increasingly troublesome. The converts joined other dissidents protesting the fiscal exactions and endemic warfare required to sustain those imperial holdings. Christians thus posed a threat to the queen's legitimacy and, in her eyes, to state stability. Ranavalona argued that to acknowledge Christ was to substitute a European "ancestor" for those of the Malagasy—by whose authority she had her title to reign. Baptisms were proscribed in 1832, and the remaining Protestant congregation, over 200 strong, suffered persecutions and martyrdom. As a consequence, the defense of Merina traditional religion was identified with anti-European political nationalism, bequeathing much confusion to twentieth-century politics.[64]

The traditionalist faction of the hova prevailed in 1836, and all but a few missionaries and concessionaires were expelled from the country. Those who remained included the genial Gascon entrepreneur, Jean Laborde. A skilled craftsman marooned on the east coast, Laborde ingratiated himself with Ranavalona and many of her courtiers, particularly the hova prime minister and army commander Rainiharo and Chief Secretary Rainimaharo. Engaged in 1833 as an agent for Lastelle's powerful Rontaunay enterprises, Laborde spent decades at Antananarivo and the nearby provinces furnishing industrial manufactures, homemade armaments, and civil engineering to the crown. He built palaces in the capital, roadways to the coast, and factories at his industrial park at Lake Mantasoa, 30 kilometers east of Antananarivo. Now a resort locality, Mantasoa under Laborde employed 20,000 conscript workers to produce cannons and small arms and ammunition, paper, silk and other cloth, porcelain and glass, soap, milled sugar, and ground coffee.

Laborde worked in isolation from other Europeans, serving Ranavalona's interests almost as well as he served the needs of his own country and religion of origin. These were ultimately in contradiction, for what Ranavalona sought was economic independence, and what ultimately interested France was domination of the vast Indian Ocean landscape—if the island could be acquired without unduly antagonizing the British. A characteristic figure of colonial history, Laborde was nicknamed "the queen's foreigner" (*vazaha de la reine*); he nonetheless remained French to the core—xenophobic, intolerant of "superstition," inveterately suspicious of anything British. This favorite of the queen never acknowledged the authenticity of Malagasy culture, the religious worthiness of ancestral precedent, or the right of Ranavalona's kingdom to genuine independence.[65]

The wheel of Malagasy politics was to revolve again, even under the recalcitrant Ranavalona, and the foreigners surged back. Soon after expelling the unwelcome Europeans in 1836, the queen had sent diplomatic missions to Paris and London in a futile, almost Thucidydean attempt to explain to imperial powers how the Malagasy understood their independence. She was forced to allow the concessionaires and missionaries to return, unit by unit, to perform work for which Madagascar would have preferred to contract on more indigenously Malagasy terms. The French connived with Sakalava pretenders and took control of Nosy Be, Madagascar's stepping-stone to the Comoros and East Africa.

By 1845, the machinations of the Europeans caused the queen to try "naturalizing" them as Malagasy commoners on the spot, a move that would have permitted their ownership of property, but under traditional law. This presumption, tolerable only in a European monarch, prompted the British and French navies to join in a bloody but inconclusive bombardment of Tamatave. The foreigners fled once more, and Madagascar's international trade ground to a virtual halt. Laborde stayed on as a technical assistant without great honor, living off an allocation of (sorely diminished) royal customs duties. His role was reduced to intriguing against the depravity of England and the Protestants. France was once again tempted to occupy the island, particularly after the emancipation of Réunion's slaves in 1848. This belated act of conscience dumped thousands of unemployable Creoles onto the slender labor markets of the erstwhile Bourbon. Still, no government in Paris was ready yet to contemplate direct aggression against the Merina island, even to find a place to deport volatile, unwanted Réunionnais.

The logic of royal business nevertheless had its way at Antananarivo, and one by one, the cast of intriguers was reassembled at court. Laborde was joined by his coterie of shady Jesuits, bribed courtiers, and rapacious civilians. Across town, his mortal enemy, the LMS's William Ellis, was practicing his own Protestant form of intrigue (in Laborde's opinion)—including the scandalous act of distributing Bibles! Finally, in 1857, after a plot to depose her was uncovered by the anti-European minister Rainijohary, Queen Ranavalona reluctantly expelled them all, even this time (but most reluctantly) Laborde. The queen's foreigner spent a five-year exile in Mauritius, denouncing her (unreluctantly) as atavistic, misguided, and depraved.

However ungracious, this deprecation of the queen is echoed by Madagascar's own modern Christian historian, Edouard Ralaimihoatra. He finds her vulgar, superstitious, lasciviously self-indulgent, and cruel to Christians, particularly to the high andriana nobility, which had opposed her accession in the first place.[66] Ironically, since her intention was to save her own people from the alienations of Christianity, Ranavalona's persecutions—particularly the expulsion of the foreign Christians—only strengthened the morale of the indigenous churches, and they would eventually win the day under her successors.[67]

Europe's technological and cultural attraction had been potent for Radama and it could not be obliterated by his successor. Behind the queen's back, that attraction had long been at work. Varieties of foreign values operated on the heir apparent, Prince Rakoto, who spurned the Malagasy traditionalists on whom his aging mother relied. Once on his throne in 1861, Rakoto substituted Europe's "civilizing mission" for Ranavalona's cautious nationalism. Deliberately taking the name Radama II, he was represented as heir to the legacy of an internationally open Madagascar. The new Radama was prepared by Europhilia to call on the French and British to modernize the degraded, superstitious Malagasy. He summoned the foreign exiles, accepting Laborde, de Lastelle, and their newest tycoon colleague, Lambert, as though their values truly transcended the profits of monopoly contract. Laborde returned in 1862 with the title of French consul. Ellis was back in the same year. As Claudine Caillon-Filet puts it, "The 1857 team is reconstituted. Each returns as he left, Laborde with the protectorate on his mind, the Jesuit Fathers with their dreams of baptisms, churches, and schools, Lambert with his ambitions of mining and agriculture. The four years have been a mere parenthesis. Each resumes his words and deeds wherever the failure of the 1857 conspiracy had frozen them."[68]

The new king seemed to consider himself a European, and a relatively advanced once at that. But he was also entirely under the influence of a Falstaffian band of dubious European and Malagasy drinking companions, aptly dubbed *menamaso* (red eyes). He liberally distributed royal concessions to foreign claimants and signed a most progressive treaty with France in September 1862, pledging freedom of religion, belief, and education, as well as property rights for foreigners—a concession deemed anathema by the old queen. The British protested and obtained an equivalent treaty from the evenhanded monarch—with an added clause reaffirming abolition of the by-then-clandestine slave trade. The army was trimmed in size and reduced in importance. Foreign dress, feuds, and duels appeared at court. Riotous living outraged virtually everyone who had not become one of the king's favorites.

It was then that the spirit of Radama's dead mother began haunting the imaginations of Imerina. The living memory of Ranavalona prompted rich and poor, powerful and humble alike, to believe in her imminent return—so hateful was the prospect of Christian-European rule through a turncoat king. Believers in the royal cult, slaves torn from their ancestral land, discharged soliders—all took their visions to the roadways and marketplaces, dancing frantically, calling to their phantoms, enacting scenes of mass hysteria that have been documented for the contemplation of social pathologists. This Europhobia, known as the *ramanenjana*, represented one of several strands of nationalist reaction that coursed through the kingdom as resistance to modern values came to reinforce hatred of the Christians and foreigners. It was to break out several times later in a Christianized, colonized Madagascar, representing what Françoise Raison-Jourde calls a final agony of paganism.[69]

> Using a symbolic choice of the name to identify with the policies of Radama I, the new monarch adopted a policy of openness to the external world signified by the return of the Protestant English missionaries and the appearance of the Jesuits; it was also a policy of peace with the coastal populations, of progressive liberalism inside the realm. But—emerging from a long, vigorously nationalistic reign fiercely hostile to cultural imports—was Imerina really prepared for such abrupt and utopic liberalization? It took only two and one-half years for popular dissatisfaction with a prince once hailed as the Messiah to become transformed into the crisis of the *Ramanenjana*.[70]

This first spasm of reaction aborted the reign of Radama II. He was assassinated on May 12, 1863, by a crowd that had already murdered many of

THE VIRTUE OF INSULARITY

Palace of the Prime Ministers, Andafiavaratra district, Antananarivo. Photo courtesy of the Embassy of Madagascar, Washington, D.C.

his menamaso companions. The plot was probably the work of the strongest of the anti-European hova parties, the Andafiavaratra faction, which had played a major role in Ranavalona's nationalist policy. In July 1864, one of several competing Andafiavaratra leaders, Rainilaiarivony, married the widowed Queen Rabodo, who had ascended the throne as Rasoherina. As prime minister, he forced the trembling Europeans to renegotiate Radama's treaties and charters, particularly those guaranteeing rights to foreigners over sacred ancestral property.

When Rasoherina died in April 1868, she was succeeded by her cousin, Ranavalona II, who likewise accepted Rainilaiarivony as her consort. A man of grand ambition, assiduity, and a flair for intrigue, the prime minister had an oratorical way with crowds and an ability to use tradition for his daily purposes. He governed Madagascar (or the three-quarters of the island under Merina administration) without serious challenge for twenty-two years. Thereafter, he found himself overtaken by European duplicity and, after 1885, managed only to keep the state functioning in stagnation for another decade.[71]

The new queen promptly signed a treaty with France prepared by the prime minister together with his father's old friend, Laborde. This pact contained a clause that the older Andafiavaratra would have never conceded under Ranavalona I: It granted French nationals certain qualified property rights that had been denied even to the British and American signatories of otherwise comparable treaties the year before. This was the aged Laborde's greatest victory. But the wily Rainilaiarivony alternated his concessions. The "Anglos" won their own triumph on February 21, 1869, when the queen, prime minister, and their entire court accepted wholesale conversion to Protestantism, despite all the efforts of the devout Anglophobe Catholic Laborde.

Moreover, Ranavalona II revoked Lambert's notorious charter, under which Radama II had allowed the beneficiary a monopoly over the exportation of sundry industrial raw materials needed by France. Beef and rice kept going to the Mascarenes, and ambergris, wax, orchil dye, India rubber, copal gum, and timber were sent directly to Europe in exchange for manufactured goods, largely for court consumption. But the primacy of the French concessionaires was broken, and France would not live with its loss, even after exacting an indemnity that proved ruinous to the Merina treasury. Colonialism was becoming a matter of principle. After Laborde's death in 1878, his property, claimed by nephews, was withheld from them in apparent contravention of the treaty of 1868. This and similar cases served as pretexts for direct intervention—once the French had secured assurances of Britain's indifference—and Laborde's own legacy thus allowed his old dream of a protectorate to come true.

France established control after an inglorious bit of war in 1883–1885. In that combat, French fleets had their way along the northwest and east coasts, but they failed to suffocate the kingdom. Paris settled by imposing another ruinous bill (10 million francs) upon the exhausted monarchy. In 1883, Ranavalona III had become the third queen to succeed Radama II and to marry Rainilaiarivony, thus maintaining his position as prime minister until the end of the dynasty.

Madagascar's economy was damaged by French impositions and by the inability to pay for its imports during the world depression of the 1870s. But it had structural weaknesses as well. Having abandoned the sea several centuries before this, the Malagasy never developed a maritime industry, coast guard, or merchant marine. The Merina left this technology in the hands of foreigners, hence sacrificing the security that it might otherwise have provided. Roads, too, were neglected for fear of facilitating foreign invasion. But that invasion came without roadways, advancing on the inexorable energy of imperialism, and the dynasty collapsed.

Like most colonial bureaucracies, Merina administration in the provinces had failed to deliver the economic and psychological fruits of military conquest. Waves of proconsuls followed ineffectual wave into these territories during more than a half-century of rule from Antananarivo. Administrators collected taxes and imposed labor quotas, but they could never mobilize the productive or affective energies of the dispersed population. Like the industrializing economies of the Northern Hemisphere, Madagascar's administration sought to solve its labor shortages through exploitation. The monarchy goaded production in its dominions by slave labor—both in the provinces, where conscription was enforced by military garrisons, and in the capital, where old slaves (*mainty,* or blacks) formed a proletariat somewhat above imported slaves (*andevo*). Both servile castes ranked beneath the free people (hova) and the noble andriana, but the mainty were able to occupy positions of responsibility, even as high officers in the Merina army. The early conquests of the first Radama and Ranavalona in the south brought slaves in swarms to the plateaus.[72] Domestic traffic continued informally and on a smaller scale thereafter—often with the venal connivance of Merina governors in the west.

The whole apparatus proved highly unproductive. In 1877 a decree of the prime minister acknowledged the uselessness of slavery, freeing 150,000 bondspeople at one time. Rainilaiarivony turned for labor to the fokon'olona, exploiting those institutions strictly as agencies of central administration rather than as communal deliberative bodies. This arrangement was codified in 1885. But slavery remained until the end of the monarchy. French sources estimate the number of slaves in the country as between a half-million and one million in 1896. France thus had a "civilizing" pretext for conquest.[73]

Moreover, forced labor (*fanampoana*)—in a form of feudal obligation on village communities—remained the rule for public works. The practice was later continued by French colonial governors despairing of finding voluntary labor even for modest remuneration. Small brigand communities fed by runaway slaves and renegades peppered the areas around major centers from the 1820s onward. When France finally joined in suppression of slave trading in the 1880s, many Antalaotse and Creole entrepreneurs collapsed, but Muslim Indians holding British passports managed to convert their illicit operations into what remain lucrative commercial businesses today.[74]

Based on such exploitative inequities, the regime of the queens was inefficient, corrupt, and often cruel; its misdeeds have damaged relations between Merina and coastal peoples (*côtiers*) to the present day. This was an imperial system contained within one island, but in most respects it was scarcely unlike the imperialism of the "civilized" world. The monarchy was in contact with that world and it was presiding over the often chaotic evolution of a truly unique civilization. Considering these distinctions, the Merina regime surely deserved more than peremptory subjugation at the hands of expansionist Europeans. Ranavalona I and her ministers had sought to defend the honor of an indigenous culture while engaging in commerce with the stronger powers, who could never appreciate that culture. For the most part, the state trading strategy had been upright. Madagascar remained a steady source of sustenance for the Mascarenes, and the court did act to curtail the maritime commerce in slaves. Concurrently, Madagascar developed a modern state infrastructure by nineteenth-century standards.[75]

What the European conquerors failed to recognize was not how much a cosmopolitan monarch or prime minister could make Antananarivo appear to be London or Paris—for they applauded the short-lived Radama II for just this intention—but how strong was the title of any state to its integrity provided it was in control of its territory and willing to engage in international comity. Perhaps, in the near-century of Merina rule, only the Mauritian governor Farquhar had truly been able to appreciate this mundane, "undivine" right of Malagasy kings and queens. As Mutibwa insists, using anachronisms to establish a comparison between nineteenth- and twentieth-century Third World experience,

> Far from being in danger of falling to pieces at the time when the French conquered the island, Madagascar was already stable and developing, although no

doubt she was going through the same kind of problems that are experienced by developing nations the world over, especially when faced with the influence and even threats from the great powers. ... Through contacts with Europeans and as a result of her free and enthusiastic acceptance of foreign ideas and influence, Madagascar had achieved many of those things in the name of which European colonialism was imposed on Africa in the nineteenth century.[76]

What remained after centralized controls broke down—or where they never reached—was an indomitable substructure of peasant life. Among Merina people as well as among Betsileo and côtiers, this "unmodern" system filled the productive gaps for local, not national or imperial, purposes. Often embodied in communal deliberative councils, the fokon'olona, decentralized (or dis-organized) authority had its roots in kinship, in geographical and functional proximity, and in other natural affinities. It exercised a political legitimacy denied to the distant monarchy. As we shall see in subsequent chapters, all central regimes have tried in vain to mobilize this indigenous legitimacy for modern purposes. The autonomy of fundamental peasant communal structures has by now survived still another century of authoritarian imposition, defying the will of sovereigns whether monarchical, colonial, bourgeois, or even revolutionary socialist.

NOTES

1. To explore Madagascar's place in the great Indian Ocean system, see Pierre Vérin, *The History of Civilisation in North Madagascar,* trans. David Smith (Rotterdam and Boston: A. A. Balkema, 1986); Auguste Toussaint, *History of the Indian Ocean,* trans. June Guicharnaud (London: Routledge and Kegan Paul, 1966); Alan Villiers, *Monsoon Seas: The Story of the Indian Ocean* (New York: McGraw Hill, 1952); André Bourde, "Résurgences de l'histoire," *Annuaire des Pays de l'Océan Indien (APOI),* no. 1, 1974 (Aix-en-Provence: CERSOI, 1976), pp. 137–153; Philip M. Allen, *Security and Nationalism in the Indian Ocean: Lessons from the Latin Quarter Islands* (Boulder and London: Westview Press, 1987), ch. 1.

2. See Michel Mollat du Jourdin, "Les contacts historiques de l'Afrique et de Madagascar avec l'Asie du Sud et du Sud-Est: Le rôle de l'océan indien," *Archipel: Études interdisciplinaires sur le Monde Insulindien,* no. 21, 1981 (Paris: SECMI-CNRS), pp. 35–53.

3. Alison Jolly, *A World Like Our Own: Man and Nature in Madagascar* (New Haven and London: Yale University Press, 1980), p. xiii.

4. *Periplus maris Erythraei: The Periplus of the Erythrean Sea: Travel and Trade in the Indian Ocean by a Merchant of the First Century,* trans. and annot. Wilfred H. Schoff (London: Longmans, Green, 1912).

5. Jolly, *A World Like Our Own,* p. 11.

6. Portuguese name for the archipelago of Réunion, Mauritius, and the latter's dependent island of Rodriguez.

7. For Mauritius, see Larry W. Bowman, *Mauritius: Democracy and Development in the Indian Ocean* (Boulder and London: Westview Press, 1992); Adele Smith Simmons, *Modern Mauritius: The Politics of Decolonization* (Bloomington: Indiana University Press, 1982); Allen, *Security and Nationalism,* ch. 4. For Réunion, see André Scherer, *La Réunion,*

Que sais-je? no. 1846 (Paris: Presses Universitaires de France, 1980); Allen, *Security and Nationalism*, ch. 3.

8. For Comoros, see Malyn Newitt, *The Comoro Islands: Struggle Against Dependency in the Indian Ocean* (Boulder and London: Westview Press, 1984); Hervé Chagnoux and Ali Haribou, *Les Comores*, Que sais-je? no. 1829 (Paris: Presses Universitaires de France, 1980); Allen, *Security and Nationalism*, ch. 2.

9. For Seychelles, see Marcus Franda, *The Seychelles: Unquiet Islands* (Boulder: Westview Press, 1982); Allen, *Security and Nationalism*, ch. 5.

10. See Jean-François Dupon, *Contraintes insulaires et fait colonial aux Mascareignes et aux Seychelles*, 3 vols. (Paris: Honoré Champion, 1977).

11. See Hubert Deschamps, *Les pirates à Madagascar aux XVIIème et XVIIIème siècles* (Paris: Berger-Levrault, 1949).

12. For tourist literature on Madagascar, see Hilary Bradt, *Guide to Madagascar* (Chalfont, St. Peter, UK: Bradt Publications, 1988); Robert Willox, *Madagascar and Comoros: A Travel Survival Kit* (Hawthorn, Victoria, Australia: Lonely Planet Publications, 1989); Philip M. Allen, "Madagascar," in Philip M. Allen and Aaron Segal, *The Traveler's Africa* (New York: Hopkinson & Blake, 1973), pp. 845–868; Patrick Rajoelina and Alain Ramelet, *Madagascar: La grande île* (Paris: Harmattan, 1989).

13. Pascal Chaigneau, *Madagascar, de la première république à l'orientation socialiste: Processus et conséquences d'une évolution politique* (Thèse IIIème cycle en sociologie politique, Univ. de Paris X, 1981), p. 67; see also Jean-Pierre Raison, "Madagascar dans le sud-ouest de l'océan indien," *Hérodote: Revue de Géographie et de Géopolitique*, nos. 37, 38, 1985 (Paris: CHEAM/CNRS), pp. 211–235.

14. Chaigneau, *Première république*, p. 67. See also Raison, "Madagascar dans le sud-ouest"; and Mollat du Jourdin, "Contacts historiques."

15. See Pierre Vérin, "Austronesian Contributions to the Culture of Madagascar: Some Archaeological Problems," in H. Neville Chittick and Robert I. Rotberg, eds., *East Africa and the Orient: Cultural Syntheses in Pre-Colonial Times* (New York and London: Africana, 1975).

16. Vérin, *History of Civilisation*, pp. 32–33 and table on p. 33; Pierre Vérin, "Madagascar," in G. Mokhtar, ed., *Ancient Civilizations of Africa*, UNESCO *General History of Africa*, v. 2 (Berkeley: University of California Press, 1981), pp. 693–717. Chaigneau and other French scholars push the origins of settlement to earlier dates: Chaigneau, *Première république*, p. 2, n. 3; Jean Poirier, "Problèmes de la mise en place des couches ethniques et des couches culturelles à Madagascar," in Poirier et al., *Mouvements de populations dans l'océan indien* (Paris: Honoré Champion, 1979), pp. 51–58; see also Chittick and Rotberg, "Introduction," in *East Africa and the Orient*; Alison Jolly, "Madagascar's Lemurs on the Edge of Survival," *National Geographic* v. 174, no. 2, August 1988, pp. 132–160, speaks of human traces unearthed from ca. A.D. 750.

17. See George P. Murdock, *Africa: Its Peoples and Their Culture History* (New York: McGraw-Hill, 1959); Hubert Deschamps, *Histoire de Madagascar* (Paris: Berger-Levrault, 1961), pp. 13–54; Raymond K. Kent, *Early Kingdoms in Madagascar, 1500–1700* (New York: Holt, Rinehart & Winston, 1970), pp. 30–36 and ch. 7; Chaigneau, *Première république*, p. 70; Chittick and Rotberg are skeptical in their introduction to *East Africa and the Orient*, as are Richard Huntington, *Gender and Social Structure in Madagascar* (Bloomington and Indianapolis: Indiana University Press, 1988), pp. 4–5; Mollat du Jourdin, "Contacts historiques"; Jean-Pierre Raison, *Les hautes terres de Madagascar* (Paris: ORSTOM-Karthala, 1984), p. 97; and Poirier, "Problèmes de la mise en place."

18. Vérin, *History of Civilisation*, pp. 32–34, 40–45; Vérin, "Madagascar," pp. 709–710; Vérin, "Austronesian Contributions," pp. 15–17; Pierre Vérin, in Henri Marchal and Sarah Doulache, eds., *Madagascar: Arts de la vie et de la survie* (Paris: Musée des Arts

Africains et Océaniens, 1989), pp. 9–14; Maurice Bloch, *Placing the Dead: Tombs, Ancestral Villages, and Kinship Organization in Madagascar* (London and New York: Seminar Press, 1972), pp. 15–17; Aidan Southall, "The Problem of Malagasy Origins," in Chittick and Rotberg, *East Africa and the Orient*, pp. 192–215. John Mack, *Madagascar: Island of the Ancestors* (London: British Museum Publications, 1986), p. 23, suggests that the African coast may have been merely explored from Madagascar and the Comoros.

19. See Albert Rakoto-Ratsimamanga, "Tache pigmentaire héréditaire, et origines des Malgaches," *Revue Anthropologique*, 1940, pp. 5–130; Pascal Chaigneau, *Rivalités politiques et socialisme à Madagascar* (Paris: Centre des Hautes Etudes sur l'Afrique et l'Asie Modernes [CHEAM], 1985), pp. 15–18.

20. See Maurice Bloch, *From Blessing to Violence: History and Ideology in the Circumcision Ritual of the Merina of Madagascar* (Cambridge: Cambridge University Press, 1986), pp. 42–43.

21. Cf. the elaborate theory of Paul Ottino, "Le moyen age de l'océan indien, et les composantes du peuplement de Madagascar," *ASEMI: Asie du Sud-Est et Monde Insulindien*, v. 7, nos. 2, 3, 1976 (Paris: EHESS/CNRS), pp. 3–8, which brings the Arabized Shirazi to Madagascar first.

22. F. Fanony and N. J. Gueunier, "Quelques directions pour l'étude de l'Islam malgache," paper presented at the Colloque d'Histoire Malgache, Mahajanga, April 1981; see also Kent, *Early Kingdoms*, esp. chs. 3 and 7.

23. See Vérin, *History of Civilisation*, ch. 4; Kent, *Early Kingdoms*; S. Labib, "Islamic Expansion and Slave Trade in Medieval Africa," in Poirier et al., *Mouvements de populations*, pp. 33–49.

24. See Wang Gungwu, "The Chinese Overseas," in Poirier et al., *Mouvements de populations*, pp. 451–457; Paul Le Bourdiec, "L'implantation des minorités étrangères à Madagascar avant 1972," *APOI*, no. 5, 1978, pp. 37–67; Leon M. S. Slawecki, *French Policy Toward the Chinese in Madagascar* (Hamden, Conn.: Shoe String Press, 1971).

25. See Kent, *Early Kingdoms*, esp. ch. 2.

26. See Chittick and Rotberg, *East Africa and the Orient*, esp. "Introduction" and Southall, "The Problem of Malagasy Origins"; cf. Pierre Vérin, "Des ancêtres venus d'au-delà," pp. 9–14, and Jacques Lombard, "L'art et les ancêtres," in *Madagascar: Arts de la vie et de la survie*, pp. 16–21.

27. See Kurt Sachs, *Les instruments de musique à Madagascar* (Paris: Institut d'Ethnographie, 1938).

28. See Kent, *Early Kingdoms*, ch. 2.

29. See Vérin, "Austronesian Contributions," p. 167; Mack, *Island of the Ancestors*, p. 15.

30. See Jacques Dez, "La lecture des documents arabico-malgaches," *ASEMI*, v. 7, nos. 3–4, 1977, pp. 3–44.

31. See Huntington, *Gender and Social Structure*, p. 5.

32. Ottino, "Le moyen age," p. 3.

33. Mack, *Island of the Ancestors*, p. 17; see also Rajoelina and Ramelet, *La grande île*, pp. 80–81.

34. See Vérin, *History of Civilisation*; James C. Armstrong, "Madagascar and the Slave Trade in the 17th Century," paper presented at the Colloque d'Histoire Malgache, Mahajanga, April 1981.

35. See Toussaint, *History*; Claude Wanquet, "Quelques remarques sur les relations des Mascareignes avec les autres pays de l'océan indien à l'époque de la révolution française," *APOI*, no. 7, 1980, pp. 199–245.

36. See Le Bourdiec, "L'implantation des minorités"; Jean-Louis Miège, "Le 'settlement' européen de l'ouest de l'océan indien au XIXème siècle et au début du XXème," in Poirier et al., *Mouvements de populations*.

37. See Raison, "Madagascar dans le sud-ouest," p. 228.
38. Bloch, *From Blessing to Violence*, p. 27.
39. See Allen, *Security and Nationalism*, ch. 7.
40. See Raison, "Madagascar dans le sud-ouest"; Wanquet, "Relations des Mascareignes."
41. See Wanquet, "Les fondements historiques de la coopération régionale," *APOI*, no. 9, 1982–1983, pp. 21–45.
42. Jolly, *A World Like Our Own*, p. xv.
43. See Chaigneau, *Première république*, pp. 73–75; Nigel Heseltine, *Madagascar* (New York: Praeger, 1971), pp. 2–3.
44. Raison, *Les hautes terres*, p. 12.
45. See Kent, *Early Kingdoms*, ch. 1.
46. Ibid., esp. chs. 1, 2, 4.
47. See Deschamps, *Les pirates à Madagascar;* and Deschamps, *Histoire de Madagascar*, pp. 76–78.
48. See Kent, *Early Kingdoms*, ch. 4; Huntington, *Gender and Social Structure*.
49. See Jean-François Rabedimy, "Contribution de l'*ombiasa* à la formation du royaume menabe, le togny," *ASEMI*, v. 7, nos. 2–3, pp. 255–270; Jacques Lombard, "'Zatovo qui n'a pas été créé par Dieu': Un conte sakalava traduit et commenté," *ASEMI*, v. 7, nos. 2–3, pp. 165–223.
50. For discussions of tromba, see J.-M. Estrade, *Un culte de possession à Madagascar: Le tromba* (Paris: Editions Anthropos, 1977); Gillian Feeley-Harnik, *A Green Estate: Restoring Independence in Madagascar* (Washington and London: Smithsonian Institution, 1991), esp. pp. 303–310; Henry Rusillon, *Un culte dynastique avec évocation des morts chez les Sakalava de Madagascar: Le "tromba"* (Paris: Alphonse Picard, 1912).
51. See Vérin, *History of Civilisation;* Deschamps, *Histoire de Madagascar*, p. 104.
52. See Kent, *Early Kingdoms*, ch. 5; Feeley-Harnik, *A Green Estate*, pp. 69–113.
53. See Feeley-Harnik, *A Green Estate*, pp. 221–228.
54. Some social psychologists have classified this peculiar royal, ancestral authority as a part-feudal, part-parental relationship with a willing dependent population; see O. Mannoni, *Prospero and Caliban: The Psychology of Colonization*, trans. Pamela Powesland, 2nd ed. (New York: Praeger, 1964), pp. 61–65.
55. Among the best of many sources on the Merina monarchy are R. P. François Callet's collection of original documents, the *Tantaran' ny Andriana eto Madagasikara* (Chronicles of the Royalty of Madagascar), 1st ed. (Antananarivo, 1873), 2nd ed. (Antananarivo: Académie Malgache, 1908), and its masterful interpreter, J. Délivré, *L'histoire des rois d'Imerina: Interprétation d'une tradition orale* (Paris: Klinsieck, 1974); see also Kent, *Early Kingdoms*, ch. 6.
56. The prefix "An" or "Am" often signifies a place name. For a detailed narrative, see Edouard Ralaimihoatra, *Histoire de Madagascar*, 4th ed. (Antananarivo: Librairie de Madagascar, 1982), chs. 8–12.
57. See Yves Prats, *Le développement communautaire à Madagascar* (Paris: Pichon et Durand-Auzias, 1972), pp. 31–33.
58. Ibid., pp. 34–35; see also Raison, *Les hautes terres*, ch. 4.
59. See Bloch, *Placing the Dead*, pp. 18–20.
60. See B.E.S.J. Bastiampillai, "Ceylon (Sri Lanka) and Madagascar, Islands in the Indian Ocean: Comparison or Contrast Especially in the Context of Anglo-French Imperial Rivalry till 1850," paper presented at the Colloque d'Histoire Malgache, Mahajanga, April 1981.
61. See Simon Ayache, "Un intellectuel malgache devant la culture européenne: L'historien Raombana (1809–1854)," *Archipel*, no. 12, pp. 95–119.

62. Ibid.; see also Claudine Caillon-Filet, *Jean Laborde et l'océan indien* (Thèse IIIème cycle, Univ. d'Aix-Marseille, 1978), esp. ch. 1; Bloch, *From Blessing to Violence*, pp. 15–29.

63. P. M. Mutibwa, *The Malagasy and the Europeans: Madagascar's Foreign Relations, 1861–1895* (Ibadan, Nigeria: Humanities Press, 1974), p. 33.

64. See Bloch, *From Blessing to Violence*, ch. 2; Gérard Althabe, "Les luttes sociales à Tananarive en 1972," *Cahiers d'Etudes Africaines*, no. 80, 1984, pp. 407–447.

65. See Caillon-Filet, *Jean Laborde et l'océan indien*, pp. 340–365.

66. Ralaimihoatra, *Histoire de Madagascar*, ch. 5.

67. See Mack, *Island of the Ancestors*, p. 55.

68. Caillon-Filet, *Jean Laborde et l'océan indien*, p. 165.

69. On *ramanenjana*, see Françoise Raison-Jourde, "Les ramanenjana: Une mise en cause populaire du Christianisme en Imerina—1863," *ASEMI*, v. 7, nos. 2–3, 1976, pp. 271–293; Bloch, *Placing the Dead*, pp. 22–26; Caillon-Filet, *Jean Laborde et l'océan indien*, pp. 181–193; in his interpretation, Ralaimihoatra, in *Histoire de Madagascar*, p. 177, believes the panic to have been "orchestrated to turn a volatile population against the new king."

70. Raison-Jourde, "Les ramanenjana," p. 271.

71. See Ralaimihoatra, *Histoire de Madagascar*, pp. 184–185; Deschamps, *Histoire de Madagascar*, pp. 182–189.

72. See Gwyn Campbell, "Madagascar and the Slave Trade, 1810–1895," paper presented at the Colloque d'Histoire Malgache, Mahajanga, April 1981.

73. See Henri Vidal, "L'arrêté du 26 septembre 1896 abolissant l'esclavage à Madagascar," *APOI*, no. 5, 1978, pp. 69–93.

74. See Campbell, "Madagascar and the Slave Trade."

75. See Heseltine, *Madagascar*, p. 126.

76. Mutibwa, *The Malagasy and the Europeans*, pp. xii–xiv.

2
Politics: From Paternalism to Revolution

While the entire Southern Hemisphere was falling under domination from northern continents, nineteenth-century Madagascar played an autonomous, largely peaceful role in the life of its region.¹ That role proved short-lived, as Madagascar's assets did not include the ability to defend Malagasy autonomy. The first Europeans came upon a complex, mature, baffling civilization occupying a vast and fertile island. They eventually managed to dominate and exploit that island without having to understand its civilization. By the end of the century Madagascar's independence had been sacrificed to European ambition in exchange for a promise of the benefits offered by Europe to the technologically less advanced. Whatever the virtues of their own civilization, the Malagasy were in no position to repudiate modernization.

For three-fourths of the twentieth century, Madagascar subsisted in dependent obscurity, removed from international intercourse. As a colony, the great island could maintain only the connections established under French authority—with the European metropole, with France's Comorean and Réunionnais territories, and (in education and personal relations) with the rest of the overseas empire. The preeminent relationship with France evolved slowly through a succession of legal status changes and viceregal trustees. In 1958, Madagascar became a republic within the French Community, and in 1960, the republic acquired technical independence. Although these latter changes granted responsibility to Malagasy nationals instead of French, those authorities primarily inherited custody of the special relationship with France. Through 1972, their regime was stigmatized as neocolonial.

By 1975, the bilateral relationship had dissipated into a new plurality of partners. Although more authentically Malagasy, the second republic remained dependent on external technology, capital, and markets—hence on the institutions of the triumphant West. By 1990, the revolution of 1972–1975 had evaporated under the pressures of dependence. Three years later, entering a third republican epoch, Madagascar remains a profoundly Third World country, its national destiny still bedeviled by indigence. Revolution has forged a path to continuity.

IMPOSITION OF THE FRENCH, 1885–1905

In retrospect, the surrender of independence was not an inevitable price for development. Throughout most of the nineteenth century, Great Britain had recognized the Merina dynasty as sovereign over the entire island. During five decades, England offered Madagascar's rulers military and industrial technology, capital investment, and schooling. Not that these advantages were extended out of respect for Malagasy civilization; British missionaries were in fact concomitantly at work against that culture and its "oriental" confusion over such issues as the final destination of souls. But the governments did cooperate well. Working through its Mauritius colony, Britain traded technology and social assistance in exchange for economic concessions on the island and for royal pledges against the slave trade. After recognizing Merina sovereignty, England helped the monarchs of the central plateaus to impose political and cultural uniformity on the recalcitrant coasts.

This patronage gave England a special position at the court of Antananarivo. Rainilaiarivony's 1869 baptism, his marriage with the baptized new queen (requiring peremptory divorce from his first wife, Rasoanalina), and the renunciation of royal *sikidy* made a favorable impression on Queen Victoria. The amicable correspondence exchanged between the two sovereigns was continued under the third Ranavalona, who ascended the throne (and wedded the same prime minister) in 1883. Prevalence of the ancestral cult and the perpetuation of slavery antagonized Christian missionaries on the island, but these atavisms did not seriously impede relations with England.

By contrast, nineteenth-century French strategy was more complex. The French Indian Ocean presence had long been sustained by Malagasy foodstuffs and timber. To obtain such resources after the defeat of Napoleon, France had to follow Britain in recognition of Merina sovereignty under the rules of nations. At first, Paris sought to compete with London at the Merina court while simultaneously developing relations with the monarchy's Sakalava and Betsimisaraka rivals in the west and east. In the last two decades of the century, however, the French were able to profit from Britain's renunciation of its special privileges in Madagascar. Preoccupied in India and elsewhere in the Indian Ocean, successful along the east coast of Africa and in Egypt, England had to economize on commitments. After the opening of the Suez Canal in 1869, travelers to and from India could avoid the southern seas and the Cape of Good Hope. The realm of the Merina queens became geopolitically marginal.

To France, in contrast, the Indian Ocean remained alive with possibilities. Here lay resources for the industrialization of a retrograde French economy. In the late nineteenth century, France needed territory and world standing as much as economic concessions from what it considered barbarian monarchs. After humiliating France in 1870, Germany feared a surge of Gallic vengeance on the continent; Bismarck thus encouraged French energies outward toward the uncharted fields of empire. Spacious, productive in primary materials, standing close to France's crowded colony of Réunion, Madagascar represented a logical target for those energies. The United States and other powers entertained only casual mercantile interest in these distant shores.

So, abandoned by England yet still dependent for state survival on European capital, technology, and markets, Madagascar confronted a resurgent French imperialism without allies or major alternatives in the industrial world. Once reduced to economic dependence on France, the monarchy was unable to resist political domination. It took a virtual century, but after clinging to obscure commercial posts on the east coast and backing the losing Sakalava dynasty in the west, France managed to inch its way into favor, then power, at Antananarivo.

Succeeding the disgraced empire of Napoleon III, the third French republic used thin historical precedents to establish an otherwise preposterous claim to sovereignty over the great island. Briefly in the mid-seventeenth century, before the *parvenu* monarchy of the Merina, Louis XIV first asserted that claim by virtue of a colonial experiment at Fort Dauphin that lasted only thirty years. A century later, in 1750, Sainte Marie with its mulatto elite had come under the protection of the Tricolor. In 1840, Sakalava antagonists of the Merina ceded lovely Nosy Be to complement France's appropriation of Mayotte, the nearest Comoro. At home in those island bases, French warships nosed along the coasts. From Réunion and Sainte Marie in the east, they bombarded Toamasina twice to teach recalcitrant Ranavalona I a lesson in global politics. They had to apologize to the queen in 1853 for damaging her dominions. Ranavalona thereupon reopened her ports, but she still kept most of the Europeans away from her court. Laborde was the usual exception, and his death in 1878 marked the beginning of the end for Franco-Malagasy cordiality.

The conquest of Madagascar in 1895–1896 evolved out of imperialist demands in France and Réunion for Malagasy land, natural resources, and trading concessions. During the half-century from the start of the first Ranavalona's reign in 1828 to the death of Jean Laborde, politicians in Paris attended halfheartedly, albeit with moments of intensity, to the demands of French businessmen, the church, and the anxious landholders on Réunion. All of them appealed for pressure on the Merina monarchy for relaxation of sacred property laws that reserved land to the throne, for favorable terms in the exports of foodstuffs and industrial raw materials, and for an expansion of Roman Catholicism—especially after the court's conversion to Protestantism in 1869. The Réunionnais establishment also sought land grants and employment for a Creole population already beginning to stretch the resources of its tiny volcanic island. Réunion was electing deputies to the National Assembly whose patriotism exceeded Joan of Arc's. Always nervously watching London and Port Louis (Mauritius) for reactions, the French government inched its way toward accommodation of these demands.

Rainilaiarivony, the queen's prime minister, understood this much of the danger. He sent ambassadors to London, Paris, Washington, and Berlin in 1882–1883, finding all parties willing to negotiate on trade. The British proved unusually conciliatory over property rights. But the Malagasy did not grasp the extent of England's abdication in the southern Indian Ocean, or London's and Berlin's diplomatic need to keep the French mollified.[2] The prime minister believed, as some Malagasy still do, that official Merina Protestantism had forged a spiritual and temporal bond between Madagascar and England. In his mind, this alliance warranted fraternal British assistance against the Jesuitical French, masters of intrigue and champions of the subjected côtiers (coastal peoples).[3] Protestant missionaries reassured him of this nexus between faith and politics. But England accepted no responsibility for Malagasy security in the path of the expansive French.

A dispute over property rights provided a pretext for attack by France in 1883. Laborde's heirs had found themselves juridically blocked from his estate by the queen's assertion of suzerainty over all island property. The prime minister's intransigeance on this account invited first consular protest, then armed retaliation. Small French fleets occupied Mahajanga and Toamasina in 1883, sealing the island off from international communications. Without a navy, the monarchy was helpless against these tactics. But France, too, was preoccupied (in Indo-China this time), and its forces were insufficient to annex Madagascar. Even an Antanosy uprising around Fort Dauphin could not be sustained, and the Merina kept their holdings. Once again, the weaknesses of France prevented a decisive conclusion.

The settlement of December 1885 consecrated stalemate, and the French accepted reparations payments in lieu of their preciously defended property claims. But the Malagasy were yielding vital sovereignty; Antsiranana with its potential as a naval base became French Diego Suarez, and the island's foreign affairs fell under the authority of a French "resident" at Antananarivo. A decade passed under what Hubert Deschamps terms a "phantom protectorate" in which neither side perceived opportunities for advantage. The French obtained little satisfaction from their new rights, and Antananarivo seethed with intrigue against the aging prime minister. The south and west were in open revolt after the messy war of 1883–1885; Indian subjects of the British Crown were there, combing the coasts for slaves, selling cloth and gunpowder, lending money, founding fortunes that would finance Karana commerce and industry over the next century.[4]

For another decade, Paris had to fear that the remaining great powers might oppose an outright annexation of this large Southern Hemisphere state ruled by a respectable, nominally Christian, monarch. Ultimately, however, Europe had acquired the habit of deciding the fate of all Africa. Territory was being staked out regardless of the qualities of indigenous polities. The Merina queen might write to her "dear sister Victoria," and privileged Malagasy might argue fine points of Christian theology over tea or aperitif, but to the despoilers of the Congo and the western Sudan, Madagascar no longer appeared to be the advanced offspring of missionized enlightenment. Its civilization was categorically ignored, and its social character identified with "African barbarism" in the mass calumny of imperialism.

Having obtained a foothold on the northeast African coast at Djibouti in 1888, France wished a more certain grip over the Malagasy island. Its resident representatives advanced new demands. Antananarivo was to cease direct external relations with other governments. It must allow France to expand its military establishments on the island at will and to build naval bases and other such projects. In short, Madagascar was to disappear from the atlas of states.

In a climate of insecurity, Paris sought to consecrate the indignity by negotiation, but the prime minister held fast. He even thought against all probability that he might restore his country's status quo ante 1885. Without realizing the consequences, Rainilaiarivony was bent on making the French fight for their imperial privileges. In October 1894, French citizens were evacuated from Antananarivo, and in the subsequent January the invasion began from Mahajanga, 625 kilometers northwest of the capital. This proved no simple task, even for the well-equipped forces of General Jacques Achille Duchesne. A 15,000-man force was slowly bogged down in the unkind swampland of the Betsiboka valley, and more than half the army died of disease or had to be evacuated because of it. The Merina army fought intermittently, if not well, and Duchesne had to re-form his remaining troops into a rapidly moving commando to effect the climb into the plateaus of Imerina. This column reached Antananarivo within two weeks. A one-day bombardment was sufficient to persuade the Malagasy that their crowded capital of 50,000 might be destroyed. Worse, their hilltop palace (*rova*), injudiciously loaded with explosives, was within incendiary reach of French artillery. They surrendered on September 30, 1895.

COLONIAL ARCHITECTONICS

The task of conquering Madagascar dominated French strategy for many months after the capture of Antananarivo by General Duchesne's forces. For ten months, by virtue of what Deschamps calls "lack of imagination,"[5] Paris permitted Ranavalona III to occupy the throne of a formal protectorate modeled after the Tunisia solution of 1881. The seventy-year-old Rainilaiarivony, symbol of hova recalcitrance, was placed under house arrest. When insurrection intensified, he was exiled to Algiers, where he died in 1896. The queen's status remained theoretically intact even after her realm had been redefined as a French possession. The monarchy had, after all, been recognized internationally and had conducted its diplomatic concourse with dignity. France had no grounds to declare its mission tantamount (as elsewhere) to the delivery of "organization" to an otherwise anarchic region of benighted tribes.

But anarchy had been engendered by the French conquest of this respectable state. Rebellions—identified as the *menalamba* (red-cloak) movement—were endemic after 1896. Although much insurrectionary fury was directed against the humiliated Merina monarchy for its thirty years of capitulation to foreign, Christian ways, the movement also involved fervent supporters of the outraged queen. Eventually, political opposition degenerated into banditry or (what is not so different) sheer resistance against a hateful new authority. In any event, so acute was the symbolic rallying power of the monarchy that the French had to abandon the simple solution of a protectorate over Merina institutions. The menalamba were displaying, however perversely, what Chaigneau termed "the profound will of the Malagasy to preserve their cultural heritage and deepest traditions, as well as the origin of a tenacious capacity for insurrection."[6]

In suppressing the revolt, the French army behaved badly, antagonizing other elements of the harassed population. Civilian French authorities were embarrassed to see islanders whom they believed they had liberated turning against their saviors. Even the Sakalava refused to trade tyrannical Merina for enlightened European masters. In essence, the menalamba revolt was profoundly inspired by pre-Christian traditions, ancestral honor, and a rejection of European modernism. It was as hostile to the French as to the Merina and was found xenophobic and atavistic by both authorities.

On August 6, 1896, to subdue the island and allow for the settlement and economic activity demanded by Réunionnais and by metropolitan business interests, the French Parliament had to declare Madagascar and its dependent islands a colony. Now, as part of the French Empire, Madagascar could no longer be permitted to maintain slavery; hence, virtually a million slaves were expeditiously emancipated by a single act of that same parliamentary session. The legislation was vague, and the resident general's implementing decree left many questions unresolved. No accommodations were made to indemnify slave owners, to define the juridical status of the new "freedom" acquired in a colonial system, or to provide orderly access to employment for the newly enfranchised subjects.[7] Nevertheless, the historic decree was promulgated at Antananarivo on September 26, 1896.

In early October, the Paris government dispatched General Joseph Simon Galliéni, veteran of campaigns in North Africa and Indo-China, to exercise full powers in pacifying the country and breaking the Merina hold over the island. Galliéni replaced the sympathetic but hapless civilian resident general, Hippolyte Laroche, who had proved unable to comprehend the depth of anti-European fervor within the resistance or the ability of the Merina oligarchy to mobilize national sentiment behind the deposed queen. Henceforth, the French proposed to substitute the ministrations of local indigenous chiefs for the authority of Merina governors. In theory, the government of Antananarivo was to be reduced to one among many "tribal" administrations answering to French residents in their respective territories. In practice, as Paris proved perpetually distracted from its colonial responsibilities, the Merina continued their relative privileges even under this "tribal policy" (*politique des races*).

Nevertheless, Galliéni began France's sixty-four years of colonial control with distinction. After his decade as governor-general (1896–1905), all regimes were merely his successors.[8] A versatile leader, statesman, patriot, and political thinker, this middle-class soldier of republican sympathies dominated French colonial policy in Madagascar by force of will. Finding Queen Ranavalona an impediment to the consolidation of French authority, he deposed her summarily on February 27, 1897, exiled her to Réunion within twenty-four hours, then sought (and received) endorsement of this action from his government. Two years later, Ranavalona was transferred to Algiers, where she died in 1917. Her remains were shipped back to Antananarivo in 1938 to be buried alongside her predecessors—whose bones Galliéni had disinterred and removed from the sacred tombs of Ambohimanga. This offense to Malagasy tradition caused scandal in France, but the general held his ground and continued the organization of military rule in the great island.

Galliéni's first task, of course, was to stamp out the menalamba resistance. This he accomplished with 7,000 troops, augmented by small contingents of Foreign Legionnaires and Malagasy recruited outside Imerina. His strategy, invoking the metaphor of *taches d'huile* (literally "oil spots"; refers to the way oil spreads) was to impose coherent and ingratiating administrations wherever the army took hold. Not entirely successful in winning Malagasy minds and hearts, the policy nevertheless served effectively to wipe out the rebellion. The job was completed substantially within two years, although uprisings occurred sporadically until 1904. Much blood was shed in the repression, try as the governor-general would to minimize the carnage. By the end of the action, Galliéni had united the entire island under a single administration—a feat that for all its other achievements the Merina monarchy had failed to accomplish.

Once his "oil spots" had dried, and after a number of forays into dead ends, Galliéni established a rational territorial governance, assigning competent French military residents to administer twenty "provinces," with Malagasy officials in subordinate and clerical positions. Scion of anticlerical French liberalism, the general depended by inclination more on civilian and military agents than on missionaries, thus offending church leadership in the provinces and at the capital. Nor did he or his successors succeed in replacing Merina administrative staff in the "interior protectorates" by traditional chiefs and local kings. Although the "tribal policy" was pursued until 1926, the district commanders used what they had at hand—literate and experienced but often unreliable Merina civil servants who enjoyed the monopoly of suitable administrative skills. By encouraging a rapid expansion of the provincial school system, Galliéni sought to facilitate ethnic equilibrium in the emerging generation, but somehow the new elites continued to be predominantly populated by Merina. By practical necessity, a single ethnic group retained the status of a conventionally favored colonial class.

A number of other important cultural institutions—including a medical school (identified with impressive advances in public health)—are attributable to Galliéni's gubernatorial innovation. These, too, were located in the capital—shortened to Tananarive in the French lexicon. They were frequented primarily by the Merina and the French, with a token contingent of provincial notables' sons. Crafts and trade schools were populated largely by côtiers.[9] Galliéni himself came to admire the Merina in invidious contradistinction to other Malagasy. He thus inadvertently contributed to the Europeans' racial myth of the "light-skinned superior people"—even though Merina superiority must be attributed to a complex of historical advantages rather than to pigmentation (which is by no means uniform among them). The governor-general predicted Merina accession to French citizenship in large numbers once Paris accepted the implications of its assimilationist colonial ideology. Unfortunately for thousands of Merina aspirants, Paris never was quite prepared for this advent.

A scholar in his own right after the fashion of French officers abroad, Galliéni recorded his thoughts liberally and encouraged his officers to learn the Malagasy language. He founded the Malagasy Academy, a distinguished research forum modeled on the Académie Française. Astutely, after eliminating the institution of slavery, French authorities used the Merina-imposed fokon'olona institutions to appoint new local leaders and to open access for themselves to rural populations. But, although claiming to restore decentralized autonomy to the provinces through these institutions, the French merely tightened central control.[10] Galliéni also instituted public health and social programs designed over the long term to modernize the island as a whole. Unfortunately, the chances of these projects weakened with the vicissitudes of French metropolitan attitudes and the declining fortunes of overseas budgets.

In addition to his military, administrative, and educational achievements, Galliéni founded a new colonial economy. Finding little capital available in France to finance an islandwide system of public works—roadways, water resource projects, administrative buildings, and the beginning of the Antananarivo-Toamasina railway—he levied taxes on the entire population. Confronted with large pools of unemployed ex-slave labor, Galliéni revived the monarchy's old practice of forced labor (the *fanampoana,* or *corvée* in French). He used fiscal measures as what he called an "educational tool"—for to pay their taxes, Malagasy peasants had to produce surpluses and enter the exchange economy hitherto left to the aristocracy and the foreign concessionaires. To avoid public works conscription, a Malagasy laborer could also pay a commutational fee but would have to earn an income to meet that obligation. Galliéni's head tax may have failed to educate masses on the joys of the market, but it proved durable—lasting until it was abolished in a popular flourish of the revolutionary government of 1972. Galliéni also manipulated the fokon'olona, using them not as proto-democratic sources of decision but as instruments of the state to ensure supplies of food, labor, and agricultural raw materials.[11]

But the thrust of colonial economic development was oriented toward Europeans, not Malagasy. Isolated from the rest of the world, Madagascar became the largest non-Mediterranean possession of the French, not only in absolute size and population but also in numbers of nonindigenous residents. By the 1960s, 34,000 French passport holders endowed Madagascar with a metropolitan settler community comparable in proportion to Britain's classic Kenya colony.[12] Like Kenya, albeit with less publicity or belletristic distinction, Madagascar became the object of tough, racially discriminatory policies implemented by colonial administrators on orders from the metropole.

French colonialism in Madagascar was probably neither better nor worse than colonial rule elsewhere. By and large, the French took pride in their "civilizing mission," acknowledging little civilized virtue in the conquered and now-pacified Malagasy society. "France has established order and respect for property; it has abolished slavery, assuring the dignity of the human person."[13] Some infrastructural and social progress was recorded—

largely in order to make the colony function for the benefit of French political and corporate interests. Beyond that, the colonial achievement fell short of ambitions. It was entirely dependent on French national crises and on the shifting options of successive governments in Paris. Much that might have been done was not done. For its part, the Malagasy nation remained inveterately dependent on industrial partners and obsessed by its "ambiguous adventure" as a ward of Europe.[14]

The French administration faced an ambiguity of its own in Madagascar—a radical mistrust borne by virtually an entire population for any authority that has not emerged out of its own cultural midst. A government in this culture invites alienation whenever it challenges the authority of ancestral tradition, regarded by most Malagasy as the only legitimate power. From the time of the Merina empire, the dispersed Malagasy communities have refused the obedience normally available to a central regime that held genuine power, including the power to improve living conditions for Malagasy. Here, "the record" of a government seems to count little or not at all in the attitude of local populations regarding their *fanjakana*, or power establishment. If the authority comes from outside the community—from Paris or even Antananarivo—it is generally considered to have other interests in mind than those of the people it claims to govern.

The great island's incorporation into Overseas France fulfilled ambitions asserted from the late seventeenth century by French colonists in Réunion and (briefly) Mauritius. From the outset, society on these neighboring Mascarenes—originally called Bourbon and Île de France—demanded free access to Malagasy sources of labor and foodstuffs. A third of the slaves imported into the Mascarenes were Malagasy. The source was convenient but hardly congenial, for these bondspeople quickly earned reputations for unruliness. Mixing with European masters and with unfree mainland Africans and Asians, the Malagasy participated in the miscegenation of these Creole plantation islands. But the Mascarenes show little direct cultural influence from the great island, and there is scant evidence that the Malagasy populations of the Creole islands retained memories of their land of origin.[15] Madagascar's highly absorbent insular culture is anchored in its ancestral locality and seems little suited to expatriation.

Colonized Madagascar also served its overpopulated neighbors regularly as an unconsenting repository for Réunionnais and Comoreans in search of land and jobs. Privileged Malagasy youth attended school in Réunion; Roman Catholicism flourished in Madagascar through the work of the Diocese of St. Denis. Islam also spread in the cities of the north, thanks to contact with Sunni faithful in the Comorean diaspora. Muslims from India and Chinese from Canton also took advantage of opportunities denied to the indigenous on the great island. In contrast with the Mascarene settler colonies, however, Madagascar did not develop a substantial Creole population. Only the Chinese minority intermarried regularly among the Malagasy, creating a substantial Asian *métissage*.

From the Parisian viewpoint, Madagascar gave every reason to favor extensive colonization by farmers, tradespeople, artisans, and small-scale industrialists. Réunionnais partisans had been advocating "opening up" the Malagasy highlands for decades, and a number of their concessions had prospered on the east coast as well as on the island of Nosy Be through much of the nineteenth century. The plateaus boasted a temperate climate, comparable to the highlands of Kenya, Rhodesia, and North Africa, which had already attracted tens of thousands of European settlers. The island was scantily populated (perhaps 2 million at the turn of the century), and the colonial administration never seemed too fastidious about what the Malagasy regarded as ancestral land. It was thus disposed to reallocate areas once identified with a community but left fallow or otherwise unutilized at the time. Tax relief and other incentives were offered French and Creole settlers, and indeed, a few thousand did try their hand at farming Malagasy soil.

These immigrants were far better treated in access to capital and labor and in taxation and other concessions than the autochthonous farmers. Most of the great feudal fiefs of Merina and other Malagasy landholders were broken up. Settler agriculture was somehow supposed to supply models for the Malagasy peasantry, but few immigrant farmers remained for long; their large, diversified plantations—the early-century equivalent of agribusiness—tended to wither on the great island. They had never rivaled in numbers the agrarian colonies of Algeria or southern Africa, and their repatriatable profits were tied to overseas market fluctuations. Few colonists reinvested in Madagascar, and many retired as soon as they were comfortable. During the 1930s new efforts at enlarging agricultural credit and cooperative schemes failed to take hold among settlers or peasants.[16] In the 1940s people simply sought to survive.

The French experimented with policy through the 1950s, trying a variety of strategies for rural development—reorganizing the cantons and villages into communes with elected "notables" under the strict tutelage of the colonial administration and its technical services. Expensive campaigns of mechanization failed to mobilize the peasantry, to convert the educational system toward utilitarian functions, or to rationalize the distorted rural price mechanisms, which favored urban dwellers and foreigners.[17] All these good ideas had been imposed on the Malagasy with utmost rationality, but they never took hold in the soils of a reluctant peasantry. The "rural animation" program was regarded as a game played by the fanjakana to please itself.[18] A couple of major development schemes promised results—cotton in the Mangoky valley, rice in the region around Lake Alaotra. Bemused by the disappointment of the settlement schemes, Nigel Heseltine, like others, contends that Madagascar was simply too far removed from networks of colonial exchange to attract truly dynamic colonists.[19] Major industry never appeared, and most Malagasy raw materials were sent to France for processing.

This limited economy was what the large agrocommercial enterprises were seeking. The real fruits of colonization subsisted in a closed atmosphere of intercontinental trade dominated by the so-called Marseillaise, Lyonnaise, Rochefortaise (companies incorporated in Marseille, Lyon, Rochefort), the major shipping lines, and other privileged firms. In what the French Left identifies as a new form of slave trade (*l'économie de traite*), these inefficient oligopolies bartered raw materials for imported manufactured goods. Generally, they possessed the political influence to stifle competitive initiatives, and they operated at low volume and high prices to restrict import and export, wholesale commerce, and production for trade. In the countryside, they cooperated with networks of ethnic Chinese and Muslim Indian traders to control agricultural marketing and rural credit.

Although the Indians and Chinese operated mainly in the remoter localities, some great fortunes have also accrued to Asians in textile trade and light manufacturing. Like the Europeans and Réunionnais Creoles, many Asians acquired French passports—an asset always promised but rarely accorded to "qualified" (read French-speaking, propertied, "evolved") Malagasy. Nationality made a vast difference. French residents were entitled to the benefits of liberal legislation and metropolitan jurisprudence; Malagasy subjects fell under the jurisdiction of the *indigénat,* a potpourri of monarchical, ancestral, and colonial legislation that allowed authorities considerably greater room for exploitation.[20] The humiliation of arbitrary imprisonment and fines for failing to perform social obligations created a perpetual grievance for Malagasy nationalists until after World War II. Under the indigénat, labor could be recruited for work not only on public projects but in private businesses as well. With low labor costs and monopoly control of trade volume and credit, those businesses could set prices at will and enjoy arbitrary profit margins.

Such were the works engendered by Galliéni, enlightened scholar-administrator, sympathizer with the Merina, assimilator; he was later to have his loftiest moment as organizer of the heroic defense of Paris against the German advance to the Marne in 1914. The governors who succeeded him were a mixed lot, reflecting the circumstances of power and policy in Paris during the third and fourth republics. Their statecraft was always just keeping up with the previous stage of Malagasy national aspirations. Whereas Merina and côtier hopes remained fixed on Galliéni's promise of full participation in the French metropole, settlers and other conservatives compelled Paris to withhold the expansion of education and citizenship that might have turned the great island into something like an overseas department on a par with Corsica or the Creole islands (Réunion, Martinique, Guadeloupe). When Malagasy soldiers returned from participation in Europe's fratricides in 1918, their demands for educational privileges and the abolition of the indigénat received scant attention. So much for assimilationist aspirations.

Hence, by the time France was ready in 1946 to broadcast citizenship and French culture throughout the colonies, Malagasy intellectuals had perceived the futility of membership in a suicidal Europe. They had already begun demanding restoration of political autonomy, along with their Indo-Chinese and Arab counterparts. Twelve years later, when the de Gaulle regime of 1958 offered just such autonomy within a loose federal community, the leading edge of Malagasy nationalism required more than that—formal independence. And after fourteen more years, when merely formal independence proved unsatisfactory for national identity, the first Malagasy republic was overthrown. In revolutionary fervor, Madagascar's nationalists then decided—prematurely—that they could do without France and France's privileged relationship.

This ratcheting interaction between colonial policy and Malagasy nationalism evolved through a continuum of incidents, gestures, and policies that manage virtually to tell their own story. One of the first inadvertent achievements of French colonial policy was to heal the long breach between the Merina andriana and the middle-class hova, who had asserted control over the monarchy in 1829. Now, both hova and nobles, Protestants and traditionalists, were united in a single national surge against a common enemy—the weakening conqueror.

Malagasy nationalism was born as a struggle by the Merina to recover their lost suzerainty; after a generation of French rule, that struggle generalized itself as anticolonialism beyond particular Merina aspirations. Nevertheless, those aspirations continued to stigmatize the nationalist cause throughout the twentieth century, engendering a powerful opposition to nationalism among the coastal majority. Côtier fears that decolonization would mean resumption of Merina control offered France an unmistakable opportunity to influence great-island destinies into the 1990s.

NATIONALISM IN THE ANXIOUS EMPIRE

Each European world war eroded French credibility in Madagascar. Malagasy conscripts returned from overseas service during 1914–1918 and 1939–1945 with diminished respect for France as a power and for white Europe as a civilization. On the home front, heavy taxation and food levies for the war effort alienated the Malagasy even further. A clandestine organization called Vy Vato Sakelika (Iron, Stone, Stem, VVS) mobilized a thousand young intellectuals and students, most of them Merina, to agitate against colonial rule in the middle of World War I. Rather than focusing on outright revolt, the VVS stressed moral, physical, and political discipline—an insular version of China's earlier Boxer society. At Antananarivo, the movement united social labor ideology and radical populism with Merina ambitions and Protestant preaching. This combination of dissidence resurfaced in 1947, 1972, and the late 1980s. Although members were pledged to secrecy, the VVS was infiltrated by colonial police. On Christmas Eve 1915, it was banned and 300 of its militants arrested as potentially seditious. Virtually all were convicted of something, but most of them were subsequently granted amnesty, and the VVS episode launched a new generation of nationalist protest.[21]

Developing along with the declining fortunes of colonial France, Malagasy nationalism remained for several decades identified with Merina bitterness over the loss of empire. Outnumbered by the coastal population, the Merina nonetheless retained the economic, social, and cultural privileges of a national elite. Although Galliéni's "tribal policy" purported to balance these advantages with a new surge of côtier advancement and prosperity, realities favored the intelligentsia and middle class that had evolved on the plateaus under Merina domination. Schools and governmental institutions remained densely concentrated in the capital; export agriculture and the island's sprinkling of industries clung mainly to the coasts. These economic assets were controlled by French companies and Asian minority business families, not by the côtier people.

Comparative privilege could scarcely mollify the dedicated Merina opponents of foreign rule, but the impact of nationalism might have been diminished had France recognized the economic-cultural elite as French citizens. Despite France's pledges of faith in "assimilation," this did not occur. French nationality, as Ralaimihoatra described it, was being doled out as a rare reward, not as a right or a means to accommodate Malagasy cultural aspirations.[22] Despite the aptitude for westernization that Galliéni had applauded in the Merina—indeed, the existence of a substantial cultural aristocracy schooled by Europeans since the time of Radama I—the number of citizenship franchises granted to Malagasy reached only 8,000 by the outbreak of World War II. Malagasy were accorded an increasing number of scholarships to study in France after World War I, and a relatively free press existed in the capital and other enclaves of urban literacy. But Malagasy scholars and readers were not allowed to claim status with Europeans or even Asian and Creole immigrants. The indigenous middle class, urban and rural, persisted in seeking such acceptance and was embittered by denial while the peasantry guarded its own impenetrable anonymity.

Bolstering these social restrictions was a constant barrage of language and imagery stressing the inferiority of the colonized and the responsibility of (civilized) Europe to protect its legitimate interests.[23] The gulf between the Malagasy and the protected minorities was reinforced in virtually every act of colonial authority. Systems of legislation separated French citizens from ordinary Malagasy (viz., the indigénat). Land not registered according to European formalities could be confiscated, thus mocking ancestral and communal sources of property rights. Malagasy workers could be peremptorily conscripted into the Labor Service for General Interest Works (SMOTIG).

Much nationalist energy was absorbed in the struggle for civil rights under colonialism, but the objective gradually changed into a crusade for freedom from French authority. Protest was distilled into proverbial speeches, songs, and sermons. On May 19, 1929, police banned a public meeting scheduled in Antananarivo to support the demand for social and legal reforms and eventual incorporation into France as an overseas department. The crowd gathered illegally, and when the police overreacted with assaults and arrests, the call rose henceforth for independence and freedom, not mere assimilation. Reasonable reforms in the 1930s that might have satisfied most aspirations—broadening of citizenship and landholding rights, abolition of the SMOTIG by the Popular Front government in 1936—were insufficient. The busy Tananarive press seized on every pretext to attack colonial rule.

Betsileo and Betsimisaraka leaders to the south and east began taking up the hitherto Merina nationalist banner. By the outbreak of World War II, the French Communist Party's CGT (General Confederation of Labor) affiliate had formed fourteen Malagasy unions. Other politicized unions adhered to the Christian and social democratic movements. For nearly twenty years until his death in 1943, Jean Ralaimongo, a Betsileo teacher, worked prominently in the labor movement and among World War I veterans; his aim was equality of treatment for Malagasy, but that message was overtaken by the demand for an end to colonialism. Secret societies sustained the alienation between nationalist-minded Malagasy and their dominators.

Just before World War II, a new leader emerged from nationalism's classic crucible—the Protestant Merina elite. Ravelojaona, a VVS leader and Protestant pastor whose sermons and articles had stirred the passions of 1915 and 1929, was elected to the Colonial Council. Although more sentimental Merina chauvinism found itself overwhelmed in the rush of radical nationalism, Merina aristocrats like Ravelojaona and Dr. Joseph Ravoahangy still embodied both dimensions of the anti-colonial movement.[24] In the capital city and surrounding highlands areas, the Protestant church bred nationalist leaders who used their pulpits to claim recovery of the independence enjoyed under the Merina queens—Protestant themselves since 1869.[25]

Because France would not accommodate the early nationalist plea for citizenship and cultural recognition, the nationalist movement in Madagascar eventually repudiated French interests categorically.[26] Even after technical independence in 1960, the nationalist opposition of Merina politicians and Protestants persisted. For more than three decades this alliance was embodied by Antananarivo mayor Richard Andriamanjato, a Merina Protestant pastor who succeeded to the pulpit occupied by the revered Ravelojaona; although leader of the nominally Marxist opposition AKFM (Congress Party for the Independence of Madagascar), Andriamanjato identified himself in a strategic 1971 interview as the non-Marxist Ravelojaona's successor.[27] Resistance to imposed authority had become a seamless web.

Humiliating defeat in World War II crippled the standing of France in the colonies as everywhere else. Labor and food requisitions intensified during the war, and the unions were suspended for a time. There were 34,000 Malagasy troops in Europe and 72,000 more ready to embark when France surrendered in June 1940; the island thereupon passed two years under the unworthy administration of Vichy. Briefly, in 1939–1940, certain Nazi German officials—even, for a time, Hitler himself—had entertained what historian Raul Hilberg calls "the fantastic idea of shipping millions of Jews to the African island of Madagascar." The island was to be ceded for the purpose by France—which in 1938 under a rightist government had itself considered deporting 10,000 Jews there. Regarded in Berlin as a kind of jungle tabula rasa, Madagascar was to have German naval bases and to be operated by the Gestapo as a "Jewish reservation."[28] This project to "solve the Jewish problem" through emigration was abandoned by July 31, 1941 in favor of the supremely fantastic but infinitely more tragic policy of mass annihilation.

Apprehending a threat from Japanese submarine activity off the East African coast and an imminent invasion of India, a British and South African force stormed the Vichy French naval base at Diego Suarez on May 5, 1942. The invaders extended the campaign to the rest of the island in September and subsequently turned Madagascar over to de Gaulle's Free French.[29] If anything, the latter period of the war proved even more difficult for the Malagasy; stringent economic exactions were imposed on the population to support the marginal contributions of de Gaulle's forces in the combat theaters. Rice was constantly in short supply for a population accustomed to eating nothing but rice. In Antananarivo, General Paul Legentilhomme purged Vichy sympathizers and even sought to revive the aborted "tribal" policies of the early Galliéni period. By the end of the war, Malagasy patriotism had followed Indochina into what Chaigneau calls "a nationalism of separation" (*nationalisme de rupture*) as contrasted with the "nationalism of continuity" prevailing in most of French Africa.[30]

Seeming to repudiate wartime pledges made to the cooperating colonies, France's postwar regimes allowed them greater participation in politics without honoring their proposals for autonomy. In Madagascar, political participation entailed overwhelming support of the nationalist platform, embodied in the Democratic Movement for Malagasy Renewal (MDRM). The party was formed in Paris during early 1946 to marshal national sentiment behind Ravoahangy and another Merina doctor, Joseph Raseta; its founders included still another Antananarivo aristocrat, the expatriate intellectual Raymond William Rabemananjara. These Merina leaders were joined by Jacques Rabemananjara, a young Betsimisaraka writer who, although no relation to Raymond William, had also been stranded in France during the war.

In June 1946, to counter the anticolonial momentum that it identified with Merina revanchism, the French encouraged a Party of the Disinherited (*déshérités*, a code word for non-Merina). This PADESM formed around selected côtier dignitaries including Philibert Tsiranana, a Tsimihety schoolteacher in Majunga. Appealing to "tribal" and caste bitterness against the Merina and their aristocracy, PADESM failed to ignite electoral enthusiasms in any of the three tests in which it encountered the MDRM. The latter had 100,000 members, thousands more sympathizers, and a clear program of decolonization and national revival.[31] In January 1947, MDRM candidates swept all provincial elections except in Majunga, but the wily Governor Marcel DeCoppet combined PADESM delegates (including Majunga's majority ten) with the protected caucus of French settlers into a single college that outvoted MDRM in the Representative Assembly at Antananarivo.

The real political tests were taking place in Paris, however; there the MDRM parliamentary deputies repeatedly failed to obtain adequate hearing for legislation granting Madagascar independence "within the French Union." A demand for autonomous institutions had surfaced as early as April 1945, when French and Malagasy citizens sent letters to the new postwar government and to the press urging colonial authorities to go beyond their contemplated reforms—abolition of forced labor and the indigénat and elimination of requisitions for rice and other necessities.[32] But under the new French constitution of October 1946, Madagascar became merely a territory of the French republic without universal rights of French citizenship. Unable to obtain any measure of decolonization, the nationalists were outraged. Malagasy hopes for self-determination were ignored even by the French Communist Party. Struggling to rise from its wartime prostration, France declined to hear the aspirations of the prostrate colonized. It thus ensured that nationalists in Madagascar would refuse to stop short of independence.

France's accumulating loss of prestige helps in part to explain the rebellion of March 29, 1947, when Malagasy rage roared into violence in several parts of the island. The uprising occurred at a time of exasperation over draconian wartime policies that had extended into a corrupt, distorted postwar economy. It followed persistent refusal of national demands that were mistakenly believed by nationalists to have found international favor. The mood of rebellion grew in an atmosphere of sluggish economic recovery and against delays in the repatriation of 10,000 Malagasy troops from Europe. The year 1946 had already witnessed a series of riots, strikes, and other symptoms of political fever in Madagascar.

Earliest—and perhaps most tragic—of many postwar nationalist uprisings in Europe's colonies, the 1947 insurrection represents an aborted movement of national liberation. It was thus an attempted answer to the deep frustrations of the postwar constitutional process.[33] The insurrectionary movement seems to have been planned by two clandestine societies spawned during the war—the PANAMA (National Malagasy Party), formed in the north and east in 1941, and the JINA (National Malagasy Youth), founded in the south during 1943 by a now legendary dissenter named Monja Jaona. JINA and PANAMA overlapped the MDRM in membership and exploited the popularity and prominence of the legitimate party to pass a more radical message to the Malagasy population.

From another perspective, Malagasy patriots still accuse the French regime of provoking the entire episode in order to destroy the nationalist movement. In 1990, Jacques Rabemananjara himself revived this charge, claiming that the French Sûreté had begun the conflict in order to block him and his MDRM colleagues from further approaches to the National Assembly on the matter of independence.[34] Rabemananjara's interpretation merits respect, but it scarcely explains why the French should fear National Assembly favor for an autonomy project that had already failed three times even to come to a vote in the Chamber of Deputies. Evidence for the provocation theory remains contradictory. For instance, the police knew the timing of the insurrection at several sites on the island, but they seem to have been caught off guard at other places. Moreover, a telegram sent by the MDRM deputies urging calm on their militants probably meant something besides a naive warning.[35]

In any case, the telegraphed note of caution went unheeded. Major uprisings occurred at Moramanga on the escarpment along the critical line of rail between Antananarivo and Toamasina, and at Manakara in the coffee-growing regions of the east coast. Attacks were aimed mainly at military garrisons and police stations, the installations of the great French companies, and the concessions that supplied them. Some French and Francophile Malagasy were murdered or terrorized, but women, children, clergy, and most foreigners were spared. In the rural areas under rebel control, insurrectionary governments were formed, institutions established, and the fokon'olona spirit invoked as a kind of mythical battle cry.[36] International help seemed to be promised through the sympathetic activity of Protestant missionaries among anticolonial organizations. "It is undeniable that the conspirators found real sympathy, perhaps even encouragement, from the acting United States Consul at Tananarive," writes Jacques Tronchon. "Some concluded from their discussions with him that once the insurrection had started, foreign assistance would follow by necessity."[37] But any anticipations of the sort were entirely illusory.

Strategically, the French held the upper hand. Points of combat in the north and south remained isolated, never able to link up with the major resistance in the east. Reinforced by 18,000 West African troops ("Senegalese") and Foreign Legionnaires, the French took the initiative in July. They drove the rebels into a stubborn guerrilla action that endured through the rainy season until April 1948, a year after the start of the insurrection. Even then, in the deepest areas of combat, colonial forces were able to secure only urban centers against the guerrillas until nearly the end of 1948. The rebel sanctuaries were eventually carved into fragments and obliterated by the well-disciplined French, Senegalese, and Comorean units.[38]

France's retaliation against the uprising represents one of the most bloody acts of repression in colonial history. In the long campaign of 1947–1948, nearly 100,000 Malagasy were executed, tortured to death, starved, or driven into the desert.[39] Even officially, 89,000 Malagasy died, about 2 percent of the entire population of 4 million; over 11,000 of them were killed outright by military action. This toll contrasts with 550 French and other non-Malagasy dead out of a total of 60,000 to 70,000; 150 of these casualties were civilians, most of the others African troops in the colonial army. Despite Tronchon's fine study and other research, the intensity of the French repression remains one of the unexplained mysteries in the complex parallelogram of cause and effect related to the insurrection. The campaign transpired under a virtual blackout of news. All leftist sympathizers in the French community had been forceably repatriated, all nationalist leaders jailed for putative inculpation in the revolt. All rebel field chiefs were dead before the public could hear their story.

On October 4, 1948, the French criminal court at Antananarivo attributed the insurrection to MDRM instigation. The authorities seized the opportunity to destroy the party completely. Six of forty convicted conspirators were sentenced to death. When the French public proved unconvinced that justice had been done, its administration reacted with greater humanity. The executions were stayed, pardons issued in 1949, and an amnesty was decreed by the socialist government in 1956. Nevertheless, all three alleged principal instigators—the MDRM deputies Ravoahangy, Raseta, and Jacques Rabemananjara—remained in fixed residence until 1960. They thereupon emerged to play leading political roles in the first republic after independence.

Violence against the French had never been part of the MDRM outlook. In an embittered postwar society careening toward some form of revolt, the broadly popular party appears to have been conveniently used by JINA and PANAMA to channel their own proclivity to overt conflict.[40] The insurrection was mounted by schoolteachers, farmers, small tradesmen, artisans, catechists, and minor officials, joined by a scattering of city elites in the secret societies. Radicalized, they rose up against central authority itself—whereas the MDRM's moderate nationalist program, advocated by professionals and middle-class elites, envisaged the replacement of one authority or fanjakana by another. JINA and PANAMA leaders seem to have decided to act after concluding that the MDRM deputies were merely "playing politics" with the French—that is, joining an elitist game against the true interests of the Malagasy nation.[41] The insurrection thus exploited the myth of the revived Malagasy state, incarnated by the respectably modern MDRM, to forge a new, more revolutionary myth of a communal nation inspired by ancestral tradition.[42] As in the aftermath of the French conquest a half-century before, rebellion was a form of popular passion, a mass tromba.[43]

The rage of March 1947 had been vented upon Malagasy collaborators of the humiliated colonial regime as much as upon that regime directly. "Collaboration" at times included Christian clerical status, administrative and technical service—in effect, anything that had fanjakana associations. This repudiation of leadership exemplifies a major theme of the Malagasy public experience—a rejection of any established authority not evidently sanctioned by traditional culture.

By notable irony, national anger had even turned against the Merina for their own ambivalent collaboration in the apparatus of French rule. It appears that the vast majority of the Malagasy civil servants (most of them Merina) either collaborated with French security or remained neutral during the rebellion, using their training to accommodate, rather than challenge, the authority under which they held their jobs.[44] Many Malagasy military personnel, however, did overcome their loyalist discipline and joined the insurgents; veterans of the European war, they had been disgruntled for some time over discrimination in the French armed services.[45] But most of these were not Merina. And as outlying areas of the island burst into rebellious flame, it was noticed with extreme resentment that the capital itself didn't budge. Well prepared for that eventuality, French and Senegalese convoys patrolled the city assiduously, protecting all installations. In Fianarantsoa, too, the army seemed prepared for revolt, and the outbreak fizzled.

Although political activity remained forbidden in the aftermath of the rebellion and only 20,000 Malagasy had attained French citizenship by 1952, ideological and ethnic interests formed cultural or study groups with political motives. They were prepared for a revival of politics in 1956, burgeoning into a host of small parties (at least thirty-five, says Chaigneau) upon enactment in Paris of the socialist government's "framework law" (*loi cadre*).[46] Even that government proved wary of radical nationalist nests (and of communist eggs laid in them); deliberately refusing interest in any avatar of the banned MDRM or other apparition of Merina nationalism, French authorities deliberately gave preference to Tsiranana's new Social Democratic Party (PSD). Far from Marxist in ideology, the PSD emerged from the Cultural Association of Coastal Malagasy Intellectuals, an obvious revival of the erstwhile PADESM coalition that the French had raised in 1946 against Merina ambitions in the MDRM. The Merina themselves adhered to a spectrum of parties, from Protestant to Marxist.

As Charles de Gaulle took power in mid-1958, launching his constitutional campaign for a fifth republic, overseas parties regrouped, seeking electoral weight. With administrative support, Madagascar's PSD began a long, successful digestion of regional, ethnic, and religious factions. By now these disparate groups could join in a common apprehension over the implications of anti-French nationalism—threatening to some an opening for communists, to others a return to Merina domination. Continued French influence proved preferable to either alternative. Moreover, that influence seemed destined this time to throw electoral victory to the PSD—a strong inducement to bring Roman Catholic and nonnationalist Merina into Tsiranana's party.

Although castigated for its neocolonial implications, this antinationalist sentiment was rooted in a historical preference for France as the liberator of slaves and côtiers from domination by the Merina. According to Gérard Althabe, who interprets the rivalry of elites in modern Madagascar as an essentially ethnic conflict,

> French presence and power are invoked [by Tsiranana in the PADESM period] as the sole protection of the peoples of the periphery against Merina hegemony which would unmistakably result from the creation of the independent state desired by the nationalists. This is nothing but a repetition of a colonial propaganda theme that for more than sixty years presented the expedition of 1895 as a liberation of peoples from royal despotism. ... If the mechanisms of decolonization were allowed to operate, the power elite would unmistakably form around the bureaucratic bourgeoisie concentrated at Tananarive, social base of the nationalist adversaries of the regime. That is why the government is obliged to constrain the surge of Tananariviens into the state apparatus while slowing the departure of the French as much as possible in order to give itself time to install people from the coastal regions in that apparatus.[47]

On the opposite flank, five radical parties—out of ten who met at Tamatave (Toamasina) in May 1958—created the Congress Party for the Independence of Madagascar (AKFM) to campaign for a negative vote in de Gaulle's referendum in September. The AKFM never denied its Marxism, but it also adhered faithfully to the original principles of (anti-French) nationalism. The party was thus able to reconcile the doctrinaire Marxism-Leninism of Gisèle Rabesahala's Union of the Malagasy People (UPM) with the Protestant communalism of the high plateaus, the bread-and-butter interests of the Labor Union Alliance of Madagascar (FISEMA), and the urge of middle-class Malagasy to unseat French capital and managerial authority. The AKFM found its 20,000 members and its following among civil servants, teachers, and intellectuals in the capital city and (with less room for maneuver) at Toamasina, Antsirabe, and Antsiranana (then Diego Suarez). For its first thirty years, the party's public leader was pastor-philosopher-educator Richard Andriamanjato, aristocratic author of a study of Malagasy cultural psychology[48] who occupies Ravelojaona's revered Protestant pulpit at Antananarivo.

These two emergent coalitions, PSD and AKFM, dominated government and opposition, respectively, from the late 1950s until 1972. Regional politics was enlivened during those years by the activities of a few localized organizations such as Monja Jaona's MONIMA (Madagascar Ruled by Malagasy) in the south and Alexis Bezaka's National Malagasy Revival (RNM) in the east. Idiosyncratic in its nationalism, MONIMA survived constant PSD persecutions, obtained footholds in cities in the late 1960s, and emerged in the 1970s behind Monja Jaona as an intransigent forum for disaffected youth and peasants. In 1968, following a failure to merge with the veteran radical Raseta and other Antananarivo dissenters, Bezaka reformed his eastern forces into the Christian Democratic Party (PDCM). The PDCM subsequently lost its following to a socialist splinter group, the Union of Christian Democrats of Madagascar (UDECMA) led by Norbert Andriamorasata. UDECMA joined President Didier Ratsiraka's National Front for the Defense of the Revolution (FNDR) in 1976; Bezaka went into exile.

Of the first republic's two national parties, the PSD was by far the largest, most comprehensive, and most diverse. With its electoral ally, the east-coast Democratic and Social Union of Madagascar, or UDSM (soon to be digested in turn), Tsiranana's party delivered a 77 percent vote for union with France as preached by de Gaulle in the referendum of September 28, 1958; of 2,154,939 registered voters, 1,767,475 (82 percent) cast ballots in that plebiscitary watershed. The nationalist AKFM had failed to take Madagascar out of the French Union, but the extent of its negative vote displayed the force of Malagasy nationalism, especially in the capital and other cities. Madagascar's 392,557 no votes (22 percent) in 1958 ranked second only to that of Guinea, which alone in French Africa precipitated itself into independence as a result of a dissenting majority in the referendum.

THE PSD REPUBLIC, 1958–1972

By its 77 percent majority, Madagascar voted itself into a nebulous French Community as a quasi-republic. Whether intended or not, the September 1958 referendum produced only a transition. Within two years, the Malagasy republic had been granted sovereign powers and the "community" had failed to materialize. Overt colonial subordination ended with revocation of the 1896 Annexation Law on October 14, 1958. A new constitution expressed Madagascar's modified relationship to the fifth French republic. Modeled on the example of de Gaulle's France with little deference to the particular qualities of Malagasy society, the constitution of April 28, 1959, endowed the island with a centralized regime dominated by a strong executive president who enjoyed a renewable seven-year mandate. Unlike France, however, the first Malagasy republic never provided for a prime minister to share executive prerogatives; however useful in other respects, that office might have disrupted the sudden fiction of unity.[49]

After serving as interim premier in the preliminary phase of the republic, Philibert Tsiranana was elected president on May 1, 1959, by Madagascar's National Assembly and Senate. Designated minister-counselor of the French Community, he participated as a French delegate in the 1959 United Nations General Assembly. Nevertheless, status as a junior partner in European legislative and diplomatic affairs now made little sense to the Malagasy; those affairs were too far removed from preoccupations of the newly enfranchised citizens. Never allowed the privilege of becoming French, they expected their leaders to make decisions for them at home, not to speak for France abroad.

A sort of republic had come about, but independence had not been achieved. Virtually all of Africa was decolonizing at this time, and Madagascar asserted as strong a claim to autonomy as any territory on the continent. In 1960, following the example of Mali, the Malagasy negotiated with France a series of agreements that governed the circumstances for an ostensible transfer of sovereign powers. In effect, even these minutely crafted accords reserved several important prerogatives for the French—in foreign affairs, higher education, security, and state finance. Stigmatized by nationalists as an "amiable decolonization," the accords were signed in Tananarive on April 27, 1960, and entered into effect on June 26, now recognized with remarkably little irony as the national day. The Malagasy republic joined the United Nations in its own right on September 21, 1960. In 1962, the presidency was made subject to direct election and Tsiranana was confirmed in the post by overwhelming popular votes in 1965 and 1972.[50]

Guided by its special relationship with Paris, Tsiranana's independent republic followed a rigorously pro-Western, anticommunist course. During its twelve years, this PSD-dominated state banned Mao's *Little Red Book* and deplored Chinese railway construction deliveries to Tanzanian ports; it condemned the Soviet Indian Ocean fleet (but not the French or American) as a military threat; it kept relations with socialist states to a desultory sputter of trade missions while exchanging ambassadors with Taiwan, South Korea, and West Germany. The rehabilitated MDRM poet-militant Jacques Rabemananjara returned from twelve years in exile to assume the post of minister of economics, subsequently moving to Agriculture and then to the Foreign Ministry. Abandoning his more radical youthful reputation, Rabemananjara soon became the most Western (and pro–South African) of all Tsiranana's lieutenants. His influence countered the more nationalist orientation of André Resampa, the gifted, deceptively oafish social democrat who served as PSD secretary-general and minister of the interior. While imposing much-needed organizational discipline on the party, Resampa nudged it toward indigenous or ideological policy alternatives. In conflict with Rabemananjara's Francophilia, these motives were also at odds with the president's irreducible instinct for internal security through complete congeniality with France.[51]

Beginning in 1956, Tsiranana's Social Democratic Party had expanded from its base in Mahajanga (Majunga) City and Province to obliterate virtually all competitors in their local fiefs. Once a national presence was achieved, the PSD dominated all but the Merina citadel of Antananarivo and a few provincial cities where the AKFM or a regional party carried weight through labor unions. MONIMA and other rural opponents had little chance in the countryside against powerfully organized governmental forces equipped with the prerogatives of incumbency, the favor of France, and the ability to manipulate the vote in places too obscure for verification. By 1960 the republic had multiplied the number of communal councils from 197 under the French to 736, thus expanding enormously the number of officials electable under PSD aegis.

On September 4, 1960, Tsiranana's party obtained 75 of 107 National Assembly seats, enough to exact special executive powers for developmental legislation. In the elections of August 8, 1965, the majority rose to 104 seats, with 94 percent of the vote. On September 6, 1970, when rumors of change buzzed in the air, the PSD still obtained 2.4 million of 2.6 million valid votes in parliamentary elections; it retained its 104 delegates, the other 3 going to the AKFM in the city of Antananarivo.

So encompassing was PSD organization that, outside the capital, party membership was tantamount to participation in civic life. One could scarcely advance in commerce, the cooperative movement, women's organizations, youth affairs, or sports—let alone elected office or higher administration—except through the party. Confronted by a PSD fund-raiser in 1964, a working-class friend of mine could honestly protest that simply paying his taxes amounted to a contribution to the party. Landholders and a new bourgeoisie created by party rule dominated access to higher education and civil service jobs, public contracts, and social prestige. The PSD and its key personnel fused political and administrative roles into one function, one aim, a single identity. The principal beneficiaries were the landowners and farmers with capital, the small urban functionaries, wage earners, and entrepreneurs.[52]

Highly centralized under Resampa's dual role as party secretary-general and minister of the interior, the PSD tended solicitously to the local and regional interests of its notable members, particularly the mandarin district bosses on whom it depended for peace and productivity. For better or worse, the party embodied practically all connotations of the fanjakana, or establishment; the first republic was widely dubbed "the PSD State."[53] It controlled territorial activity through a cascade of delegations from president to six chiefs of province to eighteen prefects and nearly a hundred subprefects, all responsible to Resampa's Interior Ministry. Local "communes" represented administrative subdivisions for tax collection and other affairs, not a collectivity of members as in the neglected fokon'olona tradition. Citizens were subject to appointed village chiefs, central information services, agricultural extension, public works (often requiring "volunteer" labor from the poor), tax collection, public health, and constant speeches demanding production and confidence in the state.[54]

Eschewing ideology and unable to reach consensus on a coherent program for economic and social progress, the Social Democrats represented a typical Third World version of the pluralist catchall political organization. Resampa may have entertained more selective pretensions for the party, but Tsiranana consistently aimed at universalizing a myriad of interests in contradiction with each other. An assiduous student of Malagasy language and culture, the president embodied an ideal of pragmatic statecraft. He managed to keep his sprawling party intact by carefully listening to disparate voices, astutely sizing up strengths and defects in his collaborators, steering problems away from ideological analysis, and insisting on the main objects of government—to stay in power and to keep Madagascar from slipping into the hands of communists or the Merina.

From the outset, the national Parliament represented a forum for government supporters to argue their differences—in the tolerated presence of an insignificant AKFM opposition. The PSD's brand of socialism was more rhetorical than a policy platform. In practice, it suggested a spirit of mutual aid, an effort to mobilize peasant cooperation in state-managed grassroots economic development and producer-marketing cooperatives, some restriction on private aggrandizement at the expense of society, and lip service to national economic planning. The AKFM and other opposition factions concurred in the rhetoric of PSD development policy but deemed the projects exploited by self-serving elites under French influence.[55]

Following Francophone examples throughout Africa, the PSD state proved willing to experiment with infrastructural development, civic service, rural animation, and limited import substitution. Acting under special powers of legislation, the government issued 299 developmental ordinances in the first three years of independence. This "legislative and regulatory effervescence" redefined certain relations between individuals and the state, but, as Yves Prats analyzed it, did not attack the fundamental question remaining unsolved from Merina monarchical and French colonial experience—how to balance central direction and local participation. Was action to be generated from the grass roots, as the rhetoric claimed, or was the population to be disciplined to follow instructions?[56]

The PSD state found few effective answers to that dilemma. Yet its viability scarcely depended on the success of these policies or even the credibility of its administration. It prospered on Tsiranana's charisma and pragmatism, the efficiency of André Resampa and other lieutenants, the self-interest of local political figures, and the tolerance of French and indigenous business interests opposed to abrupt change. From these perspectives, the Malagasy state was unified so long as the president functioned; the Malagasy people for the most part did what they were told, for want of alternatives. Tensions within the PSD had to be bridged nonetheless by daily compromises—between rival ethnic and regional factions, nationalists and Francophiles, ideologues and opportunists. After the decade of the 1960s closed, Pastor Andriamanjato, leader of the AKFM opposition, was able to profess 80 percent agreement with the majority *party*—while grudgingly admiring the would-be socialism of the AKFM's mortal political enemy, Resampa; but Andriamanjato's factions had far less in common with the *government*, which followed unacceptable presidential options more slavishly.[57] Here was a new effort to separate the PSD from the state.

Nationalists within the AKFM as well as Resampists in the PSD objected to the president's viscerally anticommunist limitations on the choice of Madagascar's partners. Beyond that, nationalists were obliged to resent the implications of cultural inferiority in Madagascar's tributary relationship to French civilization.[58] Government and local party leaders profited from foreign aid disbursements and from prestigious demonstrations of French favor. For disenchanted Malagasy, the link between foreign domination and PSD elite self-interest was clear. To the Merina minority, Tsiranana's parvenu government kept Madagascar dependent in order to deny political power to its historical heirs; hence the affront to national pride in the very existence of the PSD republic.

National debate was bitter during the first republic, but the national fabric remained intact. In a recent handbook meant for foreign businesspeople—hence, deliberately avoiding controversy—Patrick Rajoelina refers to the 1960–1965 period as a "state of grace;" employment rose sharply, inflation remained tolerable, foreign debt was low, and budget deficits were manageable.[59] Most PSD programs proved unproductive, but they at least didn't explode into disaster; that happened later. The thirty-fourth poorest country in the world according to 1970 World Bank calculations, Madagascar was to sink far lower in the following two decades. PSD cabinet officer Césaire Rabenoro insists that the Tsiranana administration was "winning the development gamble" when the events of 1972 overthrew it.[60]

Yet the programs didn't produce envisaged results. Domestic production lagged behind planned growth rates. State farms, cooperatives, and extension programs rarely met their goals. They encountered resistance from an undisciplined peasantry as well as competition (or at least a lack of coordination) among themselves. The so-called human-investment campaign faltered under the heavy hand of local politics. Over 400 cooperatives stagnated without adequate financial or technical support. According to Chaigneau, the regime "had not considered in the least the importance of a diagnosis of the social fabric. It was content in fact to transpose the colonial system of cooperatives with some adaptations but without reflecting on the failure of that system which had survived only through becoming an organism of the administration."[61] The state had to intervene in both management and production without being prepared for this technical role, let alone for teaching local participants to collaborate fruitfully in the process.

Y.-G.Paillard contends that the "participatory structures" designed to induce grassroots development—the civic service, rural animation, the cooperatives, fokon'olona, and other schemes—failed under the first plan (1963–1967) because of scarcity of resources; private enterprise within a "capitalist growth model" failed to furnish the necessary investment.[62] Seeking $225 million in foreign private financing between 1964 and 1968, the Tsiranana government received slightly more than half that much; little of it went into priority agriculture, transportation, or vital services. Still, the funds were reasonably well managed; production never fell below essential needs, as it was to do in the 1970s and 1980s; and if true independence had not arrived, neither had general misery.[63]

Toward the end of the PSD's reign, major emphasis was placed on large integrated programs (*grandes opérations*) with massive state participation and external funding. These complex schemes seem to have taken a step toward idiosyncratic solutions to the problems of development. In the place of foreign experts, they charged Malagasy technicians with the adaptation of imported technology to domestic conditions. The grandes opérations entailed fuller involvement of local groups in production and marketing, training of youth, and coordination among sectors of activity. As in the past—and later in the "structural adjustment" of the late 1980s and 1990s—the paradoxical strategy was to *force* productive and distributive systems to conform to free laws of the market.

Some of the projects promised results—rice-growing schemes in the highlands; a textile plant at Mahajanga; chromite, bauxite, and nickel mines; tourist infrastructure (with South African participation); a new deep-water port at Narinda on the northwest coast; and an Israeli-assisted orange grove at Bezizika in the region of Morondava, where Resampa's communal syndicates functioned. But they seem to have burgeoned too late, and the political elite envisaged them largely as potential pork barrels. Rural animation—depending not on experts at all but on meticulously selected and trained local residents—ran into comparable problems of local jealousies, political manipulation, and sloppy administration.[64] As Raison argues, programs such as rural animation, resettlement of farmers in the underpopulated midwestern highlands, and ambitious rice production schemes on the plateaus encountered local resistance to the development of a new type of peasant expected to act spontaneously to take advantage of market conditions.[65]

In the life of the Malagasy peasantry, the transfer of powers from French to PSD fanjakana appears to have made little difference. The same forms of coercion and exhortation were employed to produce coffee, vanilla, cloves, or cotton for the national economy, and taxes for the state. Extension agents and administrators were Malagasy foreigners instead of French foreigners. Administration and education came from outside and imposed demands. To be a peasant meant passive obedience ... and silence. The village, described by Althabe in the Betsimisaraka east, remained apart from the modern world of interchangeable administrators, servile to its dominators but never part of their world.[66] Even today, two republics later, that distance has not been bridged.

Instead, a new bourgeoisie developed out of the Malagasation of key administrative and technical jobs in the PSD republic. The new technical elite stood virtually as far from the mass of Malagasy as the French or the Merina had in their respective turns. From Marxist perspectives, rural animation and the other first-republic programs left class conflict and capitalist socioeconomic structures undisturbed.[67] French interests controlled major enterprises, production, import, and export. Although the state intervened constantly in the development sectors, outright nationalization was rare, touching only industries that were essential but unprofitable. Public enterprise never began approaching the scale of activity ordained under the planned economy of 1975.

Gradually, PSD authority stagnated, revealing disputes among ambitious and often corrupt clienteles. A pro-French party faction curbed Resampa's nationalist tendencies. The party of a million Social Democrats drifted ever farther from the unpoliticized rural and urban "little people" (*madinika*), who obtained nothing from the distant fanjakana. This alienation ultimately precipitated a rural insurrection in 1971 and the urban revolution of 1972. Yet had Tsiranana maintained his health, even those movements might have failed to overturn him.

In spite of flagrantly rigged elections, venality, and intimidation in rural areas, PSD rule had distinctly democratic assets—in the tolerance of a dissenting press, the formal legality of an opposition, the independence of the courts, respect for human rights, and the raw pluralism reflected within the party itself. In the absence of real elections, the president's personal ability to stay in touch with grassroots preoccupations guaranteed some dialogue with common people. Tsiranana's instinct for compromise had been legendary, his understanding of cultural and psychological variations around the island, unmatched. On his return from hospitalization in mid-1970, he was no longer able to travel exhaustively or listen intently. On October 9 of that year, as Tsiranana composed his sixth cabinet of ministers, constitutional amendments provided for a quartet of vice presidents to supervise clusters of ministries in place of the ailing president. The premier of those four surrogates—and presumed heir apparent—was André Resampa.[68] Tsiranana presented his selections on October 13 as a gesture to youth, dynamism, and the socialist avenue to production.

Resampa was quick to use his enhanced authority—too quick. He had already purged party cadres of deadwood. Now, he brought new people (including women) into the PSD elites, implemented long-standing legislation to turn unused productive property over to landless peasants, started investigations of price-gouging by rural middlemen, and forced Rabemananjara to seek renegotiation of the agreements with France. Each of these moves mobilized enemies within the party, who were joined by opportunists fearful of Resampa's opposition to relations with South Africa. This combination of opponents beat him. By early 1971, the president was able only to turn against Resampa, not to protect his heir of the previous October.[69] Resampa first lost his command over the principal state security forces and was warned to refrain from criticizing the Tsiranana-Rabemananjara flirtation with South Africa. He was subsequently demoted to second vice president and then arrested on June 1 for plotting against the security of the state—together, it was alleged, with the MONIMA (whom Resampa had persecuted relentlessly for over a decade) and the United States (with whom, unlike Tsiranana, he had never entertained serious relations).[70] At the next party congress, his name was never even mentioned. The party conducted a vigorous purge of Resampists, declared itself in receivership, and turned its fate over to a president who had made it strong and who would be reelected once more before he finally failed. The cult of presidential wisdom was extravagantly inflated in the search for a savior.[71]

It was clear, however, that the PSD leadership had exhausted its creative resources. For a time in 1971 even a coalition with the AKFM was considered. That proverbial Marxist opposition had come a great distance toward support for the weakening regime—helping resolve student strikes in the capital and condemning MONIMA insurgency in the south. The AKFM thus opened itself to defections among the outraged youth and city dwellers who had once regarded it as their national standard-bearer. A shadowy conspiracy was unearthed in September-October 1971, leading to several dozen arrests among farmers and intellectuals of the plateaus. The conduct of trials and inquiries became chaotic, with Resampa and others never facing charges and several instances of expeditious liberation of people charged (even convicted) of subversion.[72] On June 8, 1972, three weeks after Tsiranana's fall, Resampa was released without having been arraigned or allowed to see a lawyer. A "ministerial mafia" had done him in, he said, because they opposed the principles he defended.[73] But by that time they were gone, too.

In any event, the mystique of the infallible leader was vanishing. All that was left was the regime of the local notables, that fundamental PSD that Resampa had held in check. Self-serving activity by these rural party bosses and city ward heelers had come to infuriate the common Malagasy with the same intensity as the fanjakana of the French had alienated the militants of the 1947 insurrection.

REVOLUTION: A CONGERIES OF NATIONALISM

By the late 1960s, artless, neocolonized Madagascar was catching up with Third World social and political decay. The population was rising, production was leveling, institutions were hardening, and expectations went soaring beyond realities. Crucial exports of coffee, vanilla, and cloves faced increasing competition throughout the developing world, and new markets failed to materialize. Elections became futile, as the same aging personalities kept control, offering little choice for public policy. Only in the capital could opposition become overtly manifest without fear of reprisal by the ubiquitous police. If the army had not yet upset this regime, it was out of fear of a French reaction on Tsiranana's behalf. Until May 1972, the military leadership declined to accept a role in politics for itself.

By 1968, the republic was a decade old; it had enjoyed formal independence for eight of those years. The French were supposedly gone yet remained very conspicuously in place. In fact, everything seemed to depend on 30,000 French nationals (not counting Comoreans with French passports). France maintained an air force base and a paratroop battalion just outside Antananarivo, with a regiment of Foreign Legion infantry near the joint Franco-Malagasy naval base at Diego Suarez (now Antsiranana) in the north. French and Réunionnais landowners farmed their plantations and owned the processing facilities for those crops. Great corporations named after French cities dominated overseas and much domestic commerce. French shops and services made Tananarive an admirable setting for the European way of life. In education, government, and the professions, French practitioners dominated the highest ranks. Bishops came from France, as did the most sought-after hairdressers. It was hard to persuade foreigners that Madagascar had any culture of its own—let alone a unique civilization.

The Tsiranana regime depended on its astute, discreet French advisers and on the liberality of *la coopération,* French for foreign aid. France provided $70 million annually in direct assistance, but such transfers served mainly to keep the bureaucratic and import-export machinery functioning. The grandes opérations glistened on paper and glowed in political rhetoric. At best, they advanced within their contexts, enriching a few but not contributing perceptibly to the general welfare. Imports sustained the lifestyles of the bourgeoisie, foreigners, and upper bureaucracy; working-class urbanites resented persistent surges in living costs. And still, people trickled into the towns in search of unrealized promise, imposing additional appetites on the supply of food and other basics.

Within the ruling establishment, fissures opened inevitably. The PSD had swollen with claimants, and the fruits of power proved too meager and unevenly distributed for all adherents to enjoy. Perhaps if it had yielded power in alternation with its rivals, PSD cohesion might have survived in fallow years to regenerate itself in the more fecund. But the party's discipline fell short of so democratic a concession. The opposition, nominal as it was, remained suspect in PSD eyes for its loyalty to the presumed Marxist conspiracy, or to Merina ambition—or to both at once. For better or worse, the party of Social Democrats was popularly identified with perpetual rule. Elite hunger for privileges equaled—no, it transcended—demands for economic results among the populace.[74]

There is little in this sad story of first-republic deterioration that hadn't already been experienced elsewhere in Africa. What is typically Malagasy is the way in which the process was screened by traditional deference or apathy, and by rituals of confidence in debilitated authority. But Tsiranana's proverbial habits of reconciliation no longer ensured the solidarity of his forces or the acquiescence of multitudes. It is also characteristic of this island's history that dissent should explode dramatically when authority seemed no longer able to command the volatile future.

If the crucial explosion was to occur in the cities, it is nonetheless among the peasantry that the fuse was lit. Rural grievances punctuate Malagasy history. They arise mainly in protest against the unwelcome impact of governments on local ways of life. Official exhortations toward increased output are often followed by official refusal of fair prices for that production.[75] When customary organizations like the fokon'olona are obliged to implement such impositions of authority, they too lose credibility. Governments consider the process successful whenever city folk have regular supplies of rice, oils, vegetables, sugar, even meat, at affordable prices for city incomes. For the rural population, the benefits come back indirectly, if at all—when urban family members contribute money or manufactured goods to country kinfolk or when opportunities arise for urban employment or education, enticing those cousins to try their fortunes off the farm.

All first-republic solutions compounded a fundamental inequality of power among urban and rural, privileged and peasant, classes. Country people had to acquire some of the basics for subsistence (cooking oil and fuel, soap, salt, sugar) and for costly ritual observances vital to their sense of identity. They usually ended up paying high prices to the same trader—often an Asian, occasionally a Merina "expatriate"—who provided access to capital at usurious rates. A new deal from government should have offered peasants relief from this oppressive cycle of debt and penury, providing secure access to necessary goods, credit, and services, but this the farmers did not see. Throughout the island, production costs rose with technology, and revenues sank under official price controls. City people could live off cheap peasant production and speculate in rural real estate.

In the late 1960s, exasperation was widespread throughout the countryside, most particularly in the drought-ridden, volatile south. Here, in the province of Tuléar (now Toliara), every basic element of survival was in scant supply—from water to education, from medicine to viable roads. In 1970, a hoof-and-mouth epidemic afflicted the cattle on which Malagasy families base their deepest sense of security. Flagrant official extortion was aggravated by an interministerial contest for local power. Prices for trucked-in water rose at the whim of private suppliers without relief from a distant government. The population reacted. Peasants unable to pay taxes became peasants unwilling to do so. Postharvest brushfires sent their signal of folk alienation into the empyrean for all to read; they became unusually severe after the elections of September 6, 1970, which had merely reinforced the PSD's hold without enhancing its legitimacy.[76] In November 1970, Christian churches began a long season of protests from the pulpit and in the press against abuses of authority, poverty gaps, and favoritism for the unproductive.

Tuléar Province had become what Maurice Délépine calls the graveyard of Tsiranana's grandes opérations, the terrain where "grassroots development" consisted of conscription of indentured labor for the lands of the local gentry.[77] These southern notables, from Vice President Calvin Tsiebo down to illiterate PSD section leaders, had become identified in popular parlance as foreigners (*vazaha*) in an ominous adaptation of Malagasy folk xenophobia. Famine and disease, ruthless tax extortions and profiteering, isolation from decisions, exodus of alienated youth—all attacked the slender moral authority enjoyed by any government in this congenitally impoverished semidesert, a place only ancestors could love. Resampa, PSD secretary-general, was using civil servants and technicians for partisan purposes in a particularly flagrant way. Once Resampa had fallen, his minions were replaced with new agents; some of them were local sons—yet for the people of Tuléar, all vazaha still.

From Tuléar City and other bastions of southern resistance, the MONIMA party of Monja Jaona began reaching toward the exasperated but nonpolitical peasantry. For the Tuléar PSD, stability and development required suppression of criticism, entailing constant harassment of MONIMA and its irrepressible leader. A JINA militant in the great insurrection of 1947, then for a time mayor of Tuléar City, Monja had become an archetype of popular opposition tinctured with Maoism. He fulminated in obscurity while his PSD enemies—Resampa, Tsiebo, and province minister Albert Leda—kept the obscure region ostensibly loyal to the regime. Ignored even by the opposition press of Antananarivo, shoved into and out of detention, Monja crystallized what seemed the futility of the desperate south. The action he was to lead finally transcended the proverbial "liberation fantasy" of the Malagasy.[78]

Monja and the peasant rebels could never hope to overthrow a regime. Without resources in the cities or among the military, they were no match for the rural alliance of Social Democratic Party and police. For one moment in April 1971, however, that blanket of repression came apart, and the network of protestors arose like the embattled farmers of universal fable. On the night of April 1–2, MONIMA supporters carrying clubs, knives, and pitchforks staged simultaneous assaults on a dozen gendarmerie posts—arsenals of repression—across Tuléar Province. Although Europeans and Asians shuddered for their lives, nobody was touched who was not in uniform, and all the dead were on the rebellious side.[79] Kept secret, well-orchestrated for simultaneity, the raids nevertheless lacked coherence and momentum, and the rebels quickly lost their advantage. On the counterattack, the gendarmes wiped them out within two days, except for a small pocket around the town of Ambovombe.

The 1971 MONIMA rebellion set new standards for futility. Yet it announced the assault on the PSD republic, the beginning of a revolution—in the course of which the south would once again be forgotten.

At first the government dismissed the episode as a minor aberration of godless factions serving the purposes of communist overlords. It was a "little revolt," said Tsiranana, and the national press gave it less space than it enjoyed in the French media. Vice President Tsiebo returned from a tour of inquiry in mid-April satisfied that the uprising had been spontaneous, unprovoked. No police, military, or gendarmerie personnel had mutinied, and the PSD remained intact. After declaring the crisis terminated and MONIMA illegal, all that was needed was to minimize the damage. Local estimates claimed 1,000 killed by the police and gendarmes; official reports counted the dead as 45 only. On May 31, the French chapter of the International Human Rights Federation sent two investigators to confirm charges of official brutality. Churches rang with denunciations of the repression.

With an additional 800 adherents arrested, the MONIMA again disappeared—to rise once more a year later. Monja Jaona, arrested in a village north of Tuléar City on April 23, accepted full responsibility for the revolt. He characterized the uprising as an expression of total exasperation with abusive authority. Whereas the government accused its favorite Chinese communist menace of helping Monja to "lead our Antandroy brothers astray," the Tananarive AKFM was blaming its own preferred suspect, America's CIA, for MONIMA's violent offense.[80]

But MONIMA retained a kind of Jacobin purity from this tragedy. On its own, appealing primarily to unlettered, xenophobic peasants, it had meticulously mounted a broad revolt, kept it secret from September to April, and obtained cooperation across traditional ethnic boundaries in the south. Monja had not fled to safety in Tanzania, as government-inspired rumors alleged; he was captured close to the scene. He denied accusations of alien communist masterminding; after all, his fighters had used hunting weapons, not Kalashnikovs. Still, like the patriots of 1947, he had hoped vaguely—"abstractly," as a French commentator observed—for outside help in a nationwide insurrection.[81] Five years later, party militants told of their expectation at the time that oppressed people of Antananarivo and other centers of dissent would rise up to rid themselves of a corrupt regime, bringing the movement of 1947 to final fruition.[82] Although the conflagration didn't happen that way, slow, subterranean shock waves did reach the capital as well as Diego Suarez and Fianarantsoa. In any case, the Tuléar revolt was no mere isolated tribal outrage.

The region needed access to land for dowerless youth as well as reasonable rural credit, free water resources, and open markets; these boons were unthinkable, for the revenues could not be controlled by national priorities. Moreover, the fanjakana was still blaming a mythical, retrograde peasant mentality for resisting official programs and innovations—not admitting that these had never been meant to serve peasant interests in the first place. From government and pulpit came frequent denunciations of refusal to work on taboo (*fady*) days, of sessions of spirit possession (tromba), of lavish funerals and reburials in expensively decorated tombs, even sacrifices of excessive numbers of animals for holidays and hospitality (including feasts for junketing officials).[83] These otherwise sacrosanct customs had lost their cultural charm in the anxiety over economic development and political stability. They had dwindled into ancestrally sanctioned atavism. Even Malagasy culture was now conspiring against the regime.

Given national publicity during a tour of the south, President Tsiranana announced the release of 177 prisoners and even extended his grace personally to Monja Jaona. It was a touching encounter, characteristic of Tsiranana's grand style of reconciliation. Monja again accepted the entire blame, thanked the president for his concern, but did not forswear opposition. For his part, the chief of state assured listeners that the welfare of the south had always been dear to him. Once again, Tsiranana had risen above sectarian and partisan interest. That altitude proved too high for him to sustain for more than another year.

The movement of 1972 combined a variety of ideological tendencies into a brief period of confluence. The AKFM's complex of bourgeois nationalism and classic Leninism was joined by a new opposition of peasant recalcitrance combined with the populist anarchism of the urban poor and the more chic, French-schooled radicalism of university students. Their common element consisted in resentment against what they all regarded as neo-colonialism—the PSD regime's willing accommodation of the preeminent interests of the French.

The Merina urban bourgeoisie had been inveterately antagonistic toward those interests—and toward each government—since the fall of the monarchy in 1896. Although new governmental elites had moved into the capital to challenge that middle class, it remained staunchly behind the AKFM opposition through the 1960s and beyond the crises of the early 1970s—when the PSD itself fell apart. Two-thirds of the capital electorate voted regularly for AKFM or allied candidates. Despite official persecution, labor affiliates delivered some local offices in urban Diego Suarez and Tamatave. Although shrinking in size and influence, the AKFM remained intact thanks to Andriamanjato's personal ability to reconcile Merina bourgeois nationalism with imported socialist ideology.[84] By claiming universality in 1972, the PSD lost touch with the nation, whereas the AKFM, claiming only to be progressive, held onto its essence—the affluent, educated urban core of Antananarivo Merina.

But these urban nationalist professionals were not to point the way to revolution. Like the expatriate Antalaotse sages of the old monarchy, they performed essential services for all governments into the 1990s. As André Ravatomanga had once prophesied, "Other political tendencies ... more readily attract a larger portion of the young than do the sclerotic ideologies of the two official parties and ... [they] will create the Madagascar of tomorrow, rather than the PSD or AKFM."[85] These new tendencies—in the peasantry, the urban poor, and the restless youth—soon surpassed decorous bourgeois-Marxist nationalism to create the revolution of 1972.

These groups had much to rebel against. Stagnation within the PSD state became clearly perceptible in 1971–1972. Resampa had led opposition to Rabemananjara's sponsorship of South African investors; he also blocked a massive flour-import monopoly dear to Tsiranana's wishes. By 1972, Rabenoro's colleagues were no longer implementing their straightforward options with fervor, disinterestedness, or integrity. Corruption had become notorious in the PSD upper echelons. One scandal followed another in these last years—as the stakes grew. Drifting in the air was a tempting cloud of currencies from Europe, Japan, and South Africa, and the opportunities for aggrandizement buzzed in the ears of long-standing men of power.

Discontent had been smoldering for several years as the economy unraveled and the regime failed to produce new ways to restore it. The same tired forty men were shunted around from ministerial post to post, seldom doing a day's work, rarely catching onto a useful idea, allowing no room for new blood. Budgetary dependence on foreign transfers induced the development bureaucracy of the first republic to muddle through rather than indicate directions. The imperatives of economic and social development, requiring decentralization of structures and open participation by the peasantry, never commanded the attention they deserved.[86]

Proverbially decorous Malagasy manners could no longer hide the anger of ever-larger sectors of the population. Explosions touched the domiciles of party mandarins in early 1971. Brushfires multiplied in the universal protest of a suicidal peasantry. The Tuléar MONIMA led its brief mass revolt. National leadership would minimize the seriousness of the crisis, but it nevertheless began confiscating respectable, even French-language, newspapers bearing criticism of the regime.

To cope with national crisis, the PSD chose to reassert the omnipotence of the man who had founded the republic and kept it out of communist hands. For fifteen years, Tsiranana had acted out of sharp instinct for popular Malagasy aspirations and values. Like Tanzania's Julius Nyerere, he had been the teacher, the indefatigable rural speechifier, the expert on his people's needs and wants. But the sixty-year-old president had suffered a stroke in January 1970, returning from France on May 24 visibly enfeebled. His popular touch seemed to abandon him as his health deteriorated, leaving him at the mercy of sycophants. So institutions and the power that courses through them were drawn into the single hand of a president enfeebled by illness. The official acts of 1971 and early 1972, greeted by disillusion here and outrage there, became monuments to the living ancestor, a rapidly aging Philibert Tsiranana.

The despotic burden conferred on Tsiranana would alone have been shocking enough in that relatively legitimate republic. But the distance between this institutional beatification and the squalor of "the real country" became painfully flagrant.[87] The electorate knew that much was seriously wrong. Its anxieties had been crystallized by the leader's long illness overseas. To be credible, the president would have to reform his hated monolithic party. Townsfolk and rural youth had begun to scoff at the very sound of the name of some self-serving minister credited by radio or kabary (speech) with implausible deeds for the republic. Peasants began referring to educated Malagasy as vazaha—a portent of profound cleavage in this homogenous culture ordinarily so respectful of learning.

A final flagrancy—the disgrace of the relatively youthful but controversial vice president and interior minister André Resampa—eliminated the only PSD potentate still in touch with the "real" country. On May 25, 1971, Tsiranana assumed full authority over the party apparatus, hitherto obedient to Resampa. Local officials were reshuffled in an obvious assault on the vital ganglions of Resampa's ministry. No evidence was ever produced to demonstrate Resampa's highly improbable alleged conspiracy with the United States or China.[88] The only linkage between the three collaborators (and later, an additional nest of French technicians at the ORSTOM laboratory) was the common hostility directed toward them by French intelligence and its Malagasy cohorts.

Resampa was arrested on June 1. At the end of the month, a PSD convention ended in total triumph for Tsiranana and his closest cronies. The president's second reelection was advanced to January 30, 1972, just in time to demonstrate how irrelevant the process had become. Many rank-and-file PSD were antagonized by the humiliation of their champion, Resampa; the south remained in angry alienation; the Catholic Church joined Protestants in denouncing the willful, heavy-handed anaesthetization of the leadership. Students had already been defecting from PSD-controlled organizations—unreconciled to the Frenchified diploma tracks along which they were being prodded toward a paucity of jobs. City dwellers, never a PSD bulwark, were further repelled by the sheer politicking perpetrated in the name of the northern cowherd Tsiranana. For his part, the president continued to behave like an offended and slightly crippled sky god.

Every presidential appearance was cocooned in adoration. Evil now had its symbols—one for everybody: Maoist Monja Jaona for the conservatives and urbanites; for those who liked Monja (or Mao), there was Richard Nixon's nefarious United States, always sure to be interested in dominating so critical a country as Madagascar. Later, on May 4, 1972, Tsiranana exonerated the United States from any conspiracy with Resampa; he had never produced the putative document that had led him to doubt Washington's good faith.[89] Released on June 8 after a year in custody, Resampa shrugged off Tsiranana's conspiracy psychosis as the deception of corrupt advisers. He promised to "forget the past" and was eventually reconciled with the patriarch who had turned so savagely against him. But it was the present that would prove impossible for either of them to ignore.

As it entered its new decade, the Malagasy republic had clearly exhausted the credit inherited at independence time. By late 1971, Antananarivo had again become a high, hilly cave of winds. Rumors of plots and counterplots whistled through the streets. Jails filled with conspiratorial suspects. Prices began to soar in the towns for food, coffee, gasoline, tires, textbooks; some families could no longer afford school fees. A small rise in the minimum wage had touched off a permanent flare of inflation. The conversion from French to indigenous Francophile administration, the economic stimulation of independence, the dosages of foreign aid, popular willingness to pay taxes and suffer deprivation over a short run—all had tested the nation and were now no longer available to enhance credibility.

A second national development plan, three years overdue, emerged for deployment in October 1971; it had been announced in April, without details, before cheering PSD militants at a mass congress called the National Days of Development and Planning. Speakers claimed unity without the merest glance at the south, which was already exploding in rebellion. The first plan (1964–1968) had withered under thinly disguised contempt. The 1,500 participants in the government's "development days" were notably short on representatives of the peasantry.[90]

The absence of incentives for farmers in the national economy had filled the cities with a new nonurban population. These migrant families squatted in slums and desperation, receiving great numbers of rural youth who overwhelmed the schools and the streets. Antananarivo was becoming a principality of human flies—homeless, futureless, attracted only by promises that no regime could keep. For a time this *Lumpenproletariat* linked up with the literate bourgeois elites who had always detested colonial and postcolonial authority. Together they made the revolution of 1972, and each expected to inherit its fruits. But only an elite could do that. Like the peasants of Tuléar, the street people of Antananarivo would return to the margins of public existence. Once again, the rabble rose up in social conscience, to be suppressed under a new power structure. In this respect, Madagascar's 1972 revolution is an old story.

URBAN REVOLT AND THE RAMANANTSOA INTERREGNUM

Education in Madagascar had been ready for combustion long before the Tuléar revolt, and it was the school system that disseminated the sparks from southern dissent. In 1970–1971, the University of Madagascar held 6,611 students, 87 percent of them Malagasy, 70 percent males. Two-thirds of its 240 professors were French. The campus was built with French assistance. Diplomas were recognized in France and throughout "la Francophonie." To qualify for a chair, Malagasy professors had to pass the *aggrégation* in France. To enter university, students had to obtain a virtually French baccalaureate diploma. After a decade of aspiration, students had become disillusioned with the uselessness of becoming elite in a European system without pertinence to Malagasy life or employment in Madagascar's economy. To frustrate a generation in the educational process is tantamount politically to frustrating a regiment of military. As Chaigneau described it, "More than a simple reproductive function, the [educational] system proved a true catalyst for social conflict."[91]

Petitioning government but anticipating no real concessions, university and medical school students went on strike on several occasions during 1971–1972; they were supported by professors and by younger siblings in the lycées. On March 25, 1971, the president closed the University of Madagascar sine die, not because the protests had become volatile but because they were aimed at what he regarded as political objectives—the separation of Malagasy institutions from French.[92] Despite name-calling and threats by authorities, the demonstrations were orderly for a time. They became unruly only after police invaded the campus precincts—legally out of bounds to them—and arrested those whom they regarded as leaders.

The PSD's annual congress ended on September 12, 1971, without a single reference to the turmoil of the previous spring or to the arrest of Resampa or to the challenges posed against the cooperation agreements with France. Party unity meant solidarity behind Tsiranana, and Tsiranana's party could do no wrong. AKFM protests at the opening of Parliament on October 5 were never reported on the national radio. Quick arrests were followed by expeditious release. The police proceeded with searches, interrogations, house arrests, more press confiscations. Resampa and Monja Jaona never came to trial; promised "evidence" of U.S. plotting did not materialize.[93] Uncertainties piled on top of anguish. Promised reforms of education, of the agreements with France, of government structure and the planning process, never happened. No explanations were given. Asked about the successor to Tsiranana's presidency, the new PSD secretary-general (replacing Resampa) replied that he "hadn't been born yet." That was true in a sense, for when the Father of the Republic fell, he took his state with him.

The PSD republic came down under its own weight—its body too feeble to support the heavy head. Yet in February 1972, when I visited the island, the air seemed devoid of portent. To find Madagascar's political culture, all eyes were still turning toward the president. Tsiranana seemed just vigorous enough, the population just loyal enough, and France still sufficiently interested to disguise discontent and manage the muddle of dependence. The rebellion in Tuléar Province had happened and it had been suppressed. State fathers were presumably attending to the causes of that furious, futile action. But that presumption obscured reality; the dim fuse of revolt was conveying its incendiary message over the long, desolate track from Tuléar to Tsiranana's capital.

Some sparks did reach Antananarivo and other central places in the first months of 1972. Students were becoming exasperated at the patronizing response to their paradoxical demands—for internationally honorable diplomas based on strictly national standards. Their 1971 strikes had led only to temporization and promises of dialogue. When the government closed all schools on May 12, 1972, arresting 375 "misguided children" for the distur-

Traditional hillside houses, Antananarivo, with plains of Imerina in distance. Photo courtesy of the Embassy of Madagascar, Washington, D.C.

Modern quarter near Lake Anosy, Antananarivo. Photo by Gay Kuester, © The Chicago Zoological Society.

bances, it sent labor militants, unemployed people, and other adults into the streets. Their numbers were too great for the municipal police to handle and the army refused to act, so the presidency's commando police (Mobile Police Group, GMP) did its worst: It fired into the crowd. Thirty-four were killed. Others fell in similar riots in Tuléar. Five more of the deported students died in the offshore prison of Nosy Lava. The gendarmerie and, later, the army intervened to separate the vindictive police from the crowd.

Government and people were at loggerheads. Out of these two days in May emerged a sudden irregular organization of strikers and students, the Action Committee of the Protest Movement (KIM).[94] The relatively privileged KIM was joined at a lower social echelon by another force—the ragged mob of clandestine MONIMA supporters called the Unemployed Youth of Madagascar, or ZOAM.[95] People of the ZOAM had come to Antananarivo from all corners of the island to suffer and struggle for life. They exchanged the exhausted, under-productive, profiteered countryside for the world of hustle and harassment that at least promised society, if not survival. ZOAM was the first non-Merina mass movement concentrated in the capital city. Like ZOAM, the KIM also refused affinity with the ethnically limited, middle-class Marxist AKFM. Loyal to its own role, that party had in fact denounced KIM for refusing to work through the regular political process. In the passion of the May 1972 streets, KIM and ZOAM set fire to Antananarivo's city hall, destroying the AKFM's own symbol of congenial opposition. The Merina were to suffer from both sides; disdained by the KIM and ZOAM radicals, they were nonetheless blamed for the collapse of Tsiranana's regime in the PSD's subsequent backlash against the movements of May 1972.

Confronted in the streets with an insuperable insurrection, Tsiranana looked to France for succor. He expected Paris to appreciate its stake in his regime and to brandish its force of 4,500 men stationed on the island under the 1960 defense treaty. That stake was considerable. Thanks to liberal investment codes, French business had managed to retain about two-thirds of non-real-estate capital active in the island. France still dominated import and export trade, and the Bank of France guaranteed Malagasy currency. But the Pompidou regime had grown weary of shoring up decadent Third World cronies. Its foreign business community had lost enthusiasm for a PSD policy that alienated labor and peasants while failing to satisfy basic expectations. First Tuléar, now Tananarive, had proven the absurdity of the president's recent 100 percent reelection, as well as the party's overwhelming legislative triumph a year earlier.

Once Pompidou had declined to intervene, the best long-term assurance against nationalist (that is, anti-French) revolution was the loyal (pro-French) army. Madagascar's armed forces had grown very little since independence in 1960—from 2,700 in all services to 3,500 in January 1972. Most of the troops were Merina, commanded by aristocrats, with a sprinkling of French officers remaining as advisers under the military agreements signed before independence. The gendarmerie, under separate but comparable bilateral command, was also limited—to 4,000, most of them non-Merina. Gendarmes were used for highway policing and general security as well as civic and developmental tasks; the army, navy, and air corps performed largely ornamental functions. Promotions were rare, and rank reflected prevailing social caste and class status.[96]

In 1966, Resampa had organized the Republican Security Force (FRS) under Israeli guidance. It was this corps, largely made up of côtiers, that was transferred from his Interior Ministry to the presidency in 1971 as part of Resampa's demotion. Redesignated the Mobile Police Group (GMP) under presidential adviser André Johasy, the FRS-GMP played the key police role in suppressing the May 1972 confrontation, invading the university campus and attacking the downtown mobs. When the army left its barracks, it was to separate the GMP from the people—and then to assume an important role in the sequel.

In spite of himself, the army's sixty-five-year-old commander, General Gabriel Ramanantsoa, became the inevitable guarantor of Madagascar's stability. Descended from Merina nobility, somewhat phlegmatic in temperament, Ramanantsoa had refused to do the PSD's dirty work in 1971 at Tuléar, but he remained faithful to his commission and to France, his original flag of service. On May 18, 1972, five days after the peak of crisis, this nonpolitical national servant obtained full powers from Tsiranana to eradicate the threat of anarchy stalking the regime.[97] While Tsiranana remained titular president, Ramanantsoa's task was to abort the extremist movement of ZOAM and KIM, to neutralize the antagonisms that had paralyzed Tsiranana's PSD, and to preserve a stable economic climate for this component of the overseas Franc Zone.

The general did better than that during his three-year caretaker interregnum: He prepared for serious reform of an ossified system; he balanced civilian and military protagonists; he kept Thermidorean reaction off for a time; and he allowed resurgent spirits, including the Merina bourgeoisie, to compete in a pluralistic political arena without violating the established rules of play. But this assignment required revolutionary authority, entailing the eviction of Tsiranana; Ramanantsoa won that contest with the president through referendum on October 8, 1972, but he lost control in the backwash. A pro-PSD counterrebellion surged in late 1974, opening the way for dictatorship a year later. Although balancing these extremes, the Ramanantsoa interval scored a respectable failure for democracy.

During this interregnum ideas circulated among political leaders in their quest for legitimate institutions. In the cities, KIM organized a series of seminars to focus demands on a new polity with a new constitution. Revolutionary debate crackled like fireworks in the urban air. The body politic was polarizing as old PSD and AKFM leaders struggled to their feet under barrages of denunciation from a still shadowy Left. In December 1972, the labors of KIM brought forth a new radical party, the Militants for Power to the Little People, or MFM;[98] it was led by Manandafy Rakotonirina, a sociologist who had returned from the Paris street barricades of May 1968 to the Antananarivo movement of 1972. Significantly, the urban ZOAM abandoned its alliance with Monja Jaona's rural MONIMA to follow Manandafy into the new MFM party. The Malagasy peasantry again dropped from political view. In the provinces away from home, Merina people faced vengeance from disappointed PSD côtiers, who blamed them (and Ramanantsoa, their champion) for the fall of the regime.

The urban groups that had carried out the May 1972 demonstration dominated national debates for a time, ignoring both peasantry and bourgeois reformers. This KIM-MFM-ZOAM movement held a massive national congress in September 1972, denouncing all previous politics and trade unionism. It demanded state control of the economy, with workers' associations controlling local government. Then it, too, was gradually removed from influence—feared by Ramanantsoa and others as anarchic, disdained by sedate Marxists as unscientific, ignored by the mass of Malagasy as foreign to their tradition.[99] The peasants for the most part relapsed into recalcitrant passivity, their realm of the imagination where ritual protected them from ideological intoxication and comforted them against the impositions of officialdom.

Out of the orbits of central power, the old PSD lay prostrate but awake in the hinterland, ready to call foul whenever the military misstepped or Merina interests became exposed. Obviously ill and shorn of self-discipline, President Tsiranana vitriolically opposed the Ramanantsoa mandate as an illegal effort to install a dictatorship of the Merina. He was able to broadcast his opinions without government approval, but he had no hope of blocking Ramanantsoa.[100] Many Malagasy seemed in fact to be voting against Tsiranana in the October 8, 1972, referendum. Turnout was moderate (80 percent), and the general received overwhelming endorsement (officially, 96.4 percent of the vote). His office abolished, the old president bade a dignified farewell to his capital on October 11; he was replaced as head of state by Ramanantsoa on November 7. For two more years, Tsiranana campaigned futilely for a return to power—raising funds in France, talking to exile groups, seeking to reconcile Resampa and Rabemananjara, broadcasting appeals to côtier chauvinism, and agitating among the PSD defectors to the Vonjy and other new parties.[101]

Under Ramanantsoa, real power was contested between Navy Commander Didier Ratsiraka, appointed foreign minister after a stint at the Malagasy embassy in Paris, and Colonel Richard Ratsimandrava, commanding officer of the gendarmerie. Well-connected through family ties in both the Merina and the east-coast Betsimisaraka communities, Ratsiraka attracted favor from the established classes who scorned the visionary, low-caste Merina Ratsimandrava. On May 13, 1972, Ratsimandrava had been the first to interpolate forces to protect the street crowds from the GMP. Then, as interior minister in the interregnum, the gendarmerie colonel designed a genuine grassroots administration based on the traditional fokon'olona councils, which had been receiving assignments under the PSD without ever becoming active in development.[102]

Giving local communities their first opportunity for influence over policy, this reform designated as a fokon'olona the people inhabiting a local space, *fokontany*, equivalent to a rural village or an urban neighborhood. The council of each fokon'olona obtained responsibility for law and order, justice, public works, roads, agricultural production and marketing; its ordinances (*dina*) had the force of law. Each unit had an economic committee (*vatoeka*) supported by technical assistance from the central ministries. Locally elected councils would choose delegates to district, prefectural, and provincial assemblies (*firaisam'pokonolona, fivondronam'pokonolona, faritany*). These broader groupings looked after production, marketing, economic credit, and disputes among fokontany. In theory, the councils would legislate, and only a quasi-judicial constitutional court (the redesigned Superior Institutional Council) would stand between popular will and political efficacy.

As the program began, it was riddled with defects; people had not developed the habit of making their own public decisions. Those who had—the civil servants, technicians, and former PSD notables—did everything they could to maintain their own privileges. Running for the new fokon'olona seats, they received the votes of the rural population by birthright or feudal homage, as they had always done. Jacques Rabemananjara, one of Tsiranana's most conservative ministers, supported Ramanantsoa's referendary powers and was elected mayor of Toamasina. The army, the state bureaucracy, the commercial middle class, and vestiges of the established political parties were thus assuming control of the constitutional process, successfully aborting revolution by the *madinika* (little people) of ZOAM and MFM. Some thought the new system a mere rebaptizing of the old communal structure, under which local administrators took orders directly from French colonial, then Malagasy ministerial, headquarters. By mid-1973, Manandafy and his MFM colleagues were denouncing this experiment in political culture as a revival of exploitation. According to Chaigneau, "Notwithstanding the desires of the Interior Minister [Ratsimandrava], the aim of popular sovereignty was never achieved, the future left him no time to lead it right, and the coming socialist regime soon diverted the fokon'olona institution onto an officially centralizing track."[103]

Ramanantsoa's interim coalition also proved unstable from within. Factions of the armed forces and bureaucracy lined up behind rival personages—Colonel Ratsimandrava as interior minister; the aristocratic Merina army colonel Roland Rabetafika, who held the potent post of director general of the government; and (now) Captain Didier Ratsiraka, foreign minister with a power base on the east coast as well as in Antananarivo.[104] Ratsimandrava's fokon'olona program gave the interim regime a fairly clear choice between decentralization of decisionmaking and a return to the European-oriented economy of the first republic. A more conventional alternative—revolutionary dictatorship—waited its chance with Ratsiraka and ultimately won. But when Ratsiraka came to power in 1975 as the urban elite's choice, he nevertheless paid formal deference to his rival's vision of a decentralized, popular system.

Social conditions worsened gradually during the interregnum. In 1973–1975, new ordinances provoked strikes, invited further governmental corruption, and opened lacunae in the business chain. New policies published on August 31, 1973, announced nationalizations of major foreign-owned sectors of the economy—including banking, insurance, foreign trade, transportation, energy, mining, pharmaceuticals, and cinemas. Foreign interests investing in Madagascar encountered restrictions against repatriation of their profits. Malagasation meant insertion of Merina talent to replace French experience. French street names were changed as a way of bolstering national pride. The number of foreign residents declined as 11,000 French and 1,000 Réunionnais left the country after May 1972 (half of them were military personnel).

Domestic capital never appeared in sufficient quantity to replace French banks, industries, and commerce. The national middle class was content to manage state enterprises—and to profit through the contracts issued from that management. The 1974–1977 economic plan called for investment of 169 billion FMG ($650 million), only $50 million of that from external sources; it never amassed the percentage anticipated from private Malagasy investors. Nor did Ratsiraka's popular all-horizons foreign policy turn up other foreign sources of investment for a beleaguered economy.[105] Hence, both market and state policies ensured that the country would be pauperized. Soon Madagascar would have to turn to overseas consortia to finance development schemes, thus aggravating its debt to the point of explosion.

Ramanantsoa the soldier proved indecisive as a statesman. His government hesitated for months over its major options—social, political, financial, and cultural. Promised trials of the old regime's corrupt malefactors never did get started. In the countryside, brushfires raged fiercely; farmers were refusing to send their rice to controlled markets, as inflationary conditions bid up the prices they could obtain on black markets. A grand 1974 plan to resettle farmers in the vast, neglected moors of the midwest was never implemented.[106] Educational reform, prematurely ordaining Malagasy-language pedagogy for primary and secondary institutions, drove the affluent to more dependable schools in France and Réunion. When they returned (if they did), they enjoyed competitive advantages over the disinherited masses, who were supposed to benefit from the revolution.

A fierce backlash from PSD loyalists in Tamatave and other cities endangered Merina teachers and civil servants. This reaction condemned use of the Malagasy language (as the Merina speak it) in place of French in the secondary schools. Only Merina students could be expected to master the advanced new language of textbooks and lectures—and many of the Merina were going abroad for better French educations. School boycotts, urban riots, and strikes were openly fomented by PSD militants in a half-dozen coastal cities in the interest of côtier patriotism. In Tamatave, the education riots took the dimensions of a pogrom against all resident Merina, 9,000 of whom had to flee to Antananarivo. Crowds denouncing "Merina imperialism" actually waved the French Tricolor.[107] Government supporters inevitably suspected the French of stirring trouble in the provinces to hinder the effort to revise the sacred 1960 accords. More probably, the riots represented côtier demonstrations of protest against the overthrow of a colonial-postcolonial system on which so many of them had depended for employment and security.

Pursuing national solutions on all fronts, the new government created too many enemies for its own good. In vintage Tsiranana fashion, a frustrated Ramanantsoa was heard from time to time denouncing unidentified "leftists" and other externally guided conspirators. An antigovernment côtier plot was exposed in July 1973, implicating certain French businesspeople. But no newspapers were seized, and dissenters could use virtually any platform in the country. While brushfires and strikes assaulted domestic tranquillity, by and large the government kept its head. When the economy failed to respond, however, and new scandals began to discredit the regime, the Ramanantsoa administration lost credibility in all quarters. Revolutionaries doubted its commitment to change, and conservatives saw it as a soft touch. Despite Ratsimandrava's decentralization reform, Merina elites seemed in control of the state apparatus, outraging the displaced coastal politico-bureaucrats from the Tsiranana regime. Ultimately, the interregnum succumbed to destabilizing maneuvers of the old PSD and its loyalists.[108]

The discredited Tsirananist forces regrouped around their erstwhile leaders as the Malagasy Socialist Party (PSM); they readily joined a chorus of MFM, MONIMA, and Vonjy in attacking the administration. Lacking interest in politics, Ramanantsoa declined to organize his own supporters into a mobilizable structure. But the crucial machinations took place in the PSD's bastion of security, the Mobile Police Group. Under pro-PSD colonel Bréchard Rajaonarison, the GMP blamed Merina national leadership for its humiliation of May 13, 1972, as well as for the absence of promotions and of responsible assignments in the sequel. On December 31, 1974, Rajaonarison and his brigade took control of their own barracks in the Antanimora district of the capital, declaring it off limits to the government controlled by the "Merina technocratic lobby." In effect, the GMP had constituted itself into a private army of the PSD.

Ramanantsoa was not up to this crisis. Having come to power to keep the peace, he was unwilling to use force against the mutiny, and his self-effacing qualities were not what the situation demanded. Moreover, he wearied of constant defeats for his economic program and had no tolerance for the antagonisms of Malagasy internal politics. His protégé, Colonel Rabetafika, shared Ramanantsoa's ignominy in an unworkable and corrupt economy, and they lost the loyalty of the Merina aristocracy to Ratsiraka. On January 26, 1975, invoking emergency authority, Ramanantsoa dissolved his cabinet and made an offer of full powers to Ratsimandrava, whose ministry commanded the regular police and the gendarmerie.[109] Ratsimandrava's rival, Ratsiraka, was excluded from the new leader's cabinet when Ratsimandrava became chief of state on February 5.

Opposed by the Merina, by the urban MFM radicals, and by the loyalist côtiers of the PSM, Ratsimandrava also confronted MONIMA adherents who could never forgive him for commanding the gendarmerie's sanguinary retaliation against the April 1971 uprising in Tuléar. The new president never had the time to modify his apparently hopeless position. Before he was able to quell the mutiny, Ratsimandrava was gunned down by a trio of GMP sharpshooters while traveling under minimal security in the city on February 11, less than a week after assumption of office.[110] Power was immediately claimed by a military directorate of eighteen officers under General Gilles

Andriamahazo, former military governor of Antananarivo and Ramanantsoa's minister of territorial development.

Declaring martial law, the directorate governed as a caretaker for five months and saved the country from civil war. Its combined forces stormed the Antanimora barracks, ending the GMP's mutiny and arresting three troopers for the murder of Ratsimandrava. After a highly publicized mass investigation, the regime brought 296 persons to trial for the assassination, but its prosecutors obtained convictions for only the three triggermen—and they received minimal five-year sentences. Tsiranana and Resampa were among the erstwhile PSD (now PSM) personalities released for lack of evidence. Even Rajaonarison was pardoned (to return to national politics fifteen years later). Tsiranana thereupon proposed a resumption of power through a multipartite coalition of all forces, but public opinion would not allow the directorate to rehabilitate the old PSD. The 1972 revolution had changed fundamental circumstances, and the republic was to drift toward authoritarianism of a new stripe.

Thanks to his adroit manipulation of nationalist and Marxist rhetoric and his marriage ties with the capital bourgeoisie, côtier Didier Ratsiraka became the favorite of the urban and rural radicals who had forced Tsiranana into abdication. By mid-June, Ratsiraka and his friends had outmaneuvered both the military oligarchs and the demoralized supporters of the slain Ratsimandrava. On June 26, 1975, the fifteenth anniversary of independence, the directorate named him interim chief of state and government; he was also president of the newly instituted Supreme Council of the Revolution (CSR), watchdog of the state and its revolution. Ratsiraka worked promptly to claim the legacy of the revolution and to mobilize an anarchic country in an ideologically conceived direction. The Ratsiraka regime promulgated the documents of Malagasy socialism, including the Charter of the Socialist Revolution, published on August 26, 1975. A new constitution was ratified—along with the charter and the president's own incumbency—by a triple referendum on December 21. Only the PSM and the Christian Democratic Party opposed the proposals; the AKFM continued its collaboration with the regime in power. Ratsiraka's yes vote reached the canonical 94.66 percent, and the constitution was in force at midnight on December 31, 1975.[111]

In actuality, this program had little in common with the May 1972 revolutionary impulses of the KIM-ZOAM and only a rhetorical connection with the highly original, hopeful revolution promoted by Ratsimandrava in the fokon'olona reform. Not only was the embattled gendarmerie president dead; so was the audacious reorganization he had championed. That reform had been based on a genuinely conceived "peasant ideology," granting to people the confidence that allows them to master their development, to take responsibility for their destinies. It was perhaps both utopic and atavistic as its opponents claimed, but it never had a chance. Ratsiraka's brand of socialism was to use this newly revived fokon'olona for more centralized state purposes, for the implementation of nationally ordained modernization rather than for communitarian decisionmaking.[112] So the revolution of 1972 degenerated into the autocracy of 1975–1992.

NOTES

1. See Claude Wanquet, "Les fondements historiques de la coopération régionale," *Annuaire des Pays de l'Océan Indien (APOI)*, no. 9, 1982–1983, pp. 21–45; P. M. Mutibwa, *The Malagasy and the Europeans: Madagascar's Foreign Relations, 1861–1895* (Ibadan, Nigeria: Humanities Press, 1974).
2. See Hubert Deschamps, *Histoire de Madagascar* (Paris: Berger-Levrault, 1961), p. 185.
3. See Maurice Bloch, *Placing the Dead: Tombs, Ancestral Villages, and Kinship Organization in Madagascar* (London and New York: Seminar Press, 1972), pp. 26–27.
4. See Gwyn Campbell, "Madagascar and the Slave Trade, 1810–1895," paper presented at the Colloque d'Histoire Malgache, Mahajanga, April 1981.
5. Deschamps, *Histoire de Madagascar*, p. 231.
6. See Pascal Chaigneau, *Madagascar, de la première république à l'orientation socialiste: Processus et conséquences d'une évolution politique* (Thèse IIIème cycle en sociologie politique, Univ. de Paris X, 1981), v. 1, p. 17; see also Edouard Ralaimihoatra, *Histoire de Madagascar*, 4th ed. (Antananarivo: Librairie de Madagascar, 1982), pt. 3, ch. 1.
7. See Henri Vidal, "L'arrêté du 26 septembre 1896 abolissant l'esclavage à Madagascar," *APOI*, no. 5, 1978, pp. 69–93.
8. Nigel Heseltine, *Madagascar* (New York: Praeger, 1971), pp. 138–149, provides a detailed analysis of Galliéni's administration.
9. See François Rajaoson, *L'enseignement supérieur et le devenir de la société malgache* (Thèse d'état en lettres et sciences humaines, Univ. de Paris V, 1981), pp. 129–134.
10. See Yves Prats, *Le développement communautaire à Madagascar* (Paris: Pichon et Durand-Auzias, 1972), pp. 40–43, 49–50.
11. See Prats, *Développement communautaire*, pp. 42–46; Maurice Bloch, "The Changing Relationship Between Rural Communities and the State in Central Madagascar During the Nineteenth and Twentieth Centuries," in *Les communautés rurales: Recueils de la société Jean Bodin pour l'histoire comparative des institutions* (Paris: Dessain et Tolra, 1983), p. 243; Ralaimihoatra, *Histoire de Madagascar*, pp. 229, 271.
12. Jean-Pierre Raison, "Madagascar dans le sud-ouest de l'océan indien," *Hérodote: Revue de Géographie et de Géopolitique*, nos. 37–38, 1985, p. 227.
13. *La France de l'océan indien—Madagascar, les Comores, la Réunion, la côte française*, Collection Terres Lointaines, no. 8 (Paris: Société d'Éditions Géographiques, Maritimes et Coloniales, 1952), p. 206.
14. The phrase invokes Senegalese experience celebrated in Cheikh Hamidou Kane's novel of that name, *L'aventure ambiguë* (Paris: Julliard, 1961), translated as *Ambiguous Adventure* by Katherine Woods (London: Heinemann, 1963). For the most consistent recent defense of the colonial record, see Fernand Deleris, *Ratsiraka: Socialisme et misère à Madagascar* (Paris: Harmattan, 1986), ch. 1.
15. See Raison, "Madagascar dans le sud-ouest de l'océan indien," p. 225.
16. See Prats, *Développement communautaire*, pp. 49–51.
17. Ibid., pp. 56–63.
18. See Prats's critique of the classic ideas of Condominas on local government organization in Madagascar, ibid., pp. 85–88; see also Ralaimihoatra, *Histoire de Madagascar*, pp. 288–292.
19. See Heseltine, *Madagascar*, pp. 150–151.
20. An exception was allowed for Sainte Mariens, whose nationality as defined by French courts dated from the cession of their island to France by Queen Betia in 1750.

21. See Chaigneau, *Première république,* pp. 21–24; Ralaimihoatra, *Histoire de Madagascar,* pp. 251–258; Gérard Althabe, "Les luttes sociales à Tananarive en 1972," *Cahiers d'Etudes Africaines,* no. 80, pp. 407–447; François Rajaoson, *L'enseignement supérieure,* pp. 146–149.

22. See Ralaimihoatra, *Histoire de Madagascar,* pp. 261–263.

23. The subject is exhaustively analyzed in Antoine Bouillon, *Madagascar, le colonisé et son 'âme': Essai sur le discours psychologique colonial* (Paris: Harmattan, 1981); cf. the famous earlier treatise of O. Mannoni, *Prospero and Caliban: The Psychology of Colonization,* trans. Pamela Powesland, 2nd ed. (New York: Praeger, 1964), which imposes a psychoanalytical interpretation on these relationships.

24. See Chaigneau, *Première république,* pp. 30–31.

25. See Maurice Bloch, *From Blessing to Violence: History and Ideology in the Circumcision Ritual of the Merina of Madagascar* (Cambridge: Cambridge University Press, 1986), pp. 27–33; Althabe, "Luttes sociales."

26. For a brilliant general discussion of the relationship between the anticolonialist social cause and political nationalism in Africa, see Basil Davidson, *The Black Man's Burden: Africa and the Curse of the Nation-State* (New York: Random House Times Books, 1992).

27. Richard Andriamanjato, interviewed in the Fianarantsoa Roman Catholic weekly newspaper *Lumière,* April 18, 1971.

28. Raul Hilberg, *The Destruction of the European Jews,* 3 vols. (New York and London: Holmes & Meier, 1985), pp. 397–399; see also pp. 211, 394–395; in the earlier one-volume edition (Chicago: Quadrangle Books, 1961), see pp. 128, 138, 141, 259.

29. See Heseltine, *Madagascar,* pp. 168–171.

30. See Chaigneau, *Première république,* pp. 31–32.

31. See Jacques Tronchon, *L'insurrection malgache de 1947: Essai d'interprétation historique* (Paris: Maspero, 1974), pp. 29–30, 137–141.

32. Ibid., pp. 144–145.

33. Ibid., pp. 151–156; Tronchon insists on calling 1947 an insurrection rather than a rebellion or revolt, thus stressing the vertical, or "rising up," quality of the movement.

34. Jacques Rabemananjara, interviewed in the Antananarivo daily *Tribune,* May 5, 1990.

35. See Chaigneau, *Première république,* pp. 35–40; Ralaimihoatra, *Histoire de Madagascar,* pp. 278–279.

36. See Tronchon, *L'insurrection malgache,* pp. 170–173.

37. Ibid., p. 133.

38. For narrative, see Chaigneau, *Première république,* pp. 36–40; Heseltine, *Madagascar,* pp. 178–181; Christian Rasoarahona, "Le personnel militaire malgache et l'insurrection de 1947," *Cahiers du Centre d'Animation Culturelle, d'Information et de Documentation (CACID)* (Paris: Ambassade de Madagascar, 1980); Tronchon, *L'insurrection malgache,* ch. 1.

39. See Bloch, *Placing the Dead,* p. 29; Tronchon, *L'insurrection malgache,* p. 73.

40. See Tronchon, *L'insurrection malgache,* pp. 73, 117–118, 163.

41. See Chaigneau, *Première république,* p. 49; Georges Balandier, "Preface," in Gérard Althabe, *Oppression et libération dans l'imaginaire: Les communautés villageoises de la côte orientale de Madagascar* (Paris: François Maspéro, 1969).

42. See Tronchon, *L'insurrection malgache,* pp. 159–170.

43. See Althabe, *Oppression et libération,* pp. 255–262; Bloch, *Placing the Dead,* pp. 28–29.

44. See Frank Raharison, "Les notables et l'insurrection de 1947," *CACID.*

45. See Rasoarahona, "Personnel militaire."
46. Pascal Chaigneau, *Rivalités politiques et socialisme à Madagascar* (Paris: Centre des Hautes Etudes sur l'Afrique et l'Asie Modernes [CHEAM], 1985), p. 28.
47. See Althabe, "Luttes sociales."
48. Richard Andriamanjato, *Le tsiny et le tody dans la pensée malgache* (Paris: Présence Africaine, 1957).
49. For a critical analysis of the constitution as violating the primacy of society over state, see Chaigneau, *Première république,* pp. 144–149.
50. For analysis of the *accords de coopération,* see Heseltine, *Madagascar,* p. 189; Chaigneau, *Première république,* pp. 157–166; Edward M. Corbett, *The French Presence in Black Africa* (Washington, D.C.: Black Orpheus Press, 1972), esp. pp. 85–87, 145–148.
51. See Harry Bryce Qualman, "Limits and Constraints on Foreign Policy in a Dependent State: Madagascar Under the Tsiranana Regime," Ph.D. dissertation, Johns Hopkins University, 1975; Césaire Rabenoro, *Les relations extérieures de Madagascar de 1960 à 1972* (Thèse d'état, Univ. d'Aix-Marseille III, 1981).
52. See Chaigneau, *Première république,* pp. 309–310.
53. See Chaigneau, *Rivalités politiques,* p. 30; Y.-G. Paillard, "The First and Second Malagasy Republics: The Difficult Road of Independence," trans. Raymond Kent, in Raymond Kent, ed., *Madagascar in History: Essays from the 1970's* (Albany, Calif.: Foundation for Malagasy Studies, 1979), pp. 298–354.
54. See Chaigneau, *Première république,* pp. 175–190.
55. Ibid., pp. 326–327.
56. See Prats, *Développement communautaire,* pp. 15–16.
57. Andriamanjato interview with *Lumière,* April 18, 1971.
58. See Bouillon, *Le colonisé et son âme;* Philip M. Allen, "New Round for the Western Islands," in Alvin J. Cottrell and R. M. Burrell, eds., *The Indian Ocean: Its Political, Economic, and Military Importance* (New York: Praeger, 1972), pp. 307–329.
59. Patrick Rajoelina, *Quarante années de la vie politique de Madagascar, 1947–1987* (Paris: Harmattan, 1988), p. 31.
60. Rabenoro, *Relations extérieures,* p. 318.
61. Chaigneau, *Première république,* p. 216; cf. Prats, *Développement communautaire,* pp. 11–15 and ch. 6.
62. See Paillard, "The First and Second Malagasy Republics," pp. 298–354.
63. See Deleris, *Ratsiraka,* pp. 24–26.
64. See Prats, *Développement communautaire,* pp. 361–362.
65. See Jean-Pierre Raison, *Les hautes terres de Madagascar* (Paris: ORSTOM-Karthala, 1984), pp. 220–221; cf. projects of the Agricultural Production Development Bureau (BDPA), managed by French consulting agencies and described by Nathaniel McKitterick, "G.O.P.R. in Madagascar: A Unique Technical Assistance Project" (report to CIDA, August 1970).
66. See Althabe, pp. 47–53.
67. See Rajaoson, *L'enseignement supérieure,* pp. 193–194.
68. Second vice president was Calvin Tsiebo, Tsiranana's nominal number two since 1960; Rabemananjara, in charge of foreign affairs, and Victor Miadana, the administration's chief techno-economist, were third and fourth; these four boxed the côtier compass, west, south, east, and north; not one vice president was Merina until May 1971, when Alfred Ramangasoavina joined the quartet, taking part of the disgraced Resampa's dominion.
69. See Philip M. Allen, "Rites of Passage in Madagascar," *Africa Report,* February 1971.

70. See the extraordinary series of editorials by André Ravatomanga in *Lumière,* May 9, 16, and 30; June 6, 13, and 20; July 18; August 1 and 15, 1971.

71. See Althabe, "Luttes sociales."

72. See *Lumière,* June 20, 1971.

73. Interview with Resampa, *Jeune Afrique,* no. 598, June 24, 1972.

74. The contemporaneous accounts of André Ravatomanga in the Fianarantsoa Roman Catholic weekly *Lumière* tell the story in fine detail; it is summarized in Paillard, "First and Second Malagasy Republics"; Chaigneau, *Première république;* Althabe, "Luttes sociales"; Philip M. Allen, "Madagascar: The Authenticity of Recovery," in John M. Ostheimer, ed., *The Politics of the Western Indian Ocean Islands* (New York: Praeger, 1975), pp. 45–59; Allen, "New Round for the Western Islands."

75. See, for instance, Dominique Desjeux, *La question agraire à Madagascar: Administration et paysannat de 1895 à nos jours* (Paris: Harmattan, 1979); Desjeux, "Réforme foncière et civilisation agraire: Le cas de Madagascar," *Le Mois en Afrique,* nos. 184–185, April-May 1981, pp. 55–61; Maurice Bloch, "Changing Relationship"; Gilles Duruflé, *L'ajustement structurel en Afrique (Sénégal, Côte d'Ivoire, Madagascar)* (Paris: Karthala, 1988); Elliot Berg, "The Liberalization of Rice Marketing in Madagascar," *World Development,* v. 17, no. 5, May 1989, pp. 719–728.

76. The fires were accompanied then by acts of urban sabotage.

77. Cited in Chaigneau, *Première république,* pp. 405–406.

78. From the title of Althabe's masterful study focusing on the eastern Betsimisaraka people, *Oppression et libération dans l'imaginaire.*

79. Reported in the Antananarivo weekly *Hehy,* April 6, and in *Lumière,* April 11, 1971.

80. See Chaigneau, *Première république,* pp. 406–420; *Le Monde,* May 8, 1971; *Lumière,* April 11, May 2 and 9, 1971.

81. See *Jeune Afrique,* no. 468; see also *Le Monde,* May 8, 1971.

82. Chaigneau, *Première république,* pp. 424–428.

83. *Lumière,* October 24, 1971.

84. This cohesion lasted until 1990 when, reacting to the universal bankruptcy of Marxist solutions, Andriamanjato himself led the Merina nationalists out of the old party, AKFM, into the successful AKFM Renewal.

85. André Ravatomanga, editorial, *Lumière,* September 5, 1971.

86. See Prats, *Développement communautaire,* pp. 98–103.

87. See Chaigneau, *Première république,* pp. 429–430.

88. Ibid., pp. 433–434; see also Allen, "Rites of Passage."

89. This was possibly an emergency evacuation plan routinely filed by all U.S. Foreign Service posts in even the most friendly of countries.

90. See *Lumière,* April 25, 1971.

91. Chaigneau, *Première république,* p. 447.

92. *Lumière,* April 4, 18, July 18, 1971; see also the Antananarivo Malagasy language daily *Maresaka,* July 15, 1971.

93. See Paillard, "First and Second Malagasy Republics"; also *Jeune Afrique,* no. 564, October 30, 1971.

94. KIM: Komity iraisan'ny Mpitolona.

95. ZOAM: Zatovo orin'asa anivon'ny Madagasikara, formerly identified as ZWAM, Young Malagasy Outcasts; the letter "W" had originally stood for Western— curiously imposing a cowboy cinema image on this urban street movement. ZOAM's successors would use kung-fu films for purposes of the "imaginary revolt," identified in more rural circumstances with the cults of spirit possession, or tromba.

96. See Chaigneau, *Première république,* pp. 397–398; Chaigneau, *Rivalités politiques,* pp. 46–51.

97. See Bechir Ben Yahia, *Jeune Afrique,* no. 595; Althabe, "Luttes sociales"; Chaigneau, *Première république,* pp. 462–463; Chaigneau, *Rivalités politiques,* pp. 59–65.

98. MFM: Mpitolona ho an'ny Fanjakan'ny Madinika.

99. See Chaigneau, *Rivalités politiques,* pp. 81–84; Siradiou Diallo in *Jeune Afrique,* no. 638, March 31, 1973.

100. See *Jeune Afrique,* no. 615, October 21, 1972.

101. Vonjy Iray Tsy Mivaky, or VTM (Salvation in Unity), comprising pro-Ratsiraka renegades from the PSD. See Sennen Andriamirado in *Jeune Afrique,* nos. 730–731, January 3–10, 1975.

102. Ordinance 73-009, March 24, 1973.

103. Chaigneau, *Première république,* pp. 496–497; see also Paillard, "First and Second Malagasy Republics."

104. Chaigneau, *Rivalités politiques,* pp. 90–93.

105. See Economist Intelligence Unit, *Quarterly Economic Review,* no. 1, 1974, pp. 14–16, no. 4, 1973, p. 17; *Africa Research Bulletin,* Economic Series, May 15–June 14, 1973, pp. 2747–2749; *Jeune Afrique,* supplement to no. 716, September 28, 1974, pp. 29–73; *Marchés Tropicaux et Méditerranéens (MTM),* March 1, 1974; *Lumière,* June 30, 1974.

106. See Raison, *Les hautes terres,* p. 222.

107. See Jean-Pierre Langellier, "Madagascar, la révolution essoufflée," *Le Monde Hebdomadaire,* no. 1692, April 2–8, 1981; *Jeune Afrique,* no. 638, March 31, 1973.

108. See Rajoelina, *Quarante années,* pp. 46–50.

109. Chaigneau, *Première république,* p. 608, reports unsubstantiated charges that Ratsimandrava also held evidence of corruption incriminating the general and friends. See also Rajoelina, *Quarante années,* p. 50; Patrick Rajoelina and Alain Ramelet, *Madagascar: La grande île* (Paris: Harmattan, 1989), pp. 42–43.

110. See Maureen Covell, *Madagascar: Politics, Economics and Society* (London and New York: Frances Pinter, 1987), pp. 167–168; Rajoelina, *Quarante années,* p. 50.

111. See Chaigneau, *Première république,* pp. 621–637.

112. See Jean du Bois de Gaudusson, "Propos sur les aspects idéologiques et institutionnels des récentes réformes des fokonolona: Le fokonolona en question?" *APOI,* no. 5, 1978, pp. 17–36; Zaïveline Ramarasaona, *Les femmes malgaches dans le fokonolona* (Thèse IIIème cycle, Univ. de Paris, 1979), pp. 53–63.

3
Ratsiraka's Republic: Revolution as Myth

THE STRUCTURES OF SOCIALISM

From mid-1975 until nearly the end of the 1980s, Didier Ratsiraka's Madagascar lived under an officially assumed socialist identity. The second republic's ideological and institutional structure was declared in the Charter of the Socialist Revolution, promulgated on August 26, 1975, to legitimize everything else. Like all other major texts, the charter appeared both in Malagasy, to vindicate the revolutionary triumph of nationalism, and in French for the benefit of the world at large. Indeed, bilinguality, ambivalence, and dual personality were to characterize this republic from the outset to its expiration in 1993. In cultural expression at least, the revolution could scarcely distinguish itself from the standard neocolonial cosmopolitanism that it denounced in most other sectors of the Third World.

Promptly dubbed Ratsiraka's own "little red book," the charter offered both historical analysis and forward-looking justifications for socialist institutions. Its program incorporated all conceivable aspects of domestic and external policy, a socialism for all points of the compass (*"tous azimuts"*). The revolutionary nation was defined in terms of irreducible independence, militant Third World neutrality, and socioeconomic democracy. Proclaimed as a "socialism of the poor," the revolutionary democratic ideal followed three guiding principles: "equitable distribution of wealth and income, fair and equitable acquisition of cultural assets, power to those who produce."[1] Decolonization consisted mainly in dispossessing foreign economic interests and denouncing their local business cohorts.

In its original form Ratsiraka's charter represented a delicate blend of ingredients from various ideological sources. Without explicitly crediting those sources, the text reproduced Marxist critiques of property, factors of production, and labor value theory, endorsing "democratic centralism" in decisionmaking. The thought of Mao Tse-Tung contributed emphasis on peasant participation in crucial administrative, economic, and political organization. Leninist tradition imposed on that participation the "guidance" of the unitary state and a centrally planned economy. The triadic theory of ideological, technical, and cultural revolutions of Kim Il Sung's North Korea (the Juche theory) played a notable role in Ratsiraka's syncretism of doctrines, along with echoes of Tanzania's self-reliance and Algerian state capitalism. These elements imparted a Third World, "nonaligned" flavor to the contents of Madagascar's ideological melting pot.[2]

While the leader's red book was obtaining popular currency, its revolutionary spirit joined with traditional ideals in a new constitution declaring the Malagasy nation to be organized in a "state founded on the socialist and democratic community, the *Fokon'olona.*" This state took the name Democratic Republic of Madagascar. It refracted institutionally into the presidency (identified most significantly as "the supreme organ of state power"), a cabinet of ministers (technically termed "the government"), the Supreme Council of the Revolution (CSR), the National People's Assembly (ANP), a Military Development Committee (CMD), and the High Constitutional Court (HCC). Socialist organization was articulated through associations of liberated peasants, revolutionary youth and women, a democratized "people's" army, and workers' committees in each enterprise. In 1976, another charter established the fokon'olona structure of decentralized administration as the fulfillment of Madagascar's true political culture.[3]

Dissemination of the revolutionary charter in print and media during late 1975 tended to personify these progressive principles in the nation's new leader. Thirty-nine-year-old Didier Ratsiraka, son of the east coast Betsimisaraka, was educated by Jesuits at Antananarivo and Paris. Emerging with a diploma in engineering from the French Naval Academy at Brest, he served as Tsiranana's military attaché in Paris and was called home to become foreign minister under the Ramanantsoa interregnum. Despite his debt to French culture, Ratsiraka acquired his national reputation as liquidator of the multifarious ties that bound the first republic with Paris. After adroitly marginalizing his opposition in the brief directorate that succeeded the assassination of President Ratsimandrava, Ratsiraka became identified with the constitution of 1975, hence with fulfillment of the movement of May 1972. To seal the revolutionary compact, all three—charter, constitution, and president-designate—were approved as a package (by 94.66 percent) in the referendum of December 21, 1975, and all assumed legitimate authority ten days later. "Three different questions were compressed under electoral pressure into a single answer," comments Chaigneau. "As in all referenda-by-acclamation, the man was applauded in the adoption of a text."[4]

If this fusion of state, ideology, and person seems to mock the democratic option, it made some sense in Madagascar at the time. To separate the 1975 process into constitutional and electoral campaigns would have prolonged the struggle of irreconcilables that had flared so acutely in late 1974. The most fearsome prospect was triangular civil war between the Merina-officered military, its embittered Francophile PSD nemesis, and the remnants of Ratsimandrava's reform movement in local government and the gendarmerie. Only a year before the referendum half the country seemed to be rising up against authority; for the past century, more than half had been resisting any kind of central authority whatever. The year 1975 had witnessed the installation of four separate chiefs of state—Ramanantsoa, Ratsimandrava, Andriamahazo, Ratsiraka. Evidently, the country required stability before anything else.

Leader number four did indeed answer that demand. Ratsiraka's east coast origins and his professed Roman Catholicism reassured the côtier majority against a resumption of Merina domination, prefigured in the 1972 Ramanantsoa coup d'état. Yet his privileged school years in the highlands and his naval officer training, his marriage ties with Merina families, and his distinctly nationalist (that is, Francophobe) policies as foreign minister during the interregnum all identified the young president with the interests that had opposed and replaced Tsiranana. Moreover, despite his open rivalry with Ratsimandrava, Ratsiraka's rhetorical appropriation of his opponent's fokon'-olona ideology seemed to link him with the indigenous popular spirit at the heart of the revolution of 1972.

By 1990, Ratsiraka had surpassed Tsiranana's fourteen years in the presidency (counting the latter's two years prior to independence). His reelections in 1982 and 1989 were contested and protested, although not to the point of civic uproar. His incumbency embodied both the revolution and its contradiction, for his authoritarian regime alienated workers and peasantry alike. Moreover, his socialist commitment did not enjoy such longevity. From the mid-1980s, Ratsiraka had to concede minor failures and to command major changes of direction away from revolutionary options and toward the international neoliberal mainstream. He ensured continuity of leadership into the early 1990s by compromising the theses on which his revolutionary republic had been built.

Notwithstanding these concessions, Ratsiraka sustained official primacy through October 1991, retaining his title until the runoff election won by Albert Zafy in February 1993. The president chose two-thirds of the CSR membership; he appointed and dismissed the prime minister and could be outvoted only by two-thirds of the 137-seat National People's Assembly (ANP). In the course of events, the CSR became merely honorific; the government existed to execute presidential policy; and the ANP at its best rose from a registry office to a critical conscience that could object to, but not repudiate, the executive will.

Once the second republic had synthesized state structure and ideological principles, its foreign and domestic policy options seemed logically entailed. Democratic Madagascar was to adhere to central planning, "progressive" indoctrination of institutions, and external alignment with Cuba, Algeria, and other anticapitalist countries. Unfortunately for Madagascar, this political course encountered two main obstacles: the need for external capital to invigorate a retrograde economy and the profound and fervent Malagasy distrust of fanjakana, the central state.

In the late 1970s, conforming to international trends of the time, the Ratsiraka regime launched a deliberate campaign for funds to invest in newly nationalized industries. When the projects failed as interest rates rose, and when production lagged across almost all sectors of the economy—and world markets scorned the little that was produced—Ratsiraka's republic, like many others, had to confess its indigence. Unable to liquidate those 1977–1979 debts or to service their consequences, Madagascar has been a ward of the international system of credit since the early 1980s. By the middle of that decade, its options had been largely constrained by abject dependence; the remnants of Ratsiraka's red book blanched under international market system heat.

On the domestic scene, despite lip service to the indigenous ideal of fokon'olona, the regime was unable to concede genuine authority to local government units. Before his assassination in 1975, Ratsimandrava and his adherents could endorse a communal right to impose taxes and spend public revenues without overweening central controls. To them this devolution of confidence seemed both administratively feasible and consistent with traditional Malagasy decisionmaking. By contrast, the republic chartered by Ratsiraka entrenched a class of urban administrators, technicians, and ideologues who could scarcely be expected to release such authority to 10,000 unschooled and unmanageable localities. Moreover, the fragile security of a state newly emergent from regional and class conflict seemed to demand guidance from party, official ideology, and technical bureaucracy. Once established, the fokontany, basic units of the fokon'olona structure, deteriorated into chit-issuing offices for regulated routine and into electoral incubators for delegates to high offices. Thus, the republic renounced its opportunity to inspire Madagascar's first real partnership between central regime and autonomous localities.

The constitution of 1975 endowed the presidency with concentrated powers unknown in Madagascar since before 1958. Yet that structure was approved by a population that innately distrusts central authority. Exhorted to socialist discipline, all institutions were dominated by a heavy, coercive bureaucracy only too reminiscent of the French governor-general's administration and the exploitative PSD apparatus. Moreover, Malagasy society and culture constantly butted against the rock-ribs of ideological centralism. It was always central authority that had to be defended for the sake of stability; any alternative invited inadmissible anarchy. Local offices were channels of advice and implementation, not of initiation and consent. In this confrontation, fokon'olona autonomy appeared as a defect in national solidarity. Ratsiraka's state thus became one more in the sequence of fanjakana that failed to mobilize popular loyalties.

Centrality may have dominated the island's administration, but it never prevailed in the arena of partisan politics. For a year after the 1975 watershed, political parties remained inactive (except as "committees of support" for Ratsiraka) while the new president vainly sought consensus on the standard statist model of the single party.[5] He had to settle for much less. Article 8 of the constitution called for a voluntary coalescence of "the most conscientious citizens inspired by socialist and patriotic ideals functioning within progressive organizations" into a National Front for the Defense of the Revolution (FNDR). Membership in the front determined eligibility for public office, but the FNDR never forged its "progressive" constituents into a monolith, as envisaged in Articles 9 and 10. While sharing participation in government institutions, the several parties in the FNDR maintained separate identities, from crypto-Marxist to Christian Democratic. Their constituencies insisted on regular, competitive elections, and the state had to oblige—in 1977, 1982, 1983, and 1989—although ensuring in each case the survival of the president and his loyal forces.

Simply professing faith in the socialist charter sufficed to assure party politicians a place in the FNDR coalition; it was their way of remaining legal—until 1990, when Ratsiraka was obliged to recognize the legitimacy of an array of opposition factions outside the front. During the FNDR's ascendancy, conservatives and opportunists infiltrated all parties of the front, acquiring acceptance so long as they praised the revolution and renounced nostalgia for the old days of French-PSD domination. They too shared in managing the state enterprises that proliferated through external borrowing, but without successfully achieving the nationalist ideal of a socially managed economy.

Ratsiraka's own mass party, the Avant-Garde of the Malagasy Revolution (AREMA), evolved out of a multitude of committees that had formed to advocate the threefold yes vote in 1975. A complex movement comparable to mass parties elsewhere, AREMA developed its own affiliate organizations of women, students, laborers, artists, and athletes. It was particularly successful in the exploitable countryside, where it could dominate subservient fokon'-olona without having to suffer competition or criticism. In towns, or wherever Malagasy were free to assert the slightest political preference, AREMA encountered opposition. It became identified by masses of Malagasy with the impositions and intimidations of an uncongenial external force, the fanjakana. AREMA suffered as well from the usual incoherence of a catchall party and from the proverbial incompetence and corruptibility of "democratic centralism."[6]

Although subject to cleavages and dissension, AREMA remained the president's political instrument, carrying home the bulk of all electoral harvests from 1977 through the end of the 1980s. Despite these victories, the party never obtained enough momentum to absorb its urban-based FNDR competitors. Until 1989–1990 those rivals included only the reborn Marxist AKFM (Congress Party for the Independence of Madagascar), which remained faithful to AREMA's president without fully joining his movement; Monja Jaona's MONIMA (Madagascar Ruled by Malagasy), never reconciled to Ratsiraka in policy or personality until it perceived a return to "neocolonialism" in the opposition; a pro-Ratsiraka splinter group, the VS (Vondrona Socialista)-MONIMA; Manandafy Rakotonirina's increasingly disputatious urban MFM coalition; the Vonjy, or VITM (Salvation in Unity) party of rehabilitated PSD adherents; and the Union of Christian Democrats (UDECMA), a Catholic-oriented force in east coast politics. These parties shifted positions and traded vicissitudes over fifteen years of nominally progressive statecraft, but they survived as formal expressions of the Malagasy determination to sustain a pluralistic political culture.

MFM (Militants for Power to the Little People) originated in informal assemblies of intellectuals from the late 1960s. It surged into limelight during the revolution of 1972 thanks to the adherence of the young urban and rural unemployed (the ZOAM). Led from the start by sociologist Rakotonirina

Manandafy, a defector from MONIMA, MFM persistently challenged the prevailing regime from the viewpoint of radical nationalist populism. Reconciled to the Ratsiraka charter in 1977 after a period of interdiction, MFM remained perilously within the FNDR and the CSR but never had a minister appointed to a Ratsiraka cabinet.

Finally declaring the bankruptcy of the regime, Manandafy ran against Ratsiraka in the 1989 elections, obtaining over 19 percent of the official tally and thus regaining some of MFM's early 1970s prominence. Since then, the party has turned wholeheartedly toward the international system of trade and finance, rendering its leader persona grata in Washington but sacrificing its original clientele of populists and radicals. During the crisis of 1991–1992, MFM (retitled Party of Malagasy Progress) cooperated with the nonpartisan administration of Guy Razanamasy, thus keeping distance from both Ratsiraka and the opposition coalition, *Forces Vives* (Vital Forces), under Albert Zafy. Cochair of the semi-official Committee for Economic and Social Recovery during that period, Manandafy proved unable to make headway against the double intransigeance of presidency and opposition. Singularly unsuccessful in the November 1992 presidential election when he finished a distant third behind Zafy and Ratsiraka, Manandafy was obliged to offer his grudging support to Zafy in the February 1993 runoffs. In the legislative elections of June 1993 the MFM had to settle for 14 seats (out of 138), and its leader subsequently finished third in the contest for prime minister. The winner of that contest, Francisque Ravony, had by then already quit the party in order to campaign unequivocally for Albert Zafy as president.

Vonjy Iray Tsy Mivaky (VITM, Salvation in Unity) broke away from the remnants of the Tsiranana PSD in 1973 and persuaded Ratsiraka of its good faith during the 1975 referendum campaign. Hence, although harboring a large number of important figures from the period dubbed neocolonial, the party of Dr. Marojama Razanabahiny retained its place among the FNDR and CSR "progressives." For a brief time in 1989 Vonjy joined the MFM and VS-MONIMA in an aborted "democratic alliance" against Ratsiraka, but Razanabahiny ended by running for the presidency against both Ratsiraka and Manandafy, winning almost 15 percent of the vote and third place. During 1990, the "unity" party was crippled by major defections, particularly those of former PSD leaders such as André Resampa; they founded their own parties outside the FNDR. Vonjy virtually vanished after the June 16, 1993, parliamentary elections, which returned only two of its candidates, including Razanabahiny.

MONIMA (Madagasikara Otrin'ny Malagasy, Madagascar Ruled by Malagasy) is an independent populist force originating in the southern region of Toliara (Tuléar). Skeletal and semiclandestine during the Tsiranana ascendancy, the party nonetheless engineered the April 1971 uprising of southern peasants. It subsequently established (then lost control of) an urban bridgehead among unemployed youth in the Antananarivo ZOAM during the 1972 revolution. Even after expanding its clientele to the cities, MONIMA was dominated by Monja Jaona, an authentic revolutionary identified with the peasantry of Toliara. Active in the 1947 insurrection, Monja became a dauntless antagonist of all regimes from the French through the first republic to Ratsiraka and, inevitably, Zafy. Never entirely reconciled with Ratsiraka's cosmopolitan values and his compromises of expediency, MONIMA lost some of its members to the ineffectual Marxist splinter group VS-MONIMA and to the MFM after 1975. Monja Jaona challenged Ratsiraka for the presidency in 1982, mobilizing a substantial protest vote against the regime; he retained his seats in the ANP and in the CSR (albeit with intervals of expulsion).

Monja's appeal has waned in later years, and he obtained only negligible support in the 1989 presidential elections against Ratsiraka. In 1991, however, fearing that Zafy's Vital Forces opposition was offering the Malagasy nothing but a false choice between a return to French (neocolonial) domination and empowerment of the imperious Merina, he and the remnants of his MONIMA joined Ratsiraka in the advocacy of a "new federalism." Repudiating the third republic after Zafy's election as president, MONIMA adherents seized control of Toliara province headquarters on May 28, 1993, and proclaimed Monja Jaona "governor of the federal state." Four days later, a combined police-gendarmerie force evicted the federalists in a seven-hour skirmish, killing two insurgents and arresting forty-seven. The eighty-four-year-old "governor" was once again assigned to house arrest for the impending legislative elections.[7]

UDECMA (Union des Démocrates Chrétiens de Madagascar, Union of Christian Democrats of Madagascar) appeared in Toamasina during 1971 to assert Roman Catholic interests in a rapidly evolving political context. It soon mobilized Catholic support for Toamasina's favorite son, Ratsiraka, driving its traditional leader, Alexis Bezaka, into self-exile. Seldom forced to choose between socialist and Christian principles, the UDECMA and its new chairman, Solo Norbert Andriamorasata, played a subdued role in national politics. They espoused the critical positions of the clergy whenever possible without jeopardy to their status inside the system. By 1990, once FNDR membership was no longer required for political activity, UDECMA faced serious rivals in the Christian Democratic movement (including a new party formed by the repatriated Bezaka).[8] UDECMA virtually lost identity in the June 1993 legislative elections.

AKFM (Antoko'ny Kongresi'ny Fahaleovantenan'i Madagasikara, the Congress Party for the Independence of Madagascar) was founded at Tamatave (Toamasina) to campaign for outright independence in France's empirewide referendum of September 28, 1958. Representing the nation's principal opposition throughout the Tsiranana period, the AKFM was led by a well-disciplined cadre of Marxist strategists, journalists, and trade union officials. Its veteran general secretary, Gisèle Rabesahala, was Ratsiraka's minister of culture for fifteen years, the only prominent woman in the regime apart from the president's immediate family. Since virtually all its leaders have been Merina, this deliberately ideological party has exerted strong appeal on the distinctly middle-class nationalism of Antananarivo, and it is there that the AKFM has always drawn most of its support. Although overtaken by the events of 1972, the party quickly joined the Ratsiraka bandwagon and served as ideological drillmaster for the larger, more inchoate AREMA.

In late 1989, party president Richard Andriamanjato led a movement into a new party, the AKFM Fanavaozana (AKFM Renewal), declaring hostility to Ratsiraka and astutely supporting Zafy and the Vital Forces movement. The Fanavaozana developed a nuanced social democratic platform, finding examples in a rapidly changing East European matrix. Without its charismatic standard-bearer the Marxist rump AKFM virtually disappeared by mid-1993; the new Fanavaozana triumphed in the June elections at Antananarivo, sending both Andriamanjato and political newcomer Frédéric Randriamamonjy to the Parliament. Disappointed in his bid for the prime ministry in August 1993—an unlikely goal in view of his quintessentially Merina identity and his long association with Marxism—Andriamanjato settled for presidency of the National Assembly, a key post in the evolution of the third republic for this veteran parliamentarian.

Such were the constituents of an unwanted pluriparty compromise confronting the would-be autocrat president. For over a decade, Ratsiraka adroitly kept his critics in constant quarrels among themselves, splitting MONIMA and later the AKFM and Vonjy into rival parties and exploiting Manandafy's and MFM's stunning metamorphosis from leftist to capitalist. By 1989, however, bureaucratic, military, religious, and business leaders were cogently demanding the opportunity of genuine opposition across a broader escutcheon than the FNDR. Their several candidates had managed in March of that year to reduce Ratsiraka's official reelection majority to 62.24 percent. This comparatively weak endorsement suggested to many that had those elections been conducted entirely in the open, the incumbent would have fallen below the 50 percent line, thus requiring a runoff contest against second-place Manandafy. In any case, the flimsy solidarity of the FNDR had been shattered. The new pluralist movement thereupon obtained moral support from Pope John Paul II, who preached open politics and multiparty democracy during his visit in April-May 1989.

In response to this ineluctable surge of opposition, Ratsiraka allowed a virtually infinite proliferation of parties, playing off the strong against one another and consigning the weak to futile fulmination. Although able to neutralize his welter of political parties, Ratsiraka could not contain the political energies released by frustrations in the national economy. Thus it was in 1991 that the antigovernmental movement of 1972 finally caught up with him and continued into a new phase.

COLLAPSE OF THE REVOLUTIONARY MYTH

Beginning in the heady promise of revolution, Didier Ratsiraka's second republic was compromised from the outset by the inadequacy of revolutionary tools for the job. Willy-nilly acceptance of a multiparty system through the FNDR represented only one of the compromises imposed on the eclectic and innovative democratic republic. Embarrassing as it seems, Ratsiraka's strategies found their most effective precedents in the discredited French and PSD systems. These include the traditional structures of cabinet ministries, local administration, and law courts; the electoral process; foreign trade and assistance channels; and the articulation of state security forces. Apart from deliberate accumulation of debt and intensified police repression, Madagascar's salient problems and even their solutions since 1975 resembled the pragmatism of Tsiranana's first republic dressed in ideological armor. As elsewhere in the revolutionary Third World, official texts failed to convert society; all doctrine notwithstanding, economic and cultural reality asserted its own more cogent dynamic. Reticent, courteous, but defiant of authority and protective of the immortal family, Malagasy culture remained intact under its socialist siege.

At the start, Ratsiraka's international alignments veered radically away from the PSD's pro-Western commitments. Eschewing dependence on France, the second republic preferred Third World militancy and formulas of support for the USSR. These options materialized reflexively in the mid-1970s, as though they would entail only obligations of rhetoric. In fact they handicapped the young republic grievously in its search for investment resources. The meticulously publicized charter and referendary constitution of December 1975 vested full powers in the presidency as a means of averting civil war. But with the crisis past, Ratsiraka needed to mobilize domestic savings and foreign capital to stabilize an incidentally socialist regime, and these were hard to obtain without compromising socialist principles.[9]

Intentionally or not, Ratsiraka was also committed to advance the interests of the national middle class. This largely Merina bourgeoisie had supported the 1972 uprising against prevailing French privileges; then it had rallied behind Ratsiraka as the best alternative three years later. Welcoming his victory over the Tsiranana resurgency and the Ratsimandrava communitarians, the urban elite favored a conception of revolution that essentially replaced foreign property interests with their own—not with the sovereignty of the masses.[10]

Needless to say, that was not the definition posited by Marxists, indigenous communitarians, or others in the vigorous Malagasy Left. Within less than a decade, most revolutionaries had been antagonized by the president's politics of expediency. But bourgeois nationalist policies could not solve the economy's problems any better than international socialism. In the absence of the French, Madagascar's middle class did not produce the investment capital, acquire the technology, or exploit markets on a scale adequate to ignite a process of development. International market capital and technology became the only recourse for a withered productive system and debilitated foreign trade apparatus. For several years those massive borrowed resources fed a bureaucratized state economy staffed largely by the entrenched bourgeoisie. That period of illusory expansion soon ended, however, and—no consolation to Malagasy socialists—the sequel has brought painful subservience to international capitalist creditors.

For their part, Malagasy conservatives were outraged by Ratsiraka's reliance on an expensive army trained by Soviets, East Germans, and North Koreans to defend his personal survival. Even the nonideological middle classes grew anxious lest the external sources of security—economic from the West

Zoma market, Antananarivo. Photo courtesy of the Embassy of Madagascar, Washington, D.C.

and political from the East—impose new rules on the system from which they profited in the sacred name of nationalism.

Whether real enemies existed or not, the island's insecurity was genuine. In truth an old ghost had arisen from French colonial and PSD burial grounds to bedevil still another Malagasy government—the specter of the regime's irrelevance to real life. As in the past, large numbers of Malagasy people took no positive interest in an administration divorced from the administered, a program of benevolence inflicted on the beneficiaries. The centrifugal force of the island's clans, communities, and classes was immune to central control. It did little good to justify state centralism in terms of national priority, for the farmers and urban laborers saw themselves mirrored no more distinctly in Ratsiraka's national program than they had in Tsiranana's, or the French, for that matter.

The unraveling of Madagascar's revolution began to show first in the failure of its prime objective—expeditious development of an autonomous economy. Nationalization had restructured the productive and distributive mechanisms of the republic without being able to give them life. Once again the fragments of an extroverted but incoherent economy were linked particle by particle to overseas markets and sources of capital. Severe rural and urban distress prevailed from the outset, worsening as production levels collapsed and distribution networks failed. In 1986, one-fourth of the capital city's families were estimated as living below the absolute poverty level. Whenever the price of a kilogram of rice reached 350 FMG (about $0.72)—and that happened often—40 percent of the population fell under the line; they had less

Fruits and vegetables at Zoma market, Antananarivo. Photo courtesy of the Embassy of Madagascar, Washington, D.C.

than 10,000 FMG (slightly over $20) a month for other necessities. Only one in ten of those families could ever hope to save any of their income.[11] Good food does grow on Malagasy trees, but city dwellers can't afford to acquire it.

Nor could rural people, for that matter. Areas afflicted by drought or monopolized by specialized export agriculture often lost access to the essentials brought to them under normal conditions by road transportation and independent tradespeople. These networks had deteriorated so lamentably by the early 1980s that farm families took to butchering their cattle (a desperation recourse for Malagasy) as the only alternative to abandoning their land.

From the early 1980s, basic needs of the rural population were served mainly by subsistence production. Trade was restricted essentially to village markets within walking distance. Trekking through central Imerina in 1983, the intrepid Irish traveler Dervla Murphy and her daughter "got the impression that the rural Malagasy have reverted to a subsistence economy. Families depend on their own and their neighbours' produce, often exchanged rather than bought, and the flow of imported foodstuffs and consumer goods, stocked in colonial and immediately post-colonial days, has dried up."[12]

Moreover, rural aspirations beyond subsistence seemed mocked by a self-serving corps of local administrators. Murphy saw new bridges linking roads that had already become untraversable, schoolhouses erected by local effort standing empty for lack of books and teachers. Communications had regressed to the rudimentary, and the central government meant little or nothing at all in the lives of people.

In the towns, until forced to submit to internationally imposed discipline in the late 1980s, government kept most people fed and housed by gouging the countryside and drawing down on vestigial export income to support consumer necessities. But distribution was even then subject to caprice and inefficiency; people everywhere had to fend for themselves. Slogans and cant replaced honest assessments of the accomplishments or problems of the state. Despite demagogic proclamations, nobody believed democracy had arrived or was even imminent. Self-fulfilling tales of instability were readily spread by opponents in a "guerrilla war of rumors."[13]

An irresponsible high-governmental elite was itself fragmented by political and ethnic rivalries. Since all disputing clients had their place in the FNDR (most of them in its presidential AREMA), the resulting cacophony did afford the president unmistakable opportunities as arbiter of all conflict. But directionless management requires that all personalities be kept in some orbit, whether their presence be constructive or otherwise, and so most of the contestants remained on the scene.

Malagasy socialism had once been a nationally popular alternative to neocolonialism, but it had no solutions for a capital-starved economy or a top-heavy power structure. Inundating the nation in unproductive bureaucracy, purblind decisions, and corrupt officialdom, the state could not finance the development program crucial to the fruition of socialism. Recourse to an abandoned borrowing spree in the late 1970s created few productive assets for the afflicted economy, and the investment never earned the exchange to pay the government's debts. Belatedly, in the mid-1980s, Madagascar set forth on the by now well-trodden cycle of penurious national economies throughout the Third World. It applied for international debt rescheduling and balance-of-payments relief, agreed to drastic cuts in social spending and imports, and endured even further decline in living standards.

Politically, Ratsiraka's administration was always unsteadily stable. Power, whenever it broke off from the presidential monolith, was available to many factions, yet perilous for any to retain. Ministerial reshuffles kept personalities off balance in the interest of greater equilibrium. Politicians and technicians alike rotated through both government and CSR as Ratsiraka reapportioned units of power skillfully enough to keep any of them from accumulating specific gravity.

For example, the fourth such reconstitution, on January 15, 1982, expelled Finance and Planning Minister Rakotovao-Razakaboana and Economics and Trade Minister Justin Rarivoson from their respective ministries. Both were statesmen of international repute considered hostile to socialist experimentation and to unbridled North Korean and Soviet influence. Politically too strong to humiliate, they entered the CSR, which had been expanded from twelve to nineteen members. To balance this removal of "conservatives," Ratsiraka also ejected one of his most outspoken ideologues, Simon Pierre, who as agriculture minister had been responsible for virtually systematic disincentives to rural production. Until elected to the new parliament in 1993, Rakotovao-Razakaboana remained in a neutralized limbo, still a hero to the Antananarivo middle class, whom Ratsiraka could not afford to alienate; Simon Pierre survived to become minister of information and ideological guidance in February 1985. That 1985 reshuffle was compared by Ratsiraka himself to a basketball dribbler: "You can go left or right so long as you score."[14]

Even as early as 1981, however, public order had begun to break down under persistent economic distress. Severe shortages of rice, meat, oils, flour, soap, and sugar led to riots on market days. Railroad and oil storage facilities were sabotaged; armed bands roamed through town and country; brushfires, a dire omen of rural dissent, increased in number and severity; hoarding and black-market (*risoriso*) activity spread; corruption became a way of life in the towns. No administration, democratic or otherwise, could admit its responsibility for social collapse, so the unrest was officially attributed to the usual counterrevolutionaries and imperialists. Seeking plausible causes to blame for the failures of the revolutionary state, Ratsiraka's apologists spent a decade castigating proverbial demons—the same "international imperialists" to whom they owed their subsistence. Having been evicted in 1972–1975, those enemies were presumed to operate indirectly on the island through conveniently unidentified "comprador" elements in the national bourgeoisie.

Very little evidence for such machinations was ever produced. Student strikes in November 1980 were so reminiscent of the 1972 dissidence against Tsiranana that the government decided to suppress them entirely. So, as in the early 1970s, Monja Jaona was again arrested for refusing to stop criticizing authority. Violence intensified through the early part of 1981. Madagascar has lived with it ever since.

None of these manifestations came near toppling the regime. Identified with all the island's constituencies, and with none of them, Ratsiraka remained in control of the ball, dribbling left and right through the courts of politics, sanctioned by powerful referees (in the World Bank and the international "clubs" of creditors), scoring against his opponents, taking some hits, never really winning the national contest. Although facing severe popular criticism, the president sat in his presidential bunker (literally and figuratively), secured by the weakness of the rival political factions and the absence of alternatives to an army takeover.[15] This invulnerability came to an end in 1991, but even then Ratsiraka still held his presidency.

MILITARY AND POLITICAL PLAYERS IN THE 1980s

Having intervened to bring both Ramanantsoa and Ratsiraka to power, Madagascar's military remained remarkably loyal to the post-1972 regimes. During the first republic, Malagasy complements had been constrained in activity and limited in size—3,500 in the armed forces of January 1972, plus 4,500 in the gendarmerie; 1,500 recruits in the Service Civique had no military role. The presence of 4,500 French troops drew considerable nationalist criticism against Tsiranana's complaisance, but they remained relatively inactive on the island. Neither the French nor the Malagasy military sought to save Tsiranana in 1972.

Madagascar's regular army has always perpetuated the great island's caste and ethnic cleavages; its officer class is drawn largely from Merina aristocracy, and its enlisted ranks are also predominantly Merina. By contrast, the gendarmerie is largely rural, côtier, and working class.[16] The côtier-dominated Mobile Police Group (GMP), security police units that had been removed from the Interior Ministry during André Resampa's humiliation in 1971, obeyed Tsiranana's quixotic effort to repress the rebellions of May 1972. Tensions between these contrasting agencies thereupon broke into conflict; they were especially virulent in 1974–1975. Hence, the role of peacemaker and trailblazer for the revolution fell ironically to the nonpartisan regular army and its upper-class officer corps.

Given an important role in the transitional system of 1972–1975 under its commander, General Ramanantsoa, the army became an instrument of socialist mobilization after 1975. Its unaccustomed role in politics subjected the military to factional disputes, particularly during the conflict between the unreconciled pro-Tsiranana GMP and the more populist gendarmerie, loyal to its ill-fated commandant, Richard Ratsimandrava. The leader of the 1974–1975 GMP mutiny in which Ratsimandrava was first made president, then killed, was Col. Bréchard Rajaonarison. This conservative côtier is also identified with the mysterious putative influence of the Masonic Order. He kept his own skin in the long, inconclusive trials of Ratsimandrava's assassins and maintained serious political ambitions into the 1990s.[17]

Built to a total of 20,000 uniformed personnel,[18] the Ratsiraka military prospered in its island bastion proportionately to the distance between Madagascar and any conceivable enemy. At its peak in 1984, when the state debt to Soviet and other suppliers mounted alarmingly, the Malagasy army absorbed almost one-third of the national budget. Its equipment certainly could have been turned to defense of the republic against hostile intruders, if there had been any. Yet without a plausible enemy on the island frontiers—for even South Africa in its most belligerent days was unlikely to attack the island—these formidable forces found little to do in their conventional mode of activity. Their advanced Soviet weaponry proved useful only to protect the regime from its own people.[19] But if nothing else, the armed forces absorb a margin of otherwise unemployable young men who might pose greater social perils out of uniform (and jobs) than in.

In addition to the regular army, the gendarmerie of 7,500, several crack units of paratroops, and a new Presidential Security Guard of 1,500 men (trained by North Korea) were assigned to defend revolutionary institutions threatened by no source in particular—except the Malagasy population.[20] On August 10, 1991, the Presidential Guard fired upon a crowd of 400,000 demonstrators at Ratsiraka's suburban residence, killing more than a hundred and precipitating the country into acute crisis. But the regular army remained in its barracks. Although physically able to overthrow Ratsiraka in the 1980s, it was too fragmented, secularized, or preoccupied to do the job. In 1980, a coup that was to install Merina aristocrat General Rabetafika never took place.[21] Major Richard Andriamaholison was exiled in 1983 for a putative role in this subversion; his fate became a cause célèbre in the capital, where he returned in 1993 in time to be elected to the third republic's parliament on a pro-Zafy ticket. Three mysterious aircraft crashes in the 1980s also decimated the ranks of the old military companions of Didier Ratsiraka. Sabotage can always be suspected in these events but has never been proven; the terrain of the island and the condition of its military equipment might well be to blame.

In 1984, Chief of Staff Jean Rakotoharison, another Merina aristocrat, refused an order to fire on young kung fu demonstrators in the streets of Antananarivo. Summarily retired to his villa outside the capital, General Rakotoharison eventually became a rallying point for dissidents seeking an alternative to Ratsiraka. Apparently without consultation, his name was used as presumptive beneficiary of an aborted coup d'état in May 1990, and he became, this time with his consent, symbolic head of state for the opposition's mid-1991 shadow government. In July of that year, another major defection was recorded by General Désiré Rakotoarijaona, Ratsiraka's prime minister from 1977 to 1988; after several humiliations at the hands of his chief, who sought to blame him for systematic regime failures, Rakotoarijaona resigned from the AREMA party and joined the opposition. But, being Merina, neither of these contestants could pose an effective challenge to Ratsiraka in the presidential elections of 1992–1993. Rakotoharison subsequently broke with Zafy and retired once more.

For most of the 1980s, French military training and equipment were replaced by Soviet and North Korean sponsors, thus inspiring (inaccurate) conjecture over strategic concessions that might be offered to Warsaw Pact forces in the Indian Ocean. The training school at Antsirabe, staffed by specialists from Moscow, turned out junior officers in large numbers while dozens of other military returned from training missions in Moscow, Havana, Pyongyang, East Berlin, and Budapest. But the traditional military, with its mass of draftees, became dedicated primarily to economic and public works projects; and the gendarmerie maintained civil order. In 1989–1990, radical conversions in the socialist world and transformations in South Africa reduced even further the real importance of Madagascar's military establishment. Nevertheless, the volatility of so large and inchoate an apparatus remained problematic for Ratsiraka. He rode the tiger's back and fed the beast as he went.

Hence, the revolution's army, navy, air force, gendarmerie, and GMP had to be distracted from temptations of power by roles in the socioeconomic construction of the republic. Indeed, their most dynamic officers were nominally charged with steering the course of the revolution. Some of them received appointments to the CSR, others to the Military Development Committee (CMD). This constitutionally sanctioned council of thirty army and twenty gendarmerie officers enjoyed the prestigious, if inconsequential, status of adviser in the formation of overall development policy. Its People's Army for Development, with minimal training for the work, engaged willy-nilly in countryside ideological campaigns and in an occasional internal security deployment. Subject to typical divisive loyalties among rival officers and party elites, the CMD served mainly to provide channels for transmission of government directives to the fokon'olona. Moreover, the people's army reported on political attitudes and helped enforce obedience in the countryside.[22] Consequently, from the peasant viewpoint, the army was joining in fanjakana centralism.

Realizing his vulnerability to the military, Ratsiraka kept the Ministry of Defense within his own secretariat (as Tsiranana had done) until the late 1980s, when he turned the portfolio over to his brother-in-law. Self-promoted to fleet admiral with the title of supreme armed forces commander, the president neutralized the military institution while entrusting his personal security to the Presidential Guard. The army's allocation of cabinet portfolios waxed and waned according to presidential need for equilibrium. In July 1991, the last of the military prime ministers gave way to a civilian who enjoyed popularity in the capital.

Formally endowed with guardianship of the revolution, the CSR retained constitutional status just under the president's own until 1991. In June of that year it received a transient name change to Supreme Council of the Republic (instead of the Revolution) and in November was eliminated entirely. Throughout its existence the CSR had been subject to Ratsiraka's complete control; the president appointed most of its membership and determined its agenda. The council had been useful at times as a monitor for the implementation of policy as well as a dumping ground for politicians and an antechamber for aspiring ministers. Hence, like the bureaucracy itself, the CSR was hamstrung by internal rivalries—the very plurality that inhibited Ratsiraka from creating the central party organism he sought. Marxists and IMF-oriented marketeers, ethnic chauvinists, bourgeois nationalists, military and civilian opponents, perpetually jostled one another there as in the halls of ministerial prerogative. Ratsiraka and his close presidential advisers had to break the logjams themselves.

The structure of local administrative councils (fokon'olona) also became subject to the counterplay of politicians and central regime surveillance. Representatives were elected periodically by the country's 11,000 fokontany, but they obtained their roles from central authority and were supervised by military and civilian legates in the field. Thus they lacked substantive influence over policy or resources to commit autonomously to local projects. Its socialism reduced to a national network of parastatal and local governance bureaucracies, the democratic republic became what Chaigneau dubbed a "people's monocracy." Centralism prevailed in decisionmaking, and rhetorical appeals for support disguised the absence of popular participation in the process.[23]

The concept of socialist orientation acquired more substance in Malagasy external policy than in domestic matters. Ratsiraka's few satisfactions in statecraft came through foreign affairs, where Madagascar exerted some weight in the forums of nonalignment. There the republic was praised for its defiance of French ambitions, patronized for its resistance to great-power strategy, tolerated in its abject dependence on those powers and their multinational lenders, and ignored when the USSR seemed too close to calling the

Malagasy tune. Borrowing statist centralism from the Soviet Union and North Korea, Madagascar participated discreetly on the periphery of the international socialist network. Socialist information programs, cultural activity, exchange of students, and official delegations once far outweighed what the West contributed in propaganda and public relations on the great island. Several dozen Soviet and French-speaking Vietnamese instructors worked as university faculty in contact with Malagasy elites. Even today, bookstores overflow with unclaimed stocks of literature celebrating the victories of Marxist, Maoist, and Korean socialism.

Madagascar's new partners joined in a modest network of exchange and cooperation. Chinese participation, although important, was deliberately subordinated to the principal Soviet "liberator." Reference to Kim Il Sung's Juche doctrine allowed Ratsiraka to proclaim the simultaneity of his ideological, technical, and cultural revolutions. North Korea also provided a Third World precedent for solidarity, if not overt alignment, with the USSR on global matters. Moscow coordinated strategy and took on a few big-ticket projects; Cuba sent personnel for the government's security and development apparatus; and the East European states, along with Vietnam and North Korea, offered bits of technical assistance.

Although these collaborations had little measurable effect, they survived domestic vicissitudes through the end of the 1980s. Soviet activity remained relatively immune to antiimperialist criticism, although the Malagasy had to deny oft-rumored strategic base concessions to the USSR's Indian Ocean fleet. Nevertheless, in June 1980, the Paris weekly *Jeune Afrique* was banned for reporting the generally known presence of Cuban troops on the island.

Moreover, the socialist consortium paid court to Malagasy national pride, offering Marxism, Maoism, and Juche as consistent with indigenous Malagasy needs for decolonization and development. It was logical that Ratsiraka's regime should advocate the UN's New International Economic Order aligning East and South against the wicked will of the West. As Ratsiraka's diplomacy militated on the front lines of the Indian Ocean "zone of peace" movement, the republic obtained a distinct position in world politics, if not an avenue toward new developmental resources.[24] Although Western interests resented this ostensible allegiance to world communism, they did little to combat it, preferring to realize their comparative advantage in terms of international finance and trade. Ultimately they were vindicated, for the main trouble with Ratsiraka's global orientation was that it did the Malagasy no perceptible good.

This futility could remain concealed in 1980 when the Information Ministry celebrated "twenty years of independence and five years of socialist revolution" by crediting the FNDR with ending the fragmentation of the progressive movement; achieving collective local self-reliance for economic independence in a decentralized administration; nationalizing key economic sectors; democratizing access to education, health, and employment; and diversifying external relations, thus bringing new prestige and influence in the world. With unusual stress on historical continuity, editor Marc Rakotonoel explained that the colonial system had remained unchanged after 1960; a ruling class cooperated with foreign management to control key sectors of the economy, and foreign values dominated the educational circuits, generating a class of unemployed intellectuals. He praised Ramanantsoa for taking a healthy approach to national participation in business life and for building a broad portfolio of foreign relations, but the general's style had proved too indecisive and his reforms too feeble to satisfy popular demands. From February to June 1975, Andriamahazo had been obliged simply to keep the social fabric intact. Beginning in June, Rakotonoel wrote, Ratsiraka acted swiftly and decisively where Ramanantsoa had broken down; the class struggle was acknowledged, and the democratic republic arose in December to guarantee the triumph of the people.[25]

This self-confidence began breaking down shortly after that 1980 milestone. The years 1981 and 1982 were marked by riots, mutinies, and protests in all corners of the island. In part as a response to misery, violent factions began menacing the public peace from left and right—and from sheer indifference—and the institutions were tottering. Externally donated food and medical supplies were hoarded for sale at personal profit. All officials were popularly condemned as incorrigibly corrupt, and the security police was blamed for vast numbers of arbitrary arrests and tortures. In 1982–1983 a cascade of elections revealed the regime's administrative impotence, its vulnerability to real challenges, and its dependence on terror to retain ostensible legitimacy. In addition to the GMP, gendarmerie, and Presidential Guard, the feared DGID (Department of Information and Documentation) enforced political repression under the direction of Bienaimé Raveloson Mahasampa, Ratsiraka's brother-in-law. There was also an increase in acts of terrorism by the TTS (Tanora Tonga Saina, Youth Aware of Responsibilities), the AREMA party's youth league.

Reversing the legitimate sequence of elections so that he could renew his own mandate before the recriminations of the parliamentary campaigns, Ratsiraka found himself vigorously confronted in November 1982 by Monja Jaona, who captured 28 percent of the official tally; the Antandroy challenger took 49 percent of the votes in the capital city, where he had never before been particularly popular. After calling for nullification of the vote on the (plausible) argument that he would have won the election had it been as freely conducted everywhere as at Antananarivo, Monja was dismissed from the CSR and assigned to house arrest. When balloting for the legislature occurred on August 28, 1983, the president's AREMA party managed to increase its representation by 3 ANP seats to 115 (of 137), albeit with only 65 percent of the votes; AREMA's AKFM partner returned 9 delegates with 8.8 percent; the MFM garnered 11 percent but only 3 seats; Vonjy took 6 seats with 10 percent; and Monja Jaona's harassed MONIMA party registered only 3.7 percent of the tally, barely holding 2 seats in the ANP.

By New Year's Day 1985, Ratsiraka was lecturing his people on how difficult they were to govern. He had been naive, he said in his annual radio broadcast, to think that merely replacing men and institutions, as the North Koreans had done, could change essentially neocolonial habits of mind. Posing as an embarrassed victim of this cultural recalcitrance, the president charged his Malagasy with the inability to understand the industrial temper; they preferred easy speculation and soft relations to risk-taking and sacrifice, he said. Jacques DeBarrin reviewed the speech in *Le Monde* for what it did not overtly confess—Ratsiraka's pedanticism, his contradictory impulses on behalf of côtiers (among whom he was born) and Merina (with whom he was brought up), the inconsistency between his Christian piety and his socialist commitments, his nationalism and his French education, his deep insecurity among people, his failure to command respect as an elder in traditional Malagasy perspectives—and more: "the lack of truth, injustice, various forms of exploitation, the fact that he has trampled on others and regarded them as negligible quantities, his disdain for small people, his absolute refusal to perceive and hear the aspirations of the masses."[26]

Whatever it did not say, this 1985 broadcast betokened renunciation of the revolutionary myth. On the visit of Li Xiannan, Chinese chief of state, in March 1986, the Malagasy president was praising China's example of adaptable revolutionary principles, transcending verbiage and ideological conservatism. The Chinese, he said, "have proved that socialism could and should accommodate the evolution of the day without needing to be buttressed by the political theories of the beginning of the century, or even of thirty years ago. Doesn't the very idea of progressivism preclude any freezing of position?"[27] If China's current leaders could depart from Mao, why couldn't Madagascar's Third World course deviate from the far older orthodoxies of the Soviet model? (They had, of course, never conformed to that model in the first place, except in its rationalizations for centralized statism.)

Ratsiraka's new reasoning proved only that the crisis in Malagasy socialism could no longer be blamed on a hostile international climate. "Dogmatic refusal to accept the idea of profitability in the economy, universal statism, nonexistent agricultural policy are some of the reasons that explain the failure of the Malagasy system," commented another correspondent of *Le Monde* in late 1986. He saw Ratsiraka caught between his people's refusal of a socialism that had impoverished the country and the failure of the economy to respond clearly to austerity as dictated by international tutelage. "Madagascar," he concluded, "was paying dearly for its mistakes."[28]

At that watershed of 1985, the average Malagasy family (rural and urban) was earning 12,000–15,000 francs per month—sufficient, perhaps, for one-half of its monthly necessities. Lucky families supplemented these revenues by producing (or otherwise acquiring) goods and services for trade in the informal markets.

In November 1986, riots broke out in Toamasina, the principal port city, with recurrences in February 1987 at Antsirabe and in early March at Toliara, killing at least 14 and injuring more than 100. In these three uprisings, separated by hundreds of kilometers from each other, the main targets of street mobs were the homes and businesses of the Muslim Indo-Pakistani middle class, a tragically convenient ethnic target for national exasperation.

Unlike the Chinese traders of the east coast, this 25,000-person Karana community has rarely sought integration into the family and cultural life of

Madagascar. Moreover, the Muslims live in apparent affluence, controlling retail commerce and services and some branches of import trade, as well as textile processing. Even in poor times, Karana have managed to pick up the leavings of bankrupt and abandoned state corporations, including some of the erratic rice-marketing circuits on which the entire population depends. Occasionally flaunting their notorious wealth[29] and showing disrespect for customary prerogatives in landholding and ritual, Madagascar's Indo-Pakistani became a scapegoat for mass frustrations that could not reach as far as their principal objective, the "catastrophic political and economic options" of Ratsiraka's administration.[30] Another sanguinary pogrom had taken place against the relatively privileged Comorean Muslims of Mahajanga in 1977.

State institutions in Madagascar have long been accustomed to ignoring reality in favor of some official vision of how things are. The press was seriously censored, and the law courts served the revolution whether it existed or not. AREMA's domination of the ANP imposed a passivity on the legislature that was sometimes mistaken for "democratic tonality."[31] Yet on May 9, 1986, ANP president Lucien Xavier Michel Andrianarahinjaka, a veteran political ally of Ratsiraka's, frankly and concisely deplored the condition into which the country had fallen. By calling insecurity, unemployment, economic crisis, and misery by their right names, Andrianarahinjaka may have initiated a passage to political maturity on the part of regime leaders, "for one by one," as the *Revue de l'Océan Indien* observed, "the various agencies of this country are abandoning the pernicious attitude of uncritical self-satisfaction."[32]

Indulged by successive governments like no other institution, the Roman Catholic Church nonetheless eventually joined Protestants in a long, bitter debate with secular authority. In January 1980, the Catholics, French Protestant, Anglican, and Lutheran Churches formed the Fikambanan'ny Fiangonana Kristiana Malagasy (FFKM), the Malagasy Christian Council, which was to play a crucial role in the political transformations of the subsequent decade. Beginning in 1981, pastoral letters began attacking the regime for its principles as well as its failure to implement them. As a consequence, local parishes came under political counterattack; priests were ambushed, some assassinated. More conciliatory in his response to ecclesiastical authority than to other criticisms, Didier Ratsiraka professed public devotion to Christian principles, merging them into his piety for socialism. This new enrichment of classical ideology allowed visitors such as the Murphys to be assured that Ratsiraka's regime could be called "Marxist Christian."[33]

By 1989, the unraveling of authority was manifest, and the second republic's third round of major elections consecrated Madagascar's pluralism. The socialist option that had been pronounced irreversible in 1975 had never been fully implemented. As the venerable Monja Jaona charged in 1982, much of Ratsiraka's red book was acceptable to revolutionaries, but none of it was being applied.[34] The state had not really qualified as Marxist, for its centralized economy served mainly to enrich the bureaucratic middle class who continued to operate it, and its party system had never coalesced.[35] Moreover, its evolution in that direction was blocked by the imperatives of economic recovery. In 1987, the regime had taken its first genuine step toward internationally acceptable structural reform; it recognized the need to stop toying with World Bank and IMF demands and to begin the liberalization of domestic rice markets in earnest. From that point on, while antagonists scrutinized political horizons for the force that might ultimately topple a bankrupt, dysfunctional system, Ratsiraka and his companions were showing that this system might be able to turn over on its own.

Although it contained some of the seeds of alternative governance, the FNDR ultimately could not encompass Malagasy pluralism; interests contradictory to Ratsiraka's charter were formally ruled out, and aspirants to office had to hold membership in one or another of the endorsed "progressive" parties. Thus, the front primarily represented insurance for politicians who would affirm anything to serve their own political interests. Apart from irreconcilables such as Monja Jaona and Manandafy, who shuttled in and out of the FNDR structure, opposition consisted of diatribes from Christian pulpits, intermittent riots and civil disobedience, a sprinkling of rather quiet exile groups and personalities, and the pervasive recalcitrance of the Malagasy people. It was this last force that proved the most powerful. But the political parties had their go at an opposition by 1988–1989, and they have followed joyfully as the population led them thereafter.

On March 12, 1989, Ratsiraka won his third mandate when the "democratic alliance" of three renegade FNDR parties (Vonjy, MFM, VS-MONIMA) failed to agree on an alternative candidate. They had thought of General Rakotoharison, but when Ratsiraka's former chief of staff professed to have no political aspirations, the three parties went their own ways. Still, Ratsiraka came through with a mere 62 percent of the 1989 vote, and Manandafy, replacing Monja Jaona as principal contender, took 19.3 percent; Monja fell to 3 percent, below Vonjy's Marojama Razanabahiny, who scored 14.9 percent. Most remarkably, the abstention rate of only 9 percent (compared with nearly 40 percent in 1982) revealed a sudden awakening of popular interest in presidential politics.

The rest of 1989 saw a parade of elections—parliamentary in May, local on September 27, district on October 29, and regional on December 10. Disgraced by its slavish adherence to Ratsiraka's line wherever he took it, the AKFM split in half when Pastor Andriamanjato formed his party of renewal (AKFM Fanavaozana). The party's most conspicuous personality for thirty years (although never a cabinet minister), Andriamanjato was thereupon expelled from the CSR along with Manandafy and Razanabahiny, who had both dared oppose the Ratsiraka candidacy in March.

On May 28, AREMA again won 119 of 137 parliamentary seats with only 66.8 percent of the vote; AKFM dropped from 9 to 3 with 5.3 percent, 3 others going to Andriamanjato's new Fanavaozana team (4.2 percent); MFM held 7 seats with 11 percent; Vonjy also lost ground, maintaining only 3 seats, with 9.7 percent, and exposing itself in turn to a crisis of defections and regroupings; MONIMA managed to retain only Monja Jaona's seat. One-fourth of the 5.7 million registered voters did not cast ballots; 42 percent abstained in Antananarivo alone.

Like Monja Jaona in 1982, Manandafy called for a general strike to protest election fraud. He insisted on abandoning the Ratsiraka charter and embarking on new flights of capitalist investment and liberal trade. This was a dramatic conversion from the MFM, which had once been the incarnation of proletarian radicalism. It created reverberations among all opponents of Ratsiraka's regime, from moderates to Marxists. They had all been offended by the presidential scorn heaped on them in front of visiting Pope John Paul II on April 28, 1989, shortly after Ratsiraka's contested reelection. The demand for a more open system proved irresistible.

Ratsiraka was still the agent with whom the governments, banks, and agencies of the West would have to deal. He reappointed Victor Ramahatra, an army engineer, to lead a cabinet of continuity that included two veteran realists of the World Bank–IMF dialogues, Léon Rajaobelina and Jean Robiarivony. The cabinet's reconstitution with familiar faces from previous administrations resembled the last months of the Tsiranana republic. Even after pledges of constitutional change and a broadening of the political process, Ratsiraka's regime inspired little confidence that the political culture would keep up with economic imperatives.

METAMORPHOSIS OF THE REPUBLIC

As an experiment in Third World socialism, Madagascar's revolution had ended well before the elections of 1989. In fact, apart from an explosion in school accessibility, it had never progressed beyond a systematic and ruinous state acquisition of business enterprises and agricultural marketing networks. Since expropriation resulted in an endowment of economic power within the political bureaucracy, Madagascar's revolution could be dismantled by the very people responsible for it in the first place. The Malagasy nation had suffered its surfeit of deprivation, repression, and demagogy. The nation rejected the system that imposed those humiliations before rejecting its perpetrators.

Madagascar's socialist orientation under Ratsiraka had to suffer certain national idiosyncracies—political pluralism, entrenchment of an entrepreneurial class inside the bureaucracy, and rural defiance of central authority—that prevented coalescence into a functioning socialist system. The regime of 1975 tried central planning, national operation of industry, and an ideologically unified state, but it succeeded only in imposing the rhetoric, not the reality, of a socialist society. The Merina, Indo-Pakistani, and Chinese middle classes conserved privileges even in a shrinking statist economy. Too many interest groups remained undigested by the FNDR, and too many elites remained unreconciled even within the front. Too many cabinet and CSR personalities had to be given titles without regard to function or even ideology. Too many rural dwellers resented their indifferent distant citadel of power. Too many elders and entrepreneurs recalled better days under another, less repressive regime. Too little was happening, too much energy was spent on keeping it that way. And many Malagasy were all too aware that they had lost touch with the world outside the island.

In the macropolitical economy, the revolutionary experiment amounted to catastrophe. In the microeconomic world of herdspeople, rice farmers, and artisans, it meant harsher times, shortages, more ruthless administration, and general insecurity, but not radical change. Except for its achievements in universal education, the Ratsiraka revolution was equivalent to continuity, albeit in a downward direction. In 1987, a Malagasy correspondent summed up in the weekly *Jeune Afrique:* "The Malagasy live poorly, very poorly by comparison to what they deserve and what their country deserves. There perhaps lies the cause for their refusal to acknowledge what is happening elsewhere; they would be embarrassed to complain and even more to realize that they could live much better, if they had the will to do so."[36]

But political incoherence is not what defeated the regime. Even if Ratsiraka had been able to model a North Korean or Cuban state in his island, Madagascar's political economy would have been marginalized by poverty, isolation, and comparative disadvantage in a world-market system. Above all other logic, it was the desperation of economics that drove Ratsiraka to a gradual and bloodless revocation of his own design. The centrally planned economy had never been completed, although whatever was planned proved ineffective. Yet market liberalization could not happen by decree. For having lost control of the economy, the Antananarivo administration risked losing contact with society as a whole.

Revolutionary Madagascar had to appeal to the outside world for economic remedies. But conforming to an important trend in Francophone African states and throughout the Third World at the time, the economic remedies had to pass through elaborate filters of political and cultural liberalization.

In December 1989 a constitutional amendment permitted the registration of political parties outside the FNDR; sixteen new formations promptly responded to the call, and another dozen sprang up in the aftermath. Several were already demanding a third republic under completely new constitutional provisions, for as Richard Andriamanjato pointed out in January 1990 from his new status as an opponent of the regime, "parties that support the revolution" remained entrenched in some fifteen articles of the constitution.[37] In April 1990 a public forum of respected citizens called for a new constitution based on traditional principles of consensus, substituting the laborious and slow self-discipline of citizens for the peremptory rule of the state. Others demanded a clear separation of powers to preclude the autocracy abused so flagrantly during fifteen years of Malagasy misery.

Having ensured his own reelection for seven years before liberating any new parties, Ratsiraka would not disappear under the weight of political alternatives. The president retained a core of strength in AREMA, UDECMA, the remaining Marxist AKFM, and their affiliated social organizations. As in the Senegal of Senghor and Diouf, the opposition was encouraged to diffuse into several dozen incompatible formations. Moreover, from some opposition viewpoints, "King" Didier's self-reforming presidency was preferable to the military alternative that would almost inevitably follow any attempt to evict him by force.

Chief rival of Ratsiraka's AREMA, the MFM of Manandafy Rakotonirina brought its mission up to international trends, advocating an open society patterned after the Polish and Czech experiences. Seeking to mobilize domestic savings, this erstwhile party of the little people now greets every opportunity to trim the state budget and reduce the burden of the civil service on the supply side of the economy. Free of his commitment to the AKFM's Marxist ideologues, Andriamanjato and his Fanavaozana developed a new Nyererean brand of social democratic communitarianism, more suited than Marxism to Andriamanjato's profoundly Christian Malagasy mind.

Most conspicuous among the rehabilitated parties was the new-look PSD, formed by veterans of the Tsiranana regime who had emerged from exile or from Vonjy. They included André Resampa, once Tsiranana's appointed heir, former justice minister Alfred Ramangasoavina (one of Tsiranana's few Merina ministers), Emile Ramarasaona, founding director of the Civic Service and Rural Animation, Fianarantsoa PSD leader Daniel Ralaivelo, and Césaire Rabenoro, a Tsiranana minister who had returned after distinguished scholarly exile among the universities of France. These gray luminaries from the old regime were courted by Evariste Marson, a young attorney from the south, and by Ruffine Tsiranana, eldest daughter of the late president and one of the rare Malagasy women to stake a claim in national politics.

Also among them was the illustrious poet-politician Jacques Rabemananjara, returning to the island in March 1992 after his second generation-long political exile in France. Successively minister of economics, agriculture, and foreign affairs, then vice president under Tsiranana, the septuagenarian Rabemananjara promptly sought to rally nostalgics for the first republic and its French patrons. His reappearance was disturbed by crowds of Ratsiraka adherents, even in his hometown of Toamasina, for he had stayed away too long. Nevertheless, this leader of the 1947 nationalist MDRM who had become Tsiranana's most influential pro-French amanuensis was promptly hailed in international business circles as a hopeful factor in the recovery of Malagasy respectability.[38] Rabemananjara allowed himself to be flattered into campaigning for the presidency in November 1992, promising to serve only during a three-year transition, and was summarily trounced by Zafy and Ratsiraka.

Although a certain nostalgia inevitably suffused the PSD's cautious emergence into the new air of the successor republic, these repatriates were quick to repudiate a return to the old ethos. Resampa reminded the public that he had been languishing in detention under Tsiranana during the events of 1972 and that his disgrace had come in retaliation for his eagerness to bring about party reform. Rabenoro's doctoral thesis cast some criticism on the foreign policies of the first republic, and this Merina statesman proved acceptable to most factions as foreign minister in the transitional cabinet of 1991–1993.[39] Rabemananjara, Marson, and Ruffine Tsiranana ran quixotically against one another in the presidential elections of November 1992, aggregating only 11 percent of the vote. Nevertheless, the neo-PSD advocated a return to the Franc Zone, where Madagascar's currency had once been solidly pegged and its external balances rectified by the Bank of France. Fragmented into several splinter parties—and bereft by Resampa's untimely death in May 1993—the PSD fared poorly not only in the 1992 presidential campaign; it captured only eight seats in the legislative elections of 1993.

Abundant changes claimed public attention in 1990 and 1991. East European and North Korean advisers began to leave the country—impelled by contingencies in their home countries as well as by the changing Malagasy temper. France assumed responsibility for training and advising the Presidential Guard. To counter the tendency to place high military officials in posts of civilian importance, Ratsiraka appointed Henri Raharijaona as the new head of the fearsome DGID; he was a lawyer and former ambassador to Washington, and his role was to humanize that redoubtable secret service.[40] Local government began its detachment from centralized control. The million-strong municipality (*fivondronana*) of Antananarivo, incorporating six districts (*firaisana*), declared its management to be privatized on February 7, 1990. Before becoming prime minister in July 1991, Mayor Guy-Willy Razanamasy called for substantial private fund-raising to tend to the city's formidable needs.

Benefiting from new legislation abolishing censorship, the Malagasy press emerged jubilant from the stifling rule of sycophancy. In fact, newspapers even began neglecting the president and his administration. Where a presidential photograph had once been a daily requirement, the Antananarivo press of the 1990s showed Ratsiraka's face only once or twice a month and actually complained about his inaccessibility, his favoritism to foreign journalists, the lack of newsworthiness in his activity. Even the national radio broke precedent in March and April 1990 by interviewing opposition politicians Resampa and Manandafy.

Liberal reforms notwithstanding, Ratsiraka had to survive still another putsch on May 13, 1990, the eighteenth anniversary of the uprising that toppled Tsiranana. At dawn on that day, a group of fourteen young people—apparently all Merina, some of them identified with kung fu vigilantism, others with the Vonjy party—seized control of the national radio building and broadcast an hour-long appeal to celebrate the downfall of the tyrant Ratsiraka. Taking hostages and distributing leaflets, they anticipated formation of a Committee of Public Safety putatively headed by retired General Rakotoharison, Ratsiraka's former chief of staff who had declined a chance to run for the presidency against Ratsiraka in 1989.

Some 15,000 people eventually gathered outside the radio tower in downtown Antananarivo—not to engulf the tyrant but to watch the gendarmerie flush out the intruders with grenades. Crowd displeasure with these tactics thereupon precipitated riots, bringing out the regular army. Six people including one soldier were killed in the violence, with six military personnel and some forty others injured. Rakotoharison subsequently disclaimed any connection with the conspirators, but he hoped the authorities would take their grievances seriously and listen to the needs of suffering people. Other commentators followed suit, deploring the illegality of the aborted coup but denouncing the military's brutal response.[41]

In an exclusive interview for foreign journalists on May 15, 1990, President Ratsiraka defended the assault on the building and the right of the soldiers to defend themselves against an angry mob. Otherwise, the government kept its own commentary to a minimum. Evidence of instability was precisely what the authorities wished least to display, as South African and other potential investors were being welcomed to the island at that moment. The coalescing opposition retorted, of course, that the security of foreign capital was more seriously menaced by bureaucratic inefficiency and corruption than by political dissidence.

During 1990 and most of 1991, the opposition maneuvered to keep pressure on Ratsiraka to change constitutional options. The major parties could agree on little save the necessity to rid the state of the president who had led the nation into disaster. Ratsiraka responded by artful moves to consolidate support for his *policy* changes, a quite different aim, and to exploit inevitable disagreements within the opposition. Taking advantage of improvement in production, export revenues, and cost of living during 1989—attained through austerity and market liberalization at the insistence of World Bank, IMF, and other international creditors—he decided to court the urban populace by loosening domestic credit through the sole remaining state-owned bank, the BTM (National Agricultural Development Bank). This bread-and-circus strategy encouraged a new flood of consumer imports, aggravating domestic inflation and causing a 13 percent currency appreciation that resulted in a dramatic depletion of foreign exchange reserves. After correcting the inflationary effects of that move in early 1991 (under duress from international agencies), the administration found itself as unpopular with its urban constituents as ever.

Its choice was to procrastinate in negotiations over power sharing with political opponents and church intermediaries, hoping (successfully) to weaken opposition solidarity. At the end of May 1991 the government proposed a series of fifty amendments to the constitution, eliminating most references to socialism and revolution and providing for a bicameral legislature but retaining supreme powers in the presidency.[42] These concessions proved too weak for the opposition to accept. After suffering the defection of major coalition partners, Ratsiraka replaced the once monopolistic FNDR with a new Militant Movement for Malagasy Socialism (MMSM). This new coalition joined his foundering AREMA with fifteen smaller parties including the Pyongyang-oriented rump of the AKFM, abandoned when Andriamanjato joined the opposition. In what would have represented a political triumph five years earlier, Ratsiraka earned the adhesion of the MONIMA's aged leader, Monja Jaona, who now feared a return of the old PSD, the urban Merina bourgeoisie, and the French more than he feared his presidential antagonist. Together they resisted the opposition's drive for a national convention that would rid the nation of its second republic, constitution, president, and all.

Ratsiraka also tried to remobilize the press through a new law that retracted much of the two years of glasnost that had proved so important to the emergence of opposition forces. The emancipated news media had taken to covering such embarrassing social topics as epidemics, drug trafficking, and a shadowy syndicate allegedly engaged in selling kidnapped Malagasy children for adoption abroad. Convictions were obtained against some conspirators in the May 1990 putsch, but they received remarkably light sentences. Avidly courting the PSD and the Catholic parties (despite mounting church disapproval), Ratsiraka managed to lure away several conservative opposition leaders. His trophies included Resampa and the Christian Democrat Jean-Jacques Rakotoniaina, a once-powerful Resampa lieutenant who had been jailed for three years under Ratsiraka before being acquitted on charges of embezzlement.

By early June 1991, unable to force its national convention, the opposition was in danger of being overtaken by popular antagonism to Ratsiraka and impatience over the desultory negotiations. Street demonstrations began in the cities on June 10, some of them involving hundreds of thousands of people, more than the numbers that had brought down Tsiranana in 1972. The uprising continued regularly for seven months, punctuated by highly successful strikes in public and private sectors and by a state of emergency voted with special powers to the government on July 23. Public services came to a standstill, and the upward trail of the Malagasy economy petered out. On June 21, 1991, facing a recurrence of the pattern of popular violence that had obliterated the political process in 1947 and 1972, sixteen opposition parties formed a loose coalition of Vital Forces (Hery Velona, or Forces Vives in French).

That coalition broke almost immediately into two segments. Its more intransigeant wing, named for Andriamanjato's Rasalama School, where it met, formed a shadow cabinet to gain control over government ministries through the civil servants who participated in general strikes and mass demonstrations. A more conciliatory faction was led by the born-again liberals of the MFM, renamed Party for Malagasy Progress in early 1991 to express its conversion to the business ethos. This moderate opposition rejected direct challenges to government legitimacy while supporting the street demonstrations as a means of pressure on the dilatory regime. The first leader of the united Vital Forces, MFM's Francisque Ravony, sought to keep the factions together but was forced out before the end of June and was not replaced. As in 1989, when the opposition proved unable to agree on a single candidate to run against Ratsiraka, it was at risk of losing a genuine opportunity.

But opposition politics held fairly firm despite these fractious tendencies. Andriamanjato spoke eloquently in public for the militant wing but did not prejudice its popularity by claiming a shadow portfolio for himself. The MFM's Manandafy also refused to join what he called an insurrectional government, but he remained in contact with the more radical elements in it. That shadow cabinet, expanded to sixteen members, met regularly under Albert Zafy, a professor of surgery and leader of the small National Union of Democrats for Development (UNDD) in the Rasalama movement. A former minister of public health during the Ramanantsoa transition, the sixty-year-old Zafy enjoyed an untainted reputation as a public servant and medical scientist. His opposition credentials were enhanced by his never having served in a Ratsiraka government.

The French embassy and the politically mobilized churches continued to urge peaceful resolution of differences between government and opposition. They sought constitutional change but with a grace period for Ratsiraka to serve before ceding power. Unwilling to contemplate his own eviction, Ratsiraka refused to tolerate any challenge to the legitimacy that he claimed from the relatively open election of March 1989. But as the strikes began crippling both national administration and economy, he responded to intense public pressure on July 28, 1991, by dismissing Ramahatra's cabinet in favor of an entirely new government. The prime minister was the popular mayor of Antananarivo, Guy-Willy Razanamasy, a pharmacist and economic liberal who had refused to authorize police violence against protestors in his city.

A new coalition cabinet formed under Razanamasy on August 26 contained the PSD's André Resampa as minister of state for rural development and Césaire Rabenoro as foreign minister, as well as Jean-Jacques Rakotoniaina (said to have been abducted by government agents and persuaded to give up his post in the opposition's shadow cabinet for the identical portfolio, industry and mines, in Razanamasy's). Francisque Ravony joined as first deputy prime minister, bringing the MFM into administrative responsibility for the first time in its history.

Reorganizing his cabinet in November 1991, Razanamasy ran the government through the crucial elections of November 1992 and February and June 1993. His ministry served to sustain a semblance of administration under strict austerity, to organize those elections, and to keep peace between an unreconcilable presidency, opposition, and military institutions. He succeeded, as he subsequently claimed, in ensuring the continuity of the Malagasy state.[43]

Strikes and massive demonstrations continued throughout the period of negotiations between Razanamasy and the opposition regarding constitutional and regime change. Perceiving that Ratsiraka would not even leave his redoubt to join in the desired dialogue, the crowds fatefully decided to come to him. On August 10, 1991, at the presidential bunker in Antananarivo's Iavoloha suburb, a crowd of 400,000 was fired on by artillery and a helicopter gunship of the Presidential Guard. Estimates of deaths range from thirty-one to four times that many. Hundreds more were wounded, and the president, whose voice was recorded giving the order to fire, was severely compromised by the massacre.

Even Prime Minister Razanamasy denounced his own president's violent recourse against the people of Antananarivo. The incident embarrassed the French, who had assumed responsibility for the Guard from its original North Korean tutors. Paris hastily withdrew its training contingent but would still not repudiate the besieged and vindictive president. On October 15 and 16, the regular army entered the action to suppress an opposition rally in Antsiranana, leaving several dead.[44] Predictions of an imminent abdication once again proved premature, as Ratsiraka remained in his bunker, relatively inactive and immovable. The stalemate dragged on through October, with transportation and public services paralyzed, airports closed, prospective investors withdrawing their offers, foreign aid commitments suspended, and foreign banks refusing letters of credit for needed imports.

On October 30, 1991, the Vital Forces opposition leaders left for France, persuaded that, with help from the French embassy, they had successfully negotiated the removal of Ratsiraka along with a new coalition to share power among themselves and the Razanamasy legitimists. Their position was promptly undermined, however, when the official announcement of this so-called Panorama Agreement omitted mention of Ratsiraka's departure. Probably under pressure from the military, Razanamasy had agreed that the president would remain during a transitional period of eighteen months, shorn of power except those of commander in chief of the armed forces and the right to accredit diplomats.[45] On November 16, 1991, as though in corroboration of the arrangement, the new French ambassador promptly presented his credentials to Ratsiraka at Iavoloha.

Although enraged at this betrayal, the opposition obtained everything else it had been seeking. Zafy headed a new thirty-one-member High Authority of State (HAE) to replace both the CSR and the National Assembly. The AREMA-dominated Parliament was dissolved; its failure to play a significant role in the long crisis had been symbolized by the resignation of ANP president Andrianarahinjaka in early September. The CSR was abolished. Prime Minister Razanamasy obtained authority to appoint and dismiss ministers and to implement policies approved by Zafy's High Authority. Manandafy and Andriamanjato presided jointly over a 131-member National Committee for Economic and Social Recovery formed to advise the cabinet on policy and to guide the drafting of a new constitution.

Although Zafy and his colleagues denounced Razanamasy and Ratsiraka for treachery, they decided nonetheless to cooperate in the unwieldy panorama compromise. Ratsiraka retained formal privileges as head of state, and Zafy's HAE could legislate and control government policy, although not the composition of that government; this was Razanamasy's prerogative. Its unconstitutionality duly conceded, the arrangement had to be confirmed by popular referendum in December 1991.

Although a national convention, constitutional referendum, and presidential elections took place during 1992 as proposed by the opposition, the power standoff continued. Thinking himself creditably in advance of his time—in forsaking futile socialism and inviting structural change along international guidelines (while resisting many of the conditions imposed by those guidelines), in reconciling with France and anticipating French president Mitterrand's demand for multiparty democracy in Africa, even in reattracting South African business interest in the island—Ratsiraka was understandably astonished by his own unpopularity. Doubtless he considered the prejudice restricted largely to Antananarivo, where his government, like Tsiranana's, was beleaguered by ungrateful and ambitious Merina. The rural areas under AREMA control had indeed remained relatively stable during this period of urban fermentation; farmers clung to survival while the middle classes and urban laborers again took the country's destiny into their hands.

But disapproval was more far-reaching than that. On top of the misery caused by fifteen years of misrule, the reforms of economic and political institutions, necessary as they were, caused short-term suffering and accusations of favoritism for foreign commercial and financial interests. The statistical recovery failed to materialize in social spending or in the sustained availability of low-cost goods and services. A fragmented national territory was not about to enter an obvious new phase of cohesion and prosperity. Saving the vital environment meant at the outset sacrificing cultural and economic practices that had always seemed a natural birthright. World recession, aggravated by the 1991 Persian Gulf War, kept potential benefactors distracted from the needs of more obscure societies such as Madagascar. Sixteen years of promises, culminating in four years of deliberate change from 1987, failed to inspire faith in any system.

Above all, perhaps, Didier Ratsiraka discredited himself by his insistence on retaining power to reverse his own course. Denying in August 1990 that Madagascar had ever claimed to be a Marxist state, Ratsiraka nonetheless defended the wisdom of the nationalizations of 1975 while at the same time justifying reprivatization of those nationalized assets fifteen years later.[46] This inconsistency of vision would be difficult to tolerate in any culture; in the Malagasy, it amounted to folly. As they showed in 1947 and 1972, the Malagasy rarely forgive weakness in their leaders. The advent of a free press, of open political party activity, and of a liberal economy brought with it a huge and unexpected surge of bitterness over the catastrophe that those innovations had to correct. Madagascar had been reforming, commented a World Bank official in private, but it was like watching "perestroika under Brezhnev."

Isolated in his powerlessness, Ratsiraka struck out at both Zafy and Razanamasy by unilaterally urging a federal structure on the unitary state that he had himself created. Appealing to côtier mistrust of Antananarivo, he successfully encouraged the chiefs of three coastal provinces (the *faritany* of Toliara, Antsiranana, and Toamasina) to declare their autonomy from the central government. Antananarivo thereupon suffered an embargo of energy supplies from the port at "autonomous" Toamasina, Ratsiraka's own bailiwick. Already alienated by the August 10 massacre at Iavoloha, Razanamasy considered his break with the president complete. He averted civil war by negotiating with the secessionary provinces and by deploying the regular army wherever it was needed to sustain vital national communications. Toamasina returned to the transitional union although the city even now remains festooned with signs of federalist fervor; Toliara witnessed its brief and bloody experiment in autonomy during late May–early June 1993.

In his sudden advocacy of federalism for the provinces, Ratsiraka touched a sensitive historical nerve, threatening to divide his opponents irrevocably along ethnogeographic lines. But this campaign was also tantamount to a confession that his early reconciliation of Merina and côtier loyalties had collapsed and that his enemies were besieging him on the central plateaus.

Whether Zafy or other côtier alternatives can forge a national program together with legitimate Merina representatives remains to be seen. It is the century-old question that no political combination in Madagascar has ever answered successfully.

Astute as they are, today's Merina leaders have yet to establish credibility for this task of national conciliation. The embodiment of high plateau culture, Pastor Andriamanjato had never taken a cabinet portfolio or run for national office until his election as president of the National Assembly in August 1993. This isolation applies to General Rakotoharison, too, as it had to that other Merina military hero, Ramanantsoa, in 1972–1975. Merina presidential candidates have been exceedingly rare and even less successful; they include Rabetsitonta Tovonanahary, a young Antananarivo business favorite elected to Parliament in June 1993 and subsequently named minister of economics and planning after a disastrous 2 percent showing in the presidential election of November 1992.

Even Guy-Willy Razanamasy remains isolated as a Merina leader in a sea of côtier discontent. The interim prime minister negotiated successfully with all sides in the long transitional crisis, and he emerged as strongly as anybody from the deliberations of October 1991.[47] But Razanamasy also revealed weaknesses. His threat to fire civil servants on strike only led to even larger demonstrations by the strikers. His economic policy could obtain little more than a freeze on international obligations and a bare-bones austerity budget, awaiting the advent of permanent institutions. Moreover, his thinly disguised support for Rabemananjara, who was badly beaten in the November 1992 presidential election, tarnished his image as a politician. Despite a vigorous campaign that culminated in his own election to the Parliament in June 1993, Razanamasy's Fihaonana party obtained only eight seats in that contest, arriving a distant fourth in Antananarivo itself. The ex–prime minister sought the National Assembly presidency, winning a surprising fifty-eight votes against Andriamanjato's decisive seventy-six. After this creditable showing Razanamasy found himself in a somewhat isolated but benign opposition.

ANTICIPATING THE THIRD REPUBLIC

As research for this profile concludes, Madagascar's political class struggles for control of the great island's third republic. Albert Zafy has succeeded Didier Ratsiraka as president, a legislature of 138 deputies has been formed, and Francisque Ravony has launched his prime ministry. Nevertheless, the shape and direction of political institutions remain to be decided through interparty maneuvers and the other factors that forge political culture. The national economy has withered alarmingly after its semester of strikes in 1991 and a subsequent year of stalemate. The state is bankrupt, and half the population of 12 million struggles for food and shelter; more than a million people subsist beneath the level of absolute poverty. Political violence erupts intermittently among ethnic and ideologically oriented factions. Still, the scenario thus far bears confidence.

In March 1992, 1,400 delegates at a National Forum organized by the Malagasy Christian Council (FFKM) scheduled a referendum for the subsequent June to sanction a new constitution replacing Ratsiraka's autocratic second republic by a regime of separated powers, albeit still in a unitary state. Claiming that the forum had denied opportunity to discuss a confederal structure that would preserve autonomy for the coastal provinces, Ratsiraka refused at first to sanction a referendum on his own abdication.

Postponed until August 19, Madagascar's 1992 referendum finally confirmed the new constitution and announced the third republic. A boycott called by Ratsiraka's federalist supporters, accompanied by some violence in Toamasina and Antsiranana, blocked access to 300 voting stations (out of 13,000) and reduced voter turnout to 66 percent. Nevertheless, more than 4 million Malagasy endorsed the new national initiative, with a favorable margin in all provinces and an overall majority of 76.37 percent; that is, of course, what is expected of such constitutional ratifications. Observers from the European Community (which had helped finance the balloting) and the Geneva-based International Commission of Jurists (ICJ) congratulated the Malagasy for their political maturity in conducting the campaign. The new law was promulgated on September 18, 1992, by Prime Minister Razanamasy, whose transitional government of October 1991 remained intact until replaced through new elections in 1993.

Eventually, even Ratsiraka voted in the August referendum. In effect, the president abandoned his own abstention campaign in exchange for a waiver of the constitution's two-term limitation that would have excluded him from candidacy in the subsequent presidential elections.[48] During the debilitating half-year between the National Forum and the August 1992 referendum, Ratsiraka remained in his infamous bunker at Iavoloha, theoretically sharing power with Razanamasy's government and the new High State Authority (HAE) composed of a coalition of opposition leaders. Under Albert Zafy's leadership, the quasi-legislative HAE proclaimed commitments to lowering the cost of living and returning power to the people, but it produced few results. In reality, the coalition could agree on only one major political thesis: the eviction of Didier Ratsiraka.

A broadly based, nonpartisan National Committee for Observation of Elections (CNOE), organized by Madeleine Ramaholimihaso, denounced the Zafy-Razanamasy transition as nothing but a prolongation of Ratsiraka's disastrous seventeen years.[49] In another sense, this condominium also prolonged the economic paralysis brought on by the strikes in 1991. The stalemate was clearly expressed at the Organization of African Unity summit at Dakar in early July 1992. Ratsiraka insisted on attending that meeting despite OAU recognition of the HAE delegation under Vice Prime Minister Ravony. Intervention by Senegalese president Abdou Diouf allowed Ratsiraka to move to a "front bench," but the Malagasy vote was cast nonetheless by Ravony. Summing up, the correspondent for *Le Monde* saw the people's movement go into labor and bring forth a mouse.[50]

Under the new constitution, Madagascar is converted from a socialist to a liberal democratic state with guarantees for free enterprise and private property, as well as the security of foreign investment and protection of the environment. The state is organized into unitary governmental institutions but with some influence reserved for territorial collectivities. A weakened presidency, its mandate reduced from seven years to five, shares executive and legislative authority with a prime minister chosen by the National Assembly, the lower house of the bicameral Parliament. Assembly members are elected to four-year terms through a complex system of proportional representation. The Senate consists of distinguished citizens, two-thirds of them chosen by an electoral college from the local administrations, with the remainder appointed by the president on recommendations from recognized economic, social, cultural, and religious organizations. The Parliament receives legislation as well as cabinet nominations and budgetary proposals directly from the prime minister.

The particularity and possibly the success of the third republic hinge in large measure on the effective devolution of power to the decentralized collectivities. However constituted, those local authorities are to designate two-thirds of the senators to serve in the upper house. The constitution also gives them participation in ensuring local security and administration, environmental protection, social welfare, and the overall development of their respective territories. They will have taxing powers. Still, their specific prerogatives and terms of responsibility remain to be defined by the national Parliament, and their ordinances will not be able to contradict legislation or regulations of the state. Until these conditions are more precisely developed, neither the Ratsiraka federalists nor the champions of the indigenous fokon'olona institutions will know where they stand in the new system.

On July 29, 1992, Ratsiraka withstood another of his republic's perennial coup d'état digressions; ten soldiers affiliated with a Vital Forces splinter group occupied the national radio to announce Ratsiraka's fictitious replacement by Michel Fety, a Protestant pastor, former president of the national Chamber of Commerce, and a consultative leader in the 1972 Ramanantsoa transition. The putsch ended after a four-hour siege with four arrests and no casualties.[51]

Ratsiraka's tenacity as titular chief of state impressed observers who had once regarded his career as terminated by the mass movements of 1991. From October of that year, "King Didier" commanded only his Presidential Guard (rebaptized Regiments for Presidential Security, or RESEP) and the AREMA party apparatus, but AREMA continued to dominate large numbers of rural fokontany. Despite popular resentment over the impositions of these district councils, Zafy's HAE was unable to dislodge them from what remained of local administration. Some councils also resonated with support for the new federalist movement, which combated the continuing unitary state. Replacing the obsolete FNDR by the federalist MMSM gave Ratsiraka an unaccustomed ally in the venerable Monja Jaona and the remnants of his MONIMA party. Nevertheless, Monja's opposition to the new constitution was endorsed by only 17 percent of the referendary electorate in his home province of Toliara.

Once the constitution had been approved, Razanamasy's government set about organizing a hierarchy of elections, starting with the contest for the presidency in November 1992. Ratsiraka announced his candidacy for reelection, taking sustenance from rivalries within the multifarious opposition. The ambitions of HAE president Zafy were countered by Manandafy Rakotonirina, whose MFM had distanced itself in August from the prevailing Vital Forces coalition. This defection disrupted the movement that had launched the 1991 strikes and had compelled Ratsiraka into power sharing. Now the undisputed candidate of the remaining Vital Forces, Zafy found his own prestige tarnished by the HAE's inconclusive record during the transitional year from October 1991. Moreover, he was being subjected to criticism by the French and by international agencies fearful lest Zafy's promises of quick popular remedies endanger Madagascar's fragile commitment to structural austerities.

Inevitably delayed while procedures were tightened, the election series began on November 25, 1992, pitting Ratsiraka for the presidency against Zafy and Manandafy. The five other candidates included Evariste Marson, who had also bolted from the "dictatorial" Vital Forces to adhere to the PSD; Ruffine Tsiranana; and the illustrious poet-politician Jacques Rabemananjara, who enjoyed the favor of Prime Minister Razanamasy, General Rakotoharison, and much of the French business community. France was variously said to be putting its money on Marson, Manandafy, or Rabemananjara, whereas Ratsiraka was widely reported to enjoy substantial campaign financing from Libya and Iraq.[52] Although such reports induced foreign observers to expect a close race, Zafy trounced his opponents, collecting 46 percent of the ballots, Ratsiraka running a distant second with 28.67 percent; Manandafy won only 10 percent, Marson 4.4, Tsiranana 3.4, and Rabemananjara a mere 2.9 percent. In order to elect a majority president, however, Zafy and Ratsiraka had to face off in February, an exceedingly difficult moment to hold elections, particularly in rural areas subjected to bad weather and serious flooding.

After a campaign disrupted sporadically but not critically, Zafy won his indubitable title as president of the third republic on February 10, 1993, with 66.72 percent of the vote. Despite various impediments to participation, more than 80 percent of the voters managed to cast ballots. Seventy foreign observers and 7,000 volunteers from Ramaholimihaso's CNOE certified the orderliness of the procedure at 14,000 polling stations; certain of these sites were protected discreetly by the Malagasy armed forces under arrangements negotiated between Razanamasy and local officials. Contrasting Madagascar's experience with the sanguinary political transitions in Zaire, Togo, Rwanda, Somalia, and Liberia, Catherine Simon commended Madagascar in *Le Monde* for offering a reassuring example: "The patient stubbornness of the people of the great island has paid off. Violence had to give way."[53]

Such congratulations are merited by the long-suffering Malagasy, but they may have come prematurely. Much speculation has centered on prospective resistance by Ratsiraka and his followers to an orderly change of regime. Long-standing disputes rushed recurrently to the political surface in the extended crisis of 1991–1992. Zafy regards the election as a final vindication of his own presidential vocation against seventeen years of usurpation by Ratsiraka, but the federalists suspect Zafy to be a Trojan horse for Razanamasy, Andriamanjato, and other Merina patriots. Refusing even to recognize the existence of a unionist-federalist issue, Zafy had forced the so-called fédés into extreme measures to attract attention. Although Razanamasy handled the several crises and mutinies with diplomatic skill (earning more respect among côtier activists than most Merina leaders obtain), pro-Ratsiraka unruliness alarmed doubters in the foundering Vital Forces coalition, bringing them more readily into solidarity behind Zafy's candidacy.[54]

Unlike the decentralization advocated by Ratsiraka's rival, Ratsimandrava, in the early 1970s, the new confederalist camp is ethnically driven (that is, anti-Merina) and highly authoritarian within its privileged provincial structures. Having declared a frustrated autonomy in Toamasina, Antsiranana, and Toliara, entrenched federalists pledged to fight their cause in the legislative and local elections following the presidential assizes. If they succeed at the end of this long process, they will be able to frustrate national aspirations, particularly in the new parliament, formed through proportional representation among a welter of political parties and politicized professional groupings. If they fail, they may refuse to yield to adverse majorities. Such resistance could drive the new republic once again to the verge of civil war.

These omens of disaster, however, have not reappeared at the start of the third republic. The legislative elections suffered a two-month postponement to permit promulgation and clarification of an outrageously complicated process—ensuring both the distribution of parliamentary seats proportionally by lists of candidates and a guarantee of at least one seat to each of 111 fivondronona. Finally, however, they transpired on June 16, 1993, in virtually complete tranquillity throughout the island. Apportionment of seats accounts for only some of the complications in these elections, for the suddenly reopened process and the fragmentation of the Vital Forces movement produced an eruption of 122 parties, special-interest organizations, and mayfly factions contesting 138 parliamentary seats. Thirty-seven of these "lists" vied for Antananarivo's eight seats alone, obliging each of the 269,000 voters in the capital to collect thirty-seven ballots on the way to an isolation booth, where thirty-six would have to be discarded to cast a single vote. Partly as a result of these complexities, abstention rates were high throughout the island, reaching 60 percent in some remote rural areas.

Yet the voting happened with regularity, as I witnessed among a small contingent of international observers and a strong showing of national pollwatchers.[55] The results of the June 16 balloting became formally known only on July 21; it took several days for remote rural districts to be recorded and several more weeks for confirmation by the High Court. Legislative apportionment through proportional representation has favored the survival of small, locally and regionally active political factions. From the 122 "parties" that entered the electoral lists, some twenty-six parliamentary caucuses emerged, all of them looking for coalition partners in the gestation of a new system. Not surprisingly, the strongest of these belonged to the Vital Forces cartel (the Rasalama group) that had clustered behind Albert Zafy before the presidential campaign of November 1992. Although subject to defections and disagreements, the cartel maintained most of its strength in all provinces, seating 45 deputies of the National Assembly's 138 and allying in the Assembly with 14 or 15 additional adherents of the president. In early August 1993, after much maneuvering, those parties and coalitions concerted on the choice of Richard Andriamanjato as National Assembly president and Francisque Ravony as prime minister to organize the first government of the third republic.

A fifty-two-year-old lawyer from Vohipeno who left Manandafy's MFM in January 1993 to found a committee of support for Albert Zafy,[56] Ravony seems to have been everybody's second choice for the premiership except the president's, and it was Zafy's option that counted. Ravony has been a personal friend and legal advisor to Zafy for many years and is said to be on good terms with the Antananarivo French as well as the Merina business leaders of the capital.[57] Vice premier in Razanamasy's interim cabinet, Ravony acted as then–HAE president Zafy's surrogate in important domestic as well as external negotiations, including two meetings of the Organization of African Unity. Nevertheless, he won his parliamentary seat at Vohipeno by only a handful of votes against Marson; the latter had actually been declared victor before the High Court reversed those results in a controversial recount. As a consequence, the new Malagasy republic has acquired a chief executive whose title to a seat in Parliament raises doubt among some observers[58] and whose new pro-Zafy CSDDM "party" secured only one seat in addition to Ravony's.

Although Merina through his father (who served as president of the Senate in the first republic), the new prime minister is not ineluctably identified with plateau ethnicity after the manner of Andriamanjato or Razanamasy. His plurality of votes for the premiership on August 9 (55 of 134) came largely from côtiers hearkening to Zafy's preference for him against Manandafy and Vital Forces cartel choice Roger Ralison, a Merina. Ravony's cabinet of twenty-five ministers and state secretaries (two of them women) is carefully balanced among geographic, ethnic, and professional factions.[59] His policy statement, strongly endorsing free markets and private initiative, passed the Assembly on August 24 with 97 of the chamber's 138 votes, far exceeding the strength of the Vital Forces bloc in this fragmented legislature.

Since at best, the National Assembly counts sixty-four unconditional supporters of President Zafy, not all of them categoric friends of the prime minister, Ravony is obliged to negotiate coalitions for virtually all elements of his program. He depends in particular on the nonpartisan professionals and businesspeople elected on June 16 under such well-financed civic banners as Leader-Fanilo (thirteen seats), Grad Iloafo (Rabetsitonta's tiny faction), and even Razanamasy's Fihaonana. Thirteen of the twenty-five members of his cabinet belong to these and other parties outside the Vital Forces cartel and Ravony's own CSDDM. That cabinet does not include Ralison, favorite of the

Vital Forces political executive committee; although he'd lost in the Antananarivo legislative elections, Ralison obtained the cartel's nomination for prime minister (edging out Andriamanjato, who had to settle subsequently for the Assembly presidency) only to lose again—this time to Zafy's personal choice, Ravony.

The irreducible opposition includes fifteen deputies from Manandafy's MFM (deserted by Ravony in early 1993), eight from the PSD, and of course the eleven committed to ex-president Ratsiraka's FAMIMA (Faritra Miara Mandroso, Together for Progress), strong particularly in Toamasina, and two or three allies.[60] Most of the remaining FNDR forces of the second republic—including both MONIMA factions, UDECMA, the AKFM left behind by Andriamanjato, and Vonjy-VITM—either vanished altogether or dissolved into formations more readily adapted to the new circumstances of the third.

After his loss to Zafy in February 1993, Didier Ratsiraka watched impotently as such erstwhile AREMA stalwarts as Razakaboana defected to make their peace with the new president. Ratsiraka's supporters control only 13 votes in the 138-seat assembly, and the ex-president has been retired with a state pension to a state villa in Antananarivo. Although reconciled for the time being to the power of his opponents, Ratsiraka remains convinced of his own indispensability. He contested every step downward in his fight with the opposition from 1989 through February 1993, refusing to believe that angry mobs and even victorious candidates could represent the will of the millions of Malagasy.

Once permitted to run for reelection in November 1992, Ratsiraka ignored the National Forum's expectation that he vacate his office thirty days before that vote. He thus inadvertently allowed Madagascar to join the rare list of African polities that have been able to vote out a sitting chief of state. Comparing himself to Charles de Gaulle in the latter's 1946–1958 "desert passage," Ratsiraka told journalists that he would keep himself ready for recall to lead the state once the new regime had (inevitably) collapsed. He was comforted, he said, by the absence of any international censure against the August 10, 1991, massacre of demonstrators by his guards.[61] In truth, it is only his own people who can never forgive him for that atrocity.

While politicians wrestle for the handles of power, formal economic life stagnates alarmingly. Rice is once again imported, not as a drain on national reserves, which have dwindled to evanescence, but through gifts from abroad. Having risen above population growth in three previous years, national income suddenly dropped below that level in 1991 and again in 1992. Agricultural production declined under clouds of administrative confusion and labor paralysis. Coffee exports suffered from chronic world oversupply; 1992 was also a disastrous year for vanilla, cloves, and sugar. Thanks to wildcat importing, the domestic textile industry has lost 40 percent of its local market in less than two years. Confronting inflation of 13 percent in 1991 and nearly 20 percent in 1992, Razanamasy's government resisted IMF remonstrances toward another currency devaluation designed to help revive the export economy and rebuild foreign exchange reserves; the FMG actually appreciated against the dollar during the interim regime. Only a tenth of the taxes owed the state were collected in 1992.

Madagascar's external debt has risen to over $4 billion, with debt service in arrears by $450 million. Under prevailing terms negotiated with the Paris Club, Ravony himself foresaw continued payment on that debt by the current generation's great-grandchildren in 2016.[62] Investment and foreign assistance awaited greater definition in national structure and policy. The interim Economic Recovery Committee, under opposition magnates Manandafy and Andriamanjato, failed to propose the ideas needed to bring the economy back to credibility. Those ideas must now be pronounced and implemented by Ravony and his coalition team.

Most ominously, famine once again struck the island's indigent south, where precipitation during the four-month rainy season in 1992 remained at about 40 millimeters (1.5 inches), two-fifths of normal in this arid ecology. Drought conditions were aggravated that year by an invasion of locusts, the first serious devastation of the kind in a decade. The exhaustion of both subsistence stocks and of corn and cassava seed precluded farming in terrain without irrigation, subjecting one million people to starvation in early 1993. By May 14, 1992, when Prime Minister Razanamasy declared the disaster, twenty-five to thirty-five southerners were dying each day from starvation.[63] The World Food Program (WFP) responded with donations of 25,000 tons of corn and legumes and obtained additional pledges from Germany, France, the United States, Italy, China, and Réunion. Disbursing its massive food aid directly to households, the WFP aims to prevent further emigration from the afflicted countryside.[64] Although precipitation levels improved substantially in 1993, long-term rehabilitation of the chronically neglected Malagasy south will require massive investment for irrigation, water control, technology, communications, and training.

Compounding the shortages of agricultural input factors aggravated by seven months of nationwide strikes, the southern African drought restricted Madagascar's 1992 rice crop to little more than 2 million tons. Since inexpensive rice has become particularly difficult to find on world markets, the price of a kilogram of Madagascar's staple food in a newly liberalized domestic market reached nearly 1,700 FMG (US$1.00) in early 1992, remaining over 1,000 FMG ($0.60) for the year. To sustain decent nutrition, a Malagasy family of seven requires nearly 100 kilograms each month; it thus spends virtually all the median income on food alone![65] More than half of the island's families were reported by UNICEF in 1992 to be victims of malnutrition. Food was plentiful enough in the cities during 1993, for those who could afford it, but rural Malagasy in the south and west were continuing to go hungry.

Political stability may be ensured by a steady, successful inauguration of the third republic, but the physical and financial infrastructure, the factors of productivity, and the habits of a healthy economy will have to be redeveloped by that republic's institutions. Visiting his country of birth after a quarter-century in exile, *Marchés Tropicaux* editor Georges Ravel professed his horror at the "spectacle of desolation" that Madagascar had become:

The crisis has infected institutions and minds alike. Corruption and intrigue reign in decision-making, and inertia, permissiveness, passivity in the offices that affect the daily life of the Malagasy. Hospitals and schools, market places and roadways—all operate in chaos; everything must be done again. How can the great island have been allowed to sink this far into the depths of underdevelopment?[66]

In this deepening shadow of social and economic misery, the third republic's presidency came to Albert Zafy, proclaimed populist and environmentalist, liberal, man of science. Its public policy is in the hands of Francisque Ravony, lawyer, negotiator, everybody's lesser evil except Zafy's. Whether their task is feasible will depend on the ability of the third republic's institutions to respond to the mandates of international patron organizations on one imperious level and, on a very different level, to the dictates of a Malagasy population that for decades has resisted all pretensions of Antananarivo to lead.

NOTES

1. *Charte de la révolution socialiste malgache* (Antananarivo: Imprimerie d'Ouvrages Educatifs, August 26, 1975), p. 116.

2. For further analysis, see Pascal Chaigneau, *Madagascar, de la première république à l'orientation socialiste: Processus et conséquences d'une évolution politique* (Thèse IIIème cycle en sociologie politique, Univ. de Paris X, 1981), pt. 3, ch. 1; Chaigneau, *Un état à orientation socialiste: Madagascar* (Thèse d'état, Univ. de Paris X, 1984), v. 2, ch. 1; Maureen Covell, *Madagascar: Politics, Economics and Society* (London and New York: Frances Pinter, 1987), chs. 3 and 4.

3. See Covell, *Politics, Economics and Society*, pp. 111–113.

4. Pascal Chaigneau, *Rivalités politiques et socialisme à Madagascar* (Paris: Centre des Hautes Études sur l'Afrique et l'Asie Modernes [CHEAM], 1985), p. 110.

5. See Chaigneau, *Un état à orientation socialiste*, pp. 645–653, 666; see also interview with Ratsiraka in *Jeune Afrique*, no. 1544, August 1–7, 1990, p. 34.

6. See *Africa Confidential*, March 3, 1982.

7. Agence France Presse, reported in *Le Monde*, June 3, 1993; Jean-Eric Rakotoarisoa, *Dans les Media Demain*, no. 323, June 10, 1993. In its version of the incident, MONIMA claimed six killed on the government side; see *Midi-Madagasikara*, June 12, 1993.

8. See *Indian Ocean Newsletter*, no. 567, March 20, 1993.

9. For the narrative to 1981, see Charles Cadoux and Jean du Bois de Gaudusson, "Madagascar 1979–1981: Un passage difficile," in *Annuaire des Pays de l'Océan Indien (APOI)*, no. 7, 1980, pp. 357–387. (The *Annuaire* for 1980 was published after the terminal date in the article.)

10. See Robert Archer, *Madagascar depuis 1972: La marche d'une révolution* (Paris: Harmattan, 1978); Chaigneau, *Première république*, pp. 626–637; Chaigneau, *Rivalités politiques*, p. 105.

11. See *Revue de l'Océan Indien*, Antananarivo, March 1986.

12. Dervla Murphy, *Muddling Through in Madagascar* (Woodstock, N.Y.: Overlook Press, 1989), p. 92.

13. The phrase is from Roland Razafimandranto, *Essai de bilan politique, économique et social de la période révolutionnaire socialiste malgache: 1975–1982*, Mémoire

en Relations Internationales (Aix-en-Provence: Université d'Aix-Marseille, 1982–1983), p. 63.

14. Ratsiraka interviewed by "S.A." in *Jeune Afrique*, no. 1261, March 6, 1985, p. 21; for further analysis, see J.-P. Langellier, *Le Monde*, January 17–18, 1982; *Afrique Nouvelle*, January 13, 1982; Agence France Presse, February 22, 1985; *Le Monde*, February 23, 1985.

15. See *Africa Contemporary Record (ACR), 1985–1986* (New York: Africana, 1987), pp. B346–347, B352.

16. Ibid., pp. B397–399.

17. See Chaigneau, *Un état à orientation socialiste*, pp. 1164–1167; during the election campaign of June 1993, the author saw "Bréchard" chalked in fresh graffiti throughout the Toamasina region, although Rajaonarison was not a candidate.

18. Ibid.; see also *Africa Confidential*, March 3, 1982.

19. See *ACR, 1983–1984*, p. B196; Chaigneau, *Première république*, pp. 823–831.

20. See Covell, *Politics, Economics, and Society*, pp. 115–119.

21. See Chaigneau, *Un état à orientation socialiste*, p. 1163.

22. See Y.-G. Paillard, "The First and Second Malagasy Republics: The Difficult Road of Independence," trans. R. Kent, in Raymond Kent, ed., *Madagascar in History: Essays from the 1970s* (Albany, Calif.: Foundation for Malagasy Studies, 1979), pp. 298–354, esp. pp. 343–344.

23. Chaigneau, *Un état à orientation socialiste*, pp. 489–490.

24. See Philip M. Allen, *Security and Nationalism in the Indian Ocean: Lessons from the Latin Quarter Islands* (Boulder and London: Westview Press, 1987), pp. 171–172.

25. Malagasy Republic, Ministry of Information, *Madagascar Renouveau*, no. 14, 1980 (Antananarivo: Imprimerie Nationale).

26. Jacques De Barrin in *Le Monde*, March 21, 1985; for a somewhat more sentimental indictment of this "tyrannical" effort to repudiate Malagasy culture and then to blame it demagogically for its failure to metamorphose, see Ferdinand Deleris, *Ratsiraka: Socialisme et misère à Madagascar* (Paris: Harmattan, 1986), pp. 57–64, 120–121.

27. *Revue de l'Océan Indien*, no. 15, April 1985, p. 13.

28. Laurent Zecchini, *Le Monde*, November 22, 1986.

29. For an example, see Murphy, *Muddling Through*, pp. 205–206.

30. Editorial in *Le Monde*, March 9, 1987.

31. Razafimandranto's phrase in *Essai de bilan*, p. 32.

32. *Revue de l'Océan Indien*, June 1986, p. 16.

33. Murphy, *Muddling Through*, p. 39; the phrase presumably represents a rebirth of Ratsiraka's claim to "humanist Marxism" as a way of tempering the "scientific socialism" of 1975; see Covell, *Politics, Economics and Society*, p. 1.

34. Alan Cowell, *New York Times*, June 12, 1983.

35. See Jean Houbert's review of Covell's book in *Journal of Modern African Studies*, v. 26, no. 4, 1988, pp. 696–698; Covell's conclusion (pp. 157–166) asserting the development of Marxist socialism in Ratsiraka's Madagascar seems forced; Chaigneau's confirmation of socialist principles is more nuanced, especially in *Un état à orientation socialiste*, pp. 489–493.

36. Sennen Andriamirado, "Madagascar: L'enfer pour les uns peut être un paradis pour les autres," *Jeune Afrique*, no. 1368, March 25, 1987; cf. Deleris's denunciation in *Ratsiraka: Socialisme et misère*, esp. ch. 4; see also Lucile Rasoamanalina Ramanandraibe, *Le livre vert de l'espérance malgache* (Paris: Harmattan, 1987) esp. her conclusion, pp. 133–136.

37. Andriamanjato, interviewed in *Madagascar Tribune*, January 18, 1990.

38. See, for instance, Georges Ravel in *Marchés Tropicaux et Méditerranéens (MTM),* nos. 2440 and 2447, August 14 and October 2, 1992; Marie-Pierre Subtil in *Le Monde,* November 25, 1992.

39. Césaire Rabenoro, *Les relations extérieures de Madagascar de 1960 à 1972* (Thèse d'etat, Univ. d'Aix-Marseille, 1981).

40. See *Madagascar Tribune,* March 5, 1990.

41. Rakotoharison, interview with *Madagascar Tribune,* May 14, 1990; see also Franck Raharison, editorial in the same publication, May 15, 1990.

42. See *MTM,* July 5, 1991; *Midi-Madagasikara,* January 31, 1991; *Africa Research Bulletin,* Political Series, v. 28, no. 2, February 1991, p. 10008.

43. Razanamasy, interviewed in *Madagascar Tribune,* August 1, 1993.

44. Agence France Presse, October 25, 1991.

45. *Le Monde,* November 3–4, 1991.

46. Ratsiraka, interviewed by Sennen Andriamirado in *Jeune Afrique,* no. 1544, August 1–7, 1990, pp. 34–38; see also Roger Thurow in *Wall Street Journal,* December 10, 1990.

47. See Georges Ravel's interview with Razanamasy in *MTM,* no. 2483, June 11, 1993; Razanamasy's letter to *Madagascar Tribune,* August 4, 1993.

48. See *Africa Confidential,* v. 33, no. 16, August 14, 1992, p. 7; *Jeune Afrique Economie,* no. 159, September 1992, p. 98.

49. Marie-Pierre Subtil in *Le Monde,* November 25, 1992.

50. Ibid.

51. See *MTM,* no. 2438, July 31, 1992; Economist Intelligence Unit (EIU), *Country Report,* no. 4, 1992, October 12, 1992.

52. See *Africa Confidential,* v. 33, no. 23, November 20, 1992; *Jeune Afrique,* no. 1663, November 19–25, 1992; *MTM,* nos. 2452, November 6, and 2456, December 4, 1992.

53. Catherine Simon, *Le Monde,* February 16, 1993; see also ibid., February 11 and 12, 1993; for first round of elections, see *MTM,* nos. 2452, November 6, 2456, December 4, and 2458, December 18, 1992; *Jeune Afrique,* nos. 1658, October 15–21, and 1664, November 26–December 2, 1992.

54. See Jean Hélène, *Le Monde,* February 11, 1993.

55. See CNOE communiqué, July 26, 1993, which remains critical of the obfuscations in the electoral process, the buying of votes, prejudice in the nomination of candidates, the 47 percent abstention rate, the superfluity of "lists" enabling most elections to be decided by 10 to 20 percent of the votes, and the complexity of the appeal process before the High Court.

56. The Support Committee for Development and Democracy in Madagascar (CSDDM).

57. See *Indian Ocean Newsletter,* no. 557, January 9, 1993; Ravony also seems to have won favor among young voters, epitomized in the endorsement of the Tana rock star "Dama" (Rasolofondrasolo Zafimahaleo), an unpredicted victor in the June 16 parliamentary elections in the capital.

58. See interview with Norbert Ratsirahonana, HCC president, by Adelson Razafy, *Madagascar Tribune,* July 22, 1993; the court's decision appears to have been made without a vote among a politically mixed tribunal that included only five appointees (of eleven) from the pro-Ravony Vital Forces movement.

59. See Georges Ravel, *MTM,* nos. 2488, July 16, 2490, July 30, 2494, August 27, and 2495, September 3, 1993; *Le Monde,* August 12, 1993.

60. See *Dans les Media Demain,* July 22 and 29, 1993; Adelson Razafy in *Madagascar Tribune,* July 23 and 31, 1993; Rasediniarivo, *LaKroan'i Madagasikara,* August 8, 1993;

Midi-Madagasikara, August 10, 1993; "M.A.," in *La Lettre Mensuelle de JURECO*, no. 79–80, July-August 1993.

61. See *MTM*, no. 2456, December 4, 1992; Marie-Pierre Subtil, *Le Monde*, November 28, 1992; Sennen Andriamirado, *Jeune Afrique*, no. 1658, October 15–21, 1992, pp. 28–29.

62. *MTM*, no. 240, May 21, 1993.

63. For a comprehensive report on Madagascar's socioeconomic misery, see Catherine Simon, *Le Monde*, May 17–18, 1992; see also EIU, *Country Report*, no. 3, p. 16, no. 2, pp. 14–18, and no. 1, pp. 16–24, 1992; "Country Survey: Madagascar," *Africa Analysis*, no. 127, July 26, 1991, p. 6; *MTM*, esp. nos. 2428, 2429, and 2437, May 22 and 29 and July 31, 1992.

64. See *MTM*, no. 2460, January 1, 1993.

65. Per capita income is estimated at $190 per year; see Sylvia da Silva, "Saving Madagascar," *Swiss Review of World Affairs*, June 1991, pp. 22–24.

66. Georges Ravel, *MTM*, no. 2458, December 18, 1992.

4
Society in Modern Madagascar

More than a century of scholars have sought to account for the peculiar unity and diversity of the great island's culture, seldom finding what they'd been led to suppose. It would be logical, for instance, to expect greater heterogeneity in so vast a territory penetrated along various coasts by several large waves of immigrants from different points of origin over a solid milennium of time. The force of a universal language, however, should have guaranteed even greater cohesion of social institutions and cultural traits. Nationalists posit the survival of a single Malagasy nation unified by the nineteenth-century Merina monarchy; regionalists emphasize the particular identities of eighteen or twenty Malagasy ethnic groups. Regionalism (now politically associated with the so-called federalist movement) has been most conspicuous when advocating the rights of coastal people (côtiers) against the Merina. In reality, the great island contains one highly variegated, geographically dispersed culture subject to diverse economic, ethnic, and political influences.[1]

Malagasy tradition is less preoccupied with the enigmas of culture than are the outsiders. Madagascar in many respects is not unlike England or Japan. The founding ancestors spoke a common language, but they nonetheless organized differently to respond to circumstances in diverse sectors of the island. Yet as Malagasy groups migrated away from their ancestral foundations, each retained the mystique of its original point of departure elsewhere on the island. This centripetal power of origin has operated during the past two centuries in dialectical interaction with the centrifugal appeal of new land and jobs.[2]

The Malagasy do speak one basic language, but by no means is that tongue used uniformly throughout the island. Vérin calls Malagasy a "linguistic ensemble" with significant variations.[3] Derived from the Maayan (or Manjaan) of Borneo, Malagasy speech has evolved for more than a millennium in contact with other Indonesian and South Asian cultures, and with Bantu African, Arabic, and European sources. Through its own insular experience, the language refracts into three broad geographical clusters—the Merina-Betsileo center, the east and north coasts, and the west and south.

AN ITINERARY OF ETHNIC GROUPS

Starting with the central highlands of the Merina people, this survey of the great island reveals both the diversity of Madagascar's ecological endowment and the dispersal of its cultural groups (see Map 4.1). From the lofty heights of Imerina, a place of irrigated river valleys and vast, denuded pasture, our itinerary at first runs southward along the peaks and plateaus of the interior, then doubles back east- and northward along the rugged, still forested escarpment reaching the fertility of Lake Alaotra and then the mountainous northern extremity of the land; it then proceeds southward along the broad western prairie cut by narrow, soil-bearing red rivers that empty into the Mozambique Channel. This dry western savanna turns into desert in the deep south, to be succeeded by the seasonally humid east coast. Here, coffee, cloves, vanilla, and bananas thrive; the tropical forest yields its timber, fruit, and game; and the seas offer abundant fish and crustaceans. Rice on the plateaus and in the east, cassava in the west, corn in the south, cattle virtually everywhere, are the Malagasy agricultural staples.

Occupying the central plateaus, the Merina represent over one-fourth of the population, more than 3 million people today.[4] Considered by outsiders as an urban, literate, Christianized people of a city that has been the national capital for over 150 years, the Merina still identify themselves, like most Malagasy, with village clans, decentralized ancestral tombs, and cattle husbandry. Their settlements and paddy fields occupy the central portion of the high plateau, and their humped cattle roam freely over vast treks of otherwise empty central grasslands. Antananarivo holds about 25 percent of the Merina among its million permanent inhabitants and up to half the province's population on any given day (especially on Friday, *zoma*, day of the great market). To the south is Antsirabe, a favorite mountain resort in a rich agricultural neighborhood with some important manufacturing and educational establishments. Bureaucratic and mercantile Merina also reside in isolated colonies outside their homeland.

From the late eighteenth century, Merina leaders adapted political ideas from the east coast into a centralized institution of kingship able to impose military and economic cohesion. Dominance over Malagasy neighbors came through the weaponry acquired from British allies once England had taken Mauritius from France in 1810. That superiority survives today through cultural, commercial, and bureaucratic modernizations that the Merina have known how to turn to their own advantage. More than other Malagasy elites, the Merina bourgeoisie sacrifices economically to school its children and boost them into the learned professions and to accumulate capital for remunerative enterprise. Merina elites (still often identified with class or caste origins) retain enhanced access to modern educational benefits and to the economic and political strength that access entails. Nevertheless, many coastal families, literate, schooled, and Christianized in their own right, now share privileges and dispute politics with the Merina. And many Merina families, bending wearily over precious paddy in river valleys or tracing their zebu on

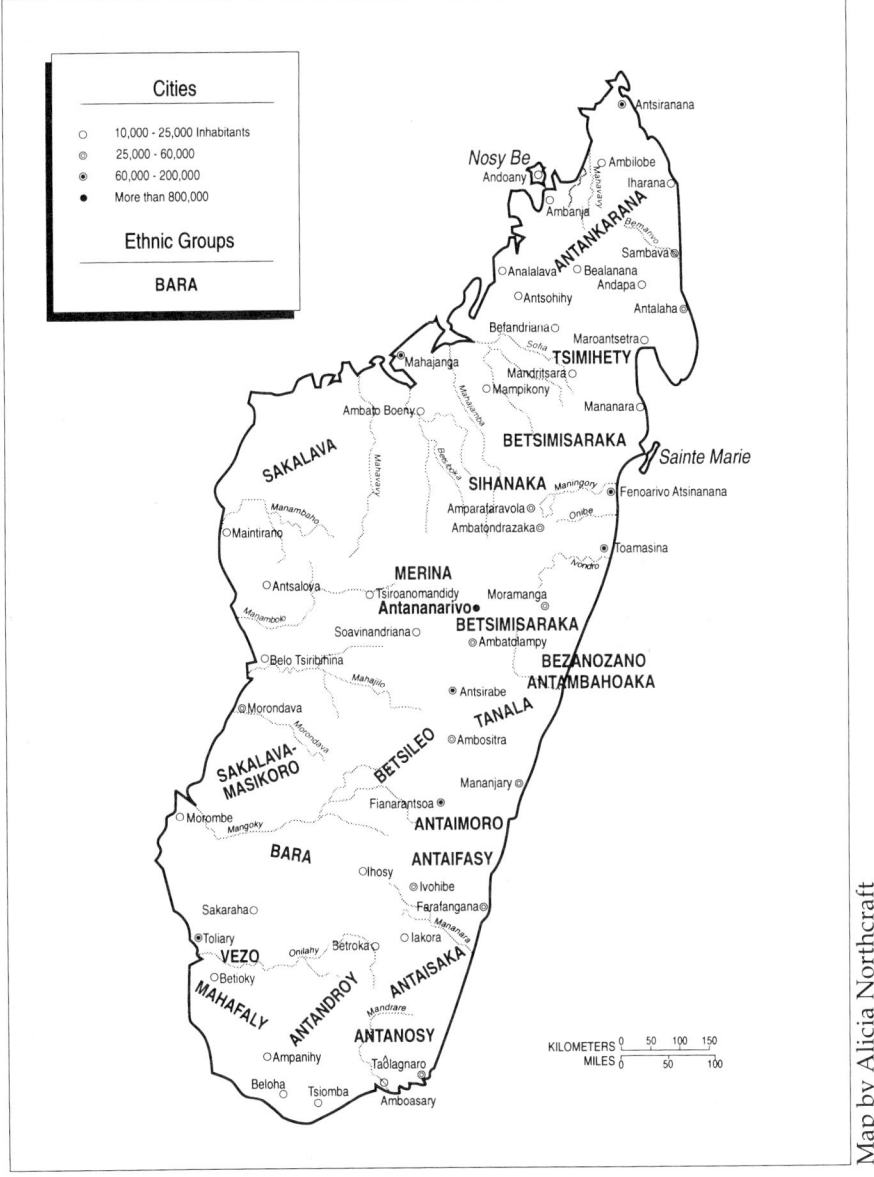

Map 4.1 Ethnic groups of Madagascar

Plateau landscape, with bags of charcoal at roadside awaiting delivery to Antananarivo. Photo by Gay Kuester, © The Chicago Zoological Society.

the long marches of savanna, share the poverty and deprivation of all Malagasy.

Proficient culturally as well as in politics and trade, the Merina occupy all refractions of the Malagasy social kaleidescope. They are exceedingly mobile, migrating to any corner of the island—or to France and other foyers of professionalism abroad. Their capital city is multifarious, their countryside relatively open to immigration from outside Imerina. Merina culture remains intrepidly verbal and musical but with a high rate of literacy. Rural and urban Merina manifest a potent gift of poetry and oratory, pervasive if highly eclectic musical traditions, and a profound conjunction of ancestral spirit and Christian piety.

The extent of "tribalism" in Malagasy politics has often been exaggerated to disguise other animosities of political elites, social classes, or religion. It is nonetheless true that political and social privileges originating in the nineteenth-century internal colonialism of the Merina have engendered considerable resentment among other Malagasy. Chaigneau identifies the role of the French colonial administration in perpetuating the conflict: "The colonial government bequeathed a practice of exploiting the bitterness emergent from situations of domination, while building an anthropological and ethnological literature aiming at "scientific" justification of this opposition. This was the product of an analysis which proved effective and convenient in controlling the country but which scarcely considered sociological realities."[5]

Nevertheless, the record of the Merina dynasts among their own coastal subjects was not without taint. Under the advantages of superior technology, fire power, and organization, Merina domination brought extensive recruitment of slaves to many of the subordinate provinces. External trade in slaves withered under British influence after 1830, when the nefarious institution was prohibited in Mauritius; France followed suit in Réunion in 1848, but Madagascar maintained domestic slavery until conquered by the French at the end of the century.

To erase Merina hegemony, the French under Galliéni proclaimed an unusually egalitarian "tribal policy" (*politique des races*). Essentially an effort to designate indigenous rulers for each ethnic group, the tribal policy also entailed an early form of affirmative action aimed at educational and economic parity between the Merina on the one hand and their Betsileo, Tsimihety, and coastal former subjects on the other. Realities of colonial administration proved stronger than principle, however, and the tribal policy was inadequate to the task.

While regularly denouncing the Merina for arrogance and cupidity, French administrators nonetheless had no choice but to give them the jobs needed to sustain a territorial system. Moreover, these advantages persisted through the decades of colonial administration as resources fell short of the levels needed to duplicate in the provinces the educational, medical, and administrative institutions established in the Merina capital of Antananarivo. At independence in 1960, educated Merina still dominated the impressive Malagasy elite available to perform the work of the nation; they do so even today despite more than three decades of côtier presidencies. Merina teachers, shopkeepers, government agents, and technicians in the provinces still find themselves relegated to the status of vazaha, or foreigner.[6] Like other migrant elites in the least-privileged parts of the Third World, they are also sometimes subjected to frightening ethnic pogroms, particularly in Toamasina, port of entry for landlocked Imerina.

From the moment of French conquest at the end of the nineteenth century, national patriotism has been identified by many Merina with the restoration of their dynastic birthright. This ethnic nationalism has a religious dimension. The mid-nineteenth-century hostility between traditional royal religion and Christianity had given way in 1869 to the establishment of Protestant Christianity at the court of Ranavalona II. Under colonialism, the several sects of Malagasy Protestantism centered in Antananarivo became a forum for nationalist opposition. Anglicans and Quakers in the city cherished their King James versions to prove that God spoke English, not French. At home they waxed nostalgic over their monarchs' loving correspondence with Queen Victoria. "Hova" patriots continued that antagonism against the heirs of the independence of 1960, the PSD coalition of coastal people and the largely Roman Catholic rural sectors of the plateau.

The anthropologist Maurice Bloch comments on the connection between nationalism and the Merina elite of the twentieth century:

> This group's relation to the colonial power was ambiguous. On one hand they depended on the institutions of the colonial state, on the other they produced the most vocal of the nationalists. In this latter role they could expect the support of the majority of the rural population, but as a dominant class, in league with the colonial power, they also aroused growing antagonism. In the religious field, because the urban bourgeoisie was closely identified with Protestantism, Protes-

tantism was both accepted and resented. The resentment did not often surface, but by the end of the 1960s and early 1970 it began to emerge more openly.[7]

During seventy years of political discrimination, the Protestant urban middle class prospered nonetheless in relative comfort and social success that tempered the revanchism of the Merina. Although it invoked revolution in the 1960s and 1970s, its interest consisted essentially in replacing French (and some Asian) privilege with privilege of its own. Prosperous urban Protestantism thus revealed its political ambivalence. Merina bourgeois nationalism was quickly transcended in the integrated movements that produced the great nationalist surges of 1947, 1960, and 1971–1975.

Outside of central Imerina, several dozen ethnic groups (*karazabe*) have developed distinct identities in their respective locations. All are more or less represented in the society of the capital city, but they find themselves truly at home elsewhere. Developing some distinctive characteristics of physiognomy and culture over time, most of these putative "tribes" nevertheless do not conceive of their descent as being from unique tribal origins. Rather, they differ from one another primarily in having occupied a certain territory and defended the specific interests of that place—including the desire to return to it at death—over an extended period of time.[8] All Malagasy groups have emerged from biological and cultural interaction among African peoples and Asians (usually including Arabs). Linked by a common language, their pluralist ethnic identity is far less pronounced than that of most African societies.[9]

To the south of Imerina, crowded into a cramped mountainous habitat, live some 1.5 million Betsileo. Rice and cattle farmers like their Merina neighbors, the Betsileo have by necessity developed intricately terraced rice fields and a migratory tendency westward when the homeland fails to sustain their needs. These mountain folk exhibit a flair for fine weaving and for wood carving as well as a rich tradition of music and oral poetics. Originating in the Arabized southeastern coastlands, the Betsileo probably mounted to the hospitable plateau in the thirteenth and fourteenth centuries. Four subareas of the Betsileo coalesced desultorily into a unitary kingdom until with some difficulty Radama I subjected them to the expanding Merina empire; his successor founded Fianarantsoa in 1830 to give central cohesion to the province. During the nineteenth century, Roman Catholicism inserted itself successfully into the sophisticated tissue of Betsileo beliefs and ritual.

In the interior east of Betsileo, the Tanala, as their name denotes, "inhabit the forests" along the steep escarpments south of the Mangoro River. Fragmented into small, mobile, fiercely independent clan groups, the 300,000 Tanala retain some of the Muslim Arab influences acquired by their ancestors on the east coast. They adopted the 1947 rebellion virtually as their own.

Second in size to the Merina is the heterogeneous eastern coastal group called Betsimisaraka, representing some 15 percent of the population—1,134,478 in 1971, perhaps 1.8 million today. Standing between the nineteenth-century Merina kingdom and the Mascarene holdings of Europe, these Afro-Asian-Arab people of forests and plantations have historically reacted with vigor against the dictates of external power. For centuries nonetheless, their separate polities maintained contact with all parts of the commercial Southern Hemisphere. They replenished European ships with food, timber, and slaves, and their families intermarried with European and American pirates along the Bay of Antongil, at Foulpointe, and on the island of Sainte Marie.[10] An emergent elite of *malata* (mulatto) people continually sought domination in the north, maintaining for a time the celebrated Republic of Libertalia and splitting the elongated Betsimisaraka nation into northern and southern halves. In 1774, an imaginative freebooting Polish adventurer named M. A. Benyowski founded the town of Louisbourg and began fabricating his own personal legend as emperor of Madagascar until he was deposed a few years later by Louis's own exasperated minions from the Île de France (Mauritius).

The Betsimisaraka have repeatedly expressed antagonism toward intrusions by unwelcome fanjakana or privileged outsiders. France had frequently intervened against lawlessness along that coast, taking possession of Sainte Marie in 1751 and controlling virtually all of Betsimisaraka by 1810. From that point, the area was subject to Anglo-French rivalry and suffered under British favoritism for the interior Merina. Betsimisaraka coastal settlements endured naval bombardments whenever Merina authorities there declined to cooperate with Britain and France. Yet the Merina not only subdued the Betsimisaraka country but also migrated there in large numbers for administrative and business purposes.

Quiescent during most of the colonial period, the Betsimisaraka rose vigorously in the powerful insurrection of 1947 when France was perceived to be inadequate to its postwar responsibilities. It was at the Betsimisaraka port of Toamasina (then Tamatave) that the 1958 congress of nationalist parties opted for independence, rejecting the qualified autonomy offered by de Gaulle and the new French fifth republic. Didier Ratsiraka, the revolutionary president of Madagascar's second republic, is Betsimisaraka; Merina-inspired challenges to his authority found the Betsimisaraka rallying to his support, as they had done a generation earlier when the Merina seemed to have engineered the overthrow of Tsimihety president Tsiranana.

Despite the vulnerability of the coasts, many Betsimisaraka have dwelt for generations without external intrusion, particularly in the denser, more traditionally oriented southeast. Betsimisaraka do what their ecology tells them to do. In their lush, humid country, they are rice farmers, fisherfolk, foresters, cultivators of the vanilla orchid and banana, miners in the graphite pits, dockworkers in their shore towns. Their elite has been penetrated deeply by Roman Catholicism, imported from Réunion across the open channel to the east, but their forest societies are enlivened by the creative spirits of ancestral animism.

Along the escarpment west of Betsimisaraka reside the Bezanozano, a small group of forest people herding their cattle and working the forests in the Mangoro River valley. As early as the eighteenth century, the Bezanozano developed village assemblies with elected leaders. Their valley was tightly occupied by Merina armed forces in the nineteenth century as a buffer against incursions through Betsimisaraka country from the east.

The 150,000 Sihanaka, whose name means "wandering in wetlands," settled in intricately fortified villages to the north of the Bezanozano. Sihanaka tradition abounds with stories about raids into the patrimony of the haughty Merina, to whom they ultimately succumbed. Today, Sihanaka inhabit the fertile lands around Lake Alaotra, territory long designated to become the richest rice beds of the entire economy.

Farther north of Imerina, the edge of the plateau is occupied by 800,000 Tsimihety, people whose name expresses a proverbial refusal to submit their hair to the shears of conquerors. Clan loyalties and decentralized power characterize Tsimihety political structure, and they developed only minimal political institutions to complicate their lives. Tsimihety cattle figure predominantly in the cultural economy. Historically, the population has ranged far westward into the northern Sakalava dominions of Boina (now Mahajanga Province), where they have traditionally been considered an abrasive presence. Madagascar's first president, Philibert Tsiranana, was a Tsimihety.

At the northern peninsula of the island dwell the Antankarana, the "rock people" of Antsiranana Province. The ruins of their ancient city of Vohemar on the northeast coast bespeak Antankarana participation over centuries in the great Indian Ocean trade systems. Familiars of the French and of the Zanzibari sultans who contested for the Comoro Islands to the west, this Muslim-influenced society fell under the control of the Sakalava Boina dynasty in the mid-eighteenth century and was later dominated by the Merina. Garrisons and traders inhabited the lovely off-shore island of Nosy Be and the great bay of Diego Suarez (now Antsiranana), where France subsequently built a formidable, if relatively inactive, naval base.

Spreading sparsely over virtually the entire west coast and across its arid inland savannas, the Sakalava live among the remnants of their political greatness. Here the rare long rivers flow gently over the sloping west to the Mozambique Channel, unlike the precipitous charge of Madagascar's eastern waters down the escarpment to the Indian Ocean. Like other Malagasy people, the original Sakalava probably settled in the west after migration from somewhere east of the plateaus. After overwhelming the ensconced Vazimba, they became farmers, cattle-keepers, and fisherfolk in their vast domains. By the late seventeenth century, they had created two powerful kingdoms, the Menabe in the south and, a generation later (from about 1712), the Boina in the north around Marovoay and Mahajanga. Both absorbed African immigrants and, whenever in need of farm labor, went on slave hunts along the East African and Comorean coasts. The northern Sakalava of Boina functioned in close cooperation with Indian Ocean Muslim tradespeople— "Moors" from Zanzibar or, if they settled on the island, generically called Antalaotse—who had their own trading colonies at Mahajanga and elsewhere on the northwest coast.

Sakalava monarchs were sacred, their relics are objects of veneration even today, and their political and cultural systems are elaborate. Dead monarchs have their will interpreted through spirit possession rites (*tromba* or *joro*). These kingdoms resisted Merina domination for much of the nineteenth century, allying with France in mid-century to hold onto the west coast and some of the interior. But they failed eventually, fragmenting from within and exposing themselves to gradual Merina domination. Their 700,000 descendants have found their patrimony eroded by newcomers—Tsimihety and Bara from the interior, Europeans and Comoreans from overseas. Merina power, the superiority of Toamasina and Antsiranana as ports, and the economic limitations of their pastoral civilization brought a decline in the Sakalava population and their overall fortune. Constantly resisting both Merina and French taxation and labor conscription, the Sakalava acquired a reputation for extreme morbidity; their numbers have indeed stagnated over the past century.[11] Yet rich Sakalava oral literature and ritual testify to the durability of the culture. The Masikoro subgroup of the Sakalava farm the lower Mangoky valley. Farther south, the subgroup known as the Vezo is among the rare Malagasy ocean-fishing cultures.

Sharing the southwest with the Vezo-Sakalava and the small population of Makoa (who are presumed to descend from predominantly Mozambican Africans) are the Mahafaly people, known for vigorous wood sculptures, mohair weaving, and other arts. In touch over centuries with all European visitors to the Bay of St. Augustine, the Mahafaly kings obtained help from French allies to keep the nineteenth-century Merina dynasts from ever fully dominating the territory around their port of Toliara.

Largest of the southern populations are the Antandroy, some 600,000 cattle-keeping people living in precarious adaptation to an arid environment. Fugitives of various origins and separate interests took to this desert wilderness at the island's southern tip, evolving over centuries into a single people with a ferocity for independence. The Antandroy developed a kind of confederal solidarity that nonetheless permitted many internal rivalries among them. Virtually nothing lives in these spiny forests except Antandroy, and they must cope with intermittent famines, plagues of locusts, failures of their crops of corn and beans, decimation of their small clan villages, and indifference from governments. When rains don't come to their place, the locusts do. Today, the Antandroy seem perpetually in search of food and fertility, sometimes having to leave the home country to do so. Isolated by the aridity of the Ivohibe basin, they have depended on their not-always-affable Mahafaly and Antanosy neighbors to ensure communication with the world outside.

Like the Antandroy, the Bara to the north, the Mahafaly to the west, and the Antanosy in the east are seminomadic cattle-owners. They all keep considerable distance between and among themselves, and they defy central or regional power ambitions in the dust of the recalcitrant south. Nevertheless, conspicuous dynasties did emerge among these peoples as the clans realized the need for collaboration against external threats. They all resisted Merina domination with success, although Antananarivo made a point of holding Fort Dauphin against the truculent Tanosy.

Occupying the vast Horombe Plateau of the deep south, the 400,000 Bara people acquired a vivid collective personality from their cattle culture, their feudal clan networks used in cattle rustling, and their cowboy insouciance. After raiding and pillaging Mahafaly and Sakalava territory to the south and west, many Bara have tended to settle in the Mangoky River valley down from their highland home. Yet the Bara still maintain their reputation for bellicosity and cattle-raiding, controlling broad territories as reserve pasture for their own herds.

The Antanosy, people of Anosy in the southeast corner, made significant contact with Portuguese and French visitors in the early seventeenth century. Temporarily mollified by the diplomacy of Etienne de Flacourt in 1648, they were never fully reconciled to the European colonists at Fort Dauphin (which they know as Taolanaro) or to the missionary activity that accompanied the settlers. In 1674, after thirty-two tense years, they expelled the remnants of France's colony. Antanosy are now often discovered in regions to the west and north, where they have migrated in groups in search of work.

The 600,000 Antaisaka traveled from their lower Menanara basin up the coast from Taolanaro; they are also found throughout Madagascar wherever labor has been needed. Likewise, their northern coastal neighbors, the Antaifasy and Zafisoro, frequently have to leave their limited bailiwicks around Farafangana, territory they once defended avidly against the Merina.

Farther north live the 400,000 Antaimoro, renowned as an ancient conduit for Islamic influence from coastal Arab contacts beginning at least as early as the fifteenth century. Islamic culture was translated and transmitted in Arabic script through a series of great books (*sorabe*), compositions of an aristocratic caste of intellectuals in this highly stratified society. Itinerant wise men (ombiassy) covered the island from Antaimoro country, giving advice to kings, including Andrianampoinimerina on his high plateau, and endowing local cultures with proverbial lore.

Northern neighbors of the Antaimoro, the Antambahoaka, inhabit the coffee-growing area around Mananjary. Their society is less tightly structured than the Antaimoro, and the penetration of Arab culture less enduring, but they, too, have developed under persistent influence from the oceanic east and north. Together, these southeastern coastal groups represent a vast transformer for people and ideas, political institutions and intelligentsia, throughout all Madagascar.

AUTHORITY OF ANCESTRAL TRADITION

Coherent yet diverse are the ritual, ceremonial, and philosophical forms through which an essentially peasant population communicates with its sources of vitality. This multifarious culture balances common beliefs—in personal kinship loyalties and the living proximity of lineage ancestors, in wealth measured by holdings of cattle, and in the integrity of the locality (often specified by ancestral tomb sites)—with the demands of external authority. The material forms assumed by that culture vary across the island, but without radical difference in meaning.

Throughout Madagascar, people define their own identities through a conjunction of kinship and locality. This character is expressed in language, religion, architecture, mythologies of fate, and priorities for the expense of personal energy.[12] Most important to the self are one's kin (*havana*), identified as people of a common environment, usually descended from an original migration (historical or mythical) that turned that locality into a homestead. Kinfolk are inhibited by the same mortal constraints (*fady*), destined for the same tomb; they are people to whom one entrusts one's land or cattle, who can be summoned in moments of need, who are bound by cords of politics and property. These lococentric affinities normally override differences of wealth or social class, and even of generation, education, and occupation.

Those considered as "others" may be classified variously as:

1. People from somewhere else living in "our" midst who remain outside the essential tomb while becoming compatriots in a common political unit; in Imerina and some other regions, acceptance of these "guest" residents (*vahiny*) represents an essential source of the fokon'olona[13]
2. Such obviously alien people (*vazaha*) as Europeans, Chinese, or South Asians
3. The more subtly "foreign" implantations of bourgeois or bureaucratic Malagasy who have come to the place recently as agents of a distant power—governmental, religious, technological, scientific, commercial (vazaha also)

Eventually, relations between the original families (*tompon'tany*, or masters of the land) and the first of these groups (vahiny) become socialized, natural, and necessary in a place; they may even evolve into havana, or family; at least, as the northwestern Sakalava told Gillian Feeley-Harnik, "strangers" turn into "friends."[14] Relations with vazaha (groups 2 and 3) are invariably products of coercion and resistance thereto. All vazaha are roughly identified with fanjakana—technically meaning "government," but in practice, any element of external establishment—including the district administrator; the priest, pastor, or missionary; the technical expert; the anthropologist; the schoolmaster; the trader; the gendarme.[15] These are the agents of municipality, the mythologized City. They come to impose new norms on rural life, to dissect cultural groups, and somehow to profit from their fragmentation.[16] As this crude typology suggests, the most tragic cleavage in contemporary Malagasy society separates westernized styles of urbanity from the traditional cultures of the rural localities, however much the latter may differ among themselves. The city is the foyer of modernity; it is believed to impose its thesis, sometimes called development, on the countryside, evidently for the city's own benefit.

Yet the fundamental focus of Malagasy personal loyalty is not the village community. A Malagasy is traditionally "at home" only in proximity to the family tomb, in the ancestral territory, or tanin'drazana. So strong is this symbolic matrix that Malagasy seem to live in two societies simultaneously—the profane everyday world in flux and the eternal unchanging, timeless dominion of the living dead. The ideal world of the dead remains only vaguely understood by their descendants in this world; hence its unpredictable, dan-

Traditional tombs and grave markers, near Morondava. Photo courtesy Service Général de l'Information de Madagascar.

gerous power. Only through ritual can that omnipresent power be partially conceived and controlled. Malagasy philosophy stresses the moral implications of all action, for a constant interpenetration of the two worlds imposes a strict responsibility for right behavior. Although ancestral intervention is always uncertain, any perverse or ambiguous behavior in this world introduces anxieties of guilt and retribution.[17]

In Imerina, studied by Maurice Bloch,[18] being creative or fertile entails mobilization of the power of the dead. Wisdom and fecundity—integrated here in the concept of *hasina*—consist in knowing and following the rules of the ancestors (*tenin'drazana*). Among the Betsimisaraka of the east coast portrayed by Gérard Althabe, villagers under external coercion tend to retreat, to coalesce in new "communities of the imagination" that transcend both lineage and ethnic particularities.[19] Coercion comes as much from Merina elites and other Malagasy vazaha (agents of the fanjakana) as from the progeny of distant continents.

To contrive contact with ancestral spirit, certain Malagasy groups have recourse to the ritual known as *tromba,* a form of religious transport identified in an early missionary work on the Sakalava.[20] The element of spirit possession in the tromba has been observed in other manifestations of Malagasy mysticism, including the *ramanenjana*, an atavistic attempt by followers of the royal religion of the late Ranavalona I in the early 1860s to dissuade her successor's court away from European and Christian influence.[21] Tromba is not the sole means for transcendantal control, however. Jacques Lombard has examined Sakalava sculpture and oral literature to discover the passionate aesthetic logic by which human beings seek influence over their destiny.[22] Similarly, Hamlet-like, the Betsileo, studied by P. H. DuBois, insist on the need to tame the errant spirits of the recent dead (*ambiroa*).[23] Perhaps even the kung fu cult prevailing among street youths in Antananarivo since the 1970s fulfills comparable needs in the urban version of community.

Malagasy tradition has been analyzed from Richard Andriamanjato's Christian vision of a guilt-driven soul and from Octave Mannoni's Freudian images of a humanity beleaguered by anxieties in its relationship to a demanding, uncompromising, yet enigmatic realm of the dead.[24] And yet, circumscribed as they are by omnipresent death—or better, by the omnipresent dead who paradoxically relieve their successors of the burden of death—Malagasy express true reverence for the life that is so scarce, so brief, so dependent on transcendant power. As followers of the Sakalava royalty expressed the mystery to Feeley-Harnik, "'Dead things have no life in them,' but ancestors do."[25]

Observing the Merina, Bloch characterized life in the actual world as "European time" in which a person must prepare for "Malagasy time" (eternity), into which the dead are integrated.[26] The clan (or "deme," as Bloch prefers) is dominated by particular elders in a clear hierarchy of rank and privilege. Once dead, however, the personality eventually dissolves into an undifferentiated quality of anonymous, bisexual ancestorhood. Individuals recently dead are kept distinctly in mind for several years, often until the ceremony of the *famadihana*, or turning of the dead. This is a highly festive familial occasion when selected ancestral remains are disinterred, brought into the common world, rewrapped, and returned in honor to the tomb.[27] Famadihana occurs by necessity whenever a family is prepared to bring home the corpse of a kinsperson who happened to die outside the tanin'drazana. That sense of "return to the tomb" is in fact the proper translation of the term famadihana; as Bakoly Domenichini-Ramiaramanana admonishes in a seldom-heeded philological distinction, the rewrapping of bodies already in the tomb *should* be called *famosan-damba*.[28]

Anything but morbid, as it may seem to Western perceptions, the famadihana is a complex ceremony of pious rejoicing, sheer play, and personal risk through contact with the powers of the dead. The ceremony links the clan together in life, reinforcing its fecundity and ensuring its continuity against the threat of death, into eternity. Thus, the centrality of the tomb in a Malagasy's personal identity.

> These tombs testify to a conception of eternity that is not just guaranteed by a single deity but also and perhaps above all by the family in its broadest sense. The extended family, the lineage, is where the living meet the dead and all the living to come as well; and the circuit is closed thanks to the presence of all their forebears as far back as can be conceived, even to God with all his children as long as they can be imagined, into the heart of the future. To honor your ancestors, to ensure your posterity, is already a way of taking your place in the eternity of the world.[29]

Eventually, the distinction of any individual dissipates and the tomb as pantheon becomes more important than the fate of its several evanescent inhabitants. Into anonymity they eventually go, but not into oblivion, for the tanin'drazana supplies vital connections to the heritage of ancestral action and to the future of an as-yet-unborn destiny.

In his classic treatise on the psychology of colonization, Mannoni interprets these relationships as a dependence complex. For Mannoni, natural Malagasy society consists of quasi-feudal clientele systems centering on indigenous patrons.[30] The European vazaha conquered and supplanted ancestors and elders in the authority structure of Malagasy dependency only to be perceived as willy-nilly abandoning their dependents during and after World War II.[31] The French had come to change Madagascar—to abolish slavery, monarchy, and superstition—thus assuming transcendant authority for the enslaved, superstitious subjects of the empire. When the historical Europeans betrayed their own weakness through a humiliating war, their mythic quality receded and with it their authority over the dependent Malagasy. This apparent abandonment invited a violent response, the revolt of 1947.

Although learned and insightful, Mannoni's analysis was limited by a colonial mentality that must posit an essentially infantile indigenous population requiring paternal authority for its survival. He thus distorts the complexity of Malagasy social psychology into a caricature of abject superstition, ignoring that society's political preference for collective autonomy, its ability to adapt, and its capacity for creative resistance to oppression. Seeing colonialism from its historical European perspective as dominion over the conquered, Mannoni appears unable to have understood the Malagasy conviction that governments and other such institutions were in fact parasitical *on the colonized*.[32]

Christian practice claims a majority of Malagasy today—and the entirety of Imerina—without having fully diverted this central allegiance from the tanin'drazana and the complex of rituals associated with it. A fertile ground for missionizing, Malagasy took readily to Protestant and Catholic liturgy, to the pragmatics of Christian schooling, and to church traditions of preaching. Christian festivals and ceremonies are folded compatibly into Madagascar's receptive spirituality. The Merina supreme deity, Andriamanitra, loaned his name to Christianity's God. The original paganism of the ancestor cults is for many adorned with Christian rationalism.

Nevertheless, the Malagasy myth of an ideal world of the dead who impinge on every aspect of the actual world of the living is a deeply etched version of animism; it endows natural and supernatural phenomena with social meaning. Manifestations of the myth are mystical, rhetorical, imagistic, informing all life's passages. So strong is this belief in the influence of the dead (even among westernized Malagasy) that Christian authority can only hope for stable blends with its own more explicit New Testament eschatology and its loving, punishing deity.[33] In fact, when Christianity confronted Malagasy tradition categorically, it was vigorously resisted as a foreign imposition—the object of violent persecutions under Ranavalona I and outbreaks of popular anti-Christian fanaticism thereafter.[34]

To protect the integrity of their own faith, Christians have had to be on constant guard against the perpetual Malagasy ethos of celebration, the pervasiveness of "idols" (*sampy*), the constant binding of taboos, premarital sexual trials, the extravagance of family festivities, and above all the apparent deification of ancestors in a mysterious, unarticulated eschatology.[35] Many early Malagasy Christians seem nonetheless to have acknowledged the value of a syncretic blend between the two antagonist cultures. They incorporated spirit possession, visions and dreams, and other manifestations of a sacred, mystical life into their testimonies of faith and conversion. Subsequently, Malagasy Christianity became urbanized, occidentalized, domesticated, and to some observers, impoverished.[36] Christian conversion also ended the Menabe Sakalava practice of adorning ancestral tombs with explicitly sexual sculptures (*volyhety*) as confirmation of the nexus between the dead and the reproductive vitality of the living.[37] By contrast, the great *aloala* pole sculptures of the Mahafaly graves farther south—less erotic and more responsive to everyday life—have been allowed to flourish and reinvigorate their style, much like Yoruba sculpture in Nigeria and Benin-Dahomey.[38]

European religion may have imposed a new sense of sin, but it has scarcely succeeded in taming all traditional observances into sedate passivity or middle-class piety. Malagasy marriages occur under complex rules of endogamy, property transfer, and prohibitions against incest. Ideal nuptial unions, contrived through elaborate, rhetorically rich negotiation, solidify the clan (*fianakavihana*). They enhance the labor supply available to family enterprise and they create new memberships and sometimes altered social rank for related tomb-families.[39] In traditional Malagasy society such ties carry as much weight as do common economic exchanges. But no Malagasy lives exclusively in the traditional society. All must inhabit two worlds at once, so that the virtues and responsibilities of kinship—from tomb to marriage to birth—must also apply to the "European," or vazaha, world of taxes and politics, with its intruders and agencies all representing another mythically conceived element, the fanjakana.

For many Malagasy boys, circumcision is obligatory, and although various explanations prevail for the ritual, Bloch interprets it among the Merina as the transmission of a transcendental force (lineage) into human action (fecundity). By vindicating male fecundity in a context of mortal risk and timeless order, circumcision turns around the terms of the famadihana, which reaffirm the dead as a power to transform and sustain life in the familial milieu.[40] Circumcision also acts to control what Malagasy understand as the erratic, savage, natural energy associated with animals and with the conquered Vazimba, especially their female dimension. Through the circumcision ritual, these forces of nature are channeled into sustained "growth fertility" associated with the ancestors. Far from Mannoni's colonial supineness, the circumcision myth refers back to the Merina ancestral conquest of nature—and of earlier ancestors. "The myth indissolubly merges the metaphysics of the symbolism with the exercise of military violence and the conquest of the Vazimba."[41]

As in the famadihana, marriage, circumcision, and other life passages link blessing and holiness with fertility—for human beings and for the natural environment. Thus religion accepts responsibility to control and focus natural potency, not to withdraw from or treat it in contemplative asceticism.[42] And yet, Bloch understands the ideological conclusion of the circumcision ritual as otherworldly and quiescent: "It is that this life is of little value, that it must be rejected, as far as is possible, and exchanged for the still transcendence where time had been vanquished by order and where therefore the relevance of birth, death and action has disappeared. It is only by this argument that power and violence can be made to appear necessary and desirable, and this applies to any power and violence that become indissolubly linked."[43]

In addition to family ritual, mediation between the temporal and eternal realms is ensured by the services of specialists. Diviners or healers, characterized by a variety of names, invoke powers of the transcendent world to transmit privileges or status in this world. Local tradition ascribes many of these powers to Islamic wisdom disseminated by Arabs or Arabic-speaking holy men (*ombiassa*), who functioned as kingmakers, magicians, and astrologers throughout the island.[44] Sorcery, a far different matter from divining, can be practiced by any person external to the group. Not to be confused with the functioning of charms or talismans (*sikidy*) and other medicines, or with spirit possession (tromba), sorcery involves deliberate witchcraft practiced against the blessing of fecundity. Recourse to talismans, divination, and sorcery all appear on the increase during the long period of tribulation traversed by Malagasy society of the 1980s.

Traditional Malagasy social life remains resilient, vital, buoyed by reference to the ideal world of the ancestors while under siege from modernity. Theoretically, tradition and modernity each produces a competing elite for the hierarchy. Controlling and interpreting the message of tradition is a proper responsibility of the elders, called *ray aman'dreny* (literally "father-and-mother," for they are thought to be at an age indifferent to sex and of virtually undifferentiated gender). This power of age should contest the politico-economic notables—village chiefs, party leaders, clergy, professionals, and technicians—who respond to the distant power impulses of the regimes of Antananarivo. In practice, the two elites often reinforce each other, especially when challenged by youth, by women, or by the landless.

In the actual world hierarchy established by tradition, most Malagasy societies maintain an elaborate caste structure. Among the Merina, *andriana* (nobles), *hova* (free commoners), *mainty* (literally blacks), and *andevo* (descendants of slaves) pass their respective heritages through endogamous practices.[45] Gender, age, parental status, and property all impose relative rank on individuals and family units. This status in turn determines access to family property and to local politics. In rural Imerina, committees of ray aman'dreny defend the rights of landed oligarchs. They control agendas of the fokon'olona, authenticating clan membership and inheritance, witnessing rites of passage, settling disputes between clans. These lineage lords may ally with administrative agents to keep an often sullen younger, poorer population in obedience to the fanjakana. Elsewhere, returned émigrés on the margins of society mediate between fanjakana and elders. Or the elders may insist on progress in the "old way," a cyclical return to a peasant-ancestor golden age. In any case, since the rituals of religion validate the authority of the elders as people closest to ancestral status, the restlessness of disenfranchised young Malagasy has become palpable.[46] This agitation of the underclass provides the foundation for the revolution of 1972.

Vigorous as they are, Madagascar's self-sufficient, conservative, patriarchal systems are easily destabilized from outside. They presuppose cyclical structures of history, where technology remains ancestral and celebrations of family solidarity may claim all surplus production. Even exogamous marriages create new status problems in the actual world. Intrusions of competitiveness and capital accumulation disturb the hierarchies sanctioned by ancestral tradition. Rural development strategy, whether conducted directly by government angecies or by external contractors, requires the fabrication of a new need for household money to pay taxes or school fees, to obtain simple commodity necessities, or to supplement cattle wealth in financing family celebrations. The strategy is to then convert that need into a market economy with diversified production, year-round employment, money exchanges, and technological progress. If the intrusion is supported by fanjakana or vazaha (including the church) the closed subsistence system tends to resist. If, as in the cases studied by Jean Pavageau in the 1970s, all the authorities act collaboratively, they marginalize the young and other natural allies for change, thus expressing a contradiction between productive forces and means of production.[47]

Although not unreceptive to improvements in living standards, Malagasy peasant tradition inhibits changes that seem of doubtful security. "The risk of innovation stands opposed to the security of the given. For the peasant, closed in a universe of poverty, the risk is intolerable; it's better to limit his ambitions to what suffices than to aim at a doubtful abundance."[48]

Moreover, the risk of change and especially of failure are not merely economic. As Prats's exhaustive study demonstrates, a peasantry cannot be expected to come into contact with a new, value-laden technology without envisioning unacceptable threats to deep-seated custom; it does not unhesitatingly pass into modernization.[49] Georges Balandier calls the results a "war of deculturation."[50] To try innovation and fail would prostrate the Malagasy soul in profound guilt before offended ancestral precedent—the *tsiny* of Andriamanjato's analysis. It is therefore no simple task persuading Malagasy to jeopardize their place in a coherent, cosmic system for the sake of mere economic gain in a very short earthly life; that decision entails far greater sacrifice than government insurance schemes or World Bank loans are likely to cover. For the Betsimisaraka of Althabe's research, money itself is only marginally useful; it serves mainly to pay off the foreigners, not to expand the possibilities of life.[51]

Of course, Malagasy do pay attention to their fortunes in this prosaic world. To subsist under economic pressure, peasants extend their plots to mountain slopes and other marginal terrain (*tanety*) or hire themselves out as day laborers or craftspeople to wealthier neighbors. But many will sell cattle or even borrow money rather than pull up stakes or try risky intensive technology. In Imerina, the very principle of tanin'drazana obstructs subdivisions and alienation of what is in theory communal property owned by the eternal clan. In the economy of cultural preference, virtually all production goes to direct consumption and family prestige; it is fanjakana that requires a portion for taxes, school fees, and church tithes. The decade of the 1960s had already witnessed stagnant per capita production in this closed, repetitive world of tradition. Later years saw even worse records of productivity.

Almost all parts of the island have become accustomed to a money economy superimposed on the traditional kinship-based mode of production in what Jean-Claude Rouveyran terms "transitional agriculture." Seldom, however, does the market economy supersede the subsistence premise of the peasant mentality, even under the best prospects for coffee and other export crops. It can only force compromises—for instance, in the leasing of marginal land for cash crops, a search for part-time remunerated employment, application of skills in craftswork, and marketing of surplus production for cash rather than bartered goods. This is the bargain that underpins all hope of rural development conceived by realistic agencies of fanjakana.

Some technological innovation has been proven successful, hence acceptable, within consumption values as well as production. In house-building and other commodities of high display, for example, Western forms have become progressively adopted even by traditional Malagasy families, sometimes to the impoverishment of a unique folk culture.[52] The price of transition, then, is ambiguous and high. It entails perpetual decisions and constant temptations of guilt as the rural family compromises between an original culture of stability, human solidarity, and mutual aid and an alluring new ideology of progress, development, enterprise, wages, and market competition.

While seeking resolution of the two contending ways of life, much agony is endured. Social disparities are aggravated, population pressures impoverish the already poor, and the landless and restless leave for areas where their labor will be remunerated. Defection of the young represents a second phase of resistance to established authority, for they perceive the ideology of *fihavanana* (community) as hypocritical. The young tend to blame their economic suffocation on the rituals and obligations of the patriarchal culture that controls a closed rural society for the benefit of the affluent elders. Pavageau concludes: "Social differentiation marks the relations among residential groups; social organization imposes on each the hierarchical and the behavioral models of dependence; political organization accentuates the relations between dominators and dominated; problems of property reinforce familial antagonisms; economic organization based on kinship conceals relations of exploitation behind the mask of an ideology of harmony."[53]

By living frugally and furtively in the cities, finding work at exploitative wages, the young migrants can hope to acquire resources for the purchase of prestige in their home villages. They shuttle constantly between the tough, volatile margins of urbanity and the inhospitable rural systems of family tra-

Traditional houses on hillside, Antananarivo. Photo by Gay Kuester, © The Chicago Zoological Society.

dition. In their villages, they help put those systems under divisive bombardments of money, schooling, Christian morality, and fanjakana policy. In town, less successful youth are impelled into public or antisocial action, some of it violent in the extreme.

Others must leave the home country permanently, for traditional technology has sorely wasted the earth. However traumatic, labor and colonist migration has long been a fact of Malagasy life. Dependent on marginal land and diminishing returns on labor and other resources in the tanin'drazana, the families do eventually colonize and populate new localities. Pressures to move out, to search for new opportunities and new land (still abundant in the west and midwest) overcome the cultural tendency to remain close to home. The Antaisaka, Betsileo, and Antanosy have become habituated to mobility, and it is such newcomers who eventually integrate into local communal institutions as vahiny without actually joining the established tombs of the resident families. New demands are then placed upon nuclear communities to ensure security through neighborhood and proximity.

New arrivals not integrated by marriage find affiliation and dialogue in the adapted institution of fokon'olona, an "as if" clan based on proximity rather than lineage. Often politicized and manipulated, the fokon'olona and its process of decision (*dinam-pokonolona*) have changed structure and constitution through the past two centuries. King Andrianampoinimerina ordained and mobilized fokon'olona for local security and political control, thus institutionalizing the tension between local options and fanjakana centralism.

Merina castes, also reorganized under Andrianampoinimerina, contained several clans, each theoretically descended from a common notable forebear and associated with that ancestor's tomb. Subsequent experience extended the *foko* concept to heterogeneous communities outside the Merina heartland.

> Retrenchment of the *foko*, their geographic isolation, their exceedingly pronounced if not absolute endogamy, seem to us a typically peasant reaction to insecurity. Threatened from every quarter, often regrouped in a place much more by fortunes of war than by a community of ancestors, the farmers were obliged spontaneously to seek to propagate ties of kinship among themselves, the only real ties they recognized. Forming closed groups united by an extremely complex network of alliances capable of integrating strangers seeking refuge was a protection against the external world, but also an assurance against the local lord, their theoretical protector; which heads should fall in a group where authority is entirely diluted?[54]

While serving primarily to ensure local security, the fokon'olona institution has acquired through time an attribute of popular (decentralized) sovereignty. It survives today as a hierarchical instrument of local landholders, party leaders, and specialists in a heterogeneous space.[55] When local needs are perceived to be incompatible with changes imposed by a tutelary fanjakana (the alien external establishment), strategies of resistance spring up, calling on both village solidarity (fokon'olona, fihavanana) and the narrower, tighter kinship of the tomb (fianakavihana). Even when the agents of change are Malagasy, their prospects for real dialogue with the village universe are inhibited by their very status[56]—hence, the frustrations of government service in the provinces even after the departure of the colonial French. Writing in the late 1960s but portraying a sorry record that persists to this day, Althabe deplores the failure of those services to change relations between power and subjects:

> Independence should have been able to trace a new path to avoid the current crisis; a forum for dialogue between the two parties could have replaced this perpetuation of the power of domination. Nothing of the kind occurred; the power created by the foreigners was preserved like an immovable monolith, the agents operating it being Malagasy. Nothing is more pitiful than the efforts over these last years to transcend domination while retaining it; moreover, failure has apparently discouraged these efforts and unfettered domination has returned.[57]

The result once again is a retreat from the shambling authority of this world into rituals of reassurance from the other, more durable, world.

LANDSCAPE OF CLASSES AND MINORITIES

Madagascar's class structure is a product of the succession of regimes imposed over centuries on cities and villages. The westernized Merina upper-middle class, mainly Protestant, is composed of a few score of tightly knit families overlapping the andriana (technically, noble) and hova castes. Urbanized by the pull of the capital city over the past century, the eminent andriana and hova families still owe their wealth to rice-growing rural property, imperial adventure, and slave trading under the Merina regime. The andriana happened to enjoy kinship with the royal family, and some hova descend from the officials who made policy under the last three queens (1863–1896). Together, the families belonging to the so-called Club of Forty-Eight owe their privilege to the outcome of several power struggles within the eighteenth- and nineteenth-century dynasty. These political successes endowed them with control of land and city real estate, as well as access to learned professions and international commerce.

A much broader hova bourgeoisie occupies urban professions, business, education, the Christian clergy, and civil service niches, often with contradictory political allegiances toward the radical Left. Middle-class status manifests itself in the acquisition of French and the capacity to season one's Malagasy-language discourse with appropriate idioms from the vocabulary of colonial mastery. These signals retained their validity even during the period of revolutionary nationalism after 1975. As Raison observes, the Malagasation of the school curriculum in that period ironically served even further to divide the dominant Francophones from the vernacular-bound subordinate classes.[58]

To face such realities, authorities have restored French as a language of instruction in primary and secondary schools, demonstrating the real depth of colonial experience. French colonial policy had clearly aimed at the selective assimilation of elites and technically qualified subelites, endowing the island with equivalent lycée and vocational education and allowing university study in France for a few. Eventually, of course, French institutions were installed directly in the evolving territory. The policy was rationalized partly in service to an articulated labor market, partly as a political reward for cooperation with administrative options. It continued under the first republic.[59] But cultural demarkation of Malagasy elites transcends the imposition of French norms; the nineteenth-century Merina aristocracy acquired facility in English and a library of London Missionary Society religious publications as a sign (which their descendants continue to display) of their social preeminence.

A Lumpenproletariat of "small folk" (*madinika*) takes up at least one-third of the urban population. Incited to political action, marginalized and pauperized youth readily joined one of the most powerful of the revolutionary forces of the 1970s, the Zatovo orin'asa anivon'ny Madagasikara (ZOAM). Disappointed at ZOAM's incorporation into the governmental coalition as a component of the MFM party, they are still vigorously unreconciled to their fate. At least half of Madagascar's urban population is neither upper nor middle class nor madinika; these are wage-earning families, dependent on government jobs and food subsidies, depressed by inflation, jeopardized by efficiency measures, descending on an ever-lower standard of living.

In parallel to the Merina class structure, the provincial elites distinguished themselves from rural and semiurban clanspeople under both the French and the republican regimes. Control of land and access to administrative privilege represent dialectical factors in the emergence of a stable class of notables under the three regimes of the twentieth century. At independence in 1960, the loyal classes of rural notables—trusted dependents and intermediaries, mild home-rule agitators under the French, collaborators in the overseas-oriented economy—inherited power under Tsiranana's Social Democratic Party (PSD). To sustain their leverage on the electorate, these new national elites promptly exploited the historical antagonism of Merina and côtiers. As Chaigneau concludes, "The ethnic theme represents a readily maintained and utilized tool for the various political parties that were anxious to conserve their regionalist constituencies parallel with an official line advocating national unity."[60]

The class structure of urban and rural elites is augmented by a variety of other middle-class residents with distinct economic and social missions that identify them clearly as vazaha or fanjakana. French colonial policy opened Madagascar to a variety of enterprising foreigners—metropolitans seeking fortunes in the imperial diaspora, Creoles from crowded mountainous Réunion eager for vacant land and colonial jobs, Muslim labor volunteers from Gujarat and Bombay in northwest India, Comoreans fleeing the hopeless poverty of their nearby islands colonized earlier in the nineteenth century; assiduous Cantonese. The Chinese colony actually dates from 1862, when the Merina monarchs imported labor to build roads and the railway between Antananarivo and the east coast; many laborers thereupon remained to enter village trade.[61]

While the other new minorities fanned out into towns and villages throughout the great island, Comoreans moved into the major cities of the north, becoming tradespeople, manual laborers, messengers, domestic servants, and guardians for European families. Their numbers grew to 43,500 in the early 1970s; more than half of them lived in Mahajanga, where the remnants of the Antalaotse colony remained in business. Occupying jobs sought by urbanizing Malagasy, the Comoreans were brutally set upon in December 1976; at least 121 were killed and 17,000 repatriated to their desperate island homelands.[62] Since then, the colony has been substantially restored in both numbers and economic vitality.

Of the 50,000 French in Madagascar in 1962, the majority were settlers and colonial employees from the Overseas Department of Réunion. Here, Mannoni's psychoanalytical approach seems to correspond most intriguingly to reality. Creoles and other metropolitans surely did come to the island not only with economic opportunity in mind but for the psychological satisfactions of cultural dominance. These motives inevitably cast the colonial class into exploitative roles, creating fundamental and mutually incomprehensible antagonisms between them and the colonized.[63] Despite official assimilation rhetoric, social and personal contact remained rare among Malagasy and Europeans. There was little intermarriage in Madagascar—more frequent for Malagasy in France than for French on the island, and seldom for European *women*. When the colonizer began to weaken during and after World War II, the response of the Malagasy was to attack them for abandoning their role; hence the great uprising of 1947.

Partly because of their putative disinterestedness, French advisers in the first republic were systematically preferred by Tsiranana over their Malagasy competitors and counterparts, thus aggravating charges of neocolonialism.[64] During the decade after the events of 1972, the resident French community was reduced from 31,000 to 18,000, where it has remained.

The French language penetrated far less deeply in linguistically autarchic Madagascar than it did in most other parts of overseas France—western and central Africa, the Antilles, and the smaller Indian Ocean islands. Ombiassy had been publishing Malagasy texts in Arabic script for five centuries, and the Merina dialect was alphabetized for official and pedagogical use by British missionaries in the 1820s. The central plateau culture thereupon became the island's lingua franca, enforced by dynastic armies and administration. For present generations, French serves primarily to identify cultural class, and English is rarer still.[65]

Reaching 18,000 by the mid-1970s, the Indo-Pakistanis (popularly called Karana, or people of the Koran) had invested savings in land and, like the Chinese, were determined to stay in the great island. Yet, unlike the Chinese, the South Asians (many of them stateless) have remained largely endogamous and exclusive in their living styles, even when only one such family dwells in a remote village surrounded by Malagasy. There were serious riots in early 1987 on the plateaus and in Toliara against Karana merchants accused of profiteering at the expense of the impoverished population. Fearing Khomeinism as much as communism in the decade of the 1980s, the Roman Catholic press had editorialized just before the 1987 riots against the expanding role of Madagascar's Muslims.[66]

Although losing some of their assets under the nationalizations of the mid-1970s, the hardy Indo-Pakistanis maintained important, viable import-export and industrial businesses throughout the second republic. These include the Sotema textile plant, one of the rare manufacturing successes on the great island. More recently, Karana have benefited from the collapse of various government economic schemes. They have weathered their internal exile and begun using capital and marketing facilities to pick up pieces of the disintegrating national economy.

Like the smaller Indo-Pakistani tradespeople in the west and south, Chinese merchants in the east operate effective networks of sale and purchase. Offering credit and barter loans on sustained personal bases, they are able to command peasant loyalties beyond those captured by more rigid government-imposed schemes for rural development. Hence, their return was welcomed upon liberalization of the domestic agricultural market between 1985 and 1988.[67]

Since the revolution of the early 1970s, Madagascar has felt the impact of other overseas minorities—Russians and North Koreans bearing socialist expertise; new groups of transient African, Asian, and Arab partners in technology; and visiting experts from anywhere including an international civil service purporting to convert Malagasy institutions from their transitional postcolonial status to modern efficacy. Apart from their respective technical fields, the influence of these cosmopolitans has been superficial. They represent a relatively disinterested foreign presence compared to the French (or the Merina, for that matter), but their efficacy has yet to be proved. Only accidentally assigned to the great island, these neovazaha enjoy minimal cultural penetration. Language has altered little under their influence except on the margins of bureaucratic patois; music, architecture, advertising imagery, production crafts, street life, all take external intrusions in self-confident Malagasy stride.

IMPACTS AND TRANSFORMATIONS IN MALAGASY SOCIETY

Caught in the tensions between a resilient indigenous culture and its enemy—the succession of nineteenth- and twentieth-century regimes—virtually all institutions of Malagasy life have undergone intense politicization. Access to and exercise of power depend on the channels of the educational system, labor organizations, churches, women's and family-interest associations, and of course the press and the military estates of modern Malagasy society. Yet those institutions never quite absorb the full political energies of a people committed to action and judgment through what Maureen Covell calls "networks of personal relationships."[68] It's in kinship and other affinities that Malagasy find the sustenance to resist the impositions of fanjakana.

Education and Youth

Traditional Madagascar has always maintained its sturdy, effective ways of acculturating young people and initiating them into their social roles. Starting in 1820, however, when a score of young nobles from King Radama's court were escorted by British missionaries to school in England and Mauritius, education has been defined in European terms. As in most societies, Malagasy families covet access to schools for the sake of personal and communal advancement; government has promoted the system as a way of ensuring the formation of privileged resources for the state. After decades of obfuscation, this distinction was finally made overt in 1981 by the Marxist rector of Madagascar's national university: "The [socialist] university in its very essence is an organism dedicated to serving the objectives of state power in higher education."[69] From the rural or urban family viewpoint, advancement in school creates a form of "intellectual capital"[70] that justifies sacrifice. The revolutionary state invested massively in education, endeavoring in the 1970s to decentralize geographically, to open access to all, and to promote mass adult instruction. Although many schools have closed for lack of resources, the beneficial effect of mass education is palpable in Madagascar today.

Whereas the pervasive culture of the island is intrepidly oral, the practice of and respect for letters runs deep. Antaimoro civilization produced Koranic scholars on the east coast as early as the fifteenth century. From 1818 under Radama I, the London Missionary Society was teaching aristocratic youth at Antananarivo and Toamasina, and the Jesuits were operating schools on Nosy Be and the northwest mainland. By the end of Radama's reign in 1828, over 100 missionary schools had taught an estimated 4,000 Malagasy to read and write. From this time, Protestant missionaries also translated and disseminated the Bible and undertook investigations of the great island's natural history and ethnography. On its return from banishment in 1861 after the anti-European reign of Ranavalona I, the LMS began training Malagasy in normal schools and seminaries; the Jesuits followed suit five years later at Antananarivo. A Royal School of Medicine opened in 1875 under British aegis.

Galliéni as governor-general secularized education and converted the system to French norms, permitting some Protestant and Catholic schools to continue. Practical and vocational courses prepared Malagasy as needed for the agricultural, commercial, administrative, and proto-industrial trades of a new economy. In 1896, the British medical academy was replaced by a five-year Ecole de Médicine, which served until it proved incapable of further reform in 1978. Sons of notables and provincial chiefs studied administration, law, agriculture, commerce, and pedagogy from 1897 at Le Myre de Villers postsecondary school, converted into a teacher-training institute in 1958. Good lycées were open to those Malagasy who qualified for French citizenship, but they were few in number and predominantly Merina in origin.

In spite of its tribal policy, France had little choice but to allow most of the secondary and all postsecondary schools to locate at the capital. The colonial government and certain missions provided scholarships for Malagasy to study abroad (almost entirely in France), but until the end of World War II, most had to be content with what they could learn on the island. This was true of artists and other creative people. The greatest of Madagascar's many poets, Jean-Joseph Rabearivelo, whose work was translated into a dozen languages during his lifetime, was never able to travel outside the island. Constant rejection of his requests for travel stipends contributed to the depression that ended in suicide for this gifted publisher's clerk in 1937 at the age of thirty-six.

"Decolonisation in amiability"[71] found France and the new Malagasy republic willing in 1960 to negotiate continuity for the independent island's educational system. A university had been created under French academic auspices in the late 1950s. During the following decade, its standard *facultés* (law, science, letters, medicine) were joined by other branches of study in vocational schools and several new institutes—administration, public works, engineering, agronomy, business administration and management, applied linguistics, art and archaeology, mathematical research and pedagogy, oceanography, and telecommunications. The diplomas of these institutions were fully recognized in France, and for a decade all academic officers and most of the regular faculty were French. The Malagasy financial contribution to higher education rose from a negligible level at the outset to roughly two-thirds of the French subsidy by 1969. Military and police academies were founded outside the university, as were certain French research centers.

Following the custom for ex-colonies, two-thirds of the university students persistently preferred intellectually prestigious degrees in letters and law to the more utilitarian channels in the sciences and technical vocations.[72] This ratio placed personal inclinations and pedagogical freedom into direct confrontation with the state's purpose for maintaining the system. Hence, the productivity of social investment in education remained low. Moreover, the attrition rate was severe; only 35 to 40 percent of baccalaureate-holders actually graduated with university degrees. Women represented only slightly more than one-fourth of the student population of the first republic.

Despite the manipulation of admissions criteria and curricula, student nationalism burgeoned during the period of academic radicalism in the late 1960s. Supported by militant faculty unions (affiliated with the French intellectual Left), the Federation of Student Associations (FAEM) even demanded renegotiation of the bilateral accords from which its own members were benefiting. This nationalist campaign provoked a conservative backlash. Loyalist students, chiefly from the coastal areas, displayed greater faith in the PSD system (or in their prospects of advancement within it); they were joined by Malagasy technical trainees (*stagiaires*) who were older and usually already employed within that system. But the Merina-dominated nationalist groups called most of the shots.

After the 1972 revolution, the university and the Education Ministry were nationalized and the agreements with France renegotiated. The university refracted in June 1973 into six regional institutions with democratized admissions and governance policies, thus enhancing access in the provinces. The connection between education and bureaucracy became far tighter, however, as socialist academics found their way into the state apparatus.

Guaranteeing all Malagasy a basic education, the Ratsiraka regime provided for a five-year elementary cycle within the village community (fokontany), followed for as many students as possible by four years of combined technical and general studies at middle schools (General Education Centers, or C.E.G.) in district centers (*firaisana*), and a three-year lycée in major towns (*fivondronona*). Two years of national service, including three months of military training, became mandatory before university study could begin. Adult education and recycling opportunities for those who had left school were also expanded.

The new concept of higher education instituted under Ratsiraka in the late 1970s regarded students as apprentice servants of the revolution. Their education was avowedly ideological: "The educational system is conceived essentially to form operating specialists for the construction of a socialist society, and to disseminate socialist ideology among the youth."[73] Institutions might function without state hindrance provided they observed the principles of the revolutionary charter. A substantial proportion of the most volatile Malagasy population remained "parked" at the six university centers. There they preferred to stay for want of remunerative alternatives in the job market, and there many guardians of order would just as soon have them remain.

So strong was the revolution's commitment to education that by 1985, in the depths of systematic depression, virtually 100 percent of Malagasy children were attending elementary school. Thirty-six percent of them went on to secondary school (43 percent of the boys, 30 percent of the girls). Six university campuses absorbed 38,000 students, compared to 6,611 in 1970–1971, 10,000 in 1978. Many were embarking on interminable cycles of repetitions and course transfers. Private (mostly church-affiliated) education remained in place while localities went on campaigns to build and equip new public schools. By the 1975–1978 period, education was obtaining 20 percent of a hard-pressed national budget. The number of elementary schools nearly doubled in five years from 1975; the middle schools almost quadrupled in number and the high schools (lycées) more than doubled, turning out 11,206 graduates in 1980, seven times as many as in 1972. So the system, laudable in itself, began producing far more graduates at every level than the economy could absorb; personal and social purposes were at loggerheads.[74]

This expansion was occurring in a rapidly growing population, most of which was under the age of twenty. The quality of schooling received by these young people left much to be desired. Faced by shortages of trained teachers and appropriate facilities, the Malagasy who heretofore had had no hope of education were submitting to a truncated, aborted, and disappointing process. Teachers had to be mass-produced through obligatory national service. The privileged persisted in sending their children to superior institutions, mostly by now in France or Réunion, absorbing a considerable cost to sustain the gap between themselves and the newly enschooled mass. Thus, commitments to egalitarian principles operated ironically against their very objectives. Madagascar's rapid democratization, mobilization of untrained diploma-holders, a language policy placing premature stress on Malagasy, and the confusions of several superimposed systems only aggravated the very social cleavage that the revolution had aimed at liquidating—the cleft between the European-educated privileged and the mass of minimally schooled Malagasy. As Charles Cadoux and Jean du Bois de Gaudusson wrote in 1985,

> Secondary and university education ... remain at the center of preoccupations, like the Achilles heel of the regime. The three goals defined in 1972—Malagasation, democratization, decentralization—encounter practical and financial obstacles (the cost of buildings and job creation in spite of obligatory National Service which assigns young secondary school graduates to teaching), as well as the galloping increase in student numbers, the aspirations of pupils and their families, the stagnation (if not absence) of job openings in the economy. What happened is a kind of flight forward which causes despair among some and serves as rationalization or pretext for others. But what government confronted by so difficult a problem could do (much) better?[75]

Even today, as ministries cope with imperious austerities, the burden of scholarships on the state budget seems ineluctable, for even tentative students demand education, sometimes violently, as a civic right. Since 1977, students have also regularly demonstrated against official manipulation of the educational process: Authorities have raised examination standards to curb the number of students graduating into the ranks of the unemployed, for instance, and have made efforts to cull a few dozen inactive matriculants from the state scholarship rolls. During the 1980s, the university's residential Cité Ankatso outside Antananarivo became a kind of autarchic commune, featuring herds of livestock, impromptu laundries, and sales of food pilfered from the school's own stocks.[76]

Although the worst of such aberrations have ended, the central and regional universities remain in crisis. Built and equipped for 26,000 students, the six campuses absorbed 37,000 in 1993, most of them living on scholarships equivalent to $1.00 a day; although deemed inadequate by recipients, that subsidy represented almost twice the minimum wage rate prevailing in the economy. Students at Toamasina simply stopped attending classes in early 1993, and even later in the year, hapless provincial administrators were confessing inability to resolve their grievances. As social pressures impinge, instructional resources diminish; the 1993 university budget of 20 billion FMG (ca. $11 million) was about equally divided between social services and pedagogy and research. The consequences are felt in a weakening of both educational quality and confidence in the system and its precious diplomas. No wonder, then, that only 10 percent of eligible students complete their degrees, often consuming eight to ten years in the effort—and that the number of candidates for the baccalaureate (ensuring university access) has been declining in recent years, along with rates of success in that examination (below 20 percent in 1992). Understandably, World Bank experts are reported to be recommending a two-year hiatus to reconstruct a completely new system of higher education.[77]

These tensions reflect a deeper alienation among Malagasy youth over at least a century of submission to uncongenial authorities. Their alienation arises in the cities and countryside both as outright revolt (in 1896, 1916, 1947, 1972, 1987, 1991) and in organized criminal gang activity, rural brushfires, and other volatile antisocial behavior. Unsatisfactory progress toward nationalist objectives in higher education kindled the 1971 urban protests that burgeoned into revolution a year later.[78] In 1972, a sudden, sociologically rare alliance between student insurgents and the Lumpenproletariat of Antananarivo brought down the Tsiranana government.

For a time that alliance sustained an important new radical party, the KIM (Action Committee of the Protest Movement). In September 1984, authorities sought to ban the capital city's numerous kung fu clubs, an urban Boxerlike form of martial protest inspired among slum youth by imported cinema from Hong Kong. The kung fu cult was officially regarded as a potentially subversive distraction from revolutionary discipline. These popular clubs persisted, however, and in December of that year they were physically attacked by the AREMA-affiliated Tanora Tonga Saina (TTS, Youth Aware of Responsibilities), a vigilante group often compared with Haiti's *tontons macoutes*. At least 100 people were killed in several days of rioting while authorities looked on apparently undisturbed by the spectacle of superfluous young men decimating their own ranks.[79]

In the provinces, Pavageau's description of a marginalized, disdainful, inarticulate youth, deprived of land and of participation in decisions, still holds true.[80] Pavageau shows poignantly, for instance, how adults became suspicious of a quasi-autonomous social club of village youth that parodied rituals of its elders, fostered diverse cultural values, and operated with little social or gender discrimination. Persecution of this organization by the elders aggravated the despair of its members. This chronic anomie tends to drive young people to towns where opportunities are more abundant and certainly more stimulating, if seldom very wholesome from society's standpoint.

The Malagasy educational system remains in high flux today, with flagrant gaps between rhetorical purpose and substantive achievement. Campaigns for universal schooling raised the adult literacy rate to 80 percent, but the economy failed to provide application for those admirable new skills. Moreover, as in some Arab countries, the existence of a noncolonial national language proved disastrously tempting. The late 1970s witnessed hopeful mass conversions of pedagogy from French into Malagasy without the capacity to train teachers or provide instructional materials of quality in the new medium. After that brief, unhappy experiment in educational decolonization, French was restored as a language of instruction in secondary and higher education; it is now returning to primacy in primary schools. By 1980, the University of Madagascar had over 200 government-employed instructors from France (compared with 160, two-thirds the entire faculty, in 1970–1971). The secondary system absorbed 700–800 French teachers, about the same level as in 1972, but four times the number remaining in 1974. But in the process of restoration, a generation of elites has been subject to deficient instruction in both languages.

The overlap of imported systems caused almost as much confusion in the revolutionary educational process as the debacle of Malagasation. On upper echelons, especially at the Ecole Normale Supérieure (the highest teacher-training institute), conventional French pedagogy encountered contradictions from more politicized Malagasy and Soviet education. There were fifty Soviet faculty members in 1982. Monoglot for the most part, East European teachers became ghettoized, their techniques and conceptions clashing with the traditional French and with the autonomy-seeking Malagasy spirit. In 1986, to counter excessive French influence and to create principles of socialist selection in the recruitment of elites, the USSR increased scholarship traffic to Moscow (already high at 2,000) and helped establish a Higher Institute of Political Studies (Institut Supérieur de l'État).

Still, by 1991 most Soviet and East European efforts had withered on the vine. Madagascar's system was left to plot its restoration to the Francophone family, but without clear definitions of the relationships between student aspirations and national purpose. As a French professor at the university had remarked in the late 1970s, "The final systems are still more or less in search of themselves."[81] That verdict holds true in 1993 as a new regime seeks to mobilize youth for social service without applying the second republic's transparent veneers of ideology—but also without commanding the quantity of resources demanded by genuinely democratic institutions.

Labor

Until the mid-1970s, Madagascar's labor movement reflected the political pluralism of the first republic and the tendency, inherited from France, for labor organizations to correspond to major political parties. At the end of the Tsiranana era in 1971, union membership was estimated at 100,000, double the number at independence a decade earlier. Virtually all the movement was urban, with greatest numerical strength in the civil service, including the government-operated railway and postal and telephone services. Membership was shared among five associations; most numerous was the social democratic Malagasy Labor Confederation (CMT); spawned by the SFIO (Section Française de l'Internationale Ouvrière) with 40,000 members, a potential mass neutralized by the organization's close affiliation with Tsiranana's PSD regime. The Catholic Christian Workers' Syndicate (SEKRIMI) group, created by the French Christian Democratic Movement (MRP), claimed 30,000. The communist-created FISEMA (in the image of France's General Confederation of Labor, CGT), held 20,000 workers; affiliated with the island's crypto-Marxist AKFM, FISEMA was the most dynamic in ideology, journalism, and political activism.

These labor clusters, thin as they were, seldom spoke to each other. Employers were easily able to divide and rule, hire and fire, without consulting them. With a few notable exceptions, none of the unions or central organizations conducted vigorous job activity, collective bargaining, or boycotts. When prospects arose for a study tour of the United States in the mid-1960s, the unions could not agree even to discuss a joint delegation; the idea was dropped as too costly.

Never powerful in an essentially unorganizable rural society, the unions did contest individual worker grievances and, especially after independence, the general rights of Malagasy labor to claim jobs occupied by Europeans and by Réunionnais Creoles. Although operating in mild antagonism to employers and overseas market interests, the unions were consistently regarded by wage-earning and rural Malagasy as part of fanjakana, an obliging if slightly more cantankerous agent of exploitation. Indeed, this assimilation of organized labor into the political apparatus became documented with the triumph of the PSD in the early 1960s and with the Revolutionary Charter, which succeeded it in the mid-1970s. Party leaders and advisers were frequently drawn from the ranks of labor; regimes regarded themselves as authentic representatives of the common person, not as partners in dialogue with, let alone adversaries of, a syndical interest.

In the period of Ratsiraka's ascendancy, unions commanded less than a third of the island's wage earners, and they were no less politicized than the educational system. To operate, they had to affiliate with a party in the government's National Front for the Defense of the Revolution (FNDR), preferably the president's own all-embracing AREMA party. This favored party's Syndicat Révolutionnaire Malgache (SEREMA), whose principal function was transmission of party ideology to the working class, absorbed more than 60 percent of the organized labor force of the 1980s. For its part, the AKFM lost control over the once vigorous FISEMA in 1976. Its remaining union affiliates, together with small allies of MONIMA (based mainly in Toliara), the UDECMA's Catholic unions in Toamasina, and the Vonjy groups in the southeast, agitated for marginal, party-bound purposes within the revolutionary charter.[82] Another charter, governing relations within the socialist enterprises, paid respect to conditions of work and the rights of labor—an institution to be consulted in the process of policy formation. But it allowed labor no rights of participation in industrial decisions or power to wield in counterpoise to the managerial bureaucracy. The enterprises never became socialist.[83]

Vigorous in public attacks on policies inimical to labor interests, the non-AREMA unions did what they could for workers under Ratsiraka. They were handicapped by intense competition for virtually every job among a desperately unemployed population. The port of Toamasina was paralyzed by a strike for eleven days in January 1986. Government had insisted the port was overstaffed and that the state had lost 1.5 billion FMG in five years; layoffs were the only answer.

This was the first major confrontation in a series of shocks suffered by the workforce under the IMF-enforced structural adjustment program. Structural adjustment entailed privatization of state enterprises, reduction of public payrolls, elimination of government subsidies, and other liberalization policies designed to create a market economy where labor would have to compete. Ultimately, labor could no longer tolerate the pressure of job losses and declining living standards. Some subsequent social relief permitted by international donors had not yet taken hold. And it was labor that threatened Ratsiraka most seriously in a cascade of highly successful strikes during June and July 1991, bringing government operations to a standstill, threatening the viability of the private sector, and forcing the president to negotiate serious social and political changes.

Labor-management troubles persisted into the third republic's debut, and union support refracted over a wide rainbow of parties contesting the June 1993 legislative elections.[84] It remains to be seen whether the working class will exert a concerted influence on policy in the new regime. President Zafy, Prime Minister Ravony, and their ministers came to power considerably indebted to labor for forcing the Ratsiraka state into a losing endgame. Still, some 200,000 youths continue to pour into a saturated job market each year, and the pressure of their demands helps force wages down. Moreover, employment expansion depends in large measure on the growth of export-oriented industries in the government's export-processing zones (EPZs), and that growth in turn relies on the availability of *cheap* labor.

Religion

Traditional religion in Madagascar is identical with traditional culture; ancestral civilization determines values and behavior as well as tenets of fundamental belief—cosmological, eschatological, and teleological. That tradition, as we have seen, is inherently wary of politics, a game played by worldly outsiders. Islam has come to prosper in Malagasy soil but remains identified with foreign minorities—the urban Comoreans of the north and the Indo-Pakistani merchant class. Both groups occupy vulnerable positions in Malagasy society, and neither can afford to experiment in Malagasy politics.

Christian activity in Madagascar is organized among a claimed 3 million Roman Catholics and a comparable number distributed over various Protestant churches. More than half the population, most of them peasants, espouse only the animist religion of their ancestors. Almost half of Madagascar's Christians are Merina. Strong on the east coast, in the cities of Fianarantsoa and Antsirabe, and in the rural areas around Antananarivo, the Catholic hierarchy has been identified successively with French colonialism and the Tsiranana PSD, which absorbed smaller Catholic parties after 1958. Nevertheless, alleged Jesuit machinations toward an anticommunist "third force" were denounced by the PSD in the early 1960s and again a decade later.

The Protestant movement shares this vulnerability to overt political suspicion and occasionally imputed clandestinity. The Protestant clergy of the capital has vigorously denounced all governments for nearly a century. American Lutheran missions in the south were regularly stigmatized for hostility to the French colonial and postcolonial administrations. Frequently throughout the 1960s, Tsiranana and his French advisers reacted suspiciously to unsubstantiated rumors that the Lutherans might be in touch with hostile external world interests, whatever they might be.

From the late 1970s, the Catholic press supported its clergy in a steady criticism against shortcomings of the Ratsiraka regime in matters of conscience. A bishops' pastoral letter read at masses in April 1980, although expressing deference to Ratsiraka's own Catholic education, excoriated his administration for its alliance with the communist world. In September 1984, nineteen bishops renewed their Jeremiad in a thirty-four-page pastoral letter denouncing all dictatorships that enjoy a monopoly of power by falsifying elections, persecuting oppositions, censoring the press, and broadcasting mendacious praise of their own leadership. They eloquently deplored regimes that insisted on being served by people rather than on serving them, regimes that exploited the many in their own name for the interest of a few, that distorted ancestral tradition into an incompatible culture, that betrayed independence, and that substituted little gods for God.[85] The domestic references were unmistakable—and not entirely tolerable. In 1984, four Catholic priests were mysteriously murdered.

On the plateaus, the main Protestant churches descend from French Evangelical missions, which inherited the position of nineteenth-century Anglicans, Methodists, and Quakers. The nationalist inclinations of these pulpits and their affiliated press have been manifest for generations. After 1975, although some Protestant leaders maintained overtly defiant attitudes, others accepted the nationalist promise inherent in the alliance between Ratsiraka's AREMA and its Antananarivo Marxist amanuensis, the AKFM—at least until the defection of Pastor Andriamanjato, the AKFM leader, in 1990.

Ratsiraka responded to church criticism with characteristic theatricality. On January 20, 1985, he was received by Pope John Paul II; on the twenty-seventh, the 150th anniversary of the publication of the Bible in the Malagasy language, he delivered a fervent sermon of his own, complete with confessions. In 1989, His Holiness returned the favor, visiting an island that was in recovery from leftist tyranny without having evicted the tyrant. Making his own position clear on the subject, the pope indirectly encouraged a relatively integrated church campaign aimed first at Ratsiraka's world socialist affiliations, subsequently at his domestic failures. The president had to confront a newly invigorated ecumenical Malagasy Christian Council (Fikambanan'ny Fiangonana Kristiana Malagasy, FFKM), formed in January 1980 by over 800 priests and 1,650 Protestant pastors. This numerical solidarity and the unflinching support of a devout middle-class clientele preserved church autonomy in the tough political and social dialogue that ensued.[86]

That strength became clear in 1990 with the success of two major congresses of intellectuals sponsored by the FFKM. Through its vigorous press, from the pulpit, and in direct action, the federation played an active role during mid-1991 in the extended battle between the political and labor opposition on the one hand and the president, who had occasionally referred to himself as a Marxist Christian, on the other. During that period, FFKM leaders urged the antagonists toward a new constitutional congress embracing all interests of the nation. Ratsiraka refused at first to acknowledge the political legitimacy of church interventions, holding out against clerical pressures to revoke the constitution of 1975. He had to yield substantially in 1992, however, as the religious and secular opposition forced Madagascar into constitutional change toward a third republic. During the interim, FFKM clerics and journalists openly served the Vital Forces opposition as intermediaries with the ministries and with the Malagasy population. Some Christian-affiliated parties scored well in the parliamentary elections of mid-1993, but overt emphasis on religious doctrine is unlikely to have much effect on Malagasy political culture in the third republic.

Women's Interests

Malagasy women retain the ambiguous distinctions common to their situation in many Third World countries. With its characteristic insular twist, Madagascar's culture pays extravagant homage to motherhood and family solidarity. It endows women with profound influence on domestic decisions, the protection of traditional values, and education. But it has not opened avenues to authority in political and institutional affairs. True to type, the Ratsiraka revolution celebrated the advent of female rights to political and social equality but allowed reality to remain lamentably far from the principle. Women are less well educated than men beyond compulsory primary school. They are paid 25 percent less for comparable work. They are rarely consulted in deliberations of the moment or on alternatives for the future of society. Female employment in education and health services has been increasing, but women are discouraged from "taking jobs away from men." Traditional male-dominated personnel hierarchies, including the professions, churches, and party politics, remain resistant to women as deserving of full opportunity in a changing society.

Rigidly organized in hierarchies, conventional political parties have resisted full participation by women. Few officeholders at any level in the first or second republic were female; the Revolutionary Women's Associations were created by the FNDR to mobilize youth for the revolution, not to promote women's status in it. Ramarasaona observes that, because Ratsiraka's charter required all candidates for office to enjoy sponsorship by an FNDR

Young women and boys parading with ritualistically purloined drums, Ampanihy Fair, Toliara Province. Photo courtesy of Service Général de l'Information de Madagascar.

party—all of them dominated by men—fewer women were elected to village councils and local committees under the revolution than during the Ramanantsoa interregnum when parties were banned.[87] Moreover, nonpolitical civic organizations struggling against illiteracy, unemployment, and pre- and postnatal neglect were also obliged to identify with an FNDR party, all of which gave little priority to those matters.[88]

Thus far the third republic appears to have followed suit. Bearing her father's illustrious name but competing with at least two other claimants to the heritage of the first republic's PSD, Soamandina Ruffine Tsiranana obtained only 3.4 percent of the vote in the first round of presidential elections in November 1992. The profusion of parties contesting for parliamentary seats in June 1993 often incorporated women candidates into their lists, but at ranks so low on those lists that only 9 were actually elected to the 138-seat Parliament under the current system of proportional representation. True to the tokenism of Malagasy regimes, Ravony's August 1993 cabinet included only one woman, Eléonore Marguerite Nerine, in the junior ministerial post of secretary of state for universities.

The island's traditional context supports subordinate status for women through customs of bride approval (*vodiondry*, often at a very young age), dowry payment, and male authority over family finances. Women are restricted to a one-third family property settlement after divorce. Women's agricultural work is often more arduous than men's—water-carrying, wood-gathering, rice-pounding—much of it to compensate for inadequate technical services in the economy. Special roles in planting and cultivating, in marketing surplus crops, preparing food, and in domestic crafts all keep women occupied throughout the day and the year; men insist on conventional periods of repose. Midwives charge higher rates for the delivery of boys than for girls.

Daughters are required to perform household obligations and to tend younger siblings; sons are schooled or allowed to play. Women are legally unprotected in concubinage liaisons.

All UN conventions on the condition of women have been formally ratified in Madagascar, and Malagasy women have made some progress under them. Women enjoy juridical autonomy for contracts, property holding, child adoption, and organizational memberships; especially important in Madagascar, wives may retain their own names. In 1976, responding to demands by national women's councils, the government established a Ministry of Population and Social Welfare with a bureau for Women's and Children's Affairs. Thanks to insistence from the World Bank, a national population policy was belatedly enacted in 1990 to reduce the 2.8 percent annual population growth rate, but it remains to be implemented with resources adequate to the objectives.

Operating against a law dating from 1920 that forbids publicity in favor of any form of contraception, the family-planning movement has worked discreetly for spacing of births and other purposes of interest to women; legal termination of pregnancy remains beyond contemplation, although affluent women can obtain abortions in Réunion. A survey conducted among Merina women in the late 1970s showed that the ancient reproduction ideal of seven boys and seven girls per household had yielded to a more modern expectation of four children. More recently, an official study concluded that the value of spacing childbirth was widely accepted among urban and educated women but that the 80 percent of Malagasy women who lived in rural areas proved nearly twice as fecund as the city minority.[89] Awareness of contraception is also restricted largely to educated and urban women, and it is that cohort that tends to bring its children regularly to immunization clinics; less than one-half of the rural women consult medical personnel or midwives at any time.[90]

Then there is the more subtle influence exerted by the distaff in most households, expressed by Ramarasaona: "Not to intervene directly, but to exert a strong influence on the activity of the other members of her family: therein lies the status and the role of the Merina woman."[91] The typical côtier situation varies scarcely from those expectations.

Yet the family norm remains partnership, not parity. Divorcees and unwed mothers bear stigmas not shared by their estranged partners. An unmarried woman is proverbially defined as a perpetual child. As Bloch interprets Merina ritual, the household, embodied in the wife-mother, stands as a nature-determined divisive force in the civilizing of the "deme" (clan). The elaborate circumcision ceremonies counter this "savage" (*mahery*) influence in humans—also associated with the archetypal imagery of the conquered Vazimba queens—by canalizing female-dominated or natural sexuality into the blessed fecundity of the permanent family. "The power of natural fertility, 'of living mother,' is something to be sought but also something to be overcome."[92] Women lack a ritual parallel to that of the circumcision, for their sexuality is a given; it can be rendered "healthy" in partnership but can't be rejected, renewed, or transformed as in the symbolism of male circumcision.

Even in a culture so indulgent of informal female power as the Merina, women acquiesce in a kind of original curse of nature, demanding correction by linkage to the community with all its hierarchical implications.

This seems a questionable record for a society ruled by four queens in the nineteenth century. Malagasy women have always responded vigorously to opportunities for training, improved hygiene, and literacy. Their society has produced several examples of powerful militants in the movements for independence and for revolutionary socialism. These models include the wily, militant confidante of Tsiranana, Zèle Rasoanoro, in the 1950s and early 1960s, and Ratsiraka's veteran culture minister, Gisèle Rabesahala of the Marxist AKFM. One of the steadiest, most diligently heeded voices in the crisis of the late 1980s was the jurist Madeleine Ramaholimihaso, founder of the National Commission for Observation of Elections (CNOE). Céline Ratsiraka played an important role in business and in family-planning policy during her husband's long tenure as president.

To a certain extent, this insular society remains cut off from cosmopolitan models. Most Malagasy women are particularly unaware of the circulation of fresh ideas in the external world—a world as close, even, as Mauritius and East Africa. Except among the sophisticated elite, awareness of liberating examples is virtually unavailable to Malagasy women.[93] The Antananarivo chapter of the International Soroptimists recently deplored the virtual absence of self-employed women, calling for enhanced access to capital and technical know-how, and publicity campaigns to increase the credibility of women entrepreneurs in the marketplace.[94] Nevertheless, highly capable and articulate Malagasy women who come into contact with external conditions often tend to express satisfaction with their own roles—enjoying influence without status—and to observe how far the rest of the world (including the United States) must go before it has practiced what it preaches.

The Press

Madagascar's insularity is alleviated by a multifarious third estate, especially in the island's plateau cities. It is a highly political press familiar with censorship and harassment over a century of regimes. Missionary publications were suppressed by the first Ranavalona in the 1850s. The Tsiranana administration permitted relatively free questioning of its broader options but not direct attacks (accurate or otherwise) on individual actions or decisions. In 1958, nineteen dailies, sixteen weeklies, and twenty other periodicals circulated in and around the capital, with a pair of strong Catholic Church papers at Fianarantsoa. The number had declined almost to half by 1966, but political polarization continued. World news was being fairly responsibly reported in the French-language daily *Le Courrier de Madagascar*. Under the Ramanantsoa interregnum, administered by Interior Minister Ratsimandrava, the press enjoyed a three-year holiday from controls and was able to participate in genuine social change.[95]

During the Ratsiraka revolution, the critical range of that effusive estate was virtually eliminated. For fifteen years, the entire national system of communication was made to serve the purposes of ideological education. "In general, this is a press which limits itself from day to day to transmitting to the reader without any analysis whatever the 'events' that happen in the country."[96] State-owned radio and audiovisual facilities have always been sycophantic, and the radio is society's main medium for mass dissemination of the established viewpoint. The island's relatively new television transmitter proved to be the last state asset over which Ratsiraka was willing to cede control.

Under a law of August 1975, censorship—in the the form of seizures, fines, or incarceration—threatened published offenses against the purposes of the revolution and the agents responsible for it. The old Francophile *Courrier* was replaced for a time by *Madagascar Matin* (circulation 15,000), with a tendency to go with the government's flow. Like the radio, it persuaded its French-speaking readership of the benefits of revolutionary socialism, the virtues of Madagascar's chosen friends, the integrity and international stature of its leaders. In external coverage, the uncultivated pluralism of the first republic gave way to more professional Marxist discipline and dependence on Tass, with carefully edited recourse to Agence France Presse, Reuters, and New China News.

Although most of the press was induced to practice self-discipline, some voices were heard from underground; and some took to providing what they regarded as sheer entertainment, as in the daily *Midi-Madagasikara*, with Antananarivo's largest circulation (28,000). Radio singers were able to complain about conditions only through ingenious insinuation.[97] Affluent Malagasy have high-powered shortwave radios capable of tuning into French Réunion; their new television system enabled them mainly to watch movies from East and West Europe and Cuba.[98]

As the years passed and the revolution's failures became undeniable, the traditional pluralism of Madagascar's political culture forced the Ratsiraka regime willy-nilly to tolerate a range of viewpoints, and eventually even of opinion.[99] Each political party published one or more journals, and the Protestant and Catholic clergy communicated through relatively lively organs of news and commentary. The Catholic diocesan press in particular always enjoyed a limited license to blame the regime directly for current troubles; this privilege was extended, albeit less liberally, to Protestant organs in the capital, where Pastor Ravelojaona had been using his *Mpanolontsaina* for nationalist purposes before World War II. In MONIMA's journals, the irrepressible Monja Jaona persistently belabored the AREMA government for its economic failures, its putative betrayal of revolutionary principles; Monja even got away with blaming the government for encouraging civil disorders, including the rural disturbances of 1982, the September 1984 kung fu-TTS massacres, and the anti-Karana riots of 1987.

Treating such charges with a mixture of silence and repression, the authorities made the habitual mistake of encouraging further speculation over the veracity of the criticism. The fact that Protestant papers had been agitating for nationalist causes since the mid-1950s established their relative credibility over that of opportunistic bureaucrats and military men. The effectiveness of this mission deteriorated somewhat, however, for the overall quality of journalism declined through the 1970s. As Chaigneau reported in 1981, "It is undeniable that the press has largely suffered from the new political orientation: scantiness of major news, obligation to present in positive terms the efforts to construct an original form of socialism, impossibility for the regime's opponents to maintain their own organs, and above all, the vigilance of strict censorship."[100]

The result was a general loss of vitality for the entire Malagasy press. Totalitarian mass communication did not function any more efficiently in Madagascar than elsewhere in the world of central planning. Constant barrages of positive imagery for the republic, its leaders, and its allies did not sink into a society long immune to affective identification with fanjakana. The mass obtained a new vocabulary for its grievances against the "foreign" central state, and the elites became more rigid, more recriminatory in their respective Marxist or bourgeois options.

In 1985–1986, a liberalization of opinion began to affect the professional, intellectual, and scholarly press of Antananarivo. The monthly *Revue de l'Océan Indien* began commenting independently on the international advantages of development through free-market operations. It exposed corruption in socialist dictatorships; advised abandoning certain unviable government projects in Madagascar; admitted that corruption, high tax levels, and black marketeering were discouraging external investment; and criticized Soviet handling of the nuclear disaster at Chernobyl.[101] Nevertheless, even in the course of such glasnost, the *Revue* remained subject to censorship; its April 1986 issue carried an editorial on page 4 praising India's Prime Minister Rajiv Gandhi for attacking corruption; the editorial appeared with several blank spaces that could be conjectured to have drawn parallels with Malagasy actuality.

By 1989, the censorship system had become so riddled with exceptions that the literate population of Antananarivo demanded legal liberalization to catch up with practice. Campaigning for reelection, Ratsiraka complied; the 1975 press law was abrogated on February 19, the scissors were removed from bureaucratic hands, and much of the national press unleashed its scorn on the heads of the regime. Newspapers emerged from obscurity and clandestinity to champion one or another exception to the revolution that had not worked. A well-edited bilingual daily, *Madagascar Tribune,* began to fill the void left by the demise of the old Tsirananist *Courrier;* it was soon joined in serious reportage by the popular *Midi-Madagasikara* (which divides its pages between Malagasy- and French-language coverage) and by a highly respected, business-oriented weekly, *Dans les Média Demain.*

In an inevitably short time, Ratsiraka's government began to deplore the consequences of its recourse to informational glasnost, and in June 1991 the president began threatening reimposition of some censorship over an almost entirely hostile press. The opposition movement proved too strong for such reversion, however, and the press has remained remarkably free to contribute to the construction of a third republic. Coverage of the presidential and parliamentary elections of 1992–1993 was remarkably balanced, even on national television, where dozens of ambitious personalities took advantage of unprecedented opportunities to make or break their political fortunes.

The Arts in Modern Madagascar

Malagasy artistic creativity finds itself in crisis today. In the past, Madagascar excelled in traditional architecture and sculpture—seen especially in the tombs of the west and south—as well as in oral and literary poetry, in textile design, and especially in music. By now much vitality has gone out of Malagasy traditional art, and the expectable successor forms, modern or Western, are more often pursued by Malagasy artists in Europe than on the island. Never purely isolated from overseas cultures, the great island has now taken to contributing its best to those far-off foreign foyers.

Once of epic and abstract power, relief sculpture has become syndicated in a few places on the island with an eye mainly on marketability, not marquetry. Mahafaly tombs' *aloala* represent the final survival of a great tradition of pole sculpture, practiced from Iakora in the east to Maintirano in the west and Betioky in the south. Few successors worthy of mention now produce sculpture on the island. Painting remains servile to French academic styles, including determination of palette choices to render typical scenes of Malagasy life, the most popular subject for oil painters and water colorists. The imitative process results in waves of local-color celebrations for the tourist market rather than a true expression of the Malagasy creative spirit.

Certain media and styles have evolved successfully, however. Gorgeous silk and cotton cloth continues to come from artisanal shops as textile arts thrive outside of Antananarivo. These arts take advantage of the dual market created by a living population's flair for body drapery and the demand of the recent dead for new vestments when they are returned to the tomb in the famadihana.[102] The capital, increasingly important as a repository for crafts aimed at foreign clientele, lacks a flair for textile design, although its cottage industries turn out large quantities of charming embroidered napkins and tablecloths for visitors.

Improvised poetry and proverbial rhetoric have been constantly in demand by Malagasy families as accompaniments to all life's starts and turns. Marriages are negotiated even today by specialists in jousts of proverbial oratory (*kabary*). Mastery of verbal lore, as Althabe explains, demonstrates proximity to ancestors.[103] As Mack puts it, "An ability to make the ancestors contemporary is the hallmark of a good speech, whatever qualities of wit or insight are otherwise displayed."[104] The classic Merina verses known as *hainteny* and their counterparts in other provinces once expressed universal themes of love, political power, and the interpenetrations of life and death.[105] Although hainteny (closely associated with the royal dynasty) are no longer composed, their proverbial tissue remains alive in vernacular speech.

The stultifying effects of linguistic codification by nineteenth-century missionaries and contemporary ideologues have gradually loosened, and the Malagasy language breathes again.[106] It is an extraordinarily imagistic vehicle for concrete poetic indirection and for abstract ideas in prose as well. This most flexible language has produced a treasury of tales and fables as well as formal poetry. As Domenichini-Ramiaramanana points out, the language of Malagasy upper classes differed little from that of the folk, so oral tradition retains the ornateness and complexity of true literature—of life itself.[107]

In more conventionally modern literary forms, the Malagasy retain considerable distinction. Malagasy poets and fiction writers have contributed powerful work to the dynamic body of Third World literature in French. Premier among them is Jean-Joseph Rabearivelo (1901-1937), gifted, tragically doomed poet of the natural correspondences of the human passions. In a later generation, Flavien Ranaivo turned out exquisite lyrics of traditional and rural life penetrated by modern sensibility. Chroniclers and transcribers of traditional tales tend now to occupy the position once dominated by such poets as Rabearivelo, Ranaivo, and Jacques Rabemananjara, although the poets have retained their audience in Malagasy and in French.[108]

For all the plastic and verbal fecundity of other arts, it is in music that the Malagasy imagination best transcends ordinary creativity. Scholarly expertise has been devoted to inventorying the various instruments of Malagasy music and to speculating on their points of origin.[109] To grasp the importance of music in Madagascar, however, requires appreciation of a musical paradigm of the world—a complex of rhythms and a revelation of cyclical structure in a partly invisible universe. In idiomatically accented melody, the musician recreates, in effect, the pulses of creation, commenting, piously or ironically, on the effects of the job through lyrical variations. Thus, players on the cylindrical bamboo zither called *valiha* give a sense of accompanying the sweet turns of life, and the flute choirs (*sodina*) of the Betsileo reproduce the harmonies of an ideal nature.

In addition to reinforcing and consecrating life, music regularly punctuates its course. Troupes of frocked singer-musicians (*mpiragasy*) visit fairs and villages of the highlands conveying news of the outside world and cautionary remonstrances (often government-sponsored) in perfect, yet largely improvised unanimity; they resound through the world like an early, socially accountable form of rap. Throughout the island, semiprofessional roadrunners turn up at fairs, family festivals, and in the presence of important politicians. Behaving with the perilous impunity of court jesters, they mock scandalous indiscretions and heavy-handed administrative bungling attributable even to the personages sitting sedately before them. Behind these singer-instrumentalists, Malagasy drum sets (*amponga*) hammer out the heartbeat of the microcosm, conveying a deeper, less ephemeral message about the cosmos.

Nevertheless, urban Madagascar rarely connects overtly with these currents of traditional culture. Mass media exert their grip on the emotions of young people in Antananarivo and Toamasina as everywhere else. Floods of pop singers now command the airwaves and local cassette markets, crowding out the powerful indigenous music that had emerged in diverse styles from all pockets of the island. One of them, Dama Zafimahaleo, even won a parliamentary seat at Antananarivo in June 1993, proving to all that youth would now be heard. Sentimental, musically obtuse, imbued with pretty imagery, church-bound harmonies, and flabby rhythms, the art of these new minstrels

Valiha player of the Bara people, Ihosy. Photo from antique post card.

nevertheless carries qualities not found among their commercial sources of origin—in Europe, America, Zaire, or Nigeria. Those qualities seem to bespeak a special relation with the land and an origin across the seas, a love of the language bequeathed to modern Malagasy by ancestors who knew no metropoles and yet managed, as the Malagasy commonly say, to "get us to where we are."

Whether the ancestors appreciate contemporary popular culture or not, they may well be awaiting the rebirth of creativity in a new republic returned to its people. For the first time in twentieth-century Malagasy history, the arts of that republic may be able to flourish without stifling preoccupation with European forms, standards, and examples.

NOTES

1. The varieties of Malagasy ethnicity and culture have been well documented for the past two centuries—flowing into and out of the politico-cultural watershed represented by the reorganizations of the Merina king Andrianampoinimerina. They continue to be studied by a highly collegial Franco-Malagasy research establishment, penetrated by an occasional British or other vazaha anthropologist. For instance, see bibliographical entries for Yoshio Abé; Maurice Bloch, Raymond Décary; Gillian Feeley-Harnik; Richard Huntington; Conrad Phillip Kottack and others; John Mack; Jean Pavageau; S. Raharijaona and Pierre Vérin; Tovonirina Rakotondrabe; Pierre Vérin. Rakontondrabe's presentation to the University of Antananarivo's May 1993 Colloquium on Democracy and Development in the Southwest Indian Ocean and in Africa, entitled "Au delà de l'ethnie: Ethnies, état-nation et démocratie à Madagascar," represents the best discussion of the contemporary politics of national unity and regionalism.

2. See Pascal Chaigneau, *Madagascar, de la première république à l'orientation socialiste: Processus et conséquences d'une évolution politique* (Thèse IIIème cycle en sociologie politique, Univ. de Paris X, 1981), p. 77; Maurice Bloch, *Placing the Dead: Tombs, Ancestral Villages and Kinship Organization in Madagascar* (London and New York: Seminar Press, 1972), p. 36; Gillian Feeley-Harnik, *A Green Estate: Restoring Independence in Madagascar* (Washington and London: Smithsonian Institution Press, 1991), pp. 156–159; Gérard Althabe, *Oppression et libération dans l'imaginaire: Les communautés villageoises de la côte orientale de Madagascar* (Paris: Maspero, 1969); Jean-Pierre Raison, *Les hautes terres de Madagascar* (Paris: ORSTOM-Karthala, 1984).

3. See Pierre Vérin, "Austronesian Contributions to the Culture of Madagascar: Some Archaeological Problems," in H. Neville Chittick and Robert I. Rotberg, eds., *East Africa and the Orient: Cultural Syntheses in Pre-Colonial Times* (New York and London: Africana, 1975), p. 167.

4. Census calculations are hazardous at best; most population data depend on extrapolations from the 1970 census.

5. Pascal Chaigneau, *Rivalités politiques et socialisme à Madagascar* (Paris: CHEAM, 1985), p. 18; for even stronger indictments of the colonial administration's role in creating ethnic conflict, see Antoine Bouillon, *Madagascar, le colonisé et son 'âme': Essai sur le discours psychologique colonial* (Paris: Harmattan, 1981) and Robert Archer, *Madagascar depuis 1972: La marche d'une révolution* (Paris: Harmattan, 1978), esp. pp. 20–25.

6. See Althabe, *Oppression et libération*, pp. 62–64.

7. Maurice Bloch, *From Blessing to Violence: History and Ideology in the Circumcision Ritual of the Merina of Madagascar* (Cambridge: Cambridge University Press, 1986), p. 164; see also Bloch, *Placing the Dead*, pp. 26–29.

8. Patrick Rajoelina and Alain Ramelet, *Madagascar: La grande île* (Paris: Harmattan, 1989), p. 79. Ethnologists have classified Malagasy groups into any number from eighteen to forty-eight; for detailed histories of the major groups see Edouard Ralaimihoatra, *Histoire de Madagascar*, 4th ed. (Antananarivo: Librairie de Madagascar, 1982), pts. 1 and 2.

9. See Frederic L. Pryor, *Malawi and Madagascar: The Political Economy of Poverty, Equity, and Growth* (Washington, D.C.: Oxford University Press for World Bank, 1990), pp. 200–201.

10. See Hubert Deschamps, *Les pirates à Madagascar aux XVIIème et XVIIIème siècles* (Paris: Berger-Levrault, 1949).

11. See Gillian Feeley-Harnik, "The Political Economy of Death: Communication and Change in Malagasy Colonial History," *American Ethnologist*, v. 11, February 1984, pp. 1–19.

12. These concepts are explored among Merina and Betsileo migrants by Raison, *Les hautes terres*, esp. ch. 3.

13. See Bloch, *Placing the Dead*, p. 46 and ch. 3; M. Guérin in *Terre Malgache*, no. 8 (Antananarivo: E.N.S.A., Université de Madagascar) p. 8, cited in Jean Pavageau, *Jeunes paysans sans terre: L'exemple malgache* (Paris: Harmattan, 1981), p. 27.

14. See Feeley-Harnik, *A Green Estate*, pp. 228–229.

15. See Jean-Claude Rouveyran, *La logique des agricultures de transition: L'exemple des sociétés paysannes malgaches* (Paris: Maisonneuve et LaRose, 1972), p. 254.

16. Ibid., pp. 257–259.

17. See Richard Andriamanjato, *Le tsiny et le tody dans la pensée malgache* (Paris: Présence Africaine, 1957); Raymond Decary, *Moeurs et coutumes des Malgaches* (Paris: Payot, 1961); Jørgen Ruud, *Taboo: A Study of Malagasy Customs and Beliefs* (Oslo: Oslo University Press, 1960); Alton C. O. Halverson, *Madagascar: Footprint at the End of the World* (Minneapolis: Augsburg Publishing, 1973), pp. 24–28.

18. In Bloch, *Placing the Dead*; see also Pavageau, *Jeunes paysans*, esp. ch. 2; Raison, *Les hautes terres*; I. Rakoto, *Parenté et mariage en droit traditionnel malgache* (Paris: Presses Universitaires de France, 1971); Paul Ramasindraibe, *Fokonolona: Revue culturelle mensuelle*, no. 7, 1965 (Antananarivo), p. 103; S. Raharijaona and P. Vérin, "Le système de parenté merina," *Annales de l'Université de Madagascar*, 1964, pp. 101–113.

19. Althabe, *Oppression et libération*; for comparable examples of this reaction—called "cultural resistance" by Roger Bastide—among the northwest coastal Sakalava, see also Feeley-Harnik, "The Political Economy of Death," and her *A Green Estate*.

20. Henry Rusillon, *Un culte dynastique avec évocation des morts chez les Sakalaves de Madagascar: Le "tromba"* (Paris: Alphonse Picard, 1912); for a more sophisticated interpretation of tromba among the northwestern Sakalava, see Feeley-Harnik, *A Green Estate*, esp. pp. 303–310.

21. See Françoise Raison-Jourde, "Les ramanenjana, une mise en cause populaire du Christianisme en Imerina—1863," *ASEMI*, v. 7, nos. 2–3, 1976, pp. 271–293; Bloch, *From Blessing to Violence*, pp. 145–148.

22. Jacques Lombard, "Zatovo qui n'a pas été créé par Dieu: Un conte sakalava traduit et commenté," *ASEMI*, v. 7, nos. 2–3, 1976, pp. 165–223; Lombard, "L'art et les ancêtres," in Henri Marchal and Sarah Doulache, eds., *Madagascar: Arts de la vie et de la survie* (Paris: ADEIAO, 1989), pp. 16–21.

23. P. H. DuBois, *Monographie des Betsileo* (Paris: Institute de l'Ethnologie, 1938); see also Conrad Phillip Kottak, *The Past in the Present: History, Ecology, and Cultural Variation in Highland Madagascar* (Ann Arbor: University of Michigan Press, 1980); Richard Huntington, in *Gender and Social Structure in Madagascar* (Bloomington and Indianapolis: Indiana University Press, 1988), studied comparable practices, called *bilo*, among the Bara.

24. Andriamanjato, *Tsiny et tody*; O. Mannoni, *Prospero and Caliban: The Psychology of Colonization*, trans. Pamela Powesland, 2nd ed. (New York: Praeger, 1964).

25. Feeley-Harnik, *A Green Estate*, p. 64.

26. Bloch, *Placing the Dead*, ch. 8.

27. Ibid., ch. 5; also Bloch, *From Blessing to Violence*, pp. 85–86; Nicole Boulfroy, "Les tissages," in Vérin, *Arts de la vie*, pp. 48–49; Nelly Graziella Raboanarijaona, *Tradi-*

tion et modernité: Analyse de deux rituels malgaches, Mémoire de DEA (Aix-en-Provence: Université d'Aix-Marseille, 1987).

28. Bakoly Doménichini-Ramiaramanana, *Du ohabolona au hainteny: Langage, littérature et politique à Madagascar* (Paris: Karthala, 1983), p. 311, n. 61.

29. Lombard, "L'art et les ancêtres," pp. 20–21; see also Narivelo Rajoanarimanana, "La poésie orale malgache et la vie," in Marchal and Doulache, *Arts de la vie*, p. 54; Bloch, *Placing the Dead*, pp. 168–169; Chaigneau, *Première république*, p. 88; Pavageau, *Jeunes paysans*, p. 38.

30. Mannoni, *Prospero and Caliban*, ch. 1 and ch. 3, p. 65.

31. Ibid., p. 8.

32. Rouveyran, *Agricultures de transition*, pp. 249–250; for alternative forms of Malagasy resistance, see theses developed by Althabe in *Oppression et libération*, and by Pavageau in *Jeunes paysans*.

33. See Mannoni, *Prospero and Caliban*, pp. 50–55; Bloch, *Placing the Dead*, pp. 26–28; Althabe, *Oppression et libération*.

34. See Bloch, *From Blessing to Violence*, pp. 127–140; Raison-Jourde, "Les ramanenjana;" Althabe, *Oppression et libération*, pp. 117–118.

35. For an example of such wariness, see Halverson, *Footprint*, pp. 18–28.

36. See Raison-Jourde, "Les ramanenjana," p. 289; yet the profanity of "ancestor worship" did not prevent an American Lutheran pastor in 1963 from declaring the contents of my stranded vehicle to be *fady* (taboo) in order to keep Antanosy villagers from looting it while we went to a distant town for help.

37. See Lombard, "L'art et les ancêtres."

38. See Nicole Boulfroy, "L'art funéraire des Mahafale," in Marchal and Doulache, *Arts de la vie*, pp. 24–29.

39. See Bloch, *Placing the Dead*, ch. 6; Chaigneau, *Première république*, p. 98.

40. See Bloch, *Placing the Dead*, p. 221; Bloch, *From Blessing to Violence*, pp. 168–175.

41. Bloch, *From Blessing to Violence*, p. 112.

42. Ibid., ch. 5.

43. Ibid., p. 195; see also Raboanarijaona, "Tradition et modernité," and reviews of Bloch's work by Feeley-Harnik in *American Ethnologist*, v. 15, August 1988, pp. 593–595, and by Michael Lambeck, in Maurice Bloch, ed., *Ritual, History and Power: Selected Papers in Anthropology* (London and Atlantic Highlands, N.J.: Athlone Press, 1989), p. 558.

44. See Jean-François Rabedimy, "Contribution de l'OMBIASA à la formation du royaume menabe, le togny," *ASEMI*, vii, nos. 2–3, pp. 255–270; Lombard, "Zatovo"; Raymond K. Kent, *Early Kingdoms in Madagascar, 1500–1700* (New York: Holt, Rinehart & Winston, 1970), ch. 3; Rajoelina and Ramelet, *La grande île*, pp. 44–71.

45. See Bar-Jaony Randriamandimby, "Le concept de hiérarchie en Imerina historique," *ASEMI*, v. 4, no. 4, 1973, pp. 3–16; Adolphe Razafintsalama, "Histoire et tradition chez les Tsimahafotsy," *ASEMI*, v. 4, no. 4, 1973, pp. 17–33.

46. See Bloch, *From Blessing to Violence*, esp. ch. 8; for other references in this argument, see Pavageau, *Jeunes paysans*, pp. 40–64; Maurice Bloch, "The Changing Relationship Between Rural Communities and the State in Central Madagascar During the Nineteenth and Twentieth Centuries," in *Les communautés rurales: Recueils de la société Jean Bodin* (Paris: Dessain et Tolra, 1983), p. 235; Althabe, *Oppression et libération*; Raison, *Les hautes terres*, pp. 539–541; Rouveyran, *Agricultures de transition*, v. 1, ch. 1.

47. See Raison, *Les hautes terres*, pp. 205–209; Pavageau, *Jeunes paysans*, ch. 5; for recent analyses of development strategy, see also David Greenaway and Chris Milner, "Industrial Incentives, Domestic Resource Costs and Resource Allocation in Madagas-

car," *Applied Economics,* no. 22, June 1990, pp. 805–821; John Crosthwaite, "Quantifying Structural Adjustment at the Grassroots: The 'Braudel' Measure of Small-Scale Entrepreneur Purchasing Power," *European Communities Courier,* no. 124, November-December 1990, pp. 12–16; Richard Szal, "Is There an Agrarian Crisis in Madagascar?" *International Labour Review,* v. 127, no. 6, 1988, pp. 735–760.

48. Rouveyran, *Agricultures de transition,* p. 212.

49. Yves Prats, *Le développement communautaire à Madagascar* (Paris: Pichon et Durand-Auzias, 1972).

50. Georges Balandier, "Preface" to Althabe, *Oppression et libération,* p. 9.

51. Althabe, *Oppression et libération,* pp. 81–91; see also Rouveyran, *Agricultures de transition,* pp. 218–230. Recently, in Toamasina, a Sino-Malagasy friend deplored this lack of enterprise among the Betsimisaraka, as contrasted with the Merina and others encountered on the east coast, but without acknowledging that the latter were a self-selected subclass—enterprising, hence truly *encountered* on the east coast.

52. See, for instance, Daniel Coulaud, "L'art et la maison," in Marchal and Doulache, *Arts de la vie,* pp. 31–38.

53. Pavageau, *Jeunes paysans,* p. 117.

54. Raison, *Les hautes terres,* p. 99.

55. The fokon'olona has been exhaustively studied; early conclusions by Alfred Grandidier and Georges Condominas have been tested and amended by Jacques Dez, in "Développement économique et tradition à Madagascar," *Cahiers de l'Institut des Sciences Économiques Appliquées,* v. 5, no. 4, 1962, pp. 79–108; Yves Prats, *Le développement communautaire;* Bloch, *Placing the Dead,* ch. 3; Andrianaivo Ravelona Rajaona, "Le Dinam-Pokonolona, mythe, mystique ou mystification?" paper presented at the Colloque d'Histoire Malgache, Mahajanga, December 1981; Chaigneau, *Première république,* ch. 3; Chaigneau, *Un état à orientation socialiste: Madagascar,* v. 3, (Paris: Université de Paris X, 1981), pp. 1112–1118; Chaigneau, *Rivalités politiques,* pp. 19–23; Rouveyran, *Agricultures de transition,* ch. 1.

56. For instance, see Althabe, *Oppression et libération,* pp. 262–265.

57. Ibid., p. 263.

58. Jean-Pierre Raison, "Madagascar dans le sud-ouest de l'océan indien," *Hérodote: Revue de Géographie et de Géopolitique,* nos. 37–38, p. 224.

59. For a forthright and detailed, if oversimplified, Marxist denunciation of this system, see François Rajaoson, *L'enseignement supérieure et le développement de la société malgache* (Paris: Université de Paris V, 1981) esp. chs. 2 and 3.

60. See Chaigneau, *Rivalités politiques,* p. 19.

61. See Wang Gungwu, "The Chinese Overseas," in Jean Poirier et al., *Mouvements de populations dans l'océan indien* (Paris: Honoré Champion, 1979), pp. 451–457; Leon M. S. Slawecki, *French Policy Toward the Chinese in Madagascar* (Hamden, Conn.: Shoestring Press, 1971).

62. See Paul Le Bourdiec, "L'implantation des minorités étrangères à Madagascar avant 1972," *APOI,* no. 5, 1978, pp. 37–67; for the Comorean authorities' claim that no fewer than 1,374 had been massacred in Mahajanga, see *Daily Telegraph,* London, January 13, 1977; *Africa Contemporary Record, 1976–1977* (London: Rex Collings, 1978), p. B174.

63. See Mannoni, *Prospero and Caliban,* pp. 28–36.

64. See Chaigneau, *Première république,* p. 364.

65. See Raison, "Madagascar dans le sud-ouest," pp. 219–224.

66. See *Marchés Tropicaux et Méditerranéens (MTM),* March 6 and 20, 1987; also Sennen Andriamirado, "Madagascar: L'enfer des uns peut être un paradis pour les autres," *Jeune Afrique,* no. 1368, March 25, 1987, pp. 30–33.

67. See Rouveyran, *Agricultures de transition*, pp. 163–203.
68. Maureen Covell, *Madagascar: Politics, Economics and Society* (London and New York: Frances Pinter, 1987), p. 76.
69. Rajaoson, *L'enseignement supérieure*, p. 49.
70. Chaigneau, *Un état à orientation socialiste*, p. 586.
71. Rajaoson's phrase, in *L'enseignement supérieure*, p. 177.
72. Ibid., pp. 233–234 and table 5.
73. Ibid., p. 412.
74. Ibid., pp. 405–411.
75. Charles Cadoux and Jean du Bois de Gaudusson, "Madagascar 1982–1984: Un tournant dans la révolution?" *APOI*, v. 9, 1980, p. 365 (the 1980 volume did not actually emerge until 1985); see also *LaKroan i'Madagasikara*, May 23 and June 6, 1982.
76. See Andriamirado, "Madagascar: L'enfer": also *MTM*, April 10, 1987.
77. See *MTM*, no. 2480, May 21, 1993.
78. See *Lumière*, esp. October 17, 1971; Rajaoson, *L'enseignement supérieure*, pp. 323–332.
79. See *Africa Confidential*, v. 25, no. 13, and v. 26, no. 13.
80. Pavageau, *Jeunes paysans*, esp. pp. 68–71 and ch. 9.
81. Jean-Louis Calvet, "Chronique politique et constitutionnelle: Madagascar," *APOI*, v. 5, p. 320.
82. See Chaigneau, *Première république*, pp. 879–884; Covell, *Politics, Economics, and Society*, p. 94.
83. See Calvet, "Chronique politique," pp. 333–334; Covell, *Politics, Economics, and Society*, p. 94.
84. See Olivier Ramahatra, *MTM*, no. 2490, July 30, 1993.
85. See *LaKroan*, January 1985; *Jeune Afrique*, no. 1261, March 6, 1985.
86. The political strength of the churches is analyzed in Justin Rakotoniaina, "Démocratie et aspirations populaires: Considérations sur la transition politique malgache," presented at the University of Antananarivo's Colloquium on Democracy and Development in the Southwest Indian Ocean and in Africa, May 1993.
87. Zaïveline Ramarasaona, *Les femmes malgaches dans le fokonolona* (Thèse IIIème cycle, Univ. de Paris, 1979), pp. 112, 225.
88. See Marie-Josette Razoeliarimboa-Ratovo, *La femme malgache: Son rôle social et politique* (Aix-en-Provence: Université d'Aix-Marseille, 1979); Ramarasaona, *Les femmes malgaches*, pp. 64–74, 230–232.
89. Centre National de Recherches sur l'Environnement and Demographic and Health Surveys, *Enquête nationale démographique et sanitaire, Madagascar, 1992*, rapport préliminaire (Antananarivo: CNRE, March 1993), pp. 5–6. Young rural women aged 15 to 19 years are particularly fertile.
90. Ibid., pp. 6–9, 14–15.
91. Ramarasaona, *Les femmes malgaches*, p. 188.
92. Bloch, *From Blessing to Violence*, p. 97; also pp. 44–45, 93–103, 169–175.
93. See Razoeliarimboa-Ratovo, *La femme malgache*; Ramarasaona, *Les femmes malgaches*, conclusion.
94. See *Lettre Mensuelle de JURECO*, May 1993 (Antananarivo), p. 33.
95. See James Ramarasaona, *Madagascar Tribune*, February 10, 1990.
96. "Les aléas de 120 années de presse malgache," *Revue de l'Océan Indien*, no. 76, May 1986, pp. 28–32.
97. See Andry Razah, *Tribune*, January 18, 1990.

98. Nevertheless, occasional world news broadcasts do make a difference, as when in spring 1991, Malagasy viewers seemed to draw obvious domestic lessons from the French report of the fall of Ethiopia's dictator Mengistu Haile Merriam.

99. The political press was inventoried by the *Revue de l'Océan Indien*, no. 76, May 1986, and earlier by Chaigneau in *Première république*, pp. 859–865, and in *Un état à orientation socialiste*, pp. 556–573; see also commentary by Adelson Razafy, *Tribune*, February 18, 1990.

100. Chaigneau, *Première république*, p. 855; see also Chaigneau, *Un état à orientation socialiste*, pp. 551–584; also see editorial in *Revue de l'Océan Indien*, no. 74, March 1986, and special issue, no. 76, May 1986.

101. See *Revue de l'Océan Indien*, nos. 76 and 77, May and June 1986.

102. See Nicole Boulfroy, "Les agréments de la vie," in Marchal and Doulache, *Arts de la vie*, pp. 44–49.

103. Althabe, *Oppression et libération*, p. 294.

104. John Mack, "Ways of the Ancestors," *Natural History*, no. 4, 1989, p. 31.

105. See Narivelo Rajaonarimanana, "La poésie orale malgache et la vie," in Marchal and Doulache, *Arts de la vie*, pp. 51–55; Doménichini-Ramiaramanana, *Du ohabolona au hainteny*; Lee Haring, *Verbal Arts in Madagascar: Performance in Historical Perspective* (Philadelphia: University of Pennsylvania Press, 1992).

106. See Raison, *Les hautes terres*, pp. 220–221.

107. Doménichini-Ramiaramanana, *Du ohabolona au hainteny*, ch. 1.

108. For the latest collection with commentary, see Régis Rajemisa-Raolison, ed., *Les poètes malgaches d'expression française* (Antananarivo: Imprimerie Catholique, 1983).

109. See Kurt Sachs, *Les instruments de musique à Madagascar* (Paris: Conservatoire de Musique, 1938); Michel Doménichini, "Musique en l'île," in Vérin, *Arts de la vie*, pp. 55–60.

5
Madagascar's Economy: Flight from Reality

For most of this century, the Malagasy people have impotently awaited the advent of prosperity. Examples of personal affluence filtering into towns and villages sufficed to show most Malagasy how wealth might appear. Such lessons arrive in lifestyles of the visible vazaha or those of the elite Malagasy who translate local political power into wealth. Moreover, every clan has urban kinspeople to report diligently on the ways of the city privileged. Although the traditional family reckons its true fortune in terms of ritual and sacrament, those spiritual assets overlap the material world substantially—particularly in land and cattle. Hence, the perquisites of wordly comfort have value to both the living and the dead. But wealth has visited only a scant few on the world's fourth largest island, where surplus production remains rare and sporadic. Sparsely settled, diversely endowed, Madagascar might soon demonstrate its capacity for economic self-sufficiency, but not yet for development.

If prosperity has proved elusive, it is scarcely for lack of strategies. French colonial administrators encouraged production through infrastructural investment, concessions to metropolitan-owned export agriculture, and fundamental education for "the indigenous." True, the intended beneficiaries of progress were metropolitan, not Malagasy, but the colonial tide was ideally to lift all boats, and the island was supposed to flourish. In reality, the colonizers had major trouble sustaining an effective transportation system and persuading peasant farmers to modernize.

The first republic, from 1960 through 1972, left foreign and Asian minority ownership of key sectors undisturbed, introducing large, integrated agricultural production schemes and inspirational grassroots extension campaigns. Relying on direct investment from France, South Africa, and other international sources, President Philibert Tsiranana's policies kept external debt low but failed to generate domestic savings or tax revenues adequate for economic transformation.

The transitional regime of 1972–1975 eliminated unpopular colonial taxes on smallhold agriculture and reduced the extent of foreign control over production. By diversifying the island's portfolio of international partners, it

TABLE 5.1 Madagascar's GDP at Current Market Prices, 1985–1993

	FMG Billion	US$ Million	Real GDP Growth Rate (%)
1985	1,553	2,344	2.3
1986	1,807	2,672	0.8
1987	2,275	2,081	1.7
1988	2,450	1,741	3.8
1989	3,451	2,152	4.9
1990	4,400	2,945	−1.7
1991	4,900	2,670	−6.4
1992	4,950	2,708	0.2
1993 forecast	–	–	3.7

NOTE: Malagasy francs; FMG 1,922 = US$1.00 (July 5, 1993).

SOURCES: Figures are compiled from various issues of Economist Intelligence Unit (EIU) *Country Report* (London: EIU *Madagascar: Comoros County Profiles, 1992–1993* and *1993–1994* (London: EIU, 1992, 1993); various issues of *Marchés Tropicaux et Méditerranéens*. Numbers are mainly extrapolations and reconciliations of varying official Malagasy data, hence are subject to wide margins of error.

threatened French prerogatives, hence weakening France's commitment. Unfortunately, this more open strategy found no source to replace those lost revenues, and the national economy stagnated.

After 1975, the revolutionary republic reversed course and, a decade later, reversed again. Eschewing direct foreign investment as a threat to independence, Ratsiraka's state took to borrowing and investing "without constraint." Thanks to this costly capital, an expanding bureaucracy could launch and manage large, ultimately unviable parastatal enterprises. The state neglected agricultural output in favor of capital-intensive industrial projects that didn't produce and social programs that didn't improve life. It ensured urban stability by favoring consumer goods over productive imports, and an overvalued currency depressed exports dramatically. By the early 1980s, Malagasy GDP began declining, and the external debt had soared to crisis levels. The economy had no hope of remedy short of capitulation to foreign financiers. Madagascar today languishes in a receivership of international agencies and creditors. Malagasy earned an average of $190 in 1988; two years later, as the international strategies took hold, per capita income rose to $235. Since then, although praising Madagascar for its responsiveness to international advice, the World Bank has ranked Madagascar's economy twelfth from the bottom of countries with more than a million people.[1]

This disheartening score seems to contradict an otherwise favorable economic record in the late 1980s—about 4 percent growth in 1990 GDP after nearly 5 percent in 1989 (see Table 5.1). Indeed, the United Nations' second report on human development in 1991 and 1993 ranked the island thirteenth highest in Africa for life expectancy, adult literacy, and purchasing power—twenty-nine positions higher than in raw per capita GNP.[2]

Low export prices, drought, and political tribulations (including 7 months of general strikes) relegated 1991 to the status of a "dead year," written off in multilateral agencies' statistical accounts. Debt-repayment obligations had to be suspended for most of that year and for the entirety of 1992, which saw no measure of economic recovery; only slight growth in national income was expected for 1993. The third Malagasy republic thus inherited a condition of political uncertainty, administrative inefficiency, and export stagnation that continued to deter new investment and commercial transactions.[3]

Some Malagasy take comfort in the inadequacy of econometrics to gauge the well-being of a culturally unique society such as their own. In the way of the world today, however, hope for regeneration of an impoverished society depends on opening markets and replacing dysfunctional state enterprises with private initiative, expanding external trade and investment, reinvigorating agricultural production, and cultivating hitherto squandered human and natural potential. Some of these processes are under way in Madagascar, but none has yet reached maturity.

ECONOMIC ENDOWMENTS AND INHIBITIONS

The Land and Its Occupations

The island has scope and resources enough to warrant reasonable expectations of development. This is a veritable continent of several complementary zones, from the dry coastal and plains ecologies of the west and south to tropical humidity in the east and north and the temperate plateaus of the center.[4] Its people have lived in sympathy with their respective localities for centuries yet are not entirely antipathetic to migration for purposes of gain. They are a manifestly educable population with a deep and practical heritage of wisdom about the world. They have developed patterns of private landholding, communal labor exchange, and family solidarity as well as a remarkable technology of rice growing—on a million hectares of irrigated paddy fields and terraced slopes—and a way of raising 15 million head of cattle with minimal labor.

When allowed latitude for rational decisions, the Malagasy know where and when to work their rice, to distribute their herds, to cultivate their coffee and other cash crops, and to leave a field for refreshment. And despite a millennium of damage from fire and erosion, the island even now retains space for subsequent fruitful moves. Beef cattle herds graze over nearly half the island; only 10 percent of the theoretically cultivable land surface is used for farming.[5]

But opportunities for sustained growth remain severely limited. The island is poorly linked by roads or other communications and poorly served by its institutions of education, health, and law enforcement. Madagascar's structural problems include a relatively closed attitude toward external trade combined paradoxically with acute dependence on international exchanges to maintain the economy's modern sector. The problem is compounded by vast distances from resources and markets and an unreliable climate beset by cyclones. Economic progress is further handicapped by a relatively rigid class structure, ancestral conservatism, degradation of the environment, and the proclivity of students and parents to choose academic fields distant from productive labor needs.

One and one-half million widely scattered farms occupy some 80 percent of the active population but create only 43 percent of the great island's wealth. Most of these are smallholds (two hectares in average size) with limited adaptability. About 45 percent of the acreage is in rice, 40 percent in other food crops, but it is the 7 percent in coffee and 3 percent in vanilla, cloves, and pepper that have traditionally earned four-fifths of the country's foreign exchange. This disparity between land use and income reflects the gap between modern and subsistence economics in Madagascar and reveals the island's great vulnerability to international fluctuations in market prices, supply, and demand. As Philippe Hugon analyzes Madagascar's economic, financial, and social paradoxes,

> The advantages which Madagascar enjoys seem in a sense to represent as many handicaps. Its diversity obstructs the effects of an economy of scale; complementarity between regions and sectors also leads to partitioning; schooling and administrative tradition are conducive to bureaucratic sluggishness, accentuating the burden of tertiary activity. Management of an unstable environment and the efficient organization of a productive system seem particularly defective.[6]

Planners and patrons of Madagascar's future are frustrated by the isolation of the island's productive localities from one another. The infrastructural networks have never sufficed and they have disintegrated from what they once were. Viable roads and lines of rail serve primarily as evacuation routes for products of interest to Europe; they were built by the French for that purpose. Maintaining even those linkages has proved daunting in the late-twentieth-century economy. Supplementing them with the genuine arterial gridwork of an integrated economy remains beyond probability.

Even as channels for exportable freight, the island's inner connections fall short of needs. Many a project for exploitation of bauxite, coal, uranium, titanium, mica, and other resources has perished through the inaccessibility of the quarry. Only chromite and graphite have been exploited consistently for European markets. Shale oil reserves abound but remain too expensive for profit, and traces of subterranean and offshore petroleum have been sounded for more than a decade by various oil-drilling contractors without yet revealing an exploitable deposit. Tourist schemes, contemplating natural and cultural marvels from north to south, have foundered on the impracticality of getting from one to another. In order to reach the island's most prominent attractions, all but the hardiest travelers must rely on air connections. The half-dozen major sites boast a total of 1,800 rooms to accommodate their guests. Most of these accommodations are located in small hotels, which have proliferated under encouragement from the investment-reform regimes of 1985 and 1990.

In 1988, the French company Savana-Pullman announced an intention to invest 1.5 billion French francs in new hotels providing 4,000 more beds. As its counterpart in this major project, the Malagasy government pledged 172 million French francs for infrastructural improvements, hoping to bring tourist traffic to 100,000 visitors per year by 1997. A recent government action plan anticipates as many as 230,000 visitors to the island by the year 2,000.[7] Tourism might thus move into second or third place in national foreign exchange earnings, particularly if the great island can join European, Asian, and Southern African circuits that already frequent Mauritius, Seychelles, and Réunion. Like other major investments, the Savana-Pullman project remains delayed until clarification of political climates and resolution of its relationship to the international environmental program.

So, in this natural wonderland with its fascinating coastal and mountainscapes and its cultural uniqueness, tourism contributed less than 1 percent of export receipts in the mid-1980s. That contribution climbed to 5 percent in 1988, when more traditional exports defaulted seriously. The major share of 34,000 visits in that year consisted of airborne businesspeople and international experts and some ship-borne passengers at Nosy Be Island; few foreigners comb the arduous but highly rewarding natural and cultural contours of this unique place. Sojourns averaged five nights at expenditures of roughly 500 French francs a day. The 1988 record was substantially exceeded in 1990, when 53,000 tourists frequented the island, but the traffic fell by 34 percent in 1991, rising to an estimated 45,000 in 1992 and an officially anticipated 68,000 visitors in 1993. These levels suffer by contrast with the annual tourist arrivals in Kenya (700,000 in 1992) and even tiny Mauritius (300,000), but Madagascar's future in tourism seems bright; after the opening of a new national park at Ranomafana and with adequate financing, promotion, and management, the tourist industry could develop into Madagascar's largest single "export" before the end of the century. Unless those initiatives are joined with social stability and conservation of national endowments, however, the traffic maximum could well remain under 100,000.[8]

The great island's inimitable biological diversity has excited much imagination—even among international civil servants. Truly this "Lemurian" chunk of ancient Gondwana represents "a world like our own," as the scientist Alison Jolly entitles her rapturous book.[9] But Madagascar is "like" the rest of the world mainly in being a separate, complete place with features and rules of its own. Only one out of twenty species identified in the spiny desert of the Malagasy south can be found anywhere else on earth. Eighty percent of the flora, more than half the birds, and 95 percent of Madagascar's reptiles survived only on this island.[10] Ancestors of the modern lemur crossed the Mozambique Channel 40 million years ago to this haven, leaving relatives to be extinguished in the course of continental Africa's evolution. Many species expired in Madagascar, too, for the present endowment was once overshadowed by larger animals—the monster-bird aepyornis, pygmy hippos, giant lemurs, and others—all wiped out by climatic change or by humankind.[11] Now the survivors turn their visages toward an unpitying humanity preoccupied by its own needs.

TABLE 5.2 Madagascar's Population, Estimated and Projected, 1900–2025

Year	Population	Year	Population
1900	2,244,000	1980	8,700,000
1913	3,295,000	1985	9,985,000
1921	3,292,000[a]	1988	10,000,000
1936	3,777,000	1990	11,503,000
1941	4,122,000	1991	11,922,000
1950	4,207,000	1992	12,232,000
1958	5,144,000	1995	13,098,000
1960	5,298,000	2000	15 to 17 million[b]
1965	6,000,000	2015	20 to 28 million[b]
1970	7,198,640	2025	24.5 to 36 million[b]
1975	7,600,000	–	–

[a]Apparent decline reflects World War I hardships, esp. infant mortality and general malnutrition.

[b]Twenty-first-century ranges calculated on projections of effectiveness of measures to reduce currently high fertility rates.

SOURCES: Figures compiled from Deschamps, Hubert. *Histoire de Madagascar*. Paris: Berger-Levrault, 1949; Heseltine, Nigel. *Madagascar*. New York: Praeger, 1971; various international agency publications. Numbers are subject to wide margins of error.

Population

Demographic projections diverge somewhat from the base point (of 7.6 million) established in the 1975 census; it is likely that the overall population surpassed 12 million in 1992 (see Table 5.2). The Malagasy nation grew at an annual rate of 2.8 percent during the 1980s, accelerating to over 3 percent at the end of the 1980s but quieting to an estimated 2.75 percent in the early 1990s. This pace of population growth stems not from falling mortality rates (which have remained at about 1.6 percent, yielding a deplorably low life expectancy of 54 years), or from negligible immigration, but from extraordinarily strong fertility. Four out of five Malagasy live in villages (places of less than 4,000 inhabitants), and although urban migration has intensified in recent decades, this preponderance of rural households induces high fertility—often for the sake of family security. If those trends continue, the Malagasy population will exceed 17 million by the year 2,000, 36 million by 2025.

With a population density of only eighteen per square kilometer, it is true that space exists for the multiplication of inhabitants. Yet the numbers of people projected for the next two decades will overtax the productive capacity of this vast but fragile landscape. More than half the 12 million Malagasy in 1992 were under twenty years of age. If current fertility trends persist, 45 percent of Madagascar's people will be under the age of fifteen by the year 2,000. Public health improvements should exert a salutary influence in the direction of longer longevity (hence, larger aggregate population), but any enhancement of the lot of the living will require birth control measures to reduce fertility rates by 50 percent within the next decade.

Population control has only recently begun to attract serious attention in the capital. Taking the lead in urging restraint on family growth, a small women's movement confronts vestigial colonial law, rural family tradition, and religious restrictions against birth control. Nevertheless, encouraged by Céline Ratsiraka, wife of the second republic's president, the movement successfully promoted the new National Population Policy Law at the end of 1990. Although family planning is now administratively encouraged and contraception is legal, implementation has been sluggish, and abortion remains prohibited except to save a mother's life.

Among the cultivated patches of the island, demographic density has forced an extension of farming to marginally fertile land. Some Malagasy groups migrate in search of opportunity; others are less mobile. Remaining farmers prefer to grow rice perilously on familiar mountaintops rather than move to distant valleys. In addition to risks of erosion, these pressures have reduced the fallow time allotted to exhausted fields, making a mockery of the ancient technology of the *tavy*.[12] Fires are set systematically to a million hectares of land each year in order to provide pasture for cattle, ashen topsoil for rice, charcoal for urban kitchens, wastelands for hunters and poachers, and scorched fields of protest for angry peasants.

Citing Madagascar as world recordholder for soil erosion, the World Bank estimated the annual cost of this environmental destruction in 1989 as $100–$300 million, or 5–15 percent of GDP.[13] Murphy called the plateaus of Imerina "a landscape long since subdued by man's needs and wounded by his ignorance."[14] Excess family members become city dwellers who, whether productive themselves or not, have to be fed by others. Over one in four Malagasy live in towns of 2,500 or more (double the ratio of 1975), and those towns have been growing at twice the rate of the territory as a whole.[15] As Ramahatra observed, the entire Malagasy productive strategy entailed an assault on the land:

> The systems of environmental exploitation typical of Malagasy societies ... engendered a vicious cycle of self-destruction of the ecosystem. In effect, an increasingly poor soil contains decreasingly dense vegetation; this entails ever weaker protection against erosion from water run-off. ... Concentrated on the productive surfaces which diminish from year to year at a spectacular pace, incapable of assuring the subsistence of a population in rapid expansion, the peasants thus tend to leave the land, joining the rural population drain.[16]

The problem is not new, but it has grown critical. Demand for food, timber, and firewood has intensified pressures on the once ubiquitous forest, which now clings to less than 20 percent of the island.

In truth, this wonderful wilderness lacks status in the unromantic Malagasy imagination. For better or worse, human techniques have disciplined the landscape; they have flooded rice fields, scorched mountain pasture, and denuded the savanna in a "suicide by fire."[17] The most rapidly growing tree for reforestation purposes, the imported Australian eucalyptus, impoverishes the soil it saves. Trees such as the clove and the litchi are being removed for firewood because their once-precious fruit suffers market vicissitudes. Hence, the remaining east coast rain forest degenerates and disappears gradually; soils drain off with it, and so do the lemurs and other beleaguered animal species. In 1988, Jolly portrayed the ravages against forest and forest creatures exerted by the overpowering demands of millions of impoverished farmers, herders, and loggers: "To subsist in a nation whose economy has stagnated for decades, they attack their island's trees—deciduous in the west, tropical in the north and east, spiny in the desert south. Slashing, burning, and sowing to create cropland, pasture, and firewood, they have reduced Madagascar's rain forest by half just since 1950, leaving lemurs besieged in the forests that remain."[18]

Other kinds of "progress" threaten the unique spiny forest in the island's south. To extract the titanium deposited there would entail removing all remaining vegetation from the sandy subsurface that is already overgrazed; already, water supplies have vanished from this area on several sad occasions in the twentieth century, including 1992. Still, titanium production may yet save the long-inert economy of the south. In the east, ilmenite may have to be mined by a Franco-Canadian consortium at the sacrifice of thousands of hectares of forest.[19] Human survival might continue to demand this price from nature. But already in the World Bank's formulation, Malagasy are living out of harmony with their own environment—consuming their natural resource capital at an accelerated pace without concern for longer-term consequences—and they must be assisted into reconciliation with it.[20]

PREPARING FOR DEVELOPMENT

The Environmental Operation

Among the first respondents to the World Bank's call for action to preserve a rapidly degrading Third World environment, the Malagasy republic concluded an agreement for that purpose with the bank and five other major partners in early 1990.[21] The action plan includes a decentralized conservation and management program for Madagascar's unique biological endowment, ranked as one of seven global "megabiodiversities" by international publicists.[22] That program is coupled with agricultural research and extension operations and with ecological or "discovery" tourism. The plan envisages mobilization of a variety of development agents—international, bilateral, and nongovernmental—to provide training, and to ensure sustainable development of natural resources, conservation and management of environmental assets, enhancement of rural and urban living conditions, institutional research and data collection, and adaptation of technology.

The tourist program, implemented by UNESCO, calls for fifty "discovery" sites for small visitor groups as well as three coastal resorts for more traditional leisure travel.[23] The program is to be incorporated into Madagascar's five-year plan. Bank sources hope to see that plan incorporate an effective design for control of population growth as well as a new environmental law code and landholding legislation; it should apply taxation strategies favoring those who work the land against prevailing customs of minimal use, *tavy*, and sharecropping.[24] The environmental action plan is already conceptually inte-

Ringtail lemurs, examples of Madagascar's unique wildlife. Photo by Gay Kuester, © The Chicago Zoological Society.

grated with the international structural adjustment scheme discussed further on.

Erosion control represents a major objective of the action plan. Within its first five years of operation, the program is to have equipped and stabilized the island's ten most threatened natural zones (of a total of fifty)—where hillsides burn for cultivation, forests turn into prairies for pasture, charcoal burners and poachers destroy existing species, and topsoil washes into the streams. This program is under way, but with hesitations and interruptions. Methodology has been tested since the mid-1980s, and culturally adapted measures exist for preparation'of the rural populations affected by the plan. An international staff has been recruited by the World Wildlife Fund in Geneva to join with local technicians and administrators, although not without complaint over the level of expertise of the first crop of personnel.[25] Landhold mapping proceeded in 1990 against some resistance in local propertied classes and their bureaucratic counterparts.[26]

Decentralized administration—difficult to conceive under the Ratsiraka regime—plays an important part in the conception of a socially effective environmental program. Fokon'olona are encouraged to contract directly with technical and financial sources, including private entrepreneurs, in order to initiate myriads of small local projects; they are also expected to adjudicate property disputes and maintain registers, collect taxes and fees, manage communally owned land, and enforce the laws. The ordinarily fragmented extension industry is to be rationalized so that a single polyvalent expert works with any particular group of farmers. Major watershed development focuses on Lake Alaotra and the Mandraka and Andekaleka river basins. A public health element includes reopening previously won combats against resurgent malaria and bilharsia. A compensatory fund operates to soften the effects of the reforms on Malagasy poor.[27]

Initial estimates of the environmental program's financial needs over twenty years is from $300–$400 million. International sources calculate this expense as little more than the current *annual* cost of environmental degradation, as a million hectares burn and wash off Madagascar's crust each year.[28]

Roughly 30 to 40 percent of the budget is to go to reforestation, soil reconstruction, and other infrastructure; 20 percent to conservation of species; 10–20 percent to training; 25 percent to mapping and land registration. Administrative costs should require only 5 percent. Before suffering postponement in the social turmoil of 1991–1993, an inaugural phase of the program (scheduled for 1991–1995) had received pledges of adequate financing from six national governments and six international organizations—the first instance of global funding for a Third World government's plan for environmental conservation.[29] National sources and beneficiary communities and enterprises are expected to bear increasing proportions of the expense as the program advances. Developmental investment provides the justification for assistance to a flourishing, privately operated tourist industry.[30]

This prototypical venture depends on the comprehension and sympathy of a population ill-accustomed to such intimacy with the purposes of *fanjakana* and its diverse dominating *vazaha*. Some peasants consider the compulsory reforestation campaign too reminiscent of forced public works under the French regime and of relatively ineffectual obligatory forestation projects of the Tsiranana period. Yet a pilot project conducted in northeast Madagascar integrated agricultural, educational, and public health projects, leading to a 70 percent reduction in deforestation over eighteen months.[31] Full economic benefits include forest, water, and species conservation; security for real estate holdings through landhold registration; and of course, technically demanding jobs for a trained population. Much more is expected from this approach to national poverty; as then-minister Maxime Zafera (Livestock, Fisheries, and Forestry) stated to the February 1990 Paris conference that approved first-phase funding, "To fight against the degradation of the environment in the third world is equivalent to combatting underdevelopment."[32]

In related actions, Madagascar also became a pioneer among the world's poorest countries by concluding in August 1989 a $2.1 million "debt for nature swap" with the United States Bankers Trust; a subsequent million-dollar swap with the World Wildlife Fund sold commercial debt from six international banks at a discount of 55 percent, three-fourths of it financed by a U.S. government loan to the WWF. The proceeds of the trade go to environmental protection programs, including national parks management, erosion control, and training of park rangers. French commercial institutions have also been buying Malagasy obligations, but debt-for-equity swaps will prove difficult until companies become more interested in direct investment in the Malagasy economy. Hence, these arrangements weigh insubstantially against a more than $4 billion debt owed by the national economy, although they provide an index for a more auspicious future.[33] Any step toward reversing environmental degradation is an advance on development for the great island.

Compared to such global development strategies as import substitution, export "push," and central planning, environmental enhancement sounds most attractively humane. Perhaps it will take hold with a population otherwise skeptical of schemes devised for its essential benefit in Washington, Paris, and even Antananarivo. Nevertheless, the action plan has thus far engendered little real action. Prior to June 1991, international functionaries and

Malagasy technicians impatiently awaited appropriate legal and administrative preparations by a sluggish Ratsiraka government. Since that time, the entire system has been paralyzed by constitutional crisis.

Perhaps Madagascar can wait until the mighty international environmental program has finally taken hold—to save vegetation, animal species, medicinal plants, oxygen, and the irreplaceable wonder of the Malagasy wilderness—all without unacceptable cost to human beings. Somehow, the aims of economic development and ecological conservation must be served simultaneously, requiring a structure of institutions and popular education that Madagascar does not yet enjoy. But at least the island has a plan with powerful international sponsorship and a sense of urgency to resolve the demands of population, production, and environment. Jolly comments on the irony of a monetarized aid program to save nature: "How absurd to think we must put a price on an alternate world of evolution—the island-continent of Madagascar—before deciding whether it is worth preserving."[34]

Absurd as it may be for terrestrial Madagascar, such practicality has not (yet) come to apply to the abundant wilderness of sea life around the island. Settled primarily by mariners, the great island gradually turned its inhabitants into lovers of the land. Alone among the coastal peoples of these undulant shores, the Vezo in the southwest regularly live from their ocean catch. Of the 150,000 tons taken annually from these waters, more than two-thirds go to French, Japanese, Russian, and other foreign fleets. By the middle of the 1980s, however, Malagasy prawns were being exported (mainly to Japan) at a rate that occupied fourth place—after coffee, vanilla, and cloves—in the Malagasy portfolio of exports; in 1991 and 1992, despite concerns over secure levels of catch, shrimp exports moved past coffee and cloves into second position, earning $41 million and (estimated) $51.5 million in those years, respectively, and attracting Japanese and European investment to fisheries off Nosy Be. To most international observers watching the degeneration of production and marketing of the island's exports of coffee, vanilla, and cloves, realization of the great island's economic promise lies in such untraditional exports as textiles, tourism, and shrimp.[35]

The absence of appropriate institutions of reform and popular education handicap even the most obvious course of constructive change in Madagascar. If not adroitly accommodated, peasant conservatism can obstruct economic progress anywhere. Whereas the Antananarivo aristocracy and bourgeoisie have proved remarkably entrepreneurial, rural class stratifications often militate against change. A need for stability in the agrarian universe tends to reinforce the authority of relatively affluent, landholding elder men against indigent, younger, landless males or women.[36] Individual enterprise challenges the cyclical (some would call it fatalistic) view of time and experience that regulates Malagasy rural life. This conservatism prevails even among such relative parvenus as the local party leaders who carried Tsiranana's PSD and Ratsiraka's AREMA to power.

In the absence of an economic dynamic, opportunities for social mobility against this grain are relatively rare. Elders tend to discount the impatience of young and underprivileged people to own land or cattle of their own, or otherwise to break the cycles of dependence. Inequality of income worsened inexorably in rural Madagascar during the Ratsiraka revolution, aggravating problems of hunger and disease among the island's poorest population.[37]

All political regimes in modern Malagasy history have respected these social cleavages in the rural environment. Government subsidies, technological incentives, tax advantages, and other perquisites went to dominant groups in that milieu so that the money economy intruded without shock to traditional structures. But this wager on the strong has by and large not paid off in rural economic growth. Agricultural cooperatives, state farms, extension technology, land distribution, taxes, all encounter mute, determined resistance. Reforms and innovations have seldom carried with them the props of security—insurance, easy credit, health and education benefits, price stability guarantees, tax concessions—so important to peasant rationality.

Under such circumstances, farmers discover abundant reasons for recalcitrance against official policy. Land is held by individuals in trust for larger families or demes (*foko*) that include the recent dead; it is not readily alienated or combined.[38] Youth are undisciplined and resist mobilization. Elders are reactionary and oppose challenges to their authority. The lore of ancestral experience renders certain days—and certain practices—inadvisable for work, even forbidden (*fady*). Technological assets can be easily sabotaged; herds can be hidden. Black markets operate in the old accustomed way whether legal markets are controlled or otherwise. As the population began increasing at a rate of 3 percent, the need for family survival inspired autarchic action that prejudiced national viability. Even in the upward-turning productivity of 1989 and 1990, growth outside agriculture exceeded the progress registered on the land.

Yet rural mobilization is possible. When able to perceive security among the accessible advantages, Malagasy farmers have responded positively to innovation, increasing production and selling through established channels.[39] Merina history invokes a two-century-old heritage of cooperation in the centralized land clearance and distribution projects, irrigation, marketing, and technological initiatives of their great king Andrianampoinimerina. This monarch's success was owed in part to an increasing population's demand for goods and in part to the need for protection, which the king's forces supplied. Nampoina's successors—subsequent monarchs, the French colonial administration, and, in a somewhat different sense, the republican regimes—increasingly had to impose their will by coercion. That strategy generates its own opposition.

In a dispersed yet harmonious cultural environment, only human-made institutions—fanjakana, the loci of authority—are foreign. This establishment became in the Tsiranana era "a quasi-mystical, fluidly shaped entity for which [the population] feels a reverential and virtually religious fear."[40] But its requirements were evaded as often as possible, for the mythologized state also represented the eternal stranger.[41] Responses to central policy become subject to a curious sociopsychological inertia, inevitably subversive yet self-protective. As Covell points out, government in Madagascar displays a reciprocal (and well-warranted) distrust of the peasantry.[42] So the cycle of coercion continues.

Exhortations to produce and to market, unless clearly compensated in price or other tangible advantage, tend to go unheeded. These efforts seem to work to the advantage only of the urban leadership or other "foreigners," not the peasant communities themselves. Under Ratsiraka, Malagasy farmers saw only bungling and chicanery in the way government agents sought to replace the profiteering middlemen of the traditional rural trade; they understood how both price and tax structures discouraged intensive production. Rice, sugar, and oils found their way into black-market outlets at double or triple the price realized through orthodox channels. In 1983, before distribution was liberalized, the parallel market was offering rice at two and one-half times the official price; even now, during the off-season of November to March (*la soudure*), the legal price more than doubles, from about 250 to 700–800 Malagasy francs (FMG) per kilogram. Antananarivo, a city of 300,000 when the author lived there in the 1960s, may hold more than 2 million now during the day; virtually all are fearfully poor, and although the country does not formally provide enough food, virtually all can eat.[43]

ECONOMICS OF THE RATSIRAKA CHARTER

Against considerable structural and cultural resistance, the revolutionary regime of 1975 sought to revitalize its national economy. Attributing previous failures to colonial and postcolonial capitalism, the Ratsiraka charter envisioned prosperity as the outcome of economic nonalignment, thanks to the victory over imperialism. Without direct reference to Marxism, the charter aimed at mobilization of national energies through state intervention to eliminate injustice and exploitation, unemployment and inflation, and scarcities of essential commodities.

In Phase 1 of the mobilization plan (1979–1984) the structural and material foundations of socialized development would include land reform, nationalized enterprises, ideological indoctrination, and productivity in the peasantry. Phase 2 (1985–1992) was to emphasize essential human needs while consolidating the socialist economy and bringing self-sufficiency in food. Phase 3 (1993–2000) entailed rapid economic diversification and accelerated growth, quadrupling the 1979 production level, building a strong cooperative movement, and limiting the private sector to one-third of GNP.[44] None of this ambition came to reality.

It is true that the ownership structure of the economy did convert—from corporate command to state command. In 1970, 80 percent of Madagascar's modern economic sector was owned by foreigners. While exporting almost one-third of their profits, these French and other non-Malagasy reinvested steadily in capital improvement and inventory. By the end of 1976, 61 percent of that economy had come under state control—70 percent by 1978. In 1980, forty-four state-owned companies and thirty-eight with majority public ownership had replaced the old colonial establishments producing coffee, vanilla, cloves, pepper, cotton, and other crops largely for export. All banks and insurance companies, electricity- and waterworks had been nationalized; export trade was 85 percent in government hands by 1983, imports 60 percent, domestic trade 70 percent; 40 percent of industry (including sugar mills and textile plants) was state-operated.

Theoretically based on agricultural production, the central-planning mystique actually considered industry to be the motor of development. Assessing the errors of the first republic, the new planners concluded that a modernized agriculture would not suffice in this world's economy. Self-sufficiency through import substitution and an exportable industrial output must complement that strong agricultural base, secure from deterioration in terms of trade.[45] Urged on by analysts of an ostensibly favorable world investment climate, the second republic embarked on a disastrous international borrowing spree to finance its industrial ambitions. Identified by the slogan "invest without restraint" (*investir à outrance*, sometimes translated as "invest to the hilt"), the program counted overoptimistically on early repayment of loans through exports of coffee and other crops at high world market prices. Catastrophically for Madagascar, those export prices did not hold into the 1980s, world interest rates rose precipitously, and creditors sought to call in their loans.

In addition to supporting new dimensions in industry, planners provided for the restructuring of agriculture through collective farms, a new cooperative movement, and universally diffused technology, all organized under the decentralized territorial administration. New energies were to invigorate transportation, agricultural marketing, and rural credit, as well as to improve conditions for the production of vanilla, sugar, coffee, cloves, groundnuts, tobacco, pepper, sisal; mining of chromite, graphite, mica, coal, bauxite; and industrial processing of textiles, timber, petroleum, and construction materials. Punctuated by ideological incentives, the new process was destined to abolish the negligent opportunism of the foreign and comprador middle class, which had sought only its jackal's share of export profits. Minds would have to be changed, of course, and parasitism had to be eradicated in city and countryside. The charter was to transform an economy hitherto globalized in the service of private transnational capital and the "negotiated imperialism" of the Lomé agreements between European and Third World governments.[46]

Central planning called on rural Madagascar once again to submit to legislation of economic and cultural change. This time, however, the experiment was supposed to conform to the inner reality of this society, thus liberating peasants from their own recalcitrance. The centralized planning of Asian socialism would combine with local management, freeing hitherto exploited labor and initiative to produce for society's needs. The several subclasses of the Malagasy bourgeoisie were to be dispossessed by state action in the people's interest. Government decisions would take their bearings from that interest, emanating out of traditional decentralized grassroots collectives and filtering through a reorganized hierarchy of decisions. Thus would triumph Madagascar's unique fokon'olona process.[47]

Endorsed by referendum on December 21, 1975, this eclectic blueprint for social revolution never had an adequate chance to prove itself. Banks and businesses were rapidly nationalized but not socialized. Cooperatives and state farms emerged, but efforts to redistribute private land foundered against the power of entrenched privilege.[48] Little changed in local administration as the proprietary, professional, and business personnel of previous regimes reshuffled themselves into an enlarged and highly privileged bureaucratic class. These officials replaced the expatriate entrepreneurs and executives of the newly nationalized French corporations, plantations, and banks. Many of those despised foreign capitalists were driven home on a wave of bureaucratized enthusiasm only to reappear as international creditors within a few years. Their Malagasy successors operated national companies (*sociétés d'intérêt national*) and other parastatal agencies in all sectors of the economy. Fully 150 of these state enterprises were subject to no competition, no countervalences. As unions were forbidden to contest policy, workers' councils never penetrated managerial situations (despite the doctrine of "socialist enterprises"); wage scales and other personnel policies were determined through peremptory decisions by government managers.[49] Many of the national companies were staffed by hastily appointed and rapidly rising incompetents. Despite their lofty purpose, these agencies behaved in much the same alienating manner as the old colonial dinosaurs, buying cheap goods from peasant producers and selling rare imported products back to them at high prices. For want of trained agents willing to serve in the "bush," technology transfers were often entrusted to military personnel who also carried rudimentary ideological slogans to a bewildered peasantry.[50]

To channel rural energies toward social goals, the new state also sought to destroy the integrated microeconomy of marketing, credit, and retail commerce operated by resourceful Chinese, Indo-Pakistani (Karana), or displaced Merina. These middlemen, "whose deviousness and toughness in business were legendary,"[51] had played essential yet often resented roles in the circulation of goods and services throughout rural Madagascar. They had held the local peasantry in perpetual servitude through face-to-face credit and pricing arrangements for farming supplies as well as consumer goods. Dismantling this predatory system, the revolutionary regime subjected each function of the rural economy to separate mismanagement through corrupt parastatal corporations, inefficient centralized collectives, undercapitalized credit agencies, and desultory technical services. The dispossessed old traders and moneylenders dwelt patiently in their boutiques, awaiting inevitable opportunities to reenter their erstwhile networks of credit and marketing. As Pryor observes,

> In his first decade of power President Ratsiraka turned the intersectoral terms of trade against agricultural producers. He established a state-owned marketing system that proved incapable of functioning adequately in purchasing crops and supplying farmers with agricultural inputs and consumer goods. As a result, ru-

ral markets literally "dis-integrated" (became misaligned with each other), total agricultural production stagnated, and agricultural exports plummeted.[52]

The revolution even retained Madagascar's inherited colonial model for domestic exchange—transferring primary products to cities and ports in exchange for capital, foreign machinery, and consumer imports. By now, however, the price-credit-supply system was being manipulated against agricultural interests. Hence, by 1977 primary production was failing to balance import needs, and both began to suffer serious decline. No longer ensured at a minimum by the foreign corporations and estates, investment capital shunned the market, and in a land capable of self-sufficiency, food was being bought in large quantity from abroad; 180,000 tons of rice had to be imported in 1980, 150,000 and an additional 100,000 in other foodstuffs in 1981.[53]

While infrastructure and technology regressed in the productive regions, the state sought to reorganize seed distribution and crop collection, with further disastrous economic results. As Razafimandranto stated in 1982, "Regularity in providing fertilizer and insecticides, punctuality in harvest collection and payment for crops and the supply of consumer goods to the rural world are no longer guaranteed."[54] Economic failure destroyed whatever early consensus Ratsiraka may have originally enjoyed, eroding capacity in the regime, which needed a second wind but reaped only the whirlwind.

For want of capital, technology, and markets for diversification, Madagascar's export policy suffered from a typical Third World contradiction; it had to persist in emphasizing robusta coffee and cloves despite declining quality in those Malagasy crops and ruinous volatility in world markets. Even so, the command system was missing its opportunities. Coffee and vanilla were being smuggled out through the Comoros for higher foreign exchange payoffs to growers and middlemen. Expensive, erratic Malagasy clove production competed with Brazil and other new major producers for the Indonesian cigarette market. Cotton acreage began to decline in 1978, continuing into the 1990s. Tobacco, sisal, and sugar quality also fell with sagging production. As the regime's defector, Ramanandraibe, judged in 1987, "Socialism administered and it administered poorly; it did not manage and still less did it innovate."[55]

Agricultural deterioration had immediate effects on Madagascar's rudimentary industrial plant. Three hundred firms had been nationalized or founded with either outright government administration or indirect control through majority shareholding. They included plants for processing of cotton, tobacco, oils and soap, meat, fruit, and baked goods as well as import-substitution ventures in batteries, paints, matches, paper, and beverages. Weak agricultural performance, inappropriate technology, and an overvalued currency lowered the export ledger; only textiles had any chance of competitiveness among the island's manufactures. Declining foreign exchange earnings forced further reduction of imports, thus depriving many plants of primary materials, fuels, and spare parts.

By the 1980s, virtually all the new industrial projects supported by the policy of investment without restraint were functioning either at a serious loss or not at all; these included poorly conceived or badly situated wheat and soya mills, urea fertilizer, pharmaceutical, and cement plants.[56] Moreover, the entire road system was left to deteriorate, and without new trucks or spare parts, both the public and private transport companies had to cut operations; officially repressed prices in state-owned trucking forced many remaining private transporters out of business.

Among the revolution's true achievements was a new educational system dedicated to self-realization according to individual aptitudes and the needs of the nation. The structure ensured almost all Malagasy five years of basic education under fokontany aegis. Indisputably good in itself, educational democratization nonetheless transpired without adequate consideration of economic consequences, especially in its secondary and post-secondary expansion. The educational apparatus was conceived to help build a socialist society and to diffuse revolutionary ideology among youth.[57] Academic freedom was restricted to conformance with the principles of the revolutionary charter. After that, the flood.

Even François Rajaoson admitted that by 1980, the system was producing too many underqualified baccalaureates: 11,206 diplomas in 1979 compared with 1,656 in 1972. Forty percent of the graduates were still in "lettres" (humanities and social sciences), for which job opportunities were virtually nonexistent.[58] This pattern was transferred into the burgeoning university environment, where students tended to reside in subsidized dormitories for six to eight years before moving (with or without degrees) into sophisticated underemployment.

The education campaign also entailed compromises of quality as well as paradoxical costs in social objectives. Genuine reform of curriculum to integrate with national needs, aspirations, and planning never materialized; nor did a well-articulated program for those who left school. Since the affluent continued to frequent the best schools and to go abroad when quality declined, the result was a reinforcement of prevailing hierarchies.

Policy remedies tended to inspire as many problems as they resolved. Raising the failure rates on national examinations, for instance, reduced the flow of credentialed job claimants—largely among the theoretically enfranchised poor. In 1980 the examination strategy cut the number of baccalaurate holders in half, with the intention of stabilizing the number of those with diplomas at about 6,000–7,000. But that strategy lacked clear alternatives for rejected students who would be less lucky, if no less qualified, than their elder siblings in the bumper crops of the late 1970s. It was therefore doubly unpopular among families to whom the glories of education had been offered as a civic right.[59]

In practice, at most exam seasons, government yielded to pressure for lower graduation standards and thus kept putative student success rates at an artificial maximum, whatever the effect on job markets. Hence, the regime was obliged, ready or not, to seek alternative ways to recruit professionals for the economy. It also had to absorb otherwise high unemployment among graduates through obligatory national service, military induction, and other schemes of dubious human resource productivity.

In the Depths of Depression

Their revolution frustrated by domestic paralysis and their national hopes overtaken by global realities, Madagascar's people spent most of the 1980s trying to sustain life. In the city, Malagasy hustled to eat and keep warm. In the countryside, they withdrew for security from larger into smaller societies. Wherever transportation links survived, intervillage exchanges certainly continued; some larger farmers and entrepreneurs made money in the parallel economy; city folk found opportunities for lucrative subcontracting, for moonlighting, or for crime.

Ordinary Malagasy nevertheless participated minimally in the official economy that was based on administered prices and negotiated international exchange adjustments. They complied only with the inevitable demands of that economy—for maintenance of property and rents, school fees, taxes. In Malagasy culture, life springs from ancestral sources; it flows into ceremony, and ceremony was financed as far as possible through cattle-trading and barter. People in the 1980s would work for those purposes but not for much else. Beyond their horizons, the bankrupt economy had to be pledged to international institutions.

In times of stress, each economic unit of the great island retreats from the national economy to attend to tangible internal needs. Villagers under administrative pressure without perceptible rewards turn inward to their families and themselves. Although aggravating the disconnections in the island's archipelago of activity, this retrenchment into autarchy kept people alive more efficiently than their national economy could manage within the global system. Growers of coffee, vanilla, groundnuts, cloves, and other exportable products either cut back production in order to fill more immediate needs or smuggled their crops into black markets or out to Réunion and the Comoros to earn foreign exchange. From a herd of at least 10 million cattle, little meat was exported, and the slaughter rate (about one head in ten) was only a third of Argentina's. Chromite exports fell by 42 percent. Lacking in domestic and imported raw materials, spare parts, and market access, industries also failed to export, producing at most for expensive import substitution. Surplus water and hydroelectric energy dissipated for want of dams and storage facilities.

Nationalization took the remaining dynamic out of the modern economy. In 1989, the largest firms on the island were in state control—the Star Breweries (68 percent public), the SNMTM maritime transportation company (59 percent), and the wholly state-owned railway system (RNCFM). The fourth largest, Ny Havana insurance syndicate, was 48 percent public. The cotton-textile cycle held up best, as fiber production revived for a time under French and World Bank aid; yet low purchasing power and the competition of imported used clothing hampered domestic marketing in this industry.[60] The largest factory, a $75 million urea fertilizer plant at Toamasina, has operated

Sisal drying, near Amboasary. Photo by Gay Kuester, © The Chicago Zoological Society.

at a loss since its opening in 1986. As a whole, industry contributes only 14 percent of GDP and occupies barely 4 percent of the labor force.

Inflation began tearing at the urban fabric in 1981 and 1982 as public finance strategies sought to keep parastatal enterprises solvent, creating formidable budgetary deficits. Rice prices rose by 87 percent, flour by 100 percent, and bread by 76.8 percent in the first half of the decade. Rice became 15 percent more expensive in 1984 alone as the overall index climbed nearly eighty points in one year. Working families were pauperized and many paupers reduced to corruption and crime.[61]

The regime of manipulated price structures engendered shortages of basic commodities (rice, natural gas, oils, sugar, salt) as well as black-market resurgence and informal strikes. Fears of shortages fired the rumor-radiators of the towns, thus helping create the shortages people feared. By 1987, the black markets in rice, sugar, and other essentials had become big business, some blaming the lawlessness on the Karana, others attributing it to prominent statesmen.[62] Cattle-rustling, always a pastime for certain feuding families of the center-west, infested the pastures as a mode of survival—or again, some say, as a recourse of vindictive authorities against recalcitrant herders. Theft of rice, in heaps, in bags, even of paddy shoots, became endemic, revealing a new theft psychosis in the Malagasy. Peasants who had declined to produce surpluses for reasons of price and delays in payment were now declining to grow anything out of sight of their own houses.

Shortages, black markets, and street crime represent only some of the elements of the morass of the Malagasy 1980s. Visitors and journalists reported the impracticality of roads, the virtual absence of medical facilities and health care, pervasive official corruption, famine in drought-stricken areas, urban housing degredation.[63] "More than a tenth of all babies die before their fifth birthday," reported Dan Baum,[64] as Malagasy parents proved unable by themselves to combat the syndrome of weaning and other problems of penury. The greater the risk of infant mortality, the greater the incentive to sustain the chain of birth, so the population grew precipitously in spite of medical inadequacies.

The breakdown of public health and a reported climatic warming trend of 0.8 degrees Celsius left the central plateaus exposed to malaria for the first time in generations. Without immunity, 100,000 are reported to have died from the dread mosquito before France, Switzerland, and Italy could send quinine suppressants for the 1988–1989 rainy season.[65] In 1989, the government opened soup kitchens (called *tsaky-pop*) in the capital, and fokontany councils were urged to try to maintain some hygiene in the neighborhoods. Provincial cities were as deplorable; in 1990, three years after Toliary's Karana-owned shops were set on fire, the stench of offal, garbage, and decay pervaded the town.[66]

One-fourth the population was estimated in 1988 to be living in or on the verge of absolute poverty (less than 28,000 FMG for a family of five); this was more than double the proportion of 1981. Urban purchasing power had declined by 10 percent between 1977 and 1984, and unemployment was epidemic. Infant mortality surged from 120 per 1,000 live births in 1980 to 250 by 1985; daily caloric intake remained at about 2,500 per person. The revolutionary regime's disastrous policies, as Frederic Pryor itemizes them, were "the relative decline of investment in agriculture, the turning of the internal terms of trade against agriculture, the overvalued exchange rate with a resulting shortage of agricultural inputs and consumer goods for the farmers, and the disintegration of both markets and the rural transportation infrastructure." These policies only increased poverty and social inequities while failing to inspire growth.[67]

Deliberate state planning had been interrupted by the 1978–1980 drive for all-out external borrowing of capital to launch the economy out of stagnation. This unrestrained investment campaign threw resources haphazardly toward ad hoc project demands. By the end of this interim, the economy was so hopelessly submerged in debt that developmental planning targets became meaningless. Thanks to frenetic acceptance of petro-dollar loans, GDP rose suddenly in 1979 by 10.3 percent and in 1980 at a like rate. But the national debt had more than quintupled from $167.3 million in 1975 to $926 million in 1980. Subject to rescheduling and other accommodations, the debt was to exceed $3 billion by the mid-1980s.

But it was not the end of the developmental tunnel that Ratsiraka was to see in 1984; it was rather the end of the experiment. Burgeoning without precautions, the ambitious investment schemes proved arbitrary and unviable, ending in a catastrophic default of debt. In the longer term, from 1972 to 1986, per capita GDP declined at an average annual rate of 2.4 percent.[68]

By now most Malagasy have forgotten that the macroeconomic slogan for the late 1970s was actually "invest *and produce* without restraint," for although the creditors responded, the producers certainly did not.[69] Debt-ridden and under-performing, the economy would surely have done better the other way around—had the investors ignored the call and the producers heeded. From 1977 to 1984, agricultural production declined at a rate of 2.3 percent annually. Little, if any, savings was recorded in the farm regions, for in a situation of scarcity and repressed prices, why should a peasant borrow? Ideological exhortations bombarded the rural world without monetary, psychological, or symbolic consequence.

By the early 1980s, passive acceptance had easily melted into passive rejection of the controlled economy, the directing state, the incoherent elites. Unable to rejoice over the replacement of French strangers with Malagasy strangers, the peasantry tended to retreat furtively into escapism. Autarchic local microeconomies remained submerged in an ostensibly permanent alienation.[70]

In counterpoint to this passive withdrawal from the official economy, the 1980s witnessed more overt popular responses to deprivation. These ranged from musical-theater satire to dream escapes (*tromba*) to civil disobedience and even insurrection. Street riots broke out in the capital city four times in 1980–1982, and the provinces were experiencing their own share of unrest. To some observers, the student strikes of February 1981 seemed a repetition of May 1972—only this time they occurred in protest not over foreign domination but against a nationalist regime, the very aspiration of the 1972 student movement.[71]

With its revenues already declining, the Ratsiraka government tried revising the old tax code in January 1978. Income taxes were refocused, but many of the 165,000 people affected found ways to avoid the full impact of the reform. In rural Madagascar, no regime could have withstood reimposition of the colonial poll and cattle taxes that had been abolished in a popular move by the Ramanantsoa interregnum. In the end, the state remained as it had been—dependent for its revenues on indirect taxation, especially from agricultural exports.[72] Most of the fiscal burden was felt by the urban poor and the peasant producers of coffee and vanilla. Rather than invest directly in agriculture or industry, the regime placed three-fourths of its revenues in relatively unproductive operating budgets (especially education, defense, and health) until the mid-1980s, when the burden of foreign debt deprived it of such discretion.

The social crisis came through hunger, shortages, alienation of young people, theft and banditry, family instability, black-market exploitation, even the abandonment and sale of unwanted children—all distorting authentic Malagasy culture from its essential norms. As its system foundered, the regime's natural reaction was to cast blame onto international mechanisms, lackeys of residual imperialism, and the bad luck of the Third World. Today, however, even the major protagonists agree that the fault lay in a poverty of conception and inadequacy of execution attending the domestic system itself.

As Pryor judges, "Madagascar's difficulties in the 1980s can be traced much more easily to governmental policies than to external forces."[73]

Nevertheless, although the state sought to blame international factors for its troubles, its recourse in 1978–1980—and its redress of that recourse throughout the 1980s—increased its dependence on that same pernicious international system. Failure to realize revolutionary goals in rapid time caused general demoralization in the second republic. Civil servants diverted state budgets to personal profit. Extension agents remained in the capital, moonlighting to make ends meet against inflation. Parastatal crop collection proved monstrously inefficient, and the bureaucracies were unable to pay even low producer prices in good time. Centralized rural credit dried up. In late 1981, Ratsiraka admitted making some errors, but he censured his finance minister, Rakotovao-Razakaboana, for regretting the rapid pace of "socialization" in food production.[74]

Two separate middle-class clienteles had developed during the first republic. One was technical, bureaucratic, and largely Merina; the other—consisting of land-based political notables identified with Tsiranana's PSD—depended on the agricultural surpluses that paid for consumer imports. The Merina bourgeoisie had developed commercial and industrial interests that were in turn frustrated by foreign domination of the modern economic sector. French-owned firms represented 65 percent of trade volume, Malagasy enterprises only 5.1 percent; 3.4 percent of all wage earners were foreigners, but they earned 27.4 percent of wages, according to an official 1969 study cited by Hugon.[75] PSD elites in the remote rural areas reserved local surpluses for their own purposes, resisting forms of accumulation that threatened the stability of the society they governed. In Hugon's terms, they tended to control, not to manage, rice field civilization.[76]

This ineffective apparatus was replaced by the revolutionary conceptions of the second republic, and that vision has in turn given way. Ratsiraka's critics contend that the entire socialist program meant little to its authors beyond a means of substituting their own national middle class for a foreign-dominated bourgeoisie. Ratsiraka declared Madagascar "open" to class conflict, wrote Robert Archer in 1978, only to mystify the Malagasy people and permit installation of the urban elites alienated by previous regimes. Pavageau understands the domination of rural middle classes over the peasantry as reinforced by that of the elders over the young; it was the latter who, if given a chance, would have combined the most progressive Western and traditional virtues and thus striven most ardently for egalitarian community.[77]

Seeing more social continuity than disruption in the Malagasy dynamics of the late 1970s, Chaigneau argued that the grand postulate of a new society consisted rather of "an inflation of juridical texts than an objective change in the social experience of the people."[78] In the new ideology, the revolution's declared enemy was not the bourgeoisie but global imperialism; hence, the compromises with national elites and landowners, religious leadership, inheritance rights, and other "reactionary" factors.[79] Pragmatic as it might seem, the socialist charter never could withstand such domestic concessions, let alone the contumelies of the contemporary world economy. It collapsed shortly after it was born and has now been all but repudiated by its own engineers.

The Path Not Taken

However disastrous, the revolution's economic strategies were responding to a manifest need for change in the mid-1970s. No momentum was left in the so-called neocolonial growth process—the economy structured on a recycled agricultural surplus determined by French agribusiness and the industries to which they were channeled. Far from conforming to capitalist incentives, Malagasy farmers were no longer willing or able to generate those surpluses. The colonial choice of coffee, vanilla, and cloves to carry the island's revenue burden encountered imperious market vicissitudes. Domestic articulation (transportation, market organization, monetarization, the fiscal base) was always too weak to supply alternative sources of productivity. Economic growth under Tsiranana, barely keeping a percentage point ahead of population, had lagged behind comparable African successes of the 1960s.

Choosing to respond radically to the call for change, the thinkers around Ratsiraka sought answers in Marxism-Leninism, in Maoist thought, in Kim Il-Sung's doctrines of Juche, and in the Algerian industrialization precedents under Boumedienne. This research ignored Madagascar's particularity, which had called the whole process into being. In Chaigneau's judgment,

> The Malagasy case represents a typical example of indifference to an imported ideology on the part of a population possessing its symbolic and conceptual social code that is foreign to the principles advanced by political decision-makers. This phenomenon of maladaptation is reinforced by the insular nature of the country, its ancestral culture, and its conception of roles and social functions (strongly hierarchized through ancestral precedent), as well as the survival of a scarcely negligeable mass of the population living on the margins of the state's jurisdiction.[80]

In addition to its own errors, the revolutionary government did have monumentally bad luck in the late 1970s. International advisers were urging the Malagasy authorities into serious indebtedness without providing good advice on project design; debt-financing plans depended on sustained coffee export prices just as that market began to drop and the second global petroleum crisis was to commence. Ratsiraka was counting on nationalist foreign policy, socialist rhetoric, and bureaucratic competence to transform the entire culture that underpinned a national economy. Given the prevailing circumstances, a successful metamorphosis was highly unlikely. Yet judged through the privilege of hindsight, economic disintegration might not have been inevitable in a Malagasy second republic.

Another strategy was available to Madagascar's leaders in 1975; since it was not tried, its prospects remain subject to endless futile conjecture. The abbreviated influence of Richard Ratsimandrava aimed at a different purpose than Ratsiraka's charter—a radical decentralization of decisions to reach essentially indigenous answers for the apparent immobility of the Malagasy economic culture. In democratic dialogue at the grass roots, new and traditional institutions were to make local law and keep order, maintain hygiene and public health, organize mutual aid and conciliation in civil litigation, plan economic development, and undertake agricultural production and marketing. Channeled through fokon'olona, such decisions would be based for better or worse on the authority of kinship and neighborhood links, not of external institutions. Traditional and technological elites would have to compete with each other for public favor.

What Covell calls "the dream of a self-taxing, self-policing community" insulated from exactions of the outside world was never to be.[81] Perhaps as Rajaona contends, it was utopic, even atavistic, to seek authenticity or national identity in a family-based, decentralized web of self-government.[82] Any number of obstacles might have arisen to subvert the decentralized process had it been allowed to transpire. Ratsimandrava's own unpopularity as gendarmerie leader and even his servile caste might have handicapped universal acceptance. The entire program would have been perceived as a threat to the entrenched bourgeoisie. Groups (especially non-Merina) who had never adopted the fokon'olona would have questioned the propriety of that institution as the locus of popular sovereignty. Yet there is reason to postulate that an authentic decentralized socialism based on consanguinity and community might have been welcomed in villages throughout the country.[83]

Instead of invoking this ideal to create the revolution, the 1975 charter turned "fokon'olona" into a mere useful label, a formalistic, juridical justifier for a very different form of activity.[84] In the new foray into socialism, the village council "was conceived from the outset as the prime forum for a campaign of awareness and indoctrination far removed from the objectives of Colonel Ratsimandrava."[85] Chaigneau portrays President Ratsiraka as incapable of conceding authority to the masses without imposing ideological impetus and discipline.[86] Rajaona sees the submission of fokon'olona to fanjakana as an inevitable assertion of direct tutelage by the *ray aman'dreny* (elders) over the forces of social change. Government domination violates the solidarity that had allowed the historical fokon'olona to embrace ever new groups and cultures, and to connect with global society.[87]

Prats believes, however, that Ratsiraka foresaw real dangers in empowering the old feudal notables, who might have seized local control in Ratsimandrava's revival of fokon'olona.[88] Hence, the revolution may have had little alternative to the imposition of democratic centralism and a command economy. Georges Serre-Ratsimandisa understands the fokon'olona institution as essentially inegalitarian in practice, despite the family solidarity that binds its unequal elements and the direct democracy through which it reaches its verdicts (*dina*).[89] Roland Razafimandranto interprets the Ratsiraka charter's references to decentralization as ambiguous; they might have allowed a sharing of state decisionmaking with popular institutions like the fokon'olona, even bringing about an equilibrium of rural wealth, capital, and power against the urban Antananarivo concentration. The chance was lost, in Razafimandranto's estimation, when the state refused to take these risks, insisting instead on the imperatives of its central plan, on ideological coherence through centralism, and on the need for bureaucratic uniformity in the face of perpetual economic crisis.[90]

In structure at least, Ratsiraka's system seemed to follow the 1973 Ratsimandrava proposals. It retained the hierarchy of 11,333 local councils (*fokontany*), 1,252 district councils (*firaisam'pokontany*), 110 regional councils (*fivondronam'pokontany*), and six provinces (*faritany*).[91] All assemblies, including the executive committees of the fokontany, were elected by the level below. In practice, however, these organisms acted as agents of the central government—delegated, as it were, by the people to govern the people. Problems of accountability became chronic. They were aggravated by a murky separation of jurisdictions between the layers of hierarchy. The system seemed at times to oblige each council simultaneously to take responsibility for every legislative, administrative, judicial, security, political, ideological, and economic problem of governance.

Under these circumstances, local autonomy could never materialize. The idea was opposed on the ground by government technicians, military personnel, and rural notables who held their advantages through licence from central authority. Even in Rajaoson's defense of "democratic centralism" under the Ratsiraka charter, the fokon'olona acts as a "channel for expression," not for decisions. It represents a linkage of people and administration, a coordinator of programs, and an executor of decisions.[92]

The spontaneity of local representation was destroyed by requiring candidates for fokontany committees and the higher councils to join certified parties in the National Front for the Defense of the Revolution (FNDR). Moreover, by the erection of "parallel pyramids" of state enterprises and cooperatives the regime drained resources from the elected community assemblies and reinforced the discipline of a top-down revolution. Instead of building on the natural ties among members of rural communities, the process relied on command, coercion, and controls imposed from above through party-dominated *vatoeka* (economic committees).[93]

To Raison and other scholars, the Ratsiraka strategy repeated the inveterate Third World exploitation of city over peasantry.[94] Pavageau sees this betrayal as a kind of epistemology, imposing on the villages "forced ideas, models of thought, official ideology."[95] And the substitution of *fokontany* (a spatial unit) as the basic cell, instead of *fokon'olona*, the more spiritual concept of human solidarity, seems indicative of the government's legalistic inspiration.

Beginning in 1976, the fokon'olona personnel were ideologically mobilized by the Direction de l'Appui Technique et Idéologique aux Collectivités Décentralisés (DATIC). This agency sponsored training programs for leaders and specialists, gave lessons on organizing the vatoeka, and promoted state cooperatives, people's banks, and the like. Its campaigns divided rural society without generating progress. The mobilizing principle of solidarity (*fihavanana*), which had prospered in defense of families against impositions of the state, did not function in the state's behalf.[96] Eventually, modest villagers elected to the councils and committees became discouraged with the denial of local autonomy, frustrated by mistakes and corruption, and bedeviled by economic crisis. The administered were again dominated by administration, as under the old colonial companies. The poor who could not pay their fines or debts in money converted them into labor obligations to the fokon'olona, just as they had been recruited for commutation of taxes under the systems of the Merina queens and the French.

By the late 1980s the fokon'olona had been relegated to delivering permits and certificates, with largely appointed officers and without the participation in social life that the movement existed to encourage. Like the rural communes in the period before 1972, they were left to exploitation by the strong, the selfish, and the opportunistic. Entangled in politics and paper directives, the fokon'olona experiment became another fanjakana imposition to be avoided whenever possible. This alienation accounts for the 50 percent abstention rate in the 1989 local elections, a defection that was particularly pronounced in urban fokontany.[97]

Nor did the agricultural cooperative movement escape control by the state. Theoretically voluntary and autonomous, the cooperatives depended for administration and finance on the party system, the specialized ministries, and the elected deputies.[98] By 1978, however, imported (mostly North Korean) models had given way to a transitional form of cooperative based on Malagasy traditions of mutual aid and feudal dues. This adaptation guaranteed to participating peasantry some ownership rights over land and tools. Cooperatives had been destined in theory to work half the cultivated land area by the year 2000. Yet without investment to finance expansion or the political courage to take unexploited land from local notables, without price incentives for peasant proprietors to increase production, without accessible credit, without technological extensions into the hinterlands, cooperatively cultivated land surface in 1980 remained about what it was in 1970, and agricultural productivity declined. In 1983, only fifty cooperatives remained, occupying some 1,500 workers in all.

RECOVERING STABILITY: STRUCTURAL ADJUSTMENT AND GLOBAL DEPENDENCE

If Madagascar's second republic was born into a world with too much money in it, the world of the third has far too little. Taking their cue from petroleum markets, prices for other primary materials shot high in the mid-1970s, and for a while some coffee producers thought themselves lords even over petroleum. Anticipating a buoyant export economy of coffee, cloves, and vanilla, Malagasy techno-ideologues took advantage of excess global liquidity in petro-dollars. They borrowed in order to launch vast parastatal agricultural and industrial schemes, with bureaucracies to match, in order to free the island once and for all from neocolonialism. This "big push" was financed at the end of a decade when much genuine economic aid had already given way to mercantile borrowing and lending. The loans came readily to Madagascar, doubling the economy's sluggish rate of investment from 12 percent of GDP in the mid-1970s to 23 percent in 1980.

But those resources arrived at high interest, especially after 1979, and at ever-higher energy costs. And they came without much consideration of project solvency, comparative advantage, infrastructural and human resource adequacy, the inflationary effects of rigid exchange policies and an overvalued currency, the psychology of farmers squeezed to pay for others' bonanzas, or the overall carrying capacity of a structurally unsound economy.[99] Madagascar's export revenues faltered when world coffee prices fell and domestic production declined for all fourteen main crops. Hence the island's GNP began falling below its total external debt in 1986. The internal dislocations caused by open-throttle borrowing were later summarized by Olivier Ramahatra in the following terms: "The wave of investment pumped revenues into the urban and assimilated economy, aggravating by imported inflation the deterioration of the terms of trade between city and countryside. This brought about a retrenchment in the rural economy and, as a consequence, a dislocation in the urban economy which in its turn demanded adjustments—by budgetary restriction, by recession in the modern sector, and by an expansion of the informal sector."[100] Like the grandes opérations of the first republic, Ratsiraka's revolutionary enterprises mostly failed, along with the export flow that was supposed to compensate the lenders.

No doubt those lenders were unwise, too, to commit overabundant millions so readily. Yet although even the most reckless creditor has a right to compensation, the reckless borrower has to pay, no matter how serious its reversals in the terms of trade. Despite Hugon's earlier warning of the prejudicial implications of such borrowing, the painfulness of this nexus has been poignantly felt in Madagascar for more than a decade.[101]

Trying to conserve foreign exchange as debt-service bills matured at the start of the 1980s, the regime had to ration imports. It chose to restrict capital goods and spare parts, thus blocking the industrial recourse that might have stimulated domestic investment. Industrial production had never climbed; it actually fell by more than 25 percent from 1980 to1982. From 1970 to 1982, GDP remained level (registering an overall annual growth rate of 0.2 percent) while the population was increasing at a rate of 2.6 percent each year. No longer was the Franc Zone there to fill essential needs for commercial capital. Terms of trade declined from an index of 100 in 1970 to 59 in 1983. Government revenues fell short of targets as the economic mechanism ratcheted downward. Exports continued to falter, and the vicious circle was closed. The institutions and strategies of the revolution fell into irredeemable disrepute.[102]

The Malagasy state seemed perpetually on the verge of dissolution throughout the 1980s. Its welter of self-serving clienteles controlled only fragments of a decentralized domestic economy (without the ability to manage even them). Hostility was erupting in riots throughout the land. The economic crisis of the 1980s was attributable to serious errors of judgment and timing based on assumptions about international markets and an ideological disposition to blame Madagascar's structural problems on the machinations of neoimperialism. While all components of production went into decline, the public sector's consumption increased relentlessly. Rising bureaucratic salaries and unproductive managerial teams worsened inflation. The gaps between rich and poor spread wider. But for some reason, the popular revolt of 1972 was not repeated during that decade—not until 1991. According to Hugon, nationalist outrage lacked a convenient foreign exploiter to rally against.[103] The only remedy—and punishment—for the folly of destitute economies within the world system was ... the world system.

Recovery of economic stability required the revolutionary Malagasy to retract the ideological victories won since 1973 over French and other putative forces of imperialism. Whatever the ideological cost, Ratsiraka's penurious regime had no alternative to the negotiation of real concessions from creditors and donors of assistance among those very adversaries.

Bilateral arrangements could provide piecemeal help for Madagascar's stabilization, but the world had changed radically from the simpler developmental paradigms of the 1960s and early 1970s. Malagasy troubles were systematic, and the solutions required broad coordination. Inability to pay a $3 billion (and growing) overall debt, to balance national accounts, and to rectify a chronic payments deficit inevitably led the Ratsiraka government to the World Bank and the International Monetary Fund. The Bretton Woods agencies gradually assumed leadership in restoring solvency through acceptable national economic performance. For societies like Madagascar, such performance entails conversion away from state control toward the liberal market system. Reluctantly at first, then with growing conviction, Malagasy policy abandoned the socialist principles that had failed—or had been undermined by reckless indebtedness. Gradually, and without changing personality, the Ratsiraka regime discarded its own revolution.

Since Madagascar has never known prosperity, the most it can expect to recover is its unprepossessing stability. That in itself is an achievement. Beyond such recovery lies uncharted terrain. After some early false starts, a series of eight major accords began in July 1982 with IMF standby (stabilization) credits, culminating in May 1989 with a full-scale Enhanced Structural Adjustment Facility (ESAF) program (see Table 5.3).[104] More important than the actual monetary sums committed, this evolution of IMF assistance demonstrated growing confidence by the international financial community in the regime's pledges of fundamental change.

Madagascar's commitments to the IMF can be broken down into four main objectives:

1. Stability in macroeconomic balances, entailing restriction of currency and credit; budget austerity (deficits under 4.7 percent of GDP); devaluation of the FMG through flexible rates pegged to a basket of foreign currencies; reduction of debt service and restraints on further borrowing; suppression of the consumer rice subsidy; and a ceiling of 10 percent on inflation
2. Restoration of agricultural producer prices to stimulate production for domestic markets
3. Gradual liberalization of industrial prices, freeing them from the administered fictions that allowed state corporations to show artificial surpluses
4. Gradual liberalization of foreign exchange allocations and exchange controls[105]

TABLE 5.3 World Bank and IMF Structural Adjustment Lending for Malagasy Stabilization (SDR millions)

Type of Facility	1980	1981	1982	1983	1984	1985	1986	1987	1988	1989
IMF standby credit	64.5[a]	109	51		33	29.5	30		113.3	
IMF compensatory	29.2		21.8		14.4	16.1				
WB consultative group aid				50	42[b]		630[b]		700[b]	
WB emergency assistance							16.6			
ESAF[c]								46.5		76.9
WB adjustment credits by sector										
Industrial						60[b]				
Agricultural							60[b]			
Industry/trade								100[b]		
Public									127.6[b]	

NOTE: SDR = Special drawing rights.
[a]Cancelled.
[b]In US$ millions.
[c]ESAF = enhanced structural adjustment facility.
SOURCES: Figures compiled from various press releases of International Monetary Fund, as well as press reports and various issues of Economist Intelligence Unit, *Country Report* (London: EIU, quarterly).

Viewed in international terms, Madagascar was to unfetter its international trade and payments, reduce government intrusion in the economy, control its debt and encourage direct foreign investment, devalue the national currency to increase exports, and rebuild foreign exchange reserves. On domestic grounds the economy was to deflate and conform to market dictates. It would be subject to tight credit and restricted money supply, reduced public spending (including consumer subsidies), and improved tax collection. Removal of price controls was combined with a freeze on civil service and other salaries.

Such conversion does not come easily for a regime that, however quixotically, had been promising its people a more agreeable life. It requires a long transition of austerity, deprivation, and personal sacrifice. The conditions imposed by international stewards are curtailment of government spending on social services and consumer price subsidies, reduced employment in the public sector, and rigorous orientation of import policies toward production rather than consumption. These measures inevitably cause suffering, particularly among urban populations. They also bring transitional dislocations of productive factors and inflationary surges while production and supply catch up with unsubsidized demand for household necessities. For a time the Malagasy government could blame international (IMF and World Bank) coercion for the social consequences of budgetary rigor. It also resisted—in the people's name—the draconian elimination of deficits and massive currency devaluations. Even in recent years it has procrastinated, temporizing with its mentors, parading structural changes for show, and sustaining some consumer imports for the benefit of the volatile urban elite.[106]

Eventually, Madagascar had to adhere to the monetarist diagnosis: Budget deficits and international price distortions led inevitably to payments blockages and insolvency. The state had to learn how to allocate resources productively, transferring as many assets as possible from the public to the private sector. Large inefficient state conglomerates had to be partitioned and sold to private entrepreneurs or dissolved entirely. Overheated demand had to be reduced and supply increased, exports priced according to market advantage. Civil service expenditures had to be curtailed, the currency devalued to reflect real costs, and public investment brought into line with national economic growth. The 1989–1992 ESAF required budget deficits to be constrained to within 5 percent of GDP.

The international prescription for Madagascar concentrated in the 1980s on export production, import substitution (in rice and textiles), and sectoral reform in agriculture, industry, and services. It reduced excess demand that had been stimulated by administered prices and other market distortions in a command economy. As conditions for assistance, prices began to be liberalized in 1986 and import restrictions were relaxed, thus stimulating some competition. The private sector benefited from a three-year program to privatize, restructure, and liquidate inefficient public enterprises.

As the second half of the decade opened, these policies were beginning to have some effect on production, financial balances, and cost of living. Even at a per capita income of $230, the 1986 Malagasy economy was characterized as "adjusting."[107] Devaluations weakened the currency by 15 percent in 1982, 37.74 percent in 1986, another 36 percent in 1987, 14 percent in 1988, and an additional 13 percent in 1991. Tariffs were lowered, domestic monopolies broken up, and the economy moved positively—even if not rapidly enough to overtake population growth until 1988–1989. In 1984, liberalization of the rice trade contributed to a 39 percent reduction in imports. By early 1985, the state that had destroyed the economy was beginning to take credit for its resuscitation.[108]

The investment code promulgated in August 1985 sought sources of capital through taxation and customs concessions while allowing repatriation of profits and payment of foreign technical assistants in hard currency. To avoid reconcentrating wealth in the hands of French or Karana capitalists, however, the state reserved rights of intervention that tied the hands of local and foreign business.[109]

Three years later, following a pattern set by neighboring Mauritius, a new program of export-processing zones (EPZs) successfully began to encourage new investment in textiles and other light manufacturing. Benefiting from duty-free import privileges, exemption from direct taxes, and some exchange controls in the EPZ areas at Antananarivo, Toamasina, and Antsiranana, manufacturers can turn primary products into Malagasy exports aimed largely at European and other Western markets. Over 300 applications have been filed for EPZ permits thus far; seventy-four agreements were negotiated by August 1993, with the first thirty-nine operating (most of them at Antananarivo) at a capacity of 19,000 employees, 5,200 of them new jobs. Most of these operations are in clothing and other textile production, handicrafts, and agricultural processing (rabbits, foie gras, wines, for instance). Sisal twine, offshore banking, and data processing seem to have prospects as well, whereas Malagasy perfume oils and leather still encounter market problems.[110]

More than half of the EPZ investment of $120 million has come from France, 20 percent of it from Mauritius; only fourteen of the firms are Malagasy-owned, although many of the French companies have Malagasy junior partners. Various Hong Kong sources have pledged a $650 million investment in textiles and food processing over a period of fifteen years, entailing an increment of 78,000 jobs. Mauritian firms once able to exploit their own skilled but hungry labor force now face the rising costs of virtually full employment at home; they look toward Madagascar for overflow-processing ventures. So hopeful was this development by mid-1990 that President Ratsiraka predicted convertibility of the Malagasy franc within four years, although the advantages of this improbable event were even then open to question.[111] EPZ growth sputtered out in the political crisis of 1991–1992, but its revival seems ensured in the new climate of the third republic provided that the exchange rates favor exports, that the investment protections are implemented, and that goods, people, and property can circulate with enhanced freedom on the island.

If the logic of structural adjustment was inexorable, its outcomes proved elusive. The liberalized import system of 1988 freed most imports under general license, hence permitting considerable international dumping that jeopardized Malagasy competitiveness. This seemed especially true for imports of French consumer goods, so desirable in the luckless Malagasy urban economy. Imported raw materials and spare parts were becoming too expensive for industrial recovery—not to mention the costs of overseas education, which middle-class families persisted in seeking. Energy costs continued to rise, underpaid technocrats and paper-pushers made faulty decisions, and market opportunities were ignored. Such would be the costs of sustained growth.[112] More serious still, the Malagasy were not yet producing exportable commodities to take advantage of the adjustment in currency prices. Cloves (always subject to cycles) recovered some export potential; sugar, vanilla, and cocoa also did reasonably well; but coffee, meat, cotton, sisal, and pepper declined in price or production in the early 1980s and never fully returned to their 1972–1975 earnings base (see Table 5.4).[113]

Traditional reliance on exports of coffee for the bulk of the island's foreign exchange has become increasingly problematic for Madagascar. Collapse of the International Coffee Agreement in 1989 opened world markets to huge gluts and falling prices, especially for the marginal-quality robusta produced in Madagascar. Ironically, producer prices rose on the island by 42 percent just as international market conditions plummeted. Earnings fell from a peak of $150 million in 1986 to $98 million in 1987, $76 million in 1988 and 1989, $42

TABLE 5.4 Production in Madagascar, 1985–1992 (thousand tons)

	1985	1986	1987	1988	1989	1990	1991	1992
Basic food crops								
Rice (paddy)	2,178	2,230	2,296	2,235	2,380	2,420	2,340	2,450
Cassava	2,140	2,421	2,178	2,200	2,277	2,292	2,777	2,292
Corn (maize)	140	153	158	156	160	155	150	–
Bananas	255	225	226	260	217	220	218	–
Yams	450	467	467	485	483	486	487	–
Main cash crops								
Coffee	53.8	59	60	66	68	65	68[a]	–
Cocoa	2.3	2	2	2.9	3.7	3.6	3.1	–
Groundnuts	31.5	33	32	30	32.2	30.4	49.3	–
Sugar (raw)	101	102	110	122	131	118[a]	124[a]	–
Tobacco	4.6	5	4	4	3.9	4	1.5	–
Sisal	19.2	19.9	21	20	19.9	20	21	–
Seed Cotton	42.7	50	27	46	41.5	32.1	26.6	–
Cloves	13.5	6.9	10	11.6	7.1	9.5	13.6	–
Prepared vanilla	1.2	0.6	1.4	1.5	1.5	0.8	–	–
Seafood	–	–	–	62.8	92.9	101.5	103.4	100.9
Minerals								
Chromium ore & concentrates	126.7	89.3	106.8	64.2	152.5	127.5	129.3	–
Graphite	14.7	16.2	13.6	14.1	15.0	18.5	13.5	–
Mica	0.6	1.8	0.4	0.6	–	–	–	–

[a]Estimates.

SOURCES: Table reconstructed from varying data from Malagasy Ministry of Agriculture, Bankin'ny Tantsaha Mpamokatra, as well as from various issues of Economist Intelligence Unit, *Country Report* (London: EIU, quarterly) and EIU *Country Profiles, 1992–1993* and *1993–1994* (London: EIU, 1993, 1994); various issues of *Marchés Tropicaux et Méditerranéens*—hence subject to wide margins of error.

million in 1990, and $28 million in 1991; an estimated rise to $55 million in 1992 and possibly $66 million in 1993 cannot conceal the steady deterioration of coffee as an export staple for the Malagasy economy. A rise in producer price in 1988 was calculated to stimulate technological improvements and to double the island's coffee production, which has remained at between 60,000 and 83,000 tons since 1986. But when smallhold coffee plantations are neglected, their yield cannot be fully recovered; average production today barely reaches 300 kilograms per hectare (elsewhere, state-of-the-art coffee farms produce from 1,000 to 2,000 kilos). Madagascar's plants are overage, and the robusta caffeine content is too high for most tastes; the industry will improve only to the extent that it converts to new strains of Arabica. Even so, farmers will improve productivity only when relative prices allow coffee surpluses to buy ample rice, rendering the export economy dependent on domestic consumption priorities.

International limitations have also been felt by the other African, Caribbean, and Pacific nations who benefit from various European Community programs under the succession of agreements signed in Lomé, capital of Togo. Lomé IV, the prevailing convention, links EC assistance to performance under structural adjustment arrangements with the IMF. It offers Madagascar generous quotas in European markets at tariff reductions of up to 90 percent. The pathfinding Stabex export-price insurance program under the Lomé regimes has been unable to adjust to massive collapse in the coffee market for many of its members. Lower export earnings obliged serious perennial cuts in the Malagasy budget, squeezing such basic priorities as health, education, and economic development ever more.

By contrast, Malagasy vanilla clings to some international advantage, accounting for approximately 20 to 30 percent of the island's exports by value. After a long test of willpower, world consumers seem persuaded to demand true vanilla, not the cheaper substitutes.[114] With production running over 900 tons of extract annually at weak but stable prices ($72 to $74 per kilogram from 1989 to 1993), Madagascar remains the world's largest producer of this gentle spice for desserts and beverages in the United States, Germany, and France. Nevertheless, Indonesian and other competition has reduced the Malagasy market share from 90 percent to under 50 percent today. Moreover, a stockpile emerged in Madagascar from 1987–1988's record production of 2,164 tons, and the world has few prospects for liquidation of those inventories at current prices. When the 1993 price dropped to $54, the government decided to burn 1,000 tons of vanilla to combat smuggling and generate supply deficits. The United States remains a major purchaser, but Malagasy primacy in the U.S. market is threatened anew by the recent appearance of a far cheaper natural vanilla product.[115] Market liberalization of this state-owned industry—demanded for years by the World Bank and IMF—might invite improvements in efficiency and other new investment to close the cost gap and retain the island's market share.

Cloves are probably destined for marginal exportability, as competition floods traditional markets; the Indonesian cigarette industry, for example, now has access to increased domestic supplies of the spice. This traditional mainstay now accounts for less than 10 percent of Malagasy exports.

Madagascar entertains some hope for marketing of its diverse mineral endowment, but no bonanzas have appeared as yet to lift the mining economy out of the same stagnation agriculture finds itself in. Petroleum imports of about 350,000 tons (mostly from Iran and Saudi Arabia) continue to consume substantial portions of the island's export revenues. The great island's foreign exchange future seems to lie in processing seafood and other food products, manufacturing textiles in the EPZs, and promoting tourism. (See Tables 5.5 and 5.6.)

Among the essential objectives of Malagasy development is the sale of viable enterprises to private investors. Beginning in 1989, a handful of major state corporations went on the market. A score or more were added in the early 1990s, reaching a total of twenty-nine firms liquidated and twenty-eight privatized. These included Air Madagascar and the vast Z-Ren fertilizer plant, (a white elephant sold to Nigerian interests at $25 million, one-third the nominal cost). If buyers are found, state cotton textile plants, the SOLIMA oil

TABLE 5.5 Madagascar's External Trade, 1980–1992 (US$ million at current prices)

	1980	1985	1986	1987	1988	1989	1990	1991	1992[c]
Exports FOB[a]	515	350	315	406	398	451	471	462	267
Imports CIF[b]	1,109	503	353	541	561	560	742	637	–
Main exports									
Coffee		104	139	98	76	75.8	42.3	41	58
Vanilla		43.8	48	80.2	44.6	41.9	57	46	60
Cloves		35.2	27.6	10	15.5	32.1	20	23	–
Sugar		9.5	6.5	8.4	8.7	24.1	20.2	–	–
Cotton cloth		12.4	7.7	12	13	13.3	8.6	14	–
Shrimp		22.1	24.7	34.1	30.5	30.4	33.5	41	–
Petroleum products		4.7	5.8	4.8	4.8	5.3	8.0	–	–
Chromite		4.8	6.5	4.3	8.0	19.4	10.4	9.4	–
Graphite		7.3	8.4	7.9	9.5	9.6	11.2	–	–
Main imports									
Capital goods		99.9	109.1	105.4	138.9	134.2	194.7	162	–
Intermediate goods		108.9	119.1	113.7	97.6	91.1	131.7	89	–
Energy products		85.2	58.5	55.3	65.5	51.5	90.7	69	–
Consumer goods		52.4	55.5	58.5	59.6	65.3	97.7	68	–
Food		46.0	51.8	49.1	17.2	39.0	40.0	35	–
Rice		30.4	36.2	30.6	11.3	26.0	17.6	–	–

[a]FOB = free on board.
[b]CIF = cost, insurance, and freight included.
[c]Estimate.
SOURCES: Figures compiled from various issues of Economist Intelligence Unit, *Country Report* (London: EIU, quarterly); EIU *Country Profiles, 1992–1993* and *1993–1994* (London: EIU, 1993, 1994). These are based on diverse Malagasy reports and are subject to wide margins of error.

refinery, and investment banks will convert as well. State monopolies on rice marketing and stabilization funds for several commodities have been surrendered to the free market; vanilla remains an exception. As the Malagasy state disengages from its inefficient enterprises in favor of private market forces, capital levels are diminished and the economy deflates. Domestic purchasing power has declined and private risk capital holds back.

To correct the ambiguities of the 1985 investment code and five-year plan of July 1986, a new code emerged in March 1990, promising enhanced taxation and import advantages for small- and medium-sized business and for low-cost manufacturing aimed at European and African markets; thirty-five existing enterprises have submitted to restructuring.[116] A new mining code (contested by domestic entrepreneurs as unduly generous to foreign interests) must encourage production of ilmenite, quartz, and gemstones, as well as petroleum and the island's traditional endowment of graphite, mica, chromite, and semiprecious stones. Nutrition, child health care, public health and population policies, and the World Bank's pioneering environmental program must be integrated into a new structure of private enterprise and open markets.[117]

TABLE 5.6 Madagascar's Direction of Trade, 1989–1991 (percent of total)

	1989	1990	1991
Exports (destination)			
France	29	27	27.4
USA	12	27	12.4
Japan	11	5	9.5
Germany	8	6	8.5
Belgium/Luxemburg	–	11	1.3
Singapore	7	4	–
Réunion	4	4	–
Imports (origin)			
France	31	34	27.7
Japan	6	6	4.8
Germany	5	5	4.1
Bahrain	–	3	4.4
Iran	6	3	4.5
United Kingdom	2	5	–
Italy	3	4	–

SOURCES: Figures compiled from Economist Intelligence Unit, *Country Profiles, 1992–1993* and *1993–1994* (London: EIU, 1993, 1994), as well as from press reports derived from various original sources. Data subject to wide margins of error.

But this is as yet insufficient mobilization. Domestic savings have not made a strong appearance to expand money supply without inflation; the savings rate remained at 16 percent of GDP in 1989. The IMF's "monetarist medicine seems to attack the manifestations of the fever more than its deeper causes," observed Hugon in 1986, and he still has a point.[118] Capital sources in the industrialized countries are turning away from questionable Third World markets, and the IMF–World Bank levels of assistance remain too modest to do more than refinance existing debt. France, subjected to its own trade and payments pressures—and to uncertainty over its place in a new German-dominated Europe—is unlikely to lavish further concessionary favors on prodigal ex-colonies such as Madagascar. Tax revenues have not increased to help sustain investment any more than they did at the point of heavy indebtedness. There is little interest in capitalizing "loser" agricultural plantations and other raw materials production except, perhaps, for mining. Buyers have not been quick to show interest in the SOLIMA refinery without guarantees of monopoly control over sources of crude or over domestic markets. Against the constraints of the international environment, the economy still seeks its uncertain future.[119]

Madagascar's first IMF structural adjustment loan ended in June 1988 with liberalization of the domestic rice market and other important reforms. The economy expanded through another ten-month standby arrangement leading to the two-year Enhanced Structural Adjustment Facility (ESAF) in May 1989.[120] Export and import diversity improved. Removal of import curbs eased the supply of soaps and oils, food and pharmaceuticals, and automobile parts. Nontraditional exports such as seafood and children's clothing became profitable, thanks to the structural reforms and what the IMF called a quality labor force.[121] Still, results proved undramatic, and the structural adjustment strategy has not yet generated sustainable growth. After the economic disaster of 1991, the jerry-built transition government of Yves Razanamasy campaigned in 1992 for renewal of World Bank and IMF commitments, flourishing a new austerity budget for the year and some recovery in essential production and export trade. It was encountering serious difficulty spending the project assistance already furnished by France, the EC, and the international agencies, however, and it had not completed privatization of the state banks that had been expanding domestic credit so irresponsibly.[122]

Given this lackluster performance over seven years of mandated reforms, Malagasy observers had to wonder whether the new strategies would ever work. Initiative and consumer interests suffered in a deflated economy. Parastatal corporations were being privatized without much publicity, complained the daily *Tribune,* asking who was buying the corporations anyway.[123]

Madagascar's adjusting economy earned a cautious "pass" from the IMF resident representative on the eve of the fund's March 1990 negotiation for a second tranche of 25.6 million SDR; politicization of the civil service, featherbedding, and other inefficiencies remained problems. But by September 1991, the World Bank was calling Madagascar an economic miracle of adjustment, as though all had happened to the good in the intervening turbulent year.[124] The bank itself had been holding back commitments as well as Club of Paris negotiation schedules during the political uncertainty of 1991–1992.

Ironically, it was in 1991 that Madagascar first decided to apply to the United Nations for least-developed-country status, finally acknowledging its continuing low income, its structural weaknesses, and its inability to mobilize human resources productively. From the state of emergency declared on July 23, 1991, until the elections of February 1993, only the subsistence economy could be said to be truly functioning—a lamentable throwback to the early 1980s. But if conditions have not as yet been met for the 1989 ESAF, Madagascar's inadequacies could be readily blamed on political uncertainties, enabling the island to obtain consent for a new try in 1993.

During the first period of structural adjustment from 1985 through 1991, the World Bank led a consultative group of thirteen major Western creditors seeking to restore Madagascar's capacity to service its foreign debt, which had absorbed 80 percent of the country's export revenues. In 1984, only $42 million of $117 million was paid on current debt service; rescheduling agreements in 1985 and 1986 offered relief opportunities of up to eleven years and allowed $177 million to be paid of the $356 million owed.

After external debt service rose above exports (to 103.6 percent) in 1987, Madagascar's Paris Club of creditors granted a sixth rescheduling of debt, reducing the ratio to 56.7 percent of exports. New loans on concessional terms came largely from France and the World Bank's "soft-loan" window, the International Development Association (IDA). In 1988 Madagascar was among the first beneficiaries of the new "Toronto" formula for preferential debt treatment based on performance according to IMF-IBRD reform schedules. Following a $516 million cancellation of debt (mostly by France), the economy

TABLE 5.7 Madagascar's External Debt and Debt Service, 1975–1991 (US$ million)

	1975	1980	1985	1986	1987	1988	1989	1990	1991
Total Public long-term debt	167	926	2157	2649	3332	3290	3346	3491	–
Concessional	142	495	871	1084	1414	1534	1744	2099	–
Nonconcess.	16	85	959	1185	1612	1411	1300	1137	–
Private	9	346	327	380	406	345	301	255	–
Composition (percent of total)									
Multilateral	47.9	20.2	22.1	23.9	25.3	28.0	30.6	36.3	–
Bilateral	46.6	42.5	62.2	62.6	63.4	62.3	60.4	56.4	–
of which % from France	20.7	5.7	16.9	18.4	20.8	21.2	22.8	24.9	–
Private	5.6	37.2	15.7	13.5	11.3	9.7	9.0	7.3	–
Debt service			155	177	203	182	206	201	160
External debt as percent of GNP			91.2	94.3	149.6	157.5	148.4	124.4	148.3

SOURCES: Figures compiled from Economist Intelligence Unit, *Country Profiles 1992–1993* and *1993–1994* (London: EIU, 1993, 1994); as well as EIU *Country Report* (London: EIU, quarterly); and press reports—hence subject to wide margins of error.

still found itself owing about $4.9 billion in 1992. (See Table 5.7.) Virtually all of this was held by governmental and international public institutions; one-fourth was owed to France, another fourth to the World Bank. But as the economy strengthened between 1988 and 1990, it was better able to service its debts through foreign exchange earnings and budgetary provisions. In 1990, payments of $231 million amounted to only 47 percent of export revenues.

At each negotiating stage the bank's prescriptions became increasingly detailed, encroaching ever more on national margins of autonomy.[125] Bank assistance credits went to both industry and agriculture, aiming at liberalized internal markets. A public investment program for 1984–1987 directed capital to rice, vegetable oils, cotton, energy, and transportation. But obstructions from old unworkable projects, lingering corruption, and structural bottlenecks inhibited capital flow. Growth remained laggard, subject to low demand, and vulnerable to external shocks. Old loans had to be rescheduled, new ones postponed. The bank allocated credits to help adjust balances in industry, agriculture, trade, and public-sector finance between 1985 and 1990.

Marked growth in rice cultivation and export manufacturing during 1988 and 1989 was offset by continued low prices on the world coffee market, so that Malagasy consumers were not realizing the benefits of their new liberal economy. In 1990, to provide some relief for the urban population, the Finance Ministry imprudently allowed credit terms to relax, thus inviting a rush of imports. This decision boosted the overall standard of living, but with disastrous effect on the 1990 current account—drawing down exchange reserves, helping bring inflation to 12 percent (aggravated by a 24 percent rise in petroleum prices attendant on the Iraq-Kuwait crisis), and suppressing real growth to 3.5 percent.

Madagascar's international mentors responded sternly, withholding important assistance commitments until the balances were corrected. Finally, the FMG was devalued by 13 percent in January 1991, and the spending binge subsided. From the middle of that year the recovery program suffered another serious setback in the long political struggle between President Ratsiraka and his opposition, a stalemate that paralyzed administrative and economic machinery for months.

Other problems of adjustment came to the social surface.[126] The liberalized economy has invited unconstructive speculation, resulting in shortages and other serious distortions; dissolution of the great parastatals created unemployment among civil servants. The relatively open economy seems to have invited dumping by Singapore, Turkey, Mauritius, and other exporters on the delicate textile market, which absorbs 30 percent of Madagascar's industrial production. On March 30, 1990, the labor union alliance, representing all but Ratsiraka's SEREMA unions, warned of lawsuits against employers who laid off workers en masse, whether prompted by structural adjustment economies or otherwise. Moreover, they contend that the skills and relative cheapness of Malagasy labor were being advertised to the world as a way of making workers pay for new investment.[127] In fact, a recent study by the French Senate demonstrated how low labor costs create the advantage enjoyed by Madagascar's EPZ program; an hour's work by a skilled Malagasy costs only 1.2 French francs, contrasted with 5.75 francs in Mauritius (home of highly successful EPZ ventures in the 1970s and 1980s), 23 francs in Taiwan, and 55 francs in France itself.[128]

Consumer import liberalization also engendered charges that Taiwanese and South Korean exporters were dumping on Malagasy markets. Malagasy coffee, meat, and sugar have not been able to compete against the overproduction of agricultural staples in the industrialized and Asian economies. Shrimp harvesting must be kept within reproductive limits, and new investment has been curtailed by the political instability of 1991–1992. Hence, exports again stagnated, and the debt-service burden reappears as a claim against lower revenues despite further rescheduling by creditors. In 1992 and 1993, competing governmental institutions perpetuated the delay in economic recovery, sustaining inefficiencies, seeking ways to depress prices for urban consumers, allowing easy credit to bring inflation to well beyond 20 percent (after that rate had been worked down to 9 percent in 1989), and supporting the currency at the artificially high level of about 1,828 FMG to US$1; the rate settled down at about 1,900 FMG to US$1 in mid-1993.

The World Bank's attention has by now focused on a strategy for sustained development through vigorous structural adjustment reforms leading to annual economic growth rates of 6 percent or higher and a doubling of per capita income within twelve years. Clearly, the multilateral agencies will begin releasing frozen credits and undertake additional debt-relief measures through the Paris Club only if the Malagasy leadership selects the difficult path of all-out austerity, market liberalization, export encouragement, and privatization that no previous government has been willing to embrace.[129]

Operations of the international agencies identify sectors of the economy for special attention; they include industry, education, health, and the environment. A regional strategy aims at

1. Enhancing high-technology rice cultivation on the densely populated, fragile soils of the high plateau, stressing conservation, diversification, and efficient marketing
2. Combating erosion caused by fire and climatic damage on the east coast
3. Improving the security of herds and countererosion measures in the midwest to encourage immigration
4. Exploiting the fisheries potential of the west while also seeking to reverse trends toward erosion
5. Stressing tourism and biodiversity in the north to correct, respectively, the region's isolation and soil erosion from climatic and fire damage
6. Funding water sources for the south, promoting ecologically sensitive tourism, and introducing new crops adapted to the region's aridity[130]

The bank's sectoral adjustment loan, based on its elaborate multilateral plan for resuscitation of the island's environment, represents the prototype for a score of programs being prepared in a variety of Third World countries.

FROM STABILIZATION TO DEVELOPMENT

During the two centuries in which Madagascar could be considered to maintain a national economy, the island's fortunes have always been determined by external conditions beyond its control. Sakalava and Merina adherence to the eighteenth-century intercontinental slave trade was followed by subservience to British Mauritius, then to French barter companies and to their successor corporations. Today that subordination has turned toward international agencies espousing global market principles. Indigenous leaders have once again surrendered their power of decision to forces at the core of the world system. Yet viewed along the continuum from malign to benign patronage, this current servitude looks like progress.

To overcome the handicaps of poverty, debt, and isolation, the Malagasy have always needed friends in the great world, where credits are held and where resources and markets appear. East Europeans, Chinese, and North Koreans never offered much help in this respect, and their disengagement from the island is by now virtually complete. French officials and business leaders have become increasingly cordial, but many remained alienated by the Ratsiraka regime's pretentious self-assertions, its radical nationalism, and its domestic ruthlessness. Eligible Third World models are either themselves deteriorating (for example, Algeria, Nicaragua, and Tanzania) or prospering (for example, nearby Mauritius) on the merry margins of the global market. South African tradespeople and bankers have paid return visits to Antananarivo, but their resources are narrower than they had been in the late 1960s when Philibert Tsiranana first hearkened to their appeal.

Most ironically, the revolution that was to free Madagascar from foreign domination only condemned the island to an even more profound dependence. From 1977 until the end of the 1980s, the Ratsiraka republic sought help abroad without overtly submitting to the island's new mentors—the World Bank, International Monetary Fund, and European Community. Negotiating debt relief and standby loans in less than perfect faith, the defiant regime postponed the inevitable, and the well-being of the Malagasy deteriorated even further. "What all this means," commented one correspondent in 1987, "is that Madagascar is still basically insolvent; that production does not finance consumption; and that foreign investment, as distinct from aid, is almost non-existent."[131]

As Pryor observes, anticipations of prosperity had risen unrealistically during Madagascar's first two decades of independence, engendering disillusion, instability, and economic fragility in the sequel.[132] Toward the end of that period, with planning choices unwisely based on an assumption of a more independent world position than the remote island actually enjoyed, Ratsiraka's nationalized economy transcended fragility into chaos.

Moreover, economic structure and social traditions sometimes militate against Malagasy developmental ambitions. Philippe Hugon, Frederic Pryor, Roger Rabetafika, Gilles Duruflé, and Olivier Ramahatra show how Madagascar has suffered from a chronically weak rate of savings, low productivity, weak tax recovery, fragmentation between its productive enclaves and sectors, and the disproportionate weight of its tertiary economy.[133] Investment and savings have always lagged behind rates prevailing in Senegal, Ivory Coast, and other French-oriented economies. The island's chief products often fail to excite world demand. Its access to the global economy is strained through long channels of resistance, and its inhabitants have yet to be persuaded that any central authority knows how to increase their happiness.

Accurate statistics have been rare in Madagascar since the 1960s.[134] Even today, variations among data on production, balance of payments, money supply, and price indices render operations and policymaking hazardous at best. For instance, the 1992 rate of inflation has been officially estimated as between 12 and 26 percent![135]

Nevertheless, in the 1980s gradual conversion of economic policy to IMF–World Bank precepts brought about a fundamental reorientation of Malagasy economic and social policy. Ratsiraka's "irreversible socialist option" turned out to be another illusion of the will to autonomy.[136] By 1989, Ratsiraka was repudiating the suffocations of socialism and looking for open air, realizing, as Deleris had put it, that in a new Europe of shifting loyalties, "the manna will stop falling from capitalist skies onto the collectivist desert."[137] Disappointed with revolution, socialists in the AKFM and other parties have resorted to urging reform of an essentially capitalist structure—hoping at least to bring some social justice to the system—as though little had changed from the time of Tsiranana and the French profiteers.

Starting in 1990, the twin Gorbachevian watchwords perestroika and glasnost became current in Madagascar among officials and critics alike, but the nation has been able to realize only their political implications. Economic reform now depends on the disciplines of structural adjustment exerted by international creditors. Although doing things differently (as always), Madagascar fell to the common destiny reserved for impecunious African and Third World debtor societies, capitalist and noncapitalist alike. The new government's job in the mid-1990s is to prepare an institutional structure for the absorption of market economics.

With Marxism renounced, Madagascar confronts another political-economic imponderable—namely, what *will* work? Is there a place for this marginally functional economy in a world grown tighter and less gracious than ever? The poorest and least dynamic of economies, trapped in sinkholes of unalleviated debt, may be refinanced and adjusted structurally, but can it be developed?

During 1989 and 1990, when economic production did increase, very ancient transportation conditions and various social obstacles kept output from reaching distribution targets. When the price of rice is up, Malagasy farmers tend to produce their staple food crop to the hilt and to neglect the alternatives of coffee, sisal, pepper, bananas, or groundnuts. Other agricultural prices tend to climb with rice, so that urban consumers find themselves in a double vise—with more expensive food and less foreign exchange for imports. Governments usually respond to such distress by depressing the agricultural market, thus eliminating incentives for farmers.

Rescheduling debts has postponed and compounded the service problem. Leaders have lost credibility, as their decisions—even regarding the structure of imports—have to be tied to externally dictated priorities of sectoral growth and financial aid rather than to the equipment of a modern economy. Already, the most responsible international benefactors are being suspected of opportunism and the "sale of illusions."[138] International cooperation has been stigmatized as a buttress for "a regime at bay ... supporting the walls of a structure whose roof has already collapsed ... a protectorate over incompetence, corruption, and beggary."[139] For whatever reason, the momentum of structural adjustment did not extend beyond 1990 in investment and production. But if structural adjustment strategies fail, the inevitable resistance to austerity and reform could burgeon into new waves of violence and suffering—and still another virtually meaningless change of regime. The IMF itself insists that stability is the first precondition for development.

What will restore health to the Malagasy system? From a global perspective, external creditors might consent to heavy trade deficits under some agreed set of advantages to Third World partners who otherwise cannot export themselves out of debt. Primary-goods prices might be allowed to rise again, after having sunk in the mid-1980s to help finance recovery in the industrialized world. The poorest countries require new financial impetus—just at the time, alas, when more attractive capital markets are opening in

Eastern Europe and Asia. Exports and investment must expand autonomously in Madagascar, but where will the external financial resources be found?

Madagascar must journey far before its people can call themselves prosperous. As ever, that population is enjoined to be patient—and thrifty. The island's reigning political-economic strategies have never succeeded in mobilizing investment for general benefit. Now, after two decades of dramatic degeneration the Malagasy have lost 40 percent of their 1971 standard of living and at best will be able to recover that (already unacceptable) level in another decade. Their current strategy is now in international hands, and their receivers are joined in a complex solution that proposes moderate growth with declining rates of population increase, containment of domestic inflation and of international payments deficits, phased alleviation of the external debt, improvement in essential public services and quality of the civil service, domestic investment in new export lines and in agriculture, and a reversal of crucial environmental degradation.

Before the political crisis of 1991–1992, world agencies and self-interested creditors had helped the island to the starting point—in domestic price reform and deregulation, international credibility, convergence toward financial stability and budget equilibrium, and participation (albeit marginal) in the market system, which alone promises the capital, markets, and technology of development. Still, in place of a sudden surge toward prosperity, Madagascar must be reconciled to lingering poverty well into the next century. Then, if its economy can grow at an annual rate of 6 percent, resources may be mobilized for development, external trade may burgeon (perhaps with currency convertibility), and social expenditures may begin to improve life substantially for subsequent generations.

A realistic scenario anticipates genuine recovery to begin around 1995 after a period of contraction, experimentation, and debate within the third republic. This evolution should be led by new investment and increased output in the EPZ industries, in tourism, and in such nontraditional exports as seafood and leather goods. It should be supported by self-sufficiency in food production (demanding a 4.6 percent annual increase); a revitalization of education, health, and training; and moderate growth in essential imports. Ilmenite and other mineral exports should contribute their share to the process toward the close of the century.

This progress depends on doubling investment from 9 to 18 percent of GDP by that millennial year, entailing a fivefold rise in domestic savings, from 2.4 to 11.4 percent of GDP. It also requires marked improvement in transportation, communications, and domestic energy production. Madagascar expects a $2 billion dose of foreign aid during the mid-1990s, half of that sum in already-approved credits that have awaited political stability and credible fiscal policies. Even a growth rate of 3 percent (that is, keeping up with population) assumes further debt forgiveness and substantial increases in flows of foreign aid for balance-of-payments equilibrium.[140] In a true development scenario, however, debt relief is essential to allow a declining

TABLE 5.8 Foreign Assistance Disbursements from OECD, OPEC, and Multilateral Sources, 1986–1991 (US$ million)

	1986	1987	1988	1989	1990	1991
Bilateral	183.3	195.8	217.6	208.6	423.8	365.5
of which % from						
France	54.7	57.0	49.9	60.5	38.0	43.0
Germany (FRG)	12.6	12.0	6.6	6.0	35.5	8.3
Japan	8.9	6.9	19.7	13.8	4.0	15.5
Multilateral	149.2	152.2	108.9	191.0	149.6	191.4
of which % from						
WB (IDA)	63.7	60.0	46.8	36.6	28.7	55.3
EC (EDF)	15.7	13.7	28.1	24.5	25.9	9.0
ADF	9.5	10.9	8.0	10.3	14.4	9.2
Total	332.5	348.0	326.5	399.6	573.4	556.9
Of which % from						
grant aid	38.7	36.4	58.6	51.9	75.4	61.4

NOTE: WB (IDA) = International Development Agency, soft-loan window of the World Bank; EC (EDF) = European Development Fund of the European Community; ADF = African Development Fund.

SOURCE: Data adapted from Economist Intelligence Unit, *Country Profile: Madagascar, 1993–1994*. London: EIU, 1993, p. 29.

quantum of imported capital to stimulate production, not merely to balance external payments.[141]

Foreign assistance to the Malagasy republic rose to exceed $570 million in 1990 from a low point of $153 million in 1984. (See Table 5.8.) The upsurge came through steady increases in project subsidies and balance-of-payments lending by France, the single largest donor; through new commitments by Germany; and through intrepid multilateral assistance dominated by the European Community and the World Bank's International Development Agency. Most concessionary assistance is by now keyed to performance in structural adjustment reforms. In that context, the 1990 lapse in domestic credit control and foreign exchange depletion and the havoc wrought by 1991–1992 sociopolitical upheavals interrupted what had been a steady advance in international development transfers. In response to that disappointment, the World Bank suspended the third phase of its Public Enterprise Adjustment credit in early 1992, and Madagascar was unable for months to draw down $40 million in outstanding IDA credits or considerable French assistance.

If the third republic's government is able to control its budget deficits and lift restrictions on capital movements; if it can privatize the remaining state bank and liberalize trading in vanilla, air transportation, insurance, and other controlled industries—avoiding price controls, consumer subsidies, and protectionism—it may anticipate multilateral adjustment program loans and credits amounting to $140 million annually. Should government performance falter, the international agencies will restrict their support to core programs at the rate of approximately $30 million, as in 1992 when IDA credits came to a mere $23 million (to finance professional training).[142] In that event, the Economist Intelligence Unit apprehended "a danger that political uncertainty and economic problems, which weakened the country in 1991, have broken the momentum of development assistance. The government of Albert Zafy will face a tough challenge to convince donors and lenders of its commitment to balanced economic policies."[143]

Now the great island must build the internal linkages of an open, coherent national economy; generate domestic capital to absorb unemployment; and find reasonable access to sources of energy, reducing pressure on its own dwindling and constantly degraded forests. It must also convert its heavy, dishonest bureaucracy into a more elegant administration fed by an efficient, equitable fiscal system. Realistic policies of direct taxation need to replace revenues lost through abolition of the unpopular cattle and head taxes in 1972. The rise in consumer prices must be accompanied by ample agricultural credit; access to seeds, materials, fertilizers, tools, and appropriate technology; and attention to irrigation and to stockpiling (if only to discourage large-scale speculation).[144] Public health services must improve, and vocational and technical education must obtain some priority over less utilitarian specializations. These changes require what Hugon called "a new mode of management and a dynamization of social forces" in Madagascar.[145]

Sympathetic observers remain skeptical, however, that this much progress can be stimulated in so short a time after the long siege of stagnation and regression suffered by the productive plant throughout the island.[146] The global coffee-price disaster of 1989 and difficulties in financing the rice market cast doubt on optimistic trade predictions. Madagascar has diversified its export portfolio without being able to ensure the viability of markets for its products. Rural demand for goods and services has to be driven in part by expanded employment and money revenues with less regard for efficiency in the short run. According to Ramahatra, "The point is to cut a deal with the rural world designed to favor the creation, no longer the seizure, of a rural surplus."[147]

In addition to requiring the monetary tools that operate through structural adjustment, development seems to demand both a new emphasis on smallhold agriculture—including a strengthened role for women in decision-making—and a return to integrated agricultural and industrial programs not unlike the grandes opérations of the Tsiranana period. These projects will be difficult to accept, especially after the disasters of Ratsiraka's massive revolutionary enterprises. They demand a new economic culture affording opportunities for private capital, supporting growth through social equity, and reversing both the agricultural torpor and the reproductive fecundity characteristic of the 1970s and 1980s.

Moreover, Malagasy savings rates in 1992 were lower even than those of the relatively stagnant 1960s. The population is increasing faster, and city folk and diploma-holders are imposing sharper claims on the quality of employment available to them. Roads and plantations have deteriorated significantly, as has the security of person and property. Population concentrations occur in the most intensely worked valley land; vast, fertile westward spaces go begging for people. Productive imports are minimal, and Madagascar no longer enjoys recourse to the neocolonial Franc Zone mechanism to correct short-term exchange deficits. Finally, many of the key players are not yet persuaded that surrender to capitalism represents the solution to their crisis.

As the World Bank's 1987 country report observed, Madagascar must create 200,000 jobs annually through the year 2,000 to soak up current unemployment (estimated at 350,000 in 1990) and accommodate 180,000 students who leave school and enter the job market each year—220,000 if the population increases at 1980s rates—hence, the auguries for export diversification and for major agricultural schemes. Invigoration of the fokon'olona could perhaps supply one avenue for the integration of production, cooperation, and marketing on local levels.[148] Farmers and farm laborers must also be encouraged to migrate from the east and center into the midwest, despite cultural preference for proximity to family tomb sites. The drought-plagued south awaits some solution to the failures of virtually all development schemes in that vast, unhappy region.

There is much more that Madagascar must do. Land-use policy must allow productive laborers to work unused plots with long-term leases. Productive areas of the economic "archipelago" must be connected with one another. Energy alternatives to firewood and charcoal must be developed. Better strains of rice would relieve dependence on seasonal flooding cycles. Tax policies must become more progressive and efficient, with more accurate data collection. Cultural institutions must inculcate conservationist habits of thought. Political authority must be enhanced, with real improvement in the ability to enforce law. Personal and property security in the relatively spacious midwest could restore the population of that otherwise promising cattle region. The government must also find sources of investment and foreign exchange while attacking social problems—conservation of the island's biodiversity, diffusion of efficient energy, improvement of the urban environment, prevention of AIDS and other public health protections, provision of jobs and appropriate education.[149]

Structural adjustment brought stability to a once-regressive economy in 1988–1990, but the program has yet to solve Madagascar's fundamental inadequacies of investment and production. Strategies were designed to stimulate export agricultural production (especially coffee), rehabilitate the existing industrial plant, and liberalize domestic markets (most crucially for rice) in order to expand production in those priority sectors and adjust prices in accordance with principles of comparative advantage. By 1989, inflation had been lowered to single digits, rural terms of trade were strengthened, and capital-goods imports were up, hence curtailing black-market activity. The new remedies did reduce deficits in payments and public finance, but without unblocking production, satisfying essential domestic needs, or sustaining growth. An economy in which per capita income had fallen by 30 percent in twelve years (1973–1985) has not responded to the pallid inspirations of austerity.

Export earnings, needed to generate the surplus for growth above debt-service levels, have become dependent on imports—resisting the logic of devaluation and comparative advantage—and imports were cut in half from 1983 to 1988. Rice imports, once nearly 300,000 tons, were capped at 42,000 in 1989 by agreement with the World Bank and IMF, requiring Malagasy producers to send 2.7 million tons into the newly free domestic market in 1990. Production fell 300,000 tons short of these expectations, however, and climatic and market factors reduced the 1991 production of rice by a further 10 percent, exhausting the state's buffer stocks. For 1991–1992, the Food and Agricultural Organization registered a lamentable need for continuing imports of some 100,000 tons of rice and similar quantities of wheat to feed a still-expanding population.[150] Rice growers thereupon held back production during 1992 in expectation of more advantageous and stable prices.[151] Current buffer stocks allow the economy somewhat more flexibility in supplying the rice market than in the past, but to reach food self-sufficiency for a population that consumes 700 grams of rice per adult each day, the liberalized market will require annual production of 2.8 to 3 million tons. This target entails either substantial expansion of acreage or improvement over the average yield of 2.5 tons of paddy rice per hectare.

Agricultural productivity, improved infrastructure, light industrial processing, cheaper energy, nontraditional exports (including tourism), and human resource enhancement represent the sectors of power for development of the Malagasy economy. French and other investors are reportedly interested in such public works as road construction and telecommunications, as well as in food-processing industries, mining, and tourism. International cooperation must continue—not only in debt relief and concessionary project assistance but in new international partnerships as well. Some of these prospects, including cooperation among the neighboring islands in the Indian Ocean Commission, are discussed in the following chapter.

NOTES

1. World Bank, *World Development Report 1991* (Washington, D.C.: World Bank, 1992); Economist Intelligence Unit (EIU), *Country Report*, no. 3, 1991, p. 21, and *Country Profile 1993–1994*, (London: EIU), p. 9.

2. United Nations Development Program (UNDP), *Second Human Development Report, 1991, Third Human Development Report, 1993* (New York: UNDP, 1991, 1993); see commentary in *Marchés Tropicaux et Méditerranéens (MTM)*, no. 2482, June 4, 1993; EIU, *Country Report*, no. 3 ,1991, p. 22, and *Africa Report*, July-August 1991, pp. 5–6, 11. With life expectancy remaining at barely fifty-five years, Madagascar's positive scores depend on the 1990 literacy indicator of 80.2 percent.

3. See *MTM*, nos. 2435, July 10, 1992, p. 1803, and 2480, May 21, 1993, pp. 1297–1300.

4. Concise inventories of the island's advantages can be found in Philippe Hugon's preface to Olivier Ramahatra, *Madagascar: Une économie en phase d'ajustement* (Paris: Harmattan, 1989); *Country Economic Memorandum*, no. 5996, 1986 (Washington, D.C.: World Bank). François Falloux and World Bank, *Plan d'action environnemental* (Washington, D.C.: World Bank, 1988), v. 1, p. R-1; Frederic L. Pryor, *Malawi and Madagascar: The Political Economy of Poverty, Equity, and Growth* (Washington, D.C.: Oxford University Press, 1990), ch. 9; Patrick Rajoelina and Alain Ramelet, *Madagascar: La*

grande île (Paris: Harmattan, 1989), pp. 15–25; Richard Szal, "Is There an Agrarian Crisis in Madagascar?" *International Labour Review,* v. 127, no. 6, 1988, pp. 735–760.

    5. See Jean-Pierre Raison, *Les hautes terres de Madagascar* (Paris: ORSTOM-Karthala, 1984); Pryor, *Malawi and Madagascar,* pp. 198–202 and ch. 11; EIU, *Country Profile 1993–1994,* p. 11.

    6. Hugon, preface to Ramahatra, *Une économie,* p. 7.

    7. See EIU, *Country Profile 1993–1994,* p. 15; EIU, *Country Report* no. 2, 1991, p. 26, and no. 3, 1993, p. 28. The World Bank's Environmental Action Plan envisions a judicious combination of resort-seekers and "adventure-discovery" travelers: World Bank, *Plan d'action,* v. 1, sec. 5, p. 2. From the government's viewpoint, South Africans are once again welcome, as they had been under the prerevolutionary regime.

    8. See World Bank, *Plan d'action,* pp. 1–7; "O.R." in *MTM,* no. 2445, September 18, 1992, p. 2442, and no. 2476, April 23, 1993, p. 1102.

    9. Alison Jolly, *A World Like Our Own: Man and Nature in Madagascar* (New Haven and London: Yale University Press, 1980).

    10. Current accounts of Madagascar's biological uniqueness have proliferated in both scholarly and popular media. In addition to Jolly's superb book, see Michel Mollat du Jourdin, "Les contacts historiques de l'Afrique et de Madagascar avec l'Asie du Sud et du Sud-Est: Le rôle de l'océan indien," *Archipel: Études Interdisciplinaires sur le Monde Insulindien* (Paris: SECMI-CNRS, 1981), no. 21, pp. 35–53; Rajoelina and Ramelet, *Madagascar: La grande île,* pp. 25–32; other coverage in English is provided by John Mack, *Madagascar: Island of the Ancestors* (London: British Museum, 1986); Russell A. Mittermeier, "Strange and Wonderful Madagascar," *International Wildlife,* July-August 1988, pp. 4–13; Alex Shoumatoff, "Look at That," *New Yorker,* v. 64, March 7, 1988, pp. 62–63; Alison Jolly, "Madagascar: A World Apart," *National Geographic,* v. 171, February 1987, pp. 148–183; and Ian Tattersall, *The Primates of Madagascar* (New York: Columbia University Press, 1982).

    11. See David A. Burney and Ross D. E. MacPhee, "Mysterious Island: What Killed Madagascar's Large Native Animals?" *Natural History,* July 1988, pp. 47–54.

    12. The practice of burning new crop- and pastureland, cultivating it for a limited period of years, and leaving it to regenerate; see Yoshio Abe, *Le riz et la riziculture à Madagascar* (Paris: CNRS, 1984), pp. 58–59; Jolly, *A World Like Our Own,* pp. 208–211.

    13. World Bank, *Plan d'action,* pp. R–1, 2.1–2.5.

    14. Dervla Murphy, *Muddling Through in Madagascar* (Woodstock, N.Y.: Overlook Press, 1989), p. 54.

    15. Rajoelina and Ramelet, *Madagascar: La grande île,* pp. 82–87; *Madagascar Tribune,* May 11, 1992, cited in EIU, *Country Report,* no. 3, 1992, p. 15.

    16. Ramahatra, *Madagascar: Une économie,* p. 73; see also Jolly, *A World Like Our Own,* pp. 39 and 208.

    17. Jolly, *A World Like Our Own,* pp. 111–120, 228.

    18. Alison Jolly, "Madagascar's Lemurs on the Edge of Survival," *National Geographic,* v. 174, no. 2, August 1988, p. 138.

    19. A new estimate calls for only 200 hectares of already deforested land for the ilmenite mine, entailing considerably less environmental impact; see EIU, *Country Report,* no. 4, 1992, p. 17.

    20. World Bank, *Plan d'action,* sec. 1, p. 2; see also World Bank Environmental Program, *Staff Appraisal Report,* no. 8348-MAG, March 19, 1990.

    21. USAID, Unesco, UNDP, Coopération Suisse, World Wildlife Fund; see World Bank, *Plan d'action;* for summary, see *IMF Survey,* April 2, 1990, pp. 97–101; also Georges Ravel, *MTM,* no. 2269, May 5, 1989, pp. 1224–1225.

    22. *IMF Survey,* April 2, 1990, p. 97.

23. *International Herald Tribune,* March 3, 1990.
24. See World Bank, *Plan d'action,* pp. 5–10.
25. See Marcel Scotto, *Le Monde,* June 12, 1990.
26. See ibid., supported by private communication from a reliable program source.
27. See World Bank, *Plan d'action,* esp. chs. 4 and 5.
28. See *IMF Survey,* April 2, 1990, p. 97; the *Plan d'action* estimates environmental damage as equal to 5 to 15 percent of annual GDP.
29. See *Le Monde,* February 17, 1990.
30. See World Bank, *Plan d'action,* ch. 6; see also EIU, *Country Report,* no. 4, 1988, p. 18, and no. 1, 1989, p. 14.
31. See *International Herald Tribune,* March 3, 1990.
32. See *IMF Survey,* April 2, 1990, p. 101.
33. See EIU, *Country Report,* no. 4, 1989, p. 19; "Debt for Nature in Madagascar," *Trade Finance* (London), August 1990, p. 17; "A Debt to Nature," *Economist,* v. 312, August 19, 1989, p. 31; EIU, *Country Report,* no. 3, 1993, p. 25.
34. Jolly, *A World Like Our Own,* p. 233.
35. See EIU, *Country Report,* no. 4, 1992, pp. 10, 16.
36. See Jean Pavageau, *Jeunes paysans sans terre: L'exemple malgache* (Paris: Harmattan, 1981), ch. 5; Gérard Althabe, *Oppression et libération dans l'imaginaire: Les communautés villageoises de la côte orientale de Madagascar* (Paris: Maspero, 1969), ch. 1; for an expression of doubt regarding the increase of landlessness, cp. Pryor, *Malawi and Madagascar,* pp. 257–258, n. 4.
37. Pryor, *Malawi and Madagascar,* ch. 16; see also Szal, "Is There an Agrarian Crisis?"
38. See Dominique Desjeux, "Réforme foncière et civilisation agraire: Le cas de Madagascar," *Le Mois en Afrique,* nos. 184–185, April-May 1981, pp. 55–61; Jolly, *A World Like Our Own,* ch. 7; Pavageau, *Jeunes paysans,* ch. 4.
39. See Pryor, *Malawi and Madagascar,* ch. 11; Szal, "Is There an Agrarian Crisis?"; Elliot Berg, "The Liberalization of Rice Marketing in Madagascar," *World Development,* v. 17, no. 5, May 1989, pp. 719–728.
40. Pascal Chaigneau, *Madagascar, de la première république à l'orientation socialiste: Processus et conséquences d'une évolution politique* (Thèse IIIème cycle en sociologie politique, Univ. de Paris X, 1981), p. ii, n. 3.
41. See Raison, *Les hautes terres,* pp. 543–544.
42. Maureen Covell, *Madagascar: Politics, Economics and Society* (London and New York: Frances Pinter, 1987), pp. 139–141.
43. See Sennen Andriamirado, "Madagascar: L'enfer des uns peut être un paradis pour les autres," *Jeune Afrique,* no. 1368, March 25, 1987, pp. 30–33.
44. Government of Madagascar, Direction Générale du Plan, *Les options fondamentales pour la planification socialiste* (Antananarivo: Ministère des Finances et du Plan, 1978), p. 70.
45. Government of Madagascar, *Charte de la révolution socialiste Malagasy* (Antananarivo: Imprimerie d'Ouvrages Éducatifs, 1975), pp. 55–75; see also Christian Roux, "Le recentrage et la restructuration de l'économie malgache depuis 1974," *Le Mois en Afrique,* v. 15, no. 176–177, August-September 1980, pp. 81–97.
46. Roux, "Le recentrage," p. 94.
47. For favorable commentary on the socioeconomics of the charter, see Roger Jouffrey, "Didier Ratsiraka et le socialisme malgache," *Afrique Contemporaine,* no. 115, May-June 1981; Roux, "Le recentrage et la restructuration"; François Rajaoson,

L'enseigement supérieure et le devenir de la société malgache (Thèse d'état en lettres, Univ. de Paris V, 1981), pt. 4, ch. 2.

48. See Desjeux, "Réforme fonçière et civilisation agraire."

49. See Pascal Chaigneau, *Un état à orientation socialiste: Madagascar* (Thèse d'état, Univ. de Paris X, 1984), pp. 779–803; Roland Razafimandranto, *Essai de bilan politique, économique et social de la période révolutionnaire socialiste malgache: 1975–1982,* (Mémoire en Relations Internationales (Aix-en-Provence: Univ. Aix-Marseille, 1983), pp. 95–96; Pryor, *Malawi and Madagascar,* pp. 317–318, 358.

50. See Pavageau, *Jeunes paysans,* p. 177.

51. Roger Rabetafika, *Réforme fiscale et révolution socialiste à Madagascar* (Paris: Harmattan, 1990), p. 41.

52. Pryor, *Malawi and Madagascar,* p. 261.

53. Madagascar had become a net importer of rice as early as 1971, but by 1977 the deficiency was critical, requiring 200,000 to 300,000 tons of food imports annually until market liberalization could effect a rise in producer prices in the late 1980s; see Berg, "Liberalization of Rice Marketing in Madagascar"; Graham Shuttleworth, "Policies in Transition: Lessons from Madagascar," *World Development,* v. 17, no. 3, March 1989, pp. 397–408.

54. Razafimandranto, *Essai de bilan politique,* p. 109.

55. Lucile Rasoamanalina Ramanandraibe, *Le livre vert de l'espérance malgache* (Paris: Harmattan, 1987), p. 17. For the economic narrative of the late 1970s, see *Madagascar: Recent Economic Developments and Future Prospects,* World Bank Country Study (Washington, D.C.: World Bank, 1980); Ramahatra, *Madagascar: Une économie,* ch. 2; Rabetafika, *Réforme fiscale,* pt. 1; Razafimandranto, *Essai de bilan politique,* ch. 2; Gilles Duruflé, *L'ajustement structurel en Afrique (Sénégal, Côte d'Ivoire, Madagascar)* (Paris: Karthala, 1988), pt. 3; Chaigneau, *Première république,* pt. 3, ch. 1.

56. See Pryor, *Malawi and Madagascar,* p. 235.

57. See Rajaoson, *L'enseignement supérieure,* p. 412.

58. Ibid., pp. 405–411.

59. Ibid., p. 419, table 28.

60. See *Revue de l'Océan Indien,* May 1986; *MTM,* June 28, 1991.

61. See Razafimandranto, *Essai de bilan politique,* pp. 128–135; Pascal Chaigneau, *Rivalités politiques et socialisme à Madagascar* (Paris: CHEAM, 1985), ch. 4; Pryor, *Malawi and Madagascar,* ch. 16.

62. See Andriamirado, "Madagascar: L'enfer des uns."

63. See *Economist,* October 15, 1988; Murphy, *Muddling Through,* esp. chs. 3, 7, and 8.

64. Dan Baum, "Indian Ocean: The Wayward Siblings," *Africa Report,* January-February 1989, p. 48.

65. *Economist,* October 15, 1988.

66. *Madagascar Tribune,* March 9, 1990.

67. Pryor, *Malawi and Madagascar,* p. 398.

68. See Rabetafika, *Réforme fiscale,* p. 78; EIU, *Country Profile 1993/94,* p. 10.

69. Government of Madagascar, Direction Générale du Plan, *Premier plan socialiste, 1979–1980* (Antananarivo: Ministère des Finances et du Plan, 1977); emphasis added.

70. See Chaigneau, *Un état à orientation socialiste,* pp. 602–605, 1203–1207; Szal, "Is There an Agrarian Crisis?" See also "Madagascar: A Weary Electorate," *Africa Contemporary Record (ACR),* 1983–1984 (New York: Africana, 1985), p. B204.

71. See *Le Monde,* February 5, 1981; Pavageau, *Jeunes paysans,* p. 194, n. 10.

72. For a full discussion, see Rabetafika, *Réforme fiscale,* esp. pt. 1, ch. 3, and pt. 2.

73. Pryor, *Malawi and Madagascar,* p. 346; see also Philippe Hugon, "La crise économique à Madagascar," *Afrique Contemporaine,* no. 144, October-December 1987, pp. 3–22; Chaigneau, *Première république,* p. 708; Chaigneau, *Un état à orientation socialiste,* v. 3, ch. 2; Ferdinand Deleris, *Ratsiraka: Socialisme et misère à Madagascar* (Paris: Harmattan, 1986); Ramanandraibe, *Livre vert.*

74. See Michael Goldsmith report for Associated Press in *Los Angeles Times,* October 25, 1981; *MTM,* January 30, 1982.

75. Hugon, "Crise économique," p. 6.

76. Ibid.; see also Duruflé, *L'ajustement structurel,* p. 154.

77. Robert Archer, *Madagascar depuis 1972: La marche d'une révolution* (Paris: Harmattan, 1978), Intro., p. 5, and ch. 1; Pavageau, *Jeunes paysans,* pp. 181, 186–191.

78. Chaigneau, *Première république,* p. iv.

79. See Covell, *Politics, Economics and Society,* pp. 97–100.

80. Chaigneau, *Première république* p. 650.

81. Covell, *Politics, Economics and Society,* p. 88.

82. Andrianaivo Ravelona Rajaona, "Le dinam-pokonolona, mythe, mystique ou mystification?" *Annuaire des Pays de l'Océan Indien (APOI),* v. 8, 1981 (Aix-en-Provence: CERSOI).

83. See Pavageau, *Jeunes paysans,* pp. 171–173; Raison, *Les hautes terres,* pp. 542–547.

84. See Jean du Bois de Gaudusson, "Propos sur les aspects idéologiques et institutionnels des récentes réformes des fokonolona: Le fokonolona en question?" *APOI,* v. 5, 1978, pp. 26–27.

85. Chaigneau, *Première république,* p. 647.

86. Chaigneau, *Un état à orientation socialiste,* p. 628; cf. Pavageau, *Jeunes paysans,* pp. 174–177.

87. Rajaona, "Le dinam-pokonolona"; see also Rajaona, *Essai sur la coopération entre pays en développement: Étude de la problématique à travers la coopération technique entre pays en développement* (Thèse de doctorat en droit, Univ. d'Aix-Marseille, 1985), pp. 77–78.

88. Yves Prats, "Les nouvelles institutions socialistes du développement économique en République Démocratique Malagasy," *APOI,* v. 4, 1977, p. 18.

89. Georges Serre-Ratsimandisa, "Théorie et pratique du 'fokonolona' moderne à Madagascar," *Revue Canadienne des Études Africaines,* v. 12, no. 1, 1978, pp. 37–58.

90. Razafimandranto, *Essai de bilan politique,* esp. ch. 1 and conclusion.

91. For an articulated chart of the decentralized administration, see Chaigneau, *Rivalités politiques,* p. 253.

92. See Rajaoson, *L'enseignement supérieur,* pp. 373–375; du Bois de Gaudusson, "Aspects idéologiques," p. 32.

93. See Razafimandranto, *Essai de bilan politique,* pp. 51–55, 68–70; Dominique Desjeux, *La question agraire à Madagascar: Administration et paysannat de 1895 à nos jours* (Paris: Harmattan, 1979), p. 176; Serre-Ratsimandisa, "Théorie et pratique du 'fokonolona' moderne."

94. Raison, *Les hautes terres,* pp. 543–546.

95. Pavageau, *Jeunes paysans,* p. 178.

96. See Covell, *Politics, Economics and Society,* p. 81.

97. See Adelson Razafy, *Madagascar Tribune,* January 26, 1990; du Bois de Gaudusson, "Aspects idéologiques," p. 34.

98. Prats, "Nouvelles institutions," p. 22.

99. See Hugon, "Crise économique"; *IMF Survey,* June 12, 1989, p. 189; Ramahatra, *Phase d'ajustement,* ch. 2; Ramanandraibe, *Livre vert,* pp. 57–58; Duruflé, *L'ajustement structurel,* pp. 149–162.

100. Ramahatra, *Phase d'ajustement,* p. 184.

101. Philippe Hugon, "Chronique économique et démographique: Madagascar," *APOI,* v. 5, 1978, pp. 423–433; see also Hugon, "L'Afrique subsaharienne face au fonds monétaire international (FMI)," *Afrique Contemporaine,* no. 139, July–September 1986, pp. 3–19.

102. See Duruflé, *L'ajustement structurel,* pp. 160–162; Michel Faure, *L'Express,* no. 2024, April 20–26, 1990; Deleris, *Ratsiraka,* ch. 3; Pryor, *Malawi and Madagascar,* ch. 17.

103. Hugon, "Crise économique," p. 20.

104. Actually, there were fourteen IMF arrangements between June 1980 and May 1989; not all of them were entirely implemented; see EIU, *Country Report,* no. 4, 1991, p. 21.

105. See Duruflé, *L'ajustement structurel,* p. 163.

106. See Pryor, *Malawi and Madagascar,* p. 401, n. 14; Hugon, "L'Afrique subsaharienne"; Ramahatra, *Phase d'ajustement,* pt. 2, ch. 1, and pt. 3, ch. 2; EIU, *Country Report,* no. 2, 1993, p. 23; *Indian Ocean Newsletter,* no. 563, February 20, 1993.

107. See Daniel Swanson and Teferra Wolde-Semait, *Africa's Public Enterprise Sector and Evidence of Reforms* (Washington, D.C.: World Bank, 1989), esp. table A-1, n. 5 to p. 34; also John R. Nellis, *Contract Plans and Public Enterprise Performance,* World Bank Discussion Paper, no. 48 (Washington, D.C.: World Bank, 1989), p. 73.

108. See *MTM,* May 3, 1985.

109. See *Revue de l'Océan Indien,* June 1986; Deleris, *Ratsiraka,* pp. 83–85; Olivier Ramahatra, *MTM,* no. 2492, August 13, 1993, p. 2086.

110. See *MTM,* no. 2455, November 27, 1992, citing an article in *Lettre Afrique-Expansion,* November 16, 1992; EIU, *Country Report,* no. 4 ,1989, no. 2, 1993, p. 26; EIU, *Country Profile 1993/94,* p. 20; *Dans les Média Demain,* (Antananarivo), April 1993.

111. See Franck Raharison, *Madagascar Tribune,* May 19, 1990.

112. See Serge Zafimahova, *Madagascar Tribune,* April 19, 1990.

113. See *MTM,* April 18, 1986.

114. See R. Jaobarison, *Madagascar Tribune,* March 6, 1990.

115. See *MTM,* no. 2465, February 5, 1993.

116. See Rabetafika, *Réforme fiscale,* p. 120.

117. See *IMF Survey,* June 12, 1989, p. 191; EIU, *Country Report,* no. 2, 1991.

118. Hugon, "L'Afrique subsaharienne," p. 18.

119. See Duruflé, *L'ajustement structurel,* pp. 15–18, 164–173; Michael Barratt Brown and Pauline Tiffen, *Short Changed: Africa and World Trade* (London and Boulder: Pluto Press, 1992), esp. pp. 10–11.

120. *IMF Survey,* June 12, 1989, p. 189, gives details; see also EIU, *Country Report,* no. 4, 1991, p. 21.

121. Interview with IMF representative Christian Schiller, *Madagascar Tribune,* January 19, 1990.

122. See EIU, *Country Report,* no. 3, 1992, pp. 13–15, and no. 4, 1992, p. 18.

123. Ibid., January 18, 1990.

124. See EIU's criticism of Jaycox speech, September 3, 1991, as "wishful thinking," *Country Report,* no. 4, 1991.

125. Ibid., p. 13. For a concise narrative on Malagasy debt adjustments through 1993, see EIU, *Country Profile 1993/94,* pp. 26–28, 29–30.

126. See Eric Fottorino, "Virage libéral à Madagascar," *Le Monde* June 12, 1990.

127. *Madagascar Tribune,* March 31, 1990.
128. Ramahatra, *MTM,* no. 2492, August 13, 1993, p. 2086.
129. See EIU, *Country Report,* no. 3, 1993, pp. 19, 24–25; *Indian Ocean Newsletter,* no. 565, March 6, 1993; Georges Ravel, *MTM,* nos. 2480, May 21, 1993, p. 1297, and 2494, August 27, 1993, p. 2183.
130. See Duruflé, *L'ajustement structurel,* ch. 4, pp. 11–13.
131. *ACR,* 1983–1984, p. B201.
132. See Pryor, *Malawi and Madagascar,* pp. 214–215, and n. 20 to ch. 9, pp. 217–218.
133. See Hugon, "Crise économique"; Duruflé, *L'ajustement structurel,* ch. 3; Pryor, *Malawi and Madagascar,* esp. ch. 10; Rabetafika, *Réforme fiscale,* ch. 2; Ramahatra, *Phase d'ajustement,* esp. pp. 66–73.
134. See Pryor, *Malawi and Madagascar;* EIU, *Country Report,* no. 4, 1990, p. 20, and no. 2, 1993, p. 23.
135. See EIU, *Country Report,* no. 4, 1992, p. 15.
136. Deleris, *Ratsiraka,* pp. 127–128; see also Ramahatra, *Phase d'ajustement,* esp. p. 174.
137. Deleris, *Ratsiraka,* p. 130.
138. Jacques De Barrin, *Le Monde,* June 7, 1990.
139. Ramanandraibe, *Livre vert,* pp. 124–125.
140. EIU, *Country Report,* no. 4, 1992, pp. 11–13.
141. EIU, *Country Report,* no. 3, 1993, p. 19; *MTM,* nos. 2458, December 18, 1992, and 2480, May 21, 1993, pp. 1297–1300; World Bank Country Economic Memorandum, Report no. 9101-MAG, June 1991, and Report no. 9817-MAG, March 1992, cited in EIU, *Country Report,* no. 4, 1992, p. 13.
142. *Country Report,* no. 4, 1992, p. 13.
143. EIU, *Country Profile 1993/94,* p. 29.
144. See Duruflé, *L'Ajustement structurel,* pp. 180–181.
145. Hugon, "Crise économique," p. 21.
146. See Duruflé, *L'ajustement structurel,* pp. 181–191; EIU, *Country Report,* no. 4, 1989, pp. 6, 15; Ramahatra, *Une economie,* p. 213; Eric Fottorino, "Virage libéral à Madagascar," *Le Monde,* June 12, 1990; Georges Ravel, *MTM,* no. 2269, May 5, 1989, pp. 1224–1225.
147. Ramahatra, *Phase d'ajustement,* p. 207.
148. See Ramanandraibe, *Livre vert,* pp. 44–49.
149. World Bank, *Plan d'action,* ch. 3.
150. EIU, *Country Report,* nos. 3 and 4, 1991.
151. See *MTM,* no. 2458, December 18, 1992.

6
Conclusion: Continuity as Revolution

While the world's limited attention for Africa was consumed by chaos in Somalia, violence in Angola and Liberia, and problematic ferment in Nigeria and South Africa, Madagascar in 1993 was experiencing a transformation of spirit. These changes occurred not dramatically from despair to hope, but surely, from exasperation to relief. Sensing that Admiral Ratsiraka's proclaimed revolution was turning upon itself, the Malagasy knew again what we ordinarily wish to forget—that in much of the Third World, authority seeks primarily to control people while claiming to develop resources. This lesson had already been manifest in the great island's monarchical, colonial, and republican fanjakana. So from the viewpoint of the people living under Ratsirakan ideology, what looked at first like policy soon revealed itself as coercion; the means became the end.[1] As revolution disclosed continuity, another even more absurd conclusion emerged from Malagasy reality: The difference to most people between one government and another has been so slight that none has merited any particular loyalty.

Madagascar spent the year 1993 in political preoccupation, cultural dormancy, and economic paralysis—a great landmass dead in the water. Eventually the island will revive, meet its international obligations, feed and occupy its people. But it will have to reinvent techniques to achieve each of those purposes, techniques that entail a new relationship between national institutions and a population that has never trusted institutions. A new republic has come forth in relative tranquillity, but its essential character remains ill-defined and perhaps compromised from the outset.

The constitution of September 18, 1992 affords a few opportunities for significant departures; it divides executive power between president and prime minister, makes the latter accountable to the National Assembly, guarantees liberties of organization and assembly, and reserves some sort of autonomy for "decentralized territorial collectivities."[2] Like its predecessors, however, that constitution rests on a doubtful premise; it presupposes a conventional, incipiently European, rather than a uniquely Malagasy, state. This state presumably manifests a welter of modern interests that, were they to be approached in public-spirited discipline, would begin to approximate those of a thriving European society. Such conventional assumptions recur naturally, perhaps, in a republic founded and led by French-trained lawyers, surgeons, and clergymen. But if Madagascar's leaders succeed only in reviving century-old colonial strategies of acculturation, their new republic, like its predecessors, will fail to encompass the interests of, or command loyalty from, the insular Malagasy mass.

Separation of powers and the investiture of executive initiative in a prime minister are still untried principles in Madagascar's governance. The coalition that brought Albert Zafy to the presidency became remarkably unstable once that purpose had been achieved. The coalition's parliamentary expression, Francisque Ravony's August 1993 cabinet, seems dangerously fragile as it begins its initial mandate without the leadership that perhaps only a president can provide. It may be this prospect of parliamentary weakness that prompted Dr. Zafy to impress his presidency's role on national life from the outset. The new president regularly presided over meetings of the Razanamasy interim government; he determined the fate of mutinous "federalist" officers at Atsiranana; Zafy manipulated the Assembly's selection of a prime minister to ensure the emergence of his man regardless of the appeal of Ravony's opponents; his palace issued edicts incorporating certain key public agencies under presidential aegis; he also made prematurely clear his own strategic options in economic development policy.[3]

Another source of compromise may be apprehended at this early stage in the republic's life. So long as the constitutional separations are respected, Francisque Ravony seems likely to conduct Malagasy affairs in directions indicated by international orthodoxies, at least until the sacrifices imposed by those policies become politically unbearable. The clients to be satisfied first are not found in the rural population; nor are they among the urban beneficiaries of public welfare. Rather, they dwell among the external creditors and mentors of the new republic.

The prime minister is already more welcome in these global forums than his presidential mentor and standard-bearer. While heading the interim High Authority of State (HAE), Zafy provoked international suspicions that he was unduly populist, prone to irresponsible gestures aimed at softening the social impact of economic austerity. Some of those inclinations—retaining of budgetary subsidies for urban consumers, holding back certain industries from privatization, and resisting the inexorable logic of currency devaluation, for instance—appeared to international economists to prejudice the fundamental strategy of structural adjustment itself. It seems likely at this point that any return to presidential authority in Malagasy governance—any empowerment of Albert Zafy over Francisque Ravony—will send a displeasing signal to the community of global creditors on whom the republic depends for its developmental resources.

Although the constitutional decentralization principle suggests hope for indigenous expression, a resurgence of the fokon'olona movement now seems improbable. The roles of the collectivities remain to be defined by national legislation, but "decentralization" has already become the international donors' euphemism for government withdrawal from the economic marketplace. A less intrusive, scaled-down state may well improve the functions of the Malagasy macroeconomy. But in itself, laissez-faire government is only that; it scarcely promises the radical devolution of governance into local autonomy, which may represent the only way to mobilize the Malagasy population toward public purpose.

Moreover, observing how quickly Ratsirakan centralism turned into an ethnocentric "federalist" obstruction, Madagascar's current leaders fear côtier separatism above all other jeopardies. Their insurance against that catastrophe consists in bestowing political authority on côtiers who speak in national, not in regional, language. Dr. Zafy and Attorneys Francisque Ravony and Jacques Sylla are in power, not "Governor" Monja Jaona, Colonel Bréchard, or their counterparts in Mahajanga and Antsiranana. This preference for the centralized European nation-state appears to preclude the evolution of "rational federalism," to use Davidson's term, which might have defined an authentic Malagasy political culture within the new constitutional mandate.[4] Thus the island's political momentum seems inevitably to be moving toward renewed reliance on central institutions of European inspiration and international credibility. This time, however, those institutions should be lighter in weight and less cumbersome in economic effect. And, at least, they will have been democratically constituted.[5]

Not that penurious Madagascar has much choice in its political and economic culture. Presenting his policies to the new parliament on August 17, 1993, Prime Minister Ravony struck the chords necessary for a revival of Madagascar's international respectability. He looked for job creation through vigorous pursuit of foreign investment—in infrastructural public works and a proliferation of industries enjoying tax holidays in the island's nascent export-processing zones. Moreover, declaring the onset of rigorous austerity in managing public accounts, the new government appears to have captured applause from creditors seeking diligent debt repayment and the cultivation of export surpluses out of the island's still-foundering economy.

Not surprisingly, the prime minister's platform resembled principles of economic revival already enunciated in Paris by the AKFM's Richard Andriamanjato, speaking for the Vital Forces movement before becoming National Assembly president, and by President Zafy himself. Whereas all three authorities promised increased rural security against rampant banditry and called on the international community to restore favor to the island's liberalizing economy, the nuances among them bear some attention. The veteran nationalist Andriamanjato had to propitiate French interests by advocating industrial revival and foreign investment, as well as agricultural credit reform. Pursuing his characteristic appeal to public opinion, Zafy stressed the eradication of government corruption and an expansion of consumer purchasing power.[6]

Invoking such measures as small-enterprise cultivation and grassroots rural development projects, the new prime minister's August 17 speech seemed to presage a return to the rural production and social development strategies of the first republic.[7] Ravony did not explain, however, how his regime would improve on the investment practices that allowed such finely tex-

School children visiting Antananarivo Zoo. Photo by Gay Kuester, © The Chicago Zoological Society.

tured projects of the 1960s to be overwhelmed by the Tsiranana regime's massive but largely dysfunctional grandes opérations.

In any case, the direction taken by the leaders of Madagascar's third republic appears determined by external, not indigenous, norms. Central control will be required to apply the investment and fiscal policies demanded by the global system, in which indigent Madagascar plays an inevitably subordinate role. To secure confidence in the world financial community, central government will have to be lighter, but firm, and this profile is likely to be etched at the expense of decentralized responsibility and priority for rural participation. The demand is now for conformity to global expectation, not for innovation to consecrate an indigenously Malagasy state seeking its own way in the world. For national leaders and their international clientele, the revolution is over, and the elements of continuity must be fashioned out of the shreds of international complicity inherited from both the first and second republics.

Because the fortunes of the great island will once again be defined by Madagascar's response to the mandates of an integrated international system, it is useful here to review the ways in which Malagasy republics of the past have been articulated with that system.

APOGEE OF THE FRENCH

In 1960, Madagascar's first independence regime inherited colonial France's great antagonist—Merina nationalism, a vigorous movement of intellectuals, Protestant pastors, and once-dominant landholders and entrepreneurs of the high plateaus. Precisely because of their antagonism to French prerogatives, it was not the nationalists who inherited power at independence in 1960. Under the regime of Philibert Tsiranana, the first Malagasy republic remained suspicious of any relationship not congenial to France. Connections with Africa and the rest of the Third World depended on their implications for the Franco-Malagasy umbilical. Relations with other major powers were hesitant, unenthusiastic, and with the socialist world virtually nonexistent.

There are two common explanations—by no means mutually exclusive—for the persistence of French influence in independent Madagascar. The first holds that French neoimperialism blocked all efforts at true decolonization, recruiting, corrupting, and mystifying a susceptible party (Tsiranana's PSD) in exchange for a transfer of nominal authority.[8] The second maintains that the lost empire of the Merina so captured the nationalist imagination that the formerly subjected côtiers and descendants of slaves came to fear nationalism itself, hence to cling to French protection. The coalition of these historically disinherited had to propose an alternative political elite, however thinly stocked and underqualified, who appealed to French interests. They justified that appeal in the name of a Malagasy security that was perpetually jeopardized by a convenient Merina-nationalist flirtation with the communist powers.[9]

The pro-Western foreign policy options of the Tsiranana regime thus reflected an overriding domestic preoccupation—to reinforce barriers against the Merina. Connections between internal and external security were dramatized by the incorporation of Merina nationalism and Protestant political preaching into a Marxist party, the AKFM. By cleaving to the West, the regime could deny access to communist influences that would presumably conspire to reinstall the Merina under foreign ideological canopies. In its foreign relations, Tsiranana's government was more cold warrior than the United States. It objected to France's recognition of Beijing in 1964, warned against global implications of socialist aid to radical regimes, and refused diplomatic relations with Soviet bloc states while exchanging ambassadors with Taiwan and South Korea.[10] Even brief calls by Soviet oceanographic and fishing vessels at Malagasy ports stirred anxiety on the part of the government in Antananarivo.

In truth, the Social Democrats often talked ideology to mask opportunism. The party soon lost all but symbolic affiliation with the parent French SFIO, preferring to see the world after the imagery of the Gaullists who had offered a peaceful transition to independence within the Franc Zone and the community of Francophones. Retaining its Social Democratic label, however, did bring the PSD and its administration into fruitful contact with the West German SDP and the Israeli Mapai; both offered technical assistance, especially in rural community development, party organization, and police training. Help was also sought from Taiwan and India, and later from South Africa.

Infrastructural and industrial development in the PSD republic was entrusted mainly to external interests under an investment code that multiplied the privileges of private capital in Madagascar and failed to require reinvestment of earnings.[11] By 1972, nine-tenths of the modern economy was owned by foreigners; 90 percent of that remained in French hands, even though both imports and exports were being steadily diversified away from the French monopoly. Development plans required three-fourths of their financing from foreign sources. Assistance projects were contracted and cycled through French firms, and all external credit was managed by the Bank of France.[12] Even the concept of large-scale monopolies protected by a benevolent and theoretically disinterested state reflected conservative French economics.

In Rabenoro's mind, the symbiosis with France had its perfectly rational side:

> The former colonizer is the type of medium-sized power that can reassure a Tsiranana who feels the need of something larger than himself, who was so disappointed by the United States after his official visit to that country [in 1964]. France guarantees his protection against the external enemy and, if he requests, against the internal enemy. Cooperation [French assistance] in its diverse forms proves very effective in the financial sector where the young state is freed from concern over its balance of payments.[13]

Under their (unpublished) military agreement of 1960, Malagasy and French forces exchanged intelligence and training services and conducted regular maneuvers together against a spectral communist enemy. France shared in administering the naval base at Diego Suarez (now Antsiranana) and maintained air force and Foreign Legion units on the island. Madagascar's military equipment was of course purchased entirely from France, although this was not completely true of the police or Special Forces apparatuses, some of which, procured by André Resampa's Interior Ministry, came from American, West German, and Israeli sources.

Privileged relations between states often extended by common consent to privileges for participant individuals. The French ambassador retained automatic status as dean of the Antananarivo diplomatic corps; students from either country attended academic institutions interchangeably; a host of specialized French officials (including Réunionnais Creoles) occupied key posts in virtually all administrative services, including the military and the educational institutions. Large colonies of Malagasy dwelt in France and in French territories, where they enjoyed considerable professional latitude and social tolerance. Freedom of investment and repatriation of revenues was ensured; transportation links and telephone lines passed through France before branching off to any other destination; public works contracts and import-export preferences were difficult for third-country nationals to obtain.

Such interpenetration of societies does not necessarily imply that French people made laws and rules for Malagasy people. True, that preemption sometimes occurred. Moreover, Tsiranana and other Malagasy leaders often preferred to have French advisers around them rather than trust the alternative experts, most of them Merina. In a larger sense, however, Malagasy elites tended to conform sympathetically to French ways of thinking and acting, for those were their own ways of thinking and acting. Important decisions were spontaneously influenced by consideration of their implications for essential Franco-Malagasy relations. There is little doubt that these cultural reflexes prevail among the leadership of the third republic today.

Madagascar's first republic found its secondary friendships among the European Community (especially after adoption of the first African treaty of association at Yaoundé in 1963), other Western democracies, and the Francophone caucus of African states. Tsiranana was far from a committed Third World patriot. He disapproved of militancy within the Organization of African Unity (OAU), fearing radical influence from Cuba, the anti-Israeli coalition, or the liberationist-minded African regimes. Preferring the comfortable community of Paris-oriented nations—the African-Malagasy Union, or UAM, subsequently dubbed the Common Organization (OCAM)—his policies rejected nonalignment as meretricious, overly politicized, and self-defeating.[14] Tsiranana had always made much of Madagascar's mixed ethnicity, never allowing the island's society to be categorically identified as African.[15] Seeking unwisely to intervene in the first of the Congo (Zaire) crises in 1961, he even developed a curious brief friendship with pro-European pariah Moïse Tshombe.

Outside Francophonia, Madagascar sought relations selectively among the more conservative African and Asian states (Liberia, Taiwan, Malawi, Philippines, South Korea) and, gradually, with Japan and South Africa. In fact, however, it was the island's unshakable alignment with France and Western Europe that isolated modern Madagascar from its closest neighbors in East and southern Africa and from the Indian Ocean's Asian nations. West Germany became the government's principal source after France for political advice, industrial investment, and cultural exchange. The United Kingdom was useful as a benign oceanic presence and as a partner in the frustrating explorations for Malagasy petroleum. Italy, Canada, and Switzerland offered marginal assistance and commerce.

The United States usually ranks second among Madagascar's clients, thanks to steady purchases of Malagasy vanilla and sporadic cane sugar quotas. Under the first republic, U.S. investment lightly touched such areas as exploring for and refining oils, raising beef cattle, constructing hotels, and operating a flour mill at Toamasina. Technical assistance from Taiwan was financed by the United States for ideological purposes, and Americans officially applauded the cordiality between Malagasy institutions and the Israelis. In 1963 Tsiranana authorized installation of a NASA satellite tracking station at Mahajanga; the station was expanded and transferred the following year to a site outside Antananarivo. Before it was closed by the revolutionary government in 1973, the NASA base brought several hundred American contractor personnel with their families and visitors to the capital. Some 200 other Americans staffed Lutheran missions in the south and on the plateaus.

As Rabenoro indicated in a passage quoted earlier, Tsiranana was more secure in the friendship of medium-sized powers than in proximity to the overgreat. He was suspicious of any initiative by the USSR in Africa or the western Indian Ocean, and he exaggerated China's capacity to realize its putative ambitions in East Africa and among Madagascar's Chinese minority. Once the United States began to focus strategic interest on the Indian Ocean, Malagasy leaders grew nervous, and Foreign Minister Rabemananjara talked of Munich and Yalta where superpowers had toyed with the fate of smaller countries. Tsiranana's official visit to the United States in 1964 brought little benefit to him or to the island apart from acknowledgement of Madagascar's valuable cooperation with NASA in the exploration of space. He remained skeptical about the development of the U.S. naval air base at Diego Garcia, about Washington's irresolute policies in the African Horn, and about U.S. condemnation of South Africa.

Throughout the first republic, French intelligence services on the island cynically fed Tsiranana's anxieties. They countered growing U.S. interest in Madagascar and its geographical environment with accusations and rumors against U.S. personnel. Such reports ultimately led to Tsiranana's unsubstantiated charges of June 1971 implicating the U.S. ambassador and staff in an alleged conspiracy with Resampa (ironically the most elusive of all major Malagasy contacts for American officials). In the weeks prior to this outburst, the United States had shown only benevolent interest in the island; regional ambassadors had attended a State Department conference at Antananarivo; an American had been named director of World Bank operations at the port of Toamasina; and new meteorological equipment had been donated by the United States to the Malagasy weather services. During his sojourn at Antananarivo, Ambassador Anthony Marshall had committed himself primarily to seeking American investment for island industry and tourism, an activity that caused nervousness among some zealous overseas French. Marshall left the country on June 6 without ceremony, claiming total ignorance of the reasons for his "quarantine."[16]

Despite this favoritism at Antananarivo, French enthusiasm for financing Madagascar's grand development projects cooled during the late 1960s, sending the Tsiranana government in search of alternative and supplementary sources of finance. It soon found a willing new friend in South Africa. Professing ideological repugnance for apartheid, the regime nonetheless appreciated Pretoria's energetic anticommunism, the interest shown in the island by South African tourism promoters, and the availability of moderately priced industrial and consumer goods at Durban.[17] As its reward for engaging in "dialogue" with Pretoria, Madagascar expected South African investors to contribute to tourist infrastructure, prospect for oil and minerals, develop a major bunkering port and dry dock at Narinda, and consider other major features of state planning.[18] South Africa was portrayed by official Antananarivo as willing to help without interfering in Malagasy affairs or requiring Madagascar's complicity in apartheid's struggle against black militancy.

From 1967 on, Foreign Minister Rabemananjara had repeatedly to deny the imminence of diplomatic relations with Pretoria, an offense that would have alienated many African partners of the great island and enraged some local patriots. The South Africans were nonetheless permitted to open an "information office" in the capital in 1971, and Madagascar joined a South Africa–inspired regional tourism council with five other participants.[19] Ironically, while dialogue with Pretoria was being defended as, after all, a private matter for businesspeople, the Tsiranana government was busy confiscating copies of Mao's *Little Red Book*, implying, perhaps, that reading was not as private as business. South Africa, said Tsiranana disingenuously in 1968 and 1969, would soon correct its official racism by nonviolent means after learning from the dialogue with Madagascar how adroitly nonwhite populations could govern themselves.[20]

This increasing fraternization induced conjecture that Tsiranana was ready to grant naval facilities and other services to South African security in the higher name of anticommunism. He had, after all, approved British arms sales to South Africa in July 1970, since they were intended for "Indian Ocean defense," not for "massacre or enslavement of our African brothers."[21] French advice probably prevailed, however, against any temptation to share naval facilities with Pretoria. By the same token, France had never welcomed the presence at Mahajanga of British reconnaissance aircraft enforcing the 1966 blockade of the self-declared independent regime in Southern Rhodesia (Zimbabwe). Paris was not displeased by Tsiranana's cancellation of those facilities in mid-June 1971.

The umbilical to France was further strained toward the end of the 1960s by French unwillingness to finance the bulk of Madagascar's ambitious five-year plan (1964–1968). Further tensions arose from the May 1968 riots in France, which nearly overthrew DeGaulle's government and did for a time interrupt communications with Antananarivo. Tsiranana then began to think more favorably of diversifying his country's external relations. Now and then, Madagascar's Francophile leaders paused to consider how accidental was the preeminent influence of France and the French culture they revered, how unlike their Creole neighbors Malagasy society was, how few people on the island actually spoke French or knew the wonders of Paris.[22] In essence, France stood for elite access to the modern world, a correction for insularity, and, in Tsiranana's view, a defense against the return of Merina tyranny. But at the beginning of the 1970s under the presidency of Georges Pompidou, a preoccupied France seemed to be approaching Madagascar and its needs with diminished enthusiasm.

Behind the unequivocal Tsiranana, certain more nationalist PSD adherents, led by Resampa, had never been reconciled to the privileged position of the French.[23] They perceived that commitment as entailing flagrant cordiality with the United States and South Africa, partners even more objectionable than the erstwhile colonizer. Thus, Madagascar's pro-Western diplomacy caused younger militants within the presidential party to object to the subservience of presidential policy, the absence of genuine social democratic commitments, and the use of Madagascar as a headquarters for French naval strategy. These critics were silenced, however, upon the demotion and imprisonment of their leader, Resampa, in 1971.

The long history of outbreaks of popular antagonism to French rule—in 1885, 1896, 1915, 1929, 1947, for example—contributed to the crises and discomfitures of the Francophile first republic. That paroxysm finally ended in the streets of Antananarivo in 1972. Philibert Tsiranana had embodied the *fanjakana vazaha,* and the revolution was aimed at ending that "establishment of strangers" once and for all.[24]

REVOLUTION AND CONTINUITY IN INTERNATIONAL RELATIONS

When the nationalist movement triumphed in 1972, it inevitably sought to weaken the bilateral connection with Paris and to spread the great island's allegiances throughout the nonaligned network of states. Abandoning its polarized status on the West-East axis, Madagascar cultivated affinities with Algeria, Ethiopia, Tanzania, and socialist Asia. One of the first achievements of the Ramanantsoa interregnum was the termination on June 23, 1972, of all cooperation with South Africa. The break with Washington, already initiated by the aberrant Tsiranana, continued through the decade. A new, highly complex equilibrium supplanted colonial dependence, with a diversity of sources to offer hope of security, stability, and prosperity. Most conspicuously, this new diplomacy brought the Malagasy into a hitherto unprecedented network of relationships with the Soviet Union, China, Cuba, and the smaller socialist states of East Europe and East Asia. Revolutionary Madagascar stagnated nonetheless, as East and West did little more through the 1970s and early 1980s than play for the favor of rival elites.

Beleaguered by global inflation and bewitched by the availability of international capital, Ratsiraka's second-republic economy plunged rapidly and profoundly into chronic debt. The unrestrained investment campaign of the late 1970s produced little substance, but it did ensure a resumption of dependence on external sources of capital, technology, and markets. Very little of this one-way traffic came from the USSR or from Madagascar's other new friends. That wasn't where the liquidity lay—although Ratsiraka visited Moscow and sibling capitals almost as often as Tsiranana had trekked to Paris. Some import credit did emerge, much of it for Soviet oil at premium prices ($26 a barrel even in 1986), most of the rest for expensive arms that no Malagasy security force would ever need. There was modest socialist state assistance in mining and maritime navigation and for a cement plant at Mahajanga, a dam at Mararara, a flour mill at Antananarivo.

In return, Moscow received very little from its investment in Madagascar. In particular, it was not granted access to the vast naval facility abandoned by the French at Diego Suarez.[25] There was a trickle of authorized East European dumping on Malagasy markets in exchange for a rare capital project here or there. Most Soviet and other communist nonmilitary assistance came in the form of scholarships for young Malagasy to learn truly foreign ways in far-off places—and to become as alienated from the East as they had been from the West. And in truth, the West had never disappeared as a source.

Political distinctions dear to the revolution receded as the beleaguered republic groped for its way. Through most of the decade Antananarivo retained educational and military links with the USSR and polite affinities with such radical states as Algeria, China, Cuba, North Korea, Seychelles, and Iraq. Its staff in New York worked diligently to realize the Third World ambition to evict major-power military forces from the Indian Ocean. But these missions and comradeships brought little tangible help; they could not even enhance revolutionary illusions for a population that had never adopted the revolution.

For investment and markets, Ratsiraka's Madagascar had tried to look inside itself—and eastward—but without results. The sunlight of development shows first in the West. As the Soviet alternative dissolved, Madagascar's leaders had no choice but to seek improved relations with the erstwhile French patron and its market-economy partners. Recultivating those relations entailed not only a compromise of anticapitalist principles; it also required the willingness to reconcile bitter disagreements from the colonial past as well as disputes over France's military deployments in the Indian Ocean. The most recalcitrant of these conflicts was resolved by Antananarivo's agreement in 1983 to compensate French businesses expropriated in the revolution of the mid-1970s. Madagascar thereupon obtained satisfaction of its claims on the intrinsically worthless neighboring islets (*les îles éparses*), resolving a dispute that had contaminated the agenda with Paris for nearly two decades.[26]

France had never turned its back entirely on its erstwhile big colony. Grants and credits kept flowing throughout the difficult decade from 1973 into the 1980s, and the French maintained 600 technical assistants (450 of them teachers) in Madagascar through 1981. The level of financial assistance also grew—from a total of 260 million French francs in 1978 to 450 million in 1981 and 870 million by 1988. Grant aid reached US$107 million in 1989, after which Paris ceased demanding reimbursement for new commitments. By then, 16,000 French nationals were living in the island, still only one-third the number there in 1972.

Moreover, the renegade ex-colony has rapidly resumed importance as a client for French goods and services and as a dependent market for French investment and technology. France has retained the primacy of its trade position, accounting for 25 to 30 percent of Madagascar's exports and imports. French exports (many of them consumer goods) usually exceed Malagasy sales to France by a substantial margin (about 30 percent in 1991). That ratio widened to 2 to 1 in 1990, as French placement of equipment, machinery, pharmaceuticals, and other products in the island rose by 17 percent while declining Malagasy coffee sales were causing an equivalent net drop in exports to France. French capital is also responsible for more than half the enterprises established in the island's export-processing zones. By the end of the 1980s, French advice was replacing Soviet and North Korean influence in the island's military institutions. Following the Franco-African political summit at La Baule in late 1990, Antananarivo joined the ranks of those Francophone African states recognizing President Mitterrand's admonition to earn French favor through democratization and observance of human rights.

Other Western powers prudently followed the French lead. Through the Cold War era, Madagascar's case for benevolent attention was bolstered by its putative geopolitical leverage on Soviet ambitions in southern Africa and the Indian Ocean. After a diplomatic hiatus, the United States and Great Britain both sent resident ambassadors to Antananarivo in the early 1980s. Six youthful technocrats were trained at Western institutions to enter Ratsiraka's government in 1982. U.S. itinerant ambassador Vernon Walters and Assistant Secretary of State Chester Crocker visited the island in 1983. By the 1990s, an ostensibly cleaner regime in Antananarivo—allowing internationally observed elections, respecting press freedoms, and complying with IMF precepts—warranted further concessions throughout the triumphant West.[27]

During the second republic, the European Community and the International Fund for Agricultural Development renewed their partnerships with France in capital aid to the Mangoky valley cotton and rice project started by the Tsiranana regime in the early 1960s. They also continued to help develop the immense rice basin around Lake Alaotra, despite weaknesses in water control and the disproportions between contractor profits and peasant income in that project.[28] In 1989, France wrote off one-third of Madagascar's $1.5 billion bilateral debt. The United States followed suit on a smaller, more selective, scale tied to performance in structural reforms.

Because of the Ratsiraka regime's broadscale borrowing campaigns, the wages of debt have had to be paid to many creditors. National integrity required—requires still today—a diversification of contributors to Madagascar's stability and growth. Indebtedness thus brought new forms of dependence on global consortia of capital, the World Bank, and the International Monetary Fund. That subservience grew steadily more cogent through the decade of the 1980s as access to world markets became inextricably linked to political and economic conditions imposed by the lenders. In a surge of 1990s practicality, the Ratsiraka regime even reissued Tsiranana's invitations to South Africa, among other prospective benefactors for a desperately impoverished island. By then, of course, this was no longer a revolutionary Madagascar, and after the independence of Namibia and the legitimization of the African National Congress, South Africa was not quite the utter pariah of the 1970s.

Even today, however, no new predominant source has been able to replace the steady if underpowered circuits of technology, markets, and capital once supplied by France. After deliberately dismantling the potent relationship with France, the second republic found itself integrated nowhere. Malagasy nationalism is at home only in Madagascar, even after decades of infiltration of the nationalist movement by Marxists and humiliation by the laws of the international market. France has played a new streamlined role of peer among peers, ensuring the European Community's continued support for Malagasy macroeconomic viability. Were it willing to pay the price, Paris might have been able to repurchase domination over Antananarivo's distressed public affairs, but that domination would have brought little material benefit to the French. Thus, the great island is at least no longer a forbidden, exotic preserve of French ambitions. Ratsiraka's diplomatic adherence to the options of the radically nonaligned—in UN, Third World, and other forums—has probably altered Malagasy foreign policy orientations permanently. There the revolution has had some lasting effect. But changing diplomacy and terms of debt brought little vital alteration for the mass of Malagasy.

THE THIRD REPUBLIC: REGIONS AND LOCALITIES

The new Madagascar may change international networks as it chooses, but the Malagasy nation has only two natural regions for close cooperation. It could turn seaward toward its sparse outskirts of small southwestern Indian Ocean islands—the Mascarenes (consisting of Réunion and Mauritius), the Comoros, and the Seychelles archipelagos. Or it could face landward toward the southeast African littoral states (Mozambique, Tanzania, and Kenya) and through them, toward the continental interior and the rapidly mutating south. Ratsiraka's diplomacy brought the Malagasy second republic into cordial contact with East Africa, but the benefits were inevitably more rhetorical than material. Although air linkages emerged desultorily on the regional map, little of substance was traded, and at no time did Malagasy commercial relations figure importantly for any continental neighbor. The Anglophone and erstwhile Portuguese societies simply did things differently than the French-thinking elites, even in a revolutionary Antananarivo. More acutely, the complex African recession that raged coextensively with the life of Ratsiraka's republic permitted little opportunity for exploring comparative advantage, complementary project development, or other common interests between the island and its hard-pressed continental neighbors.

Madagascar's third republic may have better chances to cooperate with East and southern Africa, and it will be encouraged to do so by international influences. Even during the early 1993 transition, Antananarivo announced its hope of joining the Eastern and Southern African Preferential Trade Area, seeking investment capital and export markets for its new free-trade processing industries. The fate of this venture depends in large part on the rationalization of exchange rates among the participant currencies, a situation that no Malagasy government has ever been able to manage in the direction of commercial expansion. To induce such benefits, multilateral strategies should emphasize Madagascar's gradual integration into cooperative southern African financial, commercial, tourist, and environmental planning efforts.

To its north and east, Madagascar's insular region scarcely appears to offer help for a quasi-continent of 12 million people seeking solutions for their poverty and obscurity. Although enjoying cultural status in what I have called a Latin Quarter of Afro-Asia,[29] the great island has not become a Creole version of Francophonia after the manner of the Mascarenes and Seychelles. Nor, unlike the Comoros, does it maintain vital linkages with the Swahili coast or deep historical and cultural ties with the Persian Gulf. Neither Asian nor African nor European in cultural affinity—despite centuries of influence from all three continents—Madagascar remains Malagasy. Nevertheless, there are historical linkages that may be developed to improve regional livelihood. For the better part of two centuries, Madagascar has conducted substantial trade relations with its smaller island neighbors—Mauritius, the French Overseas Department of Réunion, and Comoros. The great island has imported industrial goods and exported food and other raw materials, received surplus labor and peasant immigrants, and acted as a transportation hub in an oceanic network. Now Madagascar finds itself substantially poorer than its Mascarene and Seychelles partners and virtually as needy as the overpopulated, partially barren Comoros.[30]

Relations with these insular partners advanced sluggishly at best until the late 1980s, when the Indian Ocean Commission (IOC) took on a promise of life. A charter member of the commission, created in 1982 to promote collaborative island development, Madagascar provided IOC's first secretary-general, Henri Rasolondraibe. Still, in the early years of association, as each island passed through its own alternations of nationalism and accommodation, revolutionary Madagascar engaged itself only intermittently in IOC collaborations. For a time, moreover, South Africa's ambitions divided the insular states, frustrating their hopeful solidarity. Today, however, it is Madagascar that is "derevolutionizing," and it needs partners from Mauritius and French Réunion to reattract French investment, export markets, and tourists, hitherto diverted away from a defiant great island. Seychelles and Comoros could also participate with Madagascar in an evolving system of transportation and tourism.

Benefiting substantially through project assistance from the European Community as well as from the UN Development Program, Canada, and Australia, the IOC has undertaken projects in tuna fishing; renewable energy development; cyclone detection and communication; interisland trade; research and technology in sugar cane, rice, corn, and other shared products; aircraft maintenance; tourism and transportation; the press and radio-television; and an academy for study and research into Creole cultures.[31] The commission budget for 1993 rose by 16.7 percent, including a regional plan negotiated with the EC's European Development Fund to provide 25.5 million European Currency Units (ECUs) to facilitate transportation and tourism, environmental protection, civil security, and maritime assistance.[32] Moreover, Comoreans have returned to settle and trade in Mahajanga after a decade of brutal pogroms that had decimated their communities in Madagascar.

Mauritius alone, an economic minisuccess story with its $2,000 per capita income and full employment, offers markets and sources of capital for the emerging export industries of the larger island. Malagasy-Mauritian trade rose from 2.5 to 6.6 billion FMG between 1985 and 1989 and could expand three times again by the mid-1990s.[33] There is room for cooperation in textiles, tourism, and in cane sugar technology, where Mauritius ranks among the most efficient producers in the world.

But the evolution of regional relations will not proceed smoothly. Malagasy social critics are skeptical over the dangers of labor exploitation in the export-processing industries; they remain less than enthusiastic over offering South Africa the advantages of an open market, as Mauritius has done.[34] An IOC trade and industry fair scheduled at Toamasina in October-November 1990 was postponed when the Malagasy declared themselves unready and unable to support the costs of hosting the event. Three years later, prospective foreign investors and entrepreneurs still deplore the hesitations and apparent nonchalance of Antananarivo's administrators and the inadequacy of the island's infrastructure to support production and distribution.

So Madagascar today belongs to several networks without being incorporated into any. The years in which France determined security, economics and finance, cultural development, and diplomacy have given way to a welter of relationships and influences for the Malagasy. The island is part of a Eurafrican development complex and has logical aspirations for fruitful participation with East and southern African economies. It has further diversified its portfolio of relations without regard to ideology, so that South Koreans, Israelis, South Africans, and Moroccans have once again become welcome at Antananarivo alongside the remnants of the socialist, Arab, and nonaligned presence on which Ratsiraka had once placed his trust. Madagascar has established its island nationhood, its unique environmental personality, and its escutcheon of needs, but its most pertinent, and permanent, alignments have yet to be sorted out.

Having cultivated the components of a highly pluralistic parliamentary democracy, the third republic must begin to use the appropriate economic keys to the island's national future—mobilization of domestic capital and cultural endowments, comprehensive agricultural projects and rural stabilization policies, multiplication of jobs in export-processing and other industries, southern African and Indian Ocean regional cooperation, debt relief through multilateral mechanisms, the multifarious components of the international environmental plan, equitable taxation, burden-sharing, and distribution of benefits.

These actions will require statecraft, courage, and attention to the realities of a specifically Malagasy society. Among those realities is the need for a vast expansion of participation in public life—by women, tradespeople, and peasantry, among others. Inveterate tendencies toward clientelist politics, marginalization of the have-nots, and withdrawal of Madagascar's true "vital forces" from the affairs of state must be reversed by a government elected in the name of those forces. An entrepreneurial middle class must be offered its stake in the fruition of statecraft—through ensured savings and investment, liberal employment policies, equitable taxation structures, redress of grievances, and formal, open channels of access to power.

Such policies would be unprecedented in modern Madagascar. To deny them would destine the great island to repeat the cycle of victimization once again, a cycle that begins in neocolonial alienation and ends in political incoherence, "tribal" dissension, dictatorship. The real revolution in Madagascar—seen in 1972 if at no other time—joins national authority and popular participation, fanjakana and fokon'olona. For brief moments, the force of such bonding has overcome the essential popular resistance to central authority faced by all governments in the island's national history. Resistance has erupted in the outbreaks of 1896, 1916, 1947, 1971, 1972, and in intermittent riots and demonstrations ever since, including the massive strikes of 1991. But that resistance has been essentially passive, truculent, pervasively disobedient, and impossible to defeat. This means in effect that no strategy has been able to mobilize productive resources for sustained development, that, in the complaint of a European World Bank official in private conversation, "these people don't do what they have to do; they seem determined to starve."

Malagasy are of course not anxious to suffer, but they will not consent to develop at any cost, and they may perceive a wider zone of choice between starvation and prosperity than does the World Bank and the West. To narrow that zone of subsistence requires an unprecedented confidence in strategies of development, in what the fanjakana tells them they can achieve without surrendering their cultural identity. To begin that process, ordinary Malagasy must resolve their chronic identification of fanjakana and vazaha, or government and foreignness. Influenced by these perceptions, they rejected the first republic as a continuation of French colonialism, repudiating independence as the contradiction of both nationalism and ancestral tradition. They condemned the second republic for having imposed still another foreign import—chic ideological nationalism in Marxist rhetoric. Thanks to a new constitutional spirit, the third republic of Vital Forces will avoid these alienations, but will it succumb to still another—through deeply penetrating structural adjustments imposed by global market conditionality? Or does that republic have no choice?

Madagascar's essential culture stabilized itself for its own survival in the trauma of imperial contact. That culture sustained its family and communal traditions in defiance of imperialism, and it has yet to recover its full, autonomous dynamic. But this cultural trauma appears modest by contrast with the transformation suffered by the island's political and economic institutions in contact with the colonizers. Divorced from their inalienable traditions, the Malagasy population understandably regards political-economic Europeanization with hostility. This incompatibility between cultures has frustrated national authority to this day. It is at the heart of the fanjakana's inability to mobilize popular participation.

Such contradictions should be recognized and may be resolved by successor governments at Antananarivo; there must be hope in the dynamics of democracy. The third republic has such an opportunity, but it must implement its constitutional mandate for decentralization through consultative mechanisms from the ground up and through forms of expression inherent in traditional institutions.

To judge from the composition of Francisque Ravony's cabinet of August 1993 and to read his widely praised policy pronouncements, however, the third republic is unlikely to build its reconciliations in that sense, and perhaps it could never succeed in doing so. The uneasy coalition emergent through proportional representation in the legislative elections of June 1993 may require the hard hand of central discipline to accomplish anything whatsoever. Moreover, top-down government is probably expected by the conductors and choruses of international credit; how otherwise could national institutions come into properly adjusted relationships? Nevertheless, to obtain the necessary mobilization of human resources toward nationally fruitful purposes, it seems evident that Madagascar's third republic must heed both its international creditors and benefactors and its popular demand for unconventional channels of authority and responsibility—or it, too, risks futility.

In Madagascar, the culture that has never been permitted to emerge into political efficacy insists on the primacy of small-scale localities against the dictates of the central system. Whether through new missions for fokon'olona or a more sensitive articulation of community-fanjakana relationships, the success of the third republic will require attention to this cultural specificity. A democratic, authentically Malagasy republic cannot afford merely to fabricate one more ideologically centralized structure to be resented and resisted by a majority of the population. If its institutions dominate thought and initiative, they will be resisted; if they show uncertainty, they will be rejected as in the repudiations of weak leadership in 1947, 1972, and 1991. The third republic must not be understood merely as an Indian summer of the first. The tightrope is taut and narrow; statespeople may well lose their balance between its implacable ends.

But if the agencies of the new state can somehow be identified with the society affected by its policies, Madagascar will have started on the way toward an unprecedented achievement—the consonance of personal interest with institutional purpose on a national scale. Only through this accomplishment will the Malagasy cease requiring revolution to ensure continuity in their institutional life.

NOTES

1. Jean-Pierre Raison, in the conclusion to *Les hautes terres de Madagascar* (Paris: ORSTOM-Karthala, 1984), esp. pp. 535–538, applies this lesson to nineteenth-century Merina history but fails to detect its pertinence to the second republic.

2. République de Madagascar, *Constitution de la République de Madagascar*, 1992, préambule, Art. 2, and Title VII (Arts. 125–137).

3. See Economist Intelligence Unit (EIU), *Country Report: Mauritius, Madagascar, Seychelles*, no. 3,1993, July 5, 1993; Georges Ravel, in *Marchés Tropicaux et Méditerranéens (MTM)*, nos. 2476, April 23, 1993, and 2480, May 21, 1993. For the selection of the prime minister, see *Le Journal de Madagascar, Midi-Madagasikara, Madagascar Tribune,* August 10,1993.

4. See Basil Davidson, *The Black Man's Burden: Africa and the Curse of the Nation-State* (New York: Random House, 1992), esp. pp. 286, 294. Davidson's discussion of peasant alienation in pre–World War I Romania, pp. 144–147, provides striking parallels with the Malagasy case depicted here.

5. See D. Tovonirina Rakotondrabe, "Au delà de l'ethnie: Ethnies, état-nation, et démocratie à Madagascar," paper presented to Colloque International et Pluridisciplinaire: Démocratie et Développement dans le Sud-Ouest de l'Océan Indien et en Afrique, Université d'Antananarivo, May17–24, 1993.

6. For Andriamanjato's statement, see *Indian Ocean Newsletter*, no. 570, April 10, 1993; for Zafy's declarations, see Ravel, in *MTM*, nos. 2476, April 23, 1993, and 2494, August 27, 1993.

7. See *Madagascar Tribune*, August 10, 1993; "Anatrika," in *Madagascar Tribune*, August 19, 1993; *MTM*, no. 2494, August 27, 1993.

8. See Pascal Chaigneau, *Madagascar, de la première république à l'orientation socialiste: Processus et conséquences d'une évolution politique* (Thèse de IIIème cycle en sociologie politique, Univ. de Paris X, 1981), ch. 1; Robert Archer, *Madagascar depuis 1972: La marche d'une révolution* (Paris: Harmattan, 1978); François Rajaoson, *L'enseignement supérieur et le devenir de la société malgache* (Thèse d'état en lettres et sciences humaines, Univ. de Paris V, 1981), pt. 3; Gilles Duruflé, *L'ajustement structurel en Afrique (Sénégal, Côte d'Ivoire, Madagascar)* (Paris: Karthala, 1988), pt. 3.

9. See Gérard Althabe, "Les luttes sociales à Tananarive en 1972," *Cahiers d'Etudes Africaines*, v. 80, nos. xx-4, pp. 407–447.

10. See Chaigneau, *Première république*, pp. 240–42, 257–258; Césaire Rabenoro, *Les relations extérieures de Madagascar de 1960 à 1972* (Thèse d'état, Univ. d'Aix-Marseille III, 1981); Harry Bryce Qualman, *Limits and Constraints on Foreign Policy in a Dependent State: Madagascar Under the Tsiranana Regime*, Ph.D. dissertation, Johns Hopkins University, 1975.

11. See Rabenoro, *Relations extérieures*, p. 306.

12. See Y.-G. Paillard, "The First and Second Malagasy Republics: The Difficult Road of Independence," trans. R. Kent, in Raymond Kent, ed., *Madagascar in History: Essays from the 1970s* (Albany, Calif.: Foundation for Malagasy Studies, 1979), pp. 298–354.

13. Rabenoro, *Relations extérieures*, p. 331.

14. See Philip M. Allen, "Madagascar and OCAM: The Insular Version of Regionalism," *Africa Report*, January 1966.

15. See Raison, "Madagascar dans le sud-ouest de l'océan indien," *Hérodote: Revue de Géographie et de Géopolitique*, nos. 37–38, 1985, pp. 216–217; Allen, "Madagascar and OCAM."

16. C. L. Sulzberger's report in *New York Times*, June 25, 1971, contains inaccuracies; see Philip M. Allen, "Rites of Passage in Madagascar," *Africa Report*, February 1971.

17. Europe's prices increased after the closure of the Suez Canal in the "six-day" 1967 Middle East war.

18. See Chaigneau, *Première république*, pp. 272–275.

19. Rabemananjara interviews with *Afrique Nouvelle*, November 16, 1967, with Agence France Presse, September 3,1970, and with *La République* July 23, 1971 (Antananarivo); see Philip M. Allen, "Madagascar: The Authenticity of Recovery," in John M. Ostheimer, ed., *The Politics of the Western Indian Ocean Islands* (New York: Praeger, 1975); Allen, "New Round for the Western Islands," in Alvin J. Cottrell and R. M. Burrell, eds., *The Indian Ocean: Its Political, Economic, and Military Importance* (New York: Praeger, 1972), pp. 307–329.

20. See Allen, "New Round."

21. See Agence France Presse, July 25, and September 3, 1970.

22. See Raison, "Madagascar dans le sud-ouest de l'océan indien"; Philip M. Allen, *Security and Nationalism in the Indian Ocean: Lessons from the Latin Quarter Islands* (Boulder and London: Westview Press, 1987), ch. 7.

23. Ironically, the series of accords tying the Malagasy republic to France had been negotiated by Resampa himself in 1960 at Tsiranana's behest.

24. See Jacques Tronchon, *L'insurrection malgache de 1947: Essai d'interprétation historique* (Paris: Maspero, 1974), conclusion.

25. See Chaigneau, *Un état à orientation socialiste: Madagascar* (Thèse d'état, Univ. de Paris X, 1984), p. 999.

26. For background see Philippe Leymarie, *Océan Indien: Le nouveau coeur du monde* (Paris: Karthala, 1981), ch. 10; Allen, *Security and Nationalism*, pp. 61–62, 171–172.

27. See Michel Faure in *L'Express*, no. 2024, April 20–26, 1990.

28. See "Madagascar: The Politics of Survival," in Colin Legum, ed., *Africa Contemporary Record (ACR), 1985–1986* (New York and London: Africana, 1987), p. B353; for a subsequent record, see Graham Shuttleworth, "Policies in Transition: Lessons from Madagascar," *World Development*, v. 17, no. 3, March 1989, pp. 397–408; Elliot Berg, "The Liberalization of Rice Marketing in Madagascar," *World Development*, v. 17, no. 5, May 1989, pp. 719–728; John Crosthwaite, "Quantifying Structural Adjustment at the Grassroots: The 'Braudel' Measure of Small-Scale Entrepreneur Purchasing

Power," European Communities Commission, *Courier*, no. 124, November-December 1990, pp. 12–16; also *Courier*, no. 111, September-October 1988, pp. 25–43.

29. Allen, *Security and Nationalism*, pt. 2, esp. ch. 7.

30. For background see Ibid.; Robert LeBlond, *Les accords de coopération régionale dans le sud-ouest de l'océan indien: Recherche documentaire* (Ottowa: Author, 1990).

31. See supplement to *MTM*, no. 2277, June 30, 1989.

32. See *MTM*, no. 2457, December 11, 1992; Economist Intelligence Unit, *Country Profile 1993/94*, p. 33.

33. *Madagascar Tribune*, March 1, and April 11, 1990.

34. See for instance, interview with Richard Andriamanjato by R. Jaobarison in *Madagascar Tribune*, March 2, 1990.

Glossary

aggrégation: qualification for university professorship in French and Francophone institutions.
aloala: pole sculptures erected on graves of the southern Sakalava.
amponga: drum.
andevo: slave caste of the Merina.
andriana: Merina noble class.
Antalaotse: Muslim ocean traders in the coastal towns of the north.

Bourbon: seventeenth- and eighteenth-century name for the island of Réunion.

coopération: French foreign aid.
côtier: a Malagasy from the coast; by sociopolitical extension, any non-Merina.

fady: ancestral constraint on behavior ("taboo").
famadihana: ceremony of the turning of the dead and returning of the remains to the family tomb.
fanjakana: government, but more broadly encompassing the entire power establishment.
faritany: geographic and administrative region corresponding to French *province*.
fianakavihana: family, in the broad sense (clan).
firaisana: geographic cluster of *fokontany* corresponding roughly to town or French *commune*.
firaisam'pokontany: elected assembly of the firaisana.
fivondronana: cluster of firaisana corresponding to parliamentary electoral district or French *sous-préfecture*.
fivondronam'pokontany: elected assembly of the fivondronana.
foko (Fukun): clan or deme.
fokon'olona: assembly of the people, the generic institution of popular participation in government formed and re-formed in every regime since the Merina eighteenth-century monarchy.
fokontany: physical space inhabited by a fokon'olona; villages or urban districts; basic unit of local jurisdiction.
Forces Vives: Vital Forces, several coalitions of anti-Ratsiraka parties and organizations strengthened in the general strikes of 1991, supporting Albert Zafy in the presidential elections of 1992–1993.
Francophonie: the French-speaking world and its culture.

Grande Île: Great Island, French nickname for Madagascar.

grandes opérations: large-scale development projects launched in the late 1960s by the PSD regime.

hasina: blessedness, composed of wisdom and fertility.
havana: close family relatives.
Hery Velona: see Forces Vives.
hova: Merina commoner (middle) class.

Île de France: eighteenth-century name for Mauritius island while under French control (to 1810).
îles éparses: islets in the Indian Ocean and Mozambique Channel ceded to Madagascar by France in 1990 after long dispute.
Imerina: territory of the Merina people on the central plateaus.
indigénat: collection of exploitative French colonial laws applicable to (indigenous) Malagasy.
investir à outrance: invest without restraint; international borrowing campaign of the late 1970s.

kabary: formal speech; speech making.
Karana: Muslims ("people of the Koran"); now reserved for Indo-Malagasy population.
karazabe: large ethnic groupings, sometimes called "tribes."

loi cadre: 1956 "framework" legislation sponsored by French socialist government allowing political development in African territories.

madinika: literally, "little" people; the poor.
mainty: literally, black people; former slaves of the Merina.
menalamba: movement of resistance to French rule after 1896; so called after the red cloaks worn by some militants.
métissage: mixing of races.
mpiragasy: itinerant musicians who provide public information as well as entertainment.

ombiassa, ombiassy: itinerant Muslim scholars from the east coast, often influential politically prior to and during the nineteenth-century Merina monarchy.

politique des races: early French colonial policy seeking to advance "tribal" leaders instead of Merina.

ramanenjana: mystical anti-European popular movement of early 1860s connected with the cult of the dead Queen Ranavalona I.
ray aman'dreny: elder; literally father and mother.
risoriso: black market.

sampy: literally, idols; figures of veneration.
sikidy: royal talismans.
sodina: Bamboo flute.
sorabe: great scriptures; historical and cultural documents of the southeast, in Arabic script.

GLOSSARY 241

soudure: period (November to March) preceding rice harvest when prices rise precipitously.
Sûreté: security police.

tanin'drazana: ancestral territory, often identified with family tomb.
tavy: shifting cultivation, rotating among recently burnt-off fields.
tenin'drazana: words of the ancestors; refers to rules imposed by tradition on the living.
tompon'tany: masters of the land, often referring to Vazimba or others encountered in early migrations of Merina and other peoples.
tromba: spirit-possession rituals, often drawing power from the evocation of deceased monarchs.
tsiny: concept of guilt plaguing those who offend ancestral precedent.

vadin'tany: royal agents in provinces of the Merina empire.
vahiny: permanent residents of a locality who are politically and socially integrated yet not recognized as kinfolk of the indigenous population.
valiha: cylindrical zither, usually of bamboo, most typical of indigenous instruments.
vazaha: foreigner, usually referring to Europeans but sometimes applied to Malagasy who are strangers in an area.
Vazimba: name given to proto-Malagasy people who were probably absorbed by later waves of population.
Vy Vato Sakelika (VVS): literally, "iron, stone, stem"; clandestine movement of nationalist youth during World War I.

Selected Bibliography

The literature of Madagascar is voluminous, but little of it is available in English, and very few book-length works have emerged in recent years. This selection emphasizes works (books, primarily) that are either too seminal to ignore or more or less accessible in French libraries. More recondite and specialized material is, of course, cited in the endnotes to each chapter.

GENERAL WORKS

Allen, Philip M. *Security and Nationalism in the Indian Ocean: Lessons from the Latin Quarter Islands.* Boulder and London: Westview Press, 1987.
Cadoux, Charles. *La République Malgache.* Paris: Berger-Levrault, 1969.
Covell, Maureen. *Madagascar: Politics, Economics and Society.* London and New York: Frances Pinter, 1987.
Heseltine, Nigel. *Madagascar.* New York: Praeger, 1971.
Murphy, Dervla. *Muddling Through In Madagascar.* Woodstock, N.Y.: Overlook Press, 1989.
Nelson, Harold D. et al. *Area Handbook for the Malagasy Republic.* Washington, D.C.: U.S. Government Printing Office, 1973.
Rajoelina, Patrick, and Alain Ramelet. *Madagascar: La grande île.* Paris: Harmattan, 1989.
Thompson, Virginia, and Richard Adloff. *The Malagasy Republic: Madagascar Today.* Stanford: Stanford University Press, 1965.

GEOGRAPHICAL AND NATURAL SETTING

Attenborough, David. *Zoo Quest to Madagascar.* London: Lutterworth Press, 1961; published in the United States under the title *Bridge to the Past.* New York: Harper and Brothers, 1961.
Battistini, R., and G. Richard-Vindard, eds. *Biogeography and Ecology of Madagascar.* The Hague: Junk, 1972.
da Silva, Sylvia. "Saving Madagascar," *Swiss Review of World Affairs,* June 1991, pp. 22–24.
Decary, Raymond. *La faune malgache.* Paris: Payot, 1950.
Jolly, Alison. "Madagascar's Lemurs on the Edge of Survival," *National Geographic,* v. 174, no. 2, August 1988, pp. 132–160.
———. *A World Like Our Own: Man and Nature in Madagascar.* New Haven and London: Yale University Press, 1980.

Paulian, Renaud. *Les animaux protégés à Madagascar.* Antananarivo: Institut de Recherche Scientifique, 1955.
Tattersall, Ian. *The Primates of Madagascar.* New York: Columbia University Press, 1982.
World Bank. *Plan d'action environnemental.* Washington, D.C.: World Bank, 1988.

HISTORICAL SETTING

Boiteau, Pierre. *Contribution à l'histoire de la nation malgache.* Paris: Editions Sociales, 1958.
Bouillon, Antoine. *Madagascar: Le colonisé et son 'âme': Essai sur le discours psychologique colonial.* Paris: Harmattan, 1981.
Brown, Mervyn. *Madagascar Rediscovered: A History from Early Times to Independence.* London: Damien Tunnacliffe, 1978; Hamden, Conn.: Archon Books, 1979.
Chapus, Georges-Sully, and Gustave Mondain. *Rainilaiarivony: Un homme d'état malgache.* Paris: Editions de l'Outremer, 1953.
Davidson, Basil. *The Black Man's Burden: Africa and the Curse of the Nation-State.* New York: Random House Times Books, 1992.
Deschamps, Hubert. *Histoire de Madagascar.* Paris: Berger-Levrault, 1961.
_____. *Les pirates à Madagascar.* Paris: Berger-Levrault, 1949.
Kent, Raymond K. *Early Kingdoms in Madagascar, 1500–1700.* New York: Holt, Rinehart & Winston, 1970.
_____. ed. *Madagascar in History: Essays from the 1970s.* Albany, Calif.: Foundation for Malagasy Studies, 1979.
Poirier, Jean et al. *Mouvements de populations dans l'océan indien.* Paris: Honoré Champion, 1979.
Ralaimihoatra, Edouard. *Histoire de Madagascar.* 4th ed. Antananarivo: Librairie de Madagascar, 1982.
Spacensky, Edmond. *Madagascar: Cinquante ans de vie politique, de Ralaimongo à Tsiranana.* Paris: NEL, 1970.
Tronchon, Jacques. *L'insurrection malgache de 1947: Essai d'interprétation historique.* Paris: Maspero, 1974.
Vérin, P. *The History of Civilisation in North Madagascar.* Trans. David Smith. Rotterdam and Boston: A. A. Balkema, 1986.
_____. "Madagascar." In G. Mokhtar, ed., *UNESCO General History of Africa.* Berkeley: University of California Press, 1981.

SOCIETY AND CULTURE

Althabe, Gérard. *Oppression et libération dans l'imaginaire: Les communautés villageoises de la côte orientale de Madagascar.* Paris: Maspero, 1969.
Andriamanjato, Richard. *Le tsiny et le tody dans la pensée malgache.* Paris: Présence Africaine, 1957.
Bloch, Maurice. *From Blessing to Violence: History and Ideology in the Circumcision Ritual of the Merina of Madagascar.* Cambridge: Cambridge University Press, 1986.
_____. *Placing the Dead: Tombs, Ancestral Villages, and Kinship Organization in Madagascar.* London and New York: Seminar Press, 1972.
Decary, Raymond. *Moeurs et coutumes des Malgaches.* Paris: Payot, 1951.
Deschamps, Hubert, and Suzanne Vianès. *Les Malgaches du Sud-Est.* Paris: Presses Universitaires de France, 1959.

Domenichini-Ramiaramanana, Bakoly. *Du ohabolona au hainteny: Langue, littérature et politique à Madagascar.* Paris: Karthala, 1983.

Estrade, Jean-Marie. *Un culte de possession à Madagascar: Le tromba.* Paris: Harmattan, 1985.

Faublée, Jacques. *La cohésion des sociétés bara.* Paris: Presses Universitaires de France, 1954.

———. *Les esprits de la vie à Madagascar.* Paris: Presses Universitaires de France, 1954.

Feeley-Harnik, Gillian. *A Green Estate: Restoring Independence in Madagascar.* Washington and London: Smithsonian, 1991.

Huntington, Richard. *Gender and Social Structure in Madagascar.* Bloomington and Indianapolis: Indiana University Press, 1988.

Kottack, Conrad Phillip. *The Past in the Present: History, Ecology, and Cultural Variation in Highland Madagascar.* Ann Arbor: University of Michigan Press, 1980.

Kottack, Conrad Phillip, Jean-Aimé Rakotoarisoa, Aidan Southall, and Pierre Vérin, eds. *Madagascar: Society and History.* Durham, N.C.: Carolina Academic Press, 1986.

Longchamps, Jeanne de. *Contes malgaches.* Paris: Editions Erasme, n.d.

Mack, John. *Madagascar: Island of the Ancestors.* London: British Museum Publications, 1986.

Mannoni, O[ctave]. *Prospero and Caliban: The Psychology of Colonization.* 2nd ed. New York: Praeger, 1964. Trans. Pamela Powesland of *Psychologie de la colonisation.* Paris: Editions du Seuil, 1950; reprinted Paris: Editions Universitaires de France, 1984.

Poirier, Jean, and Aubert Rabenoro, eds. *Tradition et dynamique sociale à Madagascar.* Nice: Idéric, 1979.

Prats, Yves. *Le développement communautaire à Madagascar.* Paris: Pichon & Durand-Auzias, 1972.

Raharijaona, S., and Pierre Vérin. "Le système de parenté Merina." *Annales de l'Université de Madagascar,* 1964.

Raison, Jean-Pierre. *Les hautes terres de Madagascar.* Paris: ORSTOM-Karthala, 1984.

Rajaoson, François. *L'enseignement supérieur et le développement de la société malgache.* Paris: Université de Paris V, 1981.

Rakotondrabe, D. Tovonirina. "Au delà de l'ethnie: Ethnies, état-nation et démocratie à Madagascar." Paper presented at the Colloque Democratie et Développement dans le Sud-Ouest de l'Océan Indien et en Afrique. Université d'Antananarivo, May 17–24, 1993.

Ramandraivonona, Denis. *Le Malgache: Sa langue et sa religion.* Paris: Présence Africaine, 1959.

Rouveyran, Jean-Claude. *La logique des agricultures de transition: L'exemple des sociétés paysannes malgaches.* Paris: Maisonneuve et LaRose, 1972.

Sachs, Kurt. *Les instruments de musique à Madagascar.* Paris: Institut d'Ethnographie, 1938.

Vérin, Pierre. "Des ancêtres venus d'au-delà." In Henri Marchal and Sarah Doulache, eds., *Madagascar: Arts de la vie et de la survie.* Paris: Musée des Arts Africains et Océaniens, 1989.

POLITICS AND FOREIGN AFFAIRS

Allen, Philip M. "Madagascar: The Authenticity of Recovery." In John M. Ostehimer, ed., *The Politics of the Western Indian Ocean Islands.* New York: Praeger, 1975.

Archer, Robert. *Madagascar depuis 1972: La marche d'une révolution.* Paris: Harmattan, 1978.
du Bois de Gaudusson, J. *L'administration malgache.* Paris: Berger-Levrault, 1976.
Chaigneau, Pascal. *Madagasar, de la première république à l'orientation socialiste: Processus et conséquences d'une évolution politique.* Paris: Université de Paris X, 1981.
_____. *Un état à orientation socialiste: Madagascar.* 6 vols. Paris: Université de Paris X, 1984.
_____. *Rivalités politiques et socialisme à Madagascar.* Paris: CHEAM, 1985.
Deleris, Ferdinand. *Ratsiraka: Socialisme et misère à Madagascar.* Paris: Harmattan, 1986.
La deuxième république malgache. Talence: CEGET/CNRS and Aix-en-Provence: Presses Universitaires d'Aix-Marseille, 1989.
Leymarie, Philippe. *Océan indien: Le nouveau coeur du monde.* Paris: Karthala, 1981.
Mutibwa, P. M. *The Malagasy and the Europeans: Madagascar's Foreign Relations, 1861–1895.* Ibadan, Nigeria: Humanities Press, 1974.
Rabemananjara, Raymond William. *Chronique d'une saison carcérale en Lémurie.* Antananarivo: Editions Revue de l'Océan Indien, 1990.
Rabenoro, Césaire. *Les relations extérieures de Madagascar de 1960 à 1972.* Paris: Harmattan, 1986.
Rajoelina, Patrick. *Quarante années de la vie politique de Madagascar, 1947–1987.* Paris: Harmattan, 1988.
Ramanandraibe, Lucile Rasoamanalina. *Le livre vert de l'espérance malgache.* Paris: Harmattan, 1987.
Ratsiraka, Didier. *Charte de la révolution socialiste malagasy.* Antananarivo: Imprimerie d'Ouvrages Éducatifs, 1975.
_____. *Stratégies pour l'an 2000: Du tiers monde à la troisième puissance mondiale.* Paris: Editions Afrique Asie Amérique Latine, 1983.

ECONOMIC AFFAIRS

Abé, Yoshio. *Le riz et la riziculture à Madagascar.* Paris: Editions du CNRS, 1984.
Brown, Michael Barratt, and Pauline Tiffen. *Short Changed: Africa and World Trade.* London and Boulder: Pluto Press, 1992.
Desjeux, Dominique. *La question agraire à Madagascar: Administration et paysannat de 1895 à nos jours.* Paris: Harmattan, 1979.
Duruflé, Gilles. *L'ajustement structurel en Afrique (Sénégal, Côte d'Ivoire, Madagascar).* Paris: Karthala, 1988.
Pavageau, Jean. *Jeunes paysans sans terre: L'exemple malgache.* Paris: Harmattan, 1981.
Pryor, Frederic L. *Malawi and Madagascar: The Political Economy of Poverty.* Washington, D.C.: Oxford University Press, 1990.
Rabetafika, Roger. *Réforme fiscale et révolution socialiste à Madagascar.* Paris: Harmattan, 1990.
Ramahatra, Olivier. *Madagascar: Une économie en phase d'ajustement.* Paris: Harmattan, 1989.
World Bank. *Madagascar: Recent Economic Developments and Future Prospects.* Washington, D.C.: World Bank, 1980.

REFERENCE AND PERIODICALS

Africa Confidential. London, weekly.
Africa Contemporary Record. New York and London: Africana, annual since 1968–1969.

Annuaire des Pays de l'Océan Indien. Paris: Editions du CNRS, annual.
Archipel: Études Interdisciplinaires sur le Monde Insulindien. Paris: SECMI/CNRS, quarterly.
ASEMI: Asie du Sud-Est et Monde Insulindien. Paris: Editions du CNRS, quarterly.
Dans les Média Demain. Antananarivo: Nouvelle Société de Presse et d'Editions, weekly.
Economist Intelligence Unit. *Country Report: Madagascar, Seychelles, Comoros.* London: Economist Intelligence Unit, Ltd., quarterly.
Indian Ocean Newsletter. Paris, weekly.
Madagascar, Océan Indien. Paris: Harmattan, quarterly.
Marchés Tropicaux et Méditerranéens. Paris, weekly.

About the Book and Author

The world's fourth largest island, with a unique biological and physical endowment, Madagascar is home to an extraordinary insular civilization that has struggled for more than a century against external domination. In this sensitive introduction to the Indian Ocean's "great island," Philip Allen shows how family affinities and community loyalties at the foundation of Madagascar's culture have influenced Malagasy nationalism and forged islandwide traditions. These same principles have nonetheless engendered social cleavages and resistance to economic and political change.

In chapters on modern Madagascar, Allen analyzes the inability of a series of regimes to maintain authority among a people deeply bound to rituals of communication with their spiritual environment. He demonstrates how the first Malagasy Republic became stigmatized by its lingering identification with French colonialism and how the nationalist revolution in 1972 soon hardened into autocratic radicalism. Allen explores the complex challenges facing Madagascar's resurgent democratic forces—including a need to conserve the island's irreplaceable biodiversity and to facilitate authentic participation in public affairs without offending ancestral customs and local precedents. Finally, he discusses efforts to end Madagascar's economic and political dependence and to improve living conditions for its tragically impoverished population.

Philip M. Allen is dean of the School of Arts and Humanities at Frostburg State University in Maryland. A former U.S. Foreign Service Officer, Fulbright lecturer in Senegal and Algeria, and officer of the African-American Institute, Dr. Allen lived in Madagascar during the 1960s and was a member of an international elections observation team in 1993. He is the author of *Security and Nationalism in the Indian Ocean* (Westview, 1987).

Index

Action Committee of the Protest Movement. *See* KIM
Africa and Madagascar, 1–2, 226, 232
African and Malagasy Common Organization (OCAM), 226
African-Malagasy Union (UAM), 226
AKFM (Congress Party for the Independence of Madagascar)
  under first republic, 51–53, 56, 60–62, 65, 67, 224
  under French colonial administration, 44, 49–50
  under interregnum of 1972–1975, 73
  under second republic, 77(n84), 83, 85, 96, 99, 104
  under third republic, 115
  See also Fanavaozana AKFM
AKFM Renewal. *See* Fanavaozana AKFM
Ancestral tradition, 32, 39, 121, 127, 130–140, 161, 179
Andafiavaratra clan, 23. *See also* Hova
Andevo, 24
Andriamahazo, Gilles, 72–73, 96
Andriamaholison, Richard, 93
Andriamanjato, Richard, 44, 49, 53, 61, 77(n84), 86, 99, 101, 102, 105, 107, 109, 113, 114, 152, 222
Andriamorasata, Solo Norbert, 85
Andriana, 16, 42, 140–141
Andrianampoinimerina, 14, 16–17, 130, 139–140, 179
Andrianarahinjaka, Lucien Xavier Michel, 98, 107
Andriantsoli, 19
Antaifasy, 130
Antaimoro, 14, 130
Antaisaka, 130, 139

Antalaotse (Antalaotra), 8–9, 13, 14, 128, 142
Antambahoaka, 130
Antananarivo, 48, 52, 65–67, 103, 107, 113, 122, 180
Antandroy, 129
Antankarana, 128
Antanosy, 12, 129–130, 139
Antsirabe, 122
Antsiranana, 2. *See also* Diego Suarez
Arabs, 10, 14
AREMA (Avant-Garde of the Malagasy Revolution), 83, 96, 99, 104, 107, 111, 115

Bantu people, 9
Bara, 14, 129–130
Bassas da India, 5
Benyowski, M.A., 127
Betsileo, 14, 126, 133, 139
Betsimisaraka, 14, 126–127, 132, 137
Bezaka, Alexis, 50, 85
Bezanozano, 127
Bourbon. *See* Réunion
Boina. *See* Sakalava

Catholicism in Madagascar, 18–19, 33, 39, 126, 127, 134, 151–152
  in public affairs, 63, 85, 98, 105, 125, 143, 152–153, 156–157
Charter of the Socialist Revolution, 73, 79–80, 180–181, 189
China, 51, 63, 97, 226, 227–228, 229
Chinese residents, 9, 39, 41, 142–143, 182
Christian Democratic parties
  PDCM, 50, 52

INDEX 249

RNM, 50
UDECMA, 50, 83, 85, 115
Christianity, 18–19, 20, 21, 122, 134–135, 151–153
  in public affairs, 59. *See also* Catholicism, missionaries, Protestantism
Club of Forty-Eight, 141
Comorean residents, 9, 39, 98, 142, 233
Comoro Islands, 1, 4, 19, 232–233
Congo crisis, 226
Congress Party for the Independence of Madagascar. *See* AKFM
Constitution
  of 1959, 50
  of 1975, 73, 80
  of 1992, 110, 111, 220
Côtiers, 25, 34, 42, 45, 49, 68–69, 71, 81, 108–109, 114, 121, 222, 224
Cotton. *See* Madagascar, textile industry in
Creoles, 4, 39, 142
Cuba, 95, 229

Debt for nature, 177
DeCoppet, Marcel, 45
de Flacourt, Etienne, 12, 130
de Gaulle, Charles, 44–45, 49, 115, 127
de Hell, 5
de Lastelle, Napoléon, 19, 22
Democratic Movement for Malagasy Revival. *See* MDRM
Democratic Republic of Madagascar, 80
Department of Information and Documentation. *See* DGID
Development, economic and social, 137–138, 179, 206–211
  in colonial period, 38–40
  in first republic, 53–54, 58, 64, 228
  during interregnum, 71
  under Merina monarchy, 18, 32
  in second republic, 169, 177, 178, 190, 195, 203, 206, 207
  in third republic, 208–213, 222, 233–234
DGID, 96, 103
Diaz, Diogo, 2
Diego Garcia, 227
Diego Suarez, 34, 44, 57, 128, 225, 228, 229
Diouf, Abdou, 110
Directorate of 1975, 72–73

Disinherited, Party of. *See* PADESM
Duchesne, Jacques Achille, 35

Elections
  in 1946–1947, 45
  September 4, 1960, 52
  August 8, 1965, 52
  September 6, 1970, 52, 59
  January 30, 1972, 63, 67
  November 10; 1982, 81, 96
  August 28, 1983, 96
  March 12, 1989, 81, 84, 85, 86, 99
  May 28, 1989, 99
  September 27, 1989, 99
  October 29, 1989, 99
  December 10, 1989, 99
  November 25, 1992, 102, 106, 112
  February 10, 1993, 81, 106, 112
  June 16, 1993, 84, 103, 106, 113–114, 153, 154, 235
Ellis, William, 21, 22
Environmental Operation (World Bank), 175–177, 206
Europa islet, 5
European Community (EC), 199–200, 210, 226, 231
Export Processing Zones (EPZ), 197–198, 222, 230, 233

Famadihana, 133
Fanavaozana AKFM, 86, 99, 102
Farquhar, Robert, 18, 25
Federalist movement, 85, 121, 222
Fety, Michel, 111
Fianarantsoa, 48, 126
Fihaonana, 109, 114
First Republic, 1958–1972
  achievements and defects of, 41, 50–68, 168, 189, 190
  anti-communism in, 51, 53, 58, 224, 227, 228
  decline and fall of, 62–68, 235
  education in, 145–146
  external relations of, 51, 223–228
  French position in, 55–56, 61, 64–65, 67, 190, 223–228
  Grandes Opérations strategy, 54–55, 58, 211
  labor in, 149–150
  Rural Animation program, 40, 55
  See also Social Democratic Party; Tsiranana, Philibert

FNDR (National Front for the Defense of the Revolution), 50, 82–86, 99, 153–154, 192
Fokon'olona, 131, 139–140
  under Merina monarchy, 16–17, 25, 26, 139–140
  under French colonial administration, 38, 46
  under first republic, 58
  under interregnum (Ratsimandrava revival), 69–70, 191
  under second republic, 73, 80, 82, 94, 176, 181, 191–193
  under third republic, 111, 221–222
Fokontany. *See* Fokon'olona
Fort Dauphin settlement, 12, 33, 130
France
  colonial policy of, 31, 35–42, 43–46, 125, 134, 141–142, 168, 190
  colonial trading companies, 18, 40–41, 46
  conquest and colonization, 33, 35, 39–40
  cooperation agreements of 1960 with, 51, 56, 65
  development assistance from, 57–58, 227, 228, 230–231
  indigénat, 41, 43
  19th century relations with, 4, 11–13, 18–19, 20, 21, 23, 25, 32–35, 128–129
  relations with first republic, 55–57, 61, 63–65, 92, 223–228
  relations with second republic, 80, 103, 106, 202, 203–204, 230–231
  SMOTIG (Labor Service), 43
  tribal policy, 36, 125
Franc Zone, 194, 212, 227
Free French, 44–45
French residents, 38, 47, 71, 142–143, 230
French community, 31, 50

Galliéni, Joseph Simon, 36–38, 41, 125, 145
Gandhi, Rajiv, 158
Germany, 32, 44, 210, 224, 226
Glorieuses, 5
Gondwanaland, 2
Grad Iloafo, 114
Great Britain
  19th century relations with, 11, 18, 22, 24, 33–34, 122, 127
  Royal School of Medicine, 145

20th century relations with, 44, 226, 228, 230
Guinea, 50

High Authority of State (HAE), 107, 110, 111
Holland, 10
Hova, 16, 42, 140–141

Iavoloha massacre, 92, 106, 115
Île de France. *See* Mauritius
Îles éparses, 5, 230
Imerina, 15, 122–126, 132, 138, 174
India, 224
Indian Ocean, 1–5, 32, 95, 128, 226–227, 229, 230, 232
Indian Ocean Commission, 4, 232–233
Indo-Pakistanis. *See* Muslims
Insurrection of 1947, 46–48, 134, 142
International Development Association (IDA). *See* World Bank
International Monetary Fund (IMF), 104, 115, 195–197, 202–203, 218(n104), 231
  See also Structural Adjustment program
Interregnum of 1972–1975, 68–73, 80, 156, 168, 229
Islam, 14, 39, 151
Israel, 224, 226

Jaona, Monja. *See* Monja Jaona
Japan, 44
Jews, Nazi homeland scheme for, 44
JINA (National Malagasy Youth), 46–48
John Paul II, 86, 100, 152
Juan de Nova, 5

Karana. *See* Muslims
KIM (Action Committee of the Protest Movement), 67–68, 73, 148
Kim Il Sung, 80
Korea, Republic of, 51, 205, 224
Kung fu movement, 93, 103, 133, 148

Laborde, Jean, 20, 21, 22, 23, 33–34
Lake Alaotra, 128, 231
Lambert, 22, 24
Laroche, Hippolyte, 36
Leader-Fanilo, 114
Legentilhomme, Paul, 45
Libertalia, Republic of, 5, 14, 127
Loi cadre of 1956, 48

INDEX 251

Lomé IV Agreement, 200

Maanjan (language), 8, 121
Madagascar
  agriculture, 171, 174, 187, 208, 211
  arts in, 159–162
  biological diversity of, 172–175
  black market in, 180, 186
  cattle, 15–16, 59, 89, 122, 130, 170, 185
  circumcision ceremony, 135–136, 155
  cloves, 178, 183, 190, 200
  coffee, 115, 178, 181, 183, 190, 193, 198–200, 204
  communications, 170–171, 184, 225, 233
  communism in, 49, 59–60
  cooperative movement in, 54, 193
  decentralization of government, 190–193
  democracy in, 56, 86, 222, 234
  development assistance, 210, 210(table 5.8), 230–231
  economic production, 169(table 5.1), 183, 194, 197, 198, 199(table 5.4), 209, 211
  education, 64, 141, 144–149, 184–185, 229
  employment, 212, 222
  environment, 1, 13, 108, 174–177, 215(n28)
  ethnic groups in, 122–130
  Europeans in, 1, 10, 19
  family planning, 155, 173–174
  fisheries, 178
  forests, 2–4, 8, 13, 174–175, 177
  Gendarmerie, 67, 92, 103
  geography of, 1–4, 122–130, 170–171
  independence of, 41, 44, 45–46, 51, 140
  industry, 181, 183, 186, 194. *See also* Export Processing Zones
  investment codes, 197, 201, 224
  kinship in, 130–140, 144, 191
  labor movement in, 43–44, 49, 149–151, 182, 205
  literature in, 159–160
  market economy in, 137–138
  marriage ceremony in, 135
  migrations of labor in, 139, 174, 212
  military forces of, 57, 67–68, 87–88, 91–94, 103, 106, 108
  mining, 175, 200, 201, 214(n19)
  music in, 160–161

  nationalism, 21, 36, 41–50, 88, 152, 194–195, 228, 231
  natural resources, 170–171
  peasantry: culture of, 26, 54–55, 61, 130, 178; economy, 38, 107, 137, 186, 188; resistance to government of, 40, 58–61, 64, 68–69, 177. *See also* Revolt of 1971
  petroleum, 171, 200
  pirates in, 5, 14, 127
  police, 57, 60, 65, 67–69, 72, 92
  population, 155, 162(n4), 173–175, 179, 211–212
  poverty in, 54, 59, 61, 64, 88–89, 109, 116, 169, 179, 185–187, 209
  Presidential Guard, 92, 94, 106, 111
  press and radio/TV in, 43, 56, 98, 103, 104–105, 156–157, 160–161
  public health, 176, 187
  rice, 15, 45, 116, 122, 170, 174, 180, 183, 186, 208, 213, 216(n53)
  slavery in, 24, 25, 32, 36, 125
  social classes in, 37, 43, 49, 52–53, 55–56, 58, 63, 64, 69–70, 82, 87, 92, 100, 122, 131, 136–137, 140–144, 147, 178–179, 181–182, 189
  students in, 63–66, 91, 146
  taxation in, 38, 137, 168, 175, 188
  textile industry in, 115, 143, 159, 178, 183, 185–186, 197
  tourism in, 171–172, 175, 178, 214(n7), 233
  trade, 201(table 5.5), 202, 208, 211, 212–213, 230–231
  traditional religion, 20, 131–140, 151
  urban-rural conflict, 58–59, 90, 131, 192
  vanilla, 178, 183, 190, 200
  women's interests in, 56, 146, 153–156, 173–174, 211
  youth interests in, 119(n57), 138–139, 141, 144–149, 178–179, 189
Madagascar Ruled by Malagasy. *See* MONIMA
Mahafaly, 129, 135
Mahajanga, 128, 142
Mahasampa, Bienaimé Raveloson, 96
Mainty, 24
Makoa, 129
Malagasy Academy, 38
Malagasy Christian Council (FFKM), 98, 110, 153

Malagasy language, 8, 121, 141, 143, 149, 159–160
  people: culture, 5–7, 9–10, 12–13, 57, 121–140, 235–236; origins of, 1, 5–8, 27(n16); resistance to authority, 39, 48, 57–58, 80–83, 87–88, 99, 117, 126–127, 129, 134, 137, 140, 144, 151, 158, 177, 179–180, 207, 234, 235–236
Malagasy Socialist Party. *See* PSM
Mannoni, Octave, 134, 142
Maroserana. *See* Sakalava
Marshall, Anthony, 227
Marson, Evariste, 102, 112, 114
Mascarenes, 4, 7, 39, 232–233
Masikoro, 129
Masonic Order, 92
Mauritius, 4, 11, 17, 205, 232–233
Mayotte, 4, 19, 33. *See also* Comoro Islands
MDRM (Democratic Movement for Malagasy Renewal), 45–48
Menalamba movement, 35–37
Merina
  monarchy of, 5, 11, 14, 15–17, 24, 32–35, 127–130: foreign relations of, 17, 18, 20, 22, 23, 25, 33–35
  people, 8, 13, 37, 122–129, 133, 140–141, 155–156, 182
  politicization of, 36, 42, 44, 45, 48–49, 53, 61, 67, 69, 71–72, 80–81, 85–86, 107, 108–109, 113, 124–126, 146, 223–224, 225, 228
MFM (Militants for Power to the Little People, Party of Malagasy Progress), 68, 70, 83–84, 96, 99–100, 102, 105, 106, 115
Miadana, Victor, 76(n68)
MMSM (Militant Movement for Malagasy Socialism), 104
Militants for Power to the Little People. *See* MFM
Military Development Committee (CMD), 93
Missionaries, 17, 18, 20, 32, 34, 37, 46, 144–145, 156
Mitterrand, François, 230
MONIMA (Madagascar Ruled by Malagasy), 50, 51, 56, 59–60, 83, 84–85, 96, 99, 104, 115
Monja Jaona, 46, 50, 59–60, 63, 65, 83, 84–85, 91, 96, 98, 99, 104, 111–112, 157, 222

Mozambique Channel, 4, 122
Muslims, 1, 8–9, 25, 34, 39, 41, 97–98, 126, 143, 182

National Committee for Economic and Social Recovery, 107
National Committee for Observation of Elections (CNOE), 110, 112, 156
National Forum of 1992, 110, 115
National Front for the Defense of the Revolution. *See* FNDR
National Union of Democrats for Development (UNDD), 105
Nerine, Eléonore Marguerite, 154
North Korea, 80, 93
Nosy Be, 5, 33
Nosy Boraha. *See* Sainte Marie

Ombiassy, 9, 14, 15, 130, 136, 144
Organization of African Unity (OAU), 110, 114, 226

PADESM (Party of the Disinherited), 45, 48
PANAMA (National Malagasy Party), 46–48
Party of Malagasy Progress. *See* MFM
PDCM. *See* Christian Democratic parties
Pierre, Simon, 90–91
Polo, Marco, 2
Pompidou, Georges, 67, 228
Portugal, 10
Protestantism, 18–19, 23, 33, 134, 151–152; in public affairs, 44, 46, 63, 98, 125, 152–153, 157
PSD. *See* Social Democratic Party
PSM (Malagasy Socialist Party), 72, 73

Rabearivelo, Jean-Joseph, 145, 160
Rabemananjara, Jacques, 45, 46, 47, 51, 69–70, 76(n68), 102, 112, 160, 227
Rabemananjara, Raymond William, 45
Rabenoro, Césaire, 54, 102, 106
Rabesahala, Gisèle, 49, 85, 156
Rabetafika, Roland, 70, 72, 93
Rabetsitonta, Tovonanahary, 109, 114
Radama I, 11, 17–18, 126, 144
Radama II, 21–22
Raharijaona, Henri, 103
Rainiharo, 20
Rainijohary, 21
Rainilaiarivony, 23–25, 32–35

INDEX 253

Rainimaharo, 20
Rajaonarison, Bréchard, 72, 73, 92, 118(n17), 222
Rakoto, Prince. *See* Radama II
Rakotoarijaona, Désiré, 93
Rakotoharison, Jean, 93, 99, 103, 109, 112
Rakotoniaina, Jean-Jacques, 105, 106
Rakotonirina, Manandafy, 68, 70, 83–84, 86, 99–100, 102, 105, 107, 114, 115
Ralaimongo, Jean, 44
Ralaivelo, Daniel, 102
Ralison, Roger, 114–115
Ramahatra, Victor, 100, 106
Ramaholimihaso, Madeleine, 110, 156
Ramanantsoa, Gabriel, 68–72, 78(n109), 81, 92, 96, 109. *See also* Interregnum of 1972–1975
Ramanenjana, 22, 30(n69), 132
Ramangasoavina, Alfred, 76(n68), 102
Ramarasaona, Emile, 102
Ranaivo, Flavien, 160
Ranavalona I, 18–22, 25, 33, 125, 132, 134, 156
Ranavalona II, 23–24
Ranavalona III, 24, 32, 35–37
Raombana, 18
Rarivoson, Justin, 90
Rasalama faction. *See* Vital Forces
Raseta, Joseph, 45, 47, 50
Rasoanoro, Zèle, 156
Rasoherina, 23
Rasolondraibe, Henri, 233
Ratsimandrava, Richard, 69–70, 72–73, 78(n109), 80, 82, 92, 156, 190–191
Ratsimilaho, 14
Ratsiraka, Céline, 156, 174
Ratsiraka, Didier, 50, 69–70, 72–73, 79–112, 115, 127, 152–153, 191, 220, 229–231
Ravelojaona, 44, 157
Ravoahangy, Joseph, 44, 45, 47
Ravony, Francisque, 84, 105, 106, 109, 110, 114–117, 151, 154, 221–222, 235
Razakaboana-Rakotovao, 90–91, 115, 189
Razanabahiny, Marojama, 84, 99
Razanamasy, Guy-Willy, 84, 103, 106, 107, 108, 109, 110, 112, 113, 114, 115, 116, 203, 221
Referendum
  of September 28, 1958, 50, 85
  of October 8, 1972, 68–69
  of December 21, 1975, 73, 80, 182
  of August 19, 1992, 110
Resampa, André, 51, 52, 53, 55, 56, 57, 59, 62–65, 68–69, 73, 84, 92, 102–103, 105, 106, 225, 228, 237(n23)
Réunion, 4, 12, 17, 21, 33, 39, 232–233
Revolt of 1971, 55, 60–62, 65, 72, 84
Revolution of 1972, 61–62, 64, 81, 229, 234
  frustration of, 31, 192, 207, 231
  origins of, 137
  See also Revolt of 1971
  student radicalism in, 146, 148
  urban forces in, 55–56
RNM. *See* Christian Democratic parties

Sainte Marie, 5, 33, 74(n20), 127
Sakalava
  culture, 132–133, 135
  kingdom of, 5, 14–15, 17, 21, 33, 36, 128
Second Republic, 1975–1993, 31
  achievements and defects of, 91–97, 98, 101, 107–108, 193, 199
  economic policy, 81–82, 87–89, 98, 101, 104, 108, 169, 180–183, 185–188, 193, 196–198
  education in, 146–147, 229
  federalism in, 108–109
  foreign relations of, 79–80, 87–88, 94–95, 103, 112, 229, 232
  international debt and dependence, 81–82, 87–90, 169, 187–188, 194, 203–204, 204(table 5.7), 208, 221–223, 229, 231
  labor in, 150–151, 182
  political parties in, 82–86, 96, 99–100, 101–104. *See also* FNDR
  presidential power in, 81–82, 91, 94–95, 104. *See also* Ratsiraka, Didier
  press in, 156–157
  rejection by population of, 87–88, 105–108, 220, 235
  socialism in, 79–82, 87, 90, 97, 100, 118(n35), 150–151, 180–182, 189–191, 195, 207. *See also* Charter of the Socialist Revolution
  structure of, 80–81, 94
  Supreme Council of the Revolution (CSR), 73, 94, 107
Seychelles, 4, 232–233
Sihanaka, 128
Slave trade, 8, 10–11, 15, 17, 18, 19, 25, 32, 34, 39, 124–125, 128, 206

Social Democratic Party (PSD), 48–65, 71–73, 80, 102–103, 115
  See also First Republic
Sorabe, 9, 14, 130
Sorcery, 136
South Africa, 44, 55, 56, 104, 224, 227–228, 229, 231
Soviet Union, 93, 94–95, 149, 224, 226, 229
Strikes of 1991, 105–107, 151, 169–170, 205, 234
Structural Adjustment program, 151, 195–206, 196(table 5.3), 208, 212, 221
Suez Canal, 32
Sylla, Jacques, 222

Taiwan, 51, 205, 224, 226
Tamatave. *See* Toamasina
Tanala, 126
Tananarive. *See* Antananarivo
Tanora Tonga Saina (TTS), 96, 148
Taolanaro, 130
Tavy, 8, 15, 174
Third republic, 1993 to date, 31, 109, 231–236
  decentralization in, 111, 113, 221–222
  economic problems and policies of, 115–117, 208–213, 222
  education in, 148–149
  foreign relations of, 231–234
  labor in, 151
  leadership of, 114
  political parties in, 113–114
  structure of, 110, 111–113, 220
Toamasina, 108, 125, 127, 151
Toliara (Tuléar, Toliary), 59, 108, 129, 212. *See also* Revolt of 1971
Tromba, 15, 128, 132–133
Tshombe, Moïse, 226
Tsiebo, Calvin, 59–60, 76(n68)
Tsimihety people, 128
Tsiomeko, 5
Tsiranana, Philibert, 45, 50–69, 73, 92, 127, 128, 143, 154, 168, 223–228

Tsiranana, Ruffine, 102, 112
Tuléar. *See* Toliara

UDECMA. *See* Christian Democratic parties
United Nations 51
United States, 33, 47, 56, 63, 65, 77(n89), 152, 226–227, 228, 229, 230–231
United States Bankers Trust, 177
University of Madagascar, 64–65, 144, 145–146, 149, 184

Vazimba people, 8, 16, 135
Vezo people, 129, 178
Vital Forces, 84, 86, 105, 107, 111, 112, 113, 114, 153, 222, 235
VS-MONIMA, 83, 85, 115
Vonjy Iray Tsy Mivaky, 69, 83, 84, 99, 103, 115
VVS (Vy Vato Sakelika), 42

War of 1883–1885, 24, 34
World Bank, 104, 175, 195–197, 203–204, 205–206, 210, 231
  See also Environmental Operation
  See also International Monetary Fund
  See also Structural Adjustment program
World Food Program (WFP), 116
World War I, 41, 42
World War II, 43, 44
World Wildlife Fund (WWF), 176, 177

Zafera, Maxime, 177
Zafimahaleo, Rasolofondrasolo, "Dama," 119(n57), 160
Zafisoro, 130
Zafy, Albert, 81, 84, 85, 86, 102, 105–106, 107, 108, 109, 110, 111, 112, 113, 114, 117, 151, 211, 221–222
Zana-Malata, 14
ZOAM (Unemployed Youth of Madagascar), 67–68, 73, 77(n95), 84, 141–142

/969.1A428M>C1/

DATE DUE

DEMCO, INC. 38-2931